Mastering
Chess Sight

2

GM Vladimir Romanenko

Mastering Chess Sight 2

Contents

Introduction

To play chess successfully, you must develop chess sight. This does not happen quickly. However, solving chess puzzles daily will improve and build up sharp "chess eyes"!

This book provides many useful and interesting chess puzzles which you can solve daily. It does not take much time to solve two puzzles per day. After a half of a year, you will solve all the puzzles from this book and improve your chess sight to another level. You can do more than two puzzles per day and finish the book faster; however, I would recommend that you do not rush solving the puzzles. Try to understand the concept of the each puzzle you solve and memorize the patterns!

This book provides huge diagrams that should help you to create a good chess vision without using a chess set. You can also find many interesting phrases about chess in this book.

The level of these puzzles is between 800 – 1200 rated chess players.

Symbols:

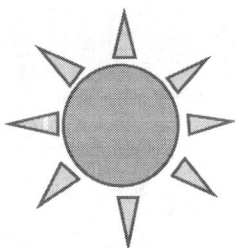

- white to move
- morning puzzle

- black to move
- evening puzzle

In all the following chess puzzles, you should find the best continuation!

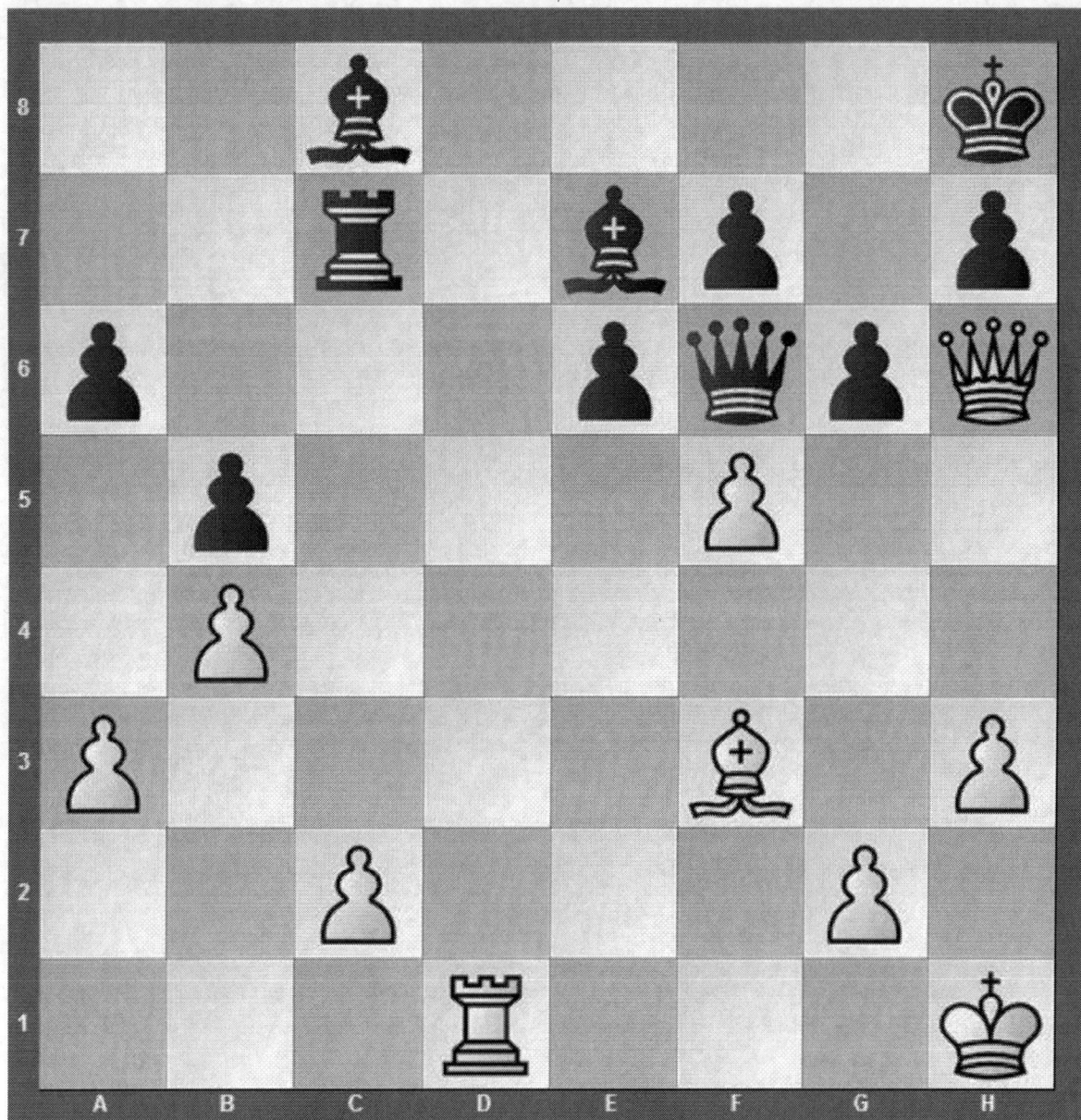

1		
2		

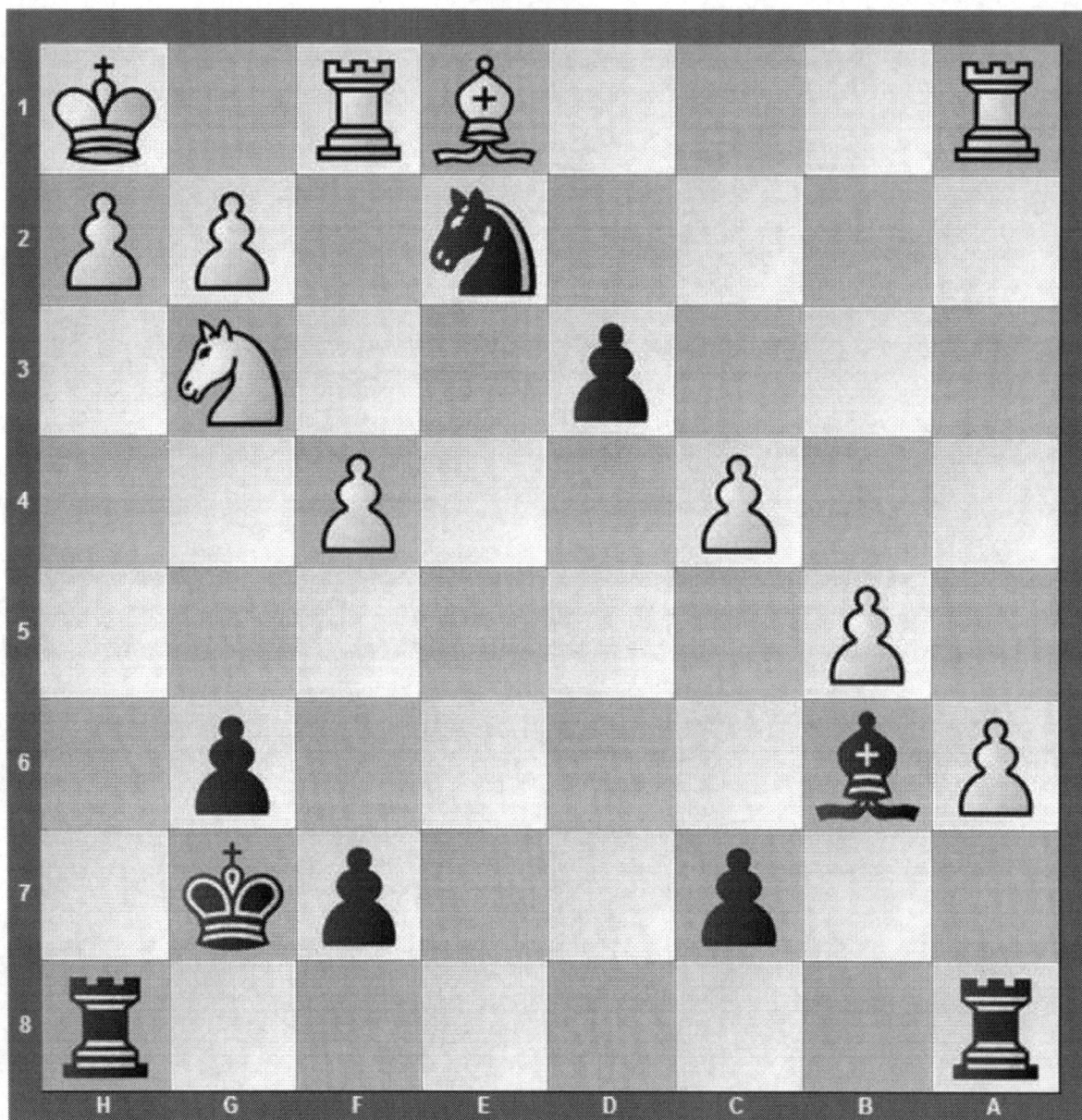

1		
2		

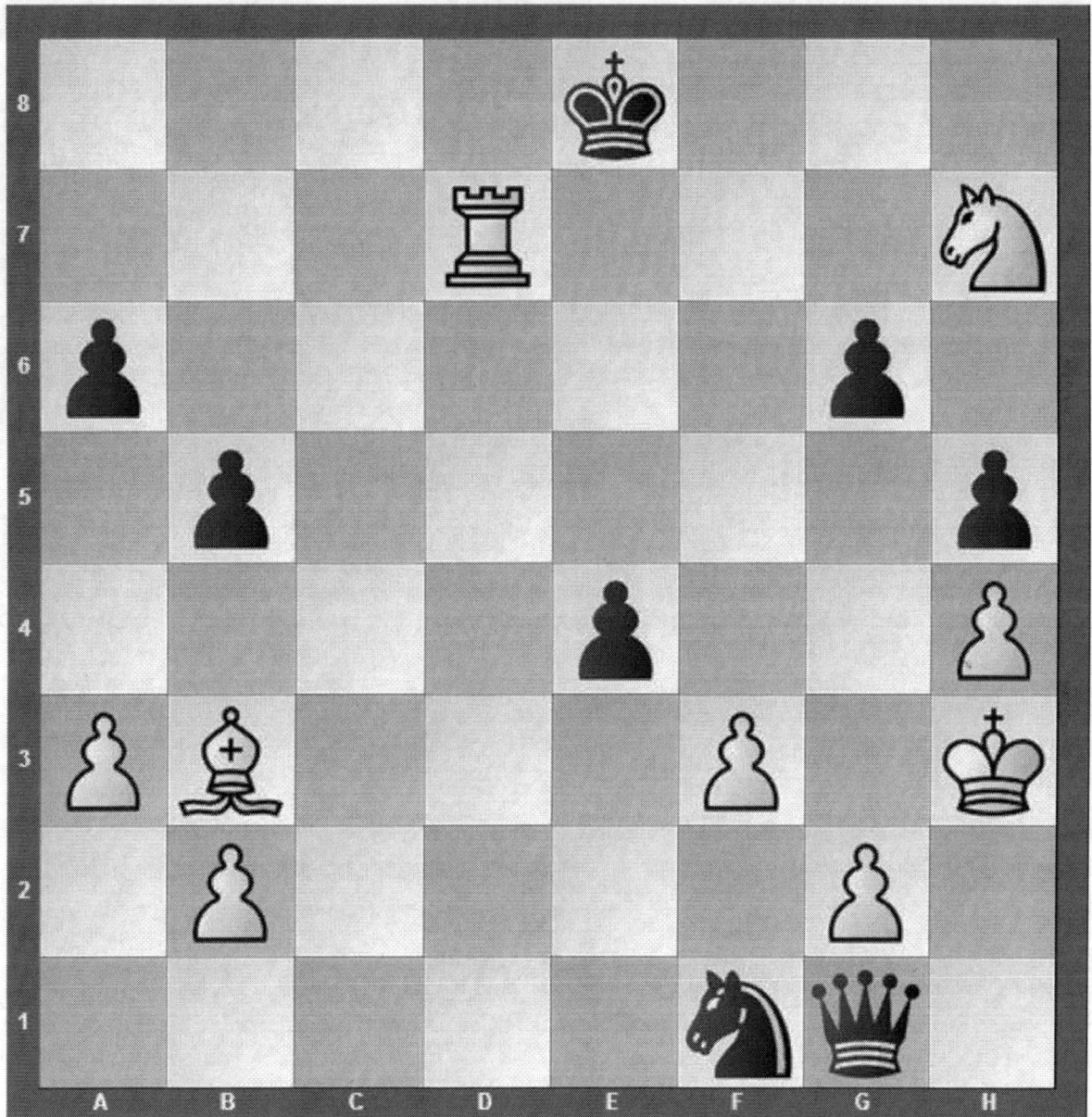

1		
2		

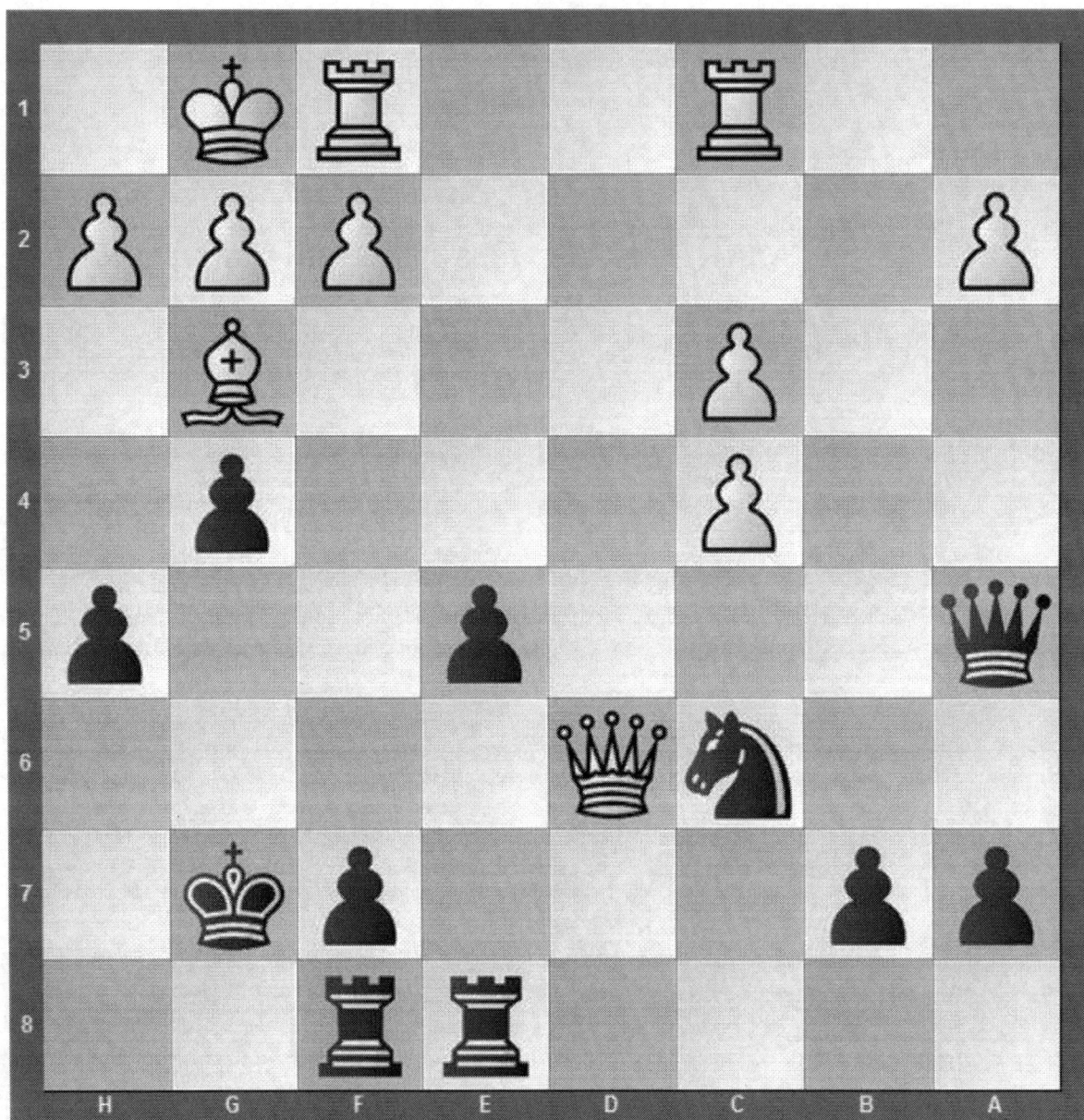

1		
2		

1		
2		

1		
2		

1		
2		

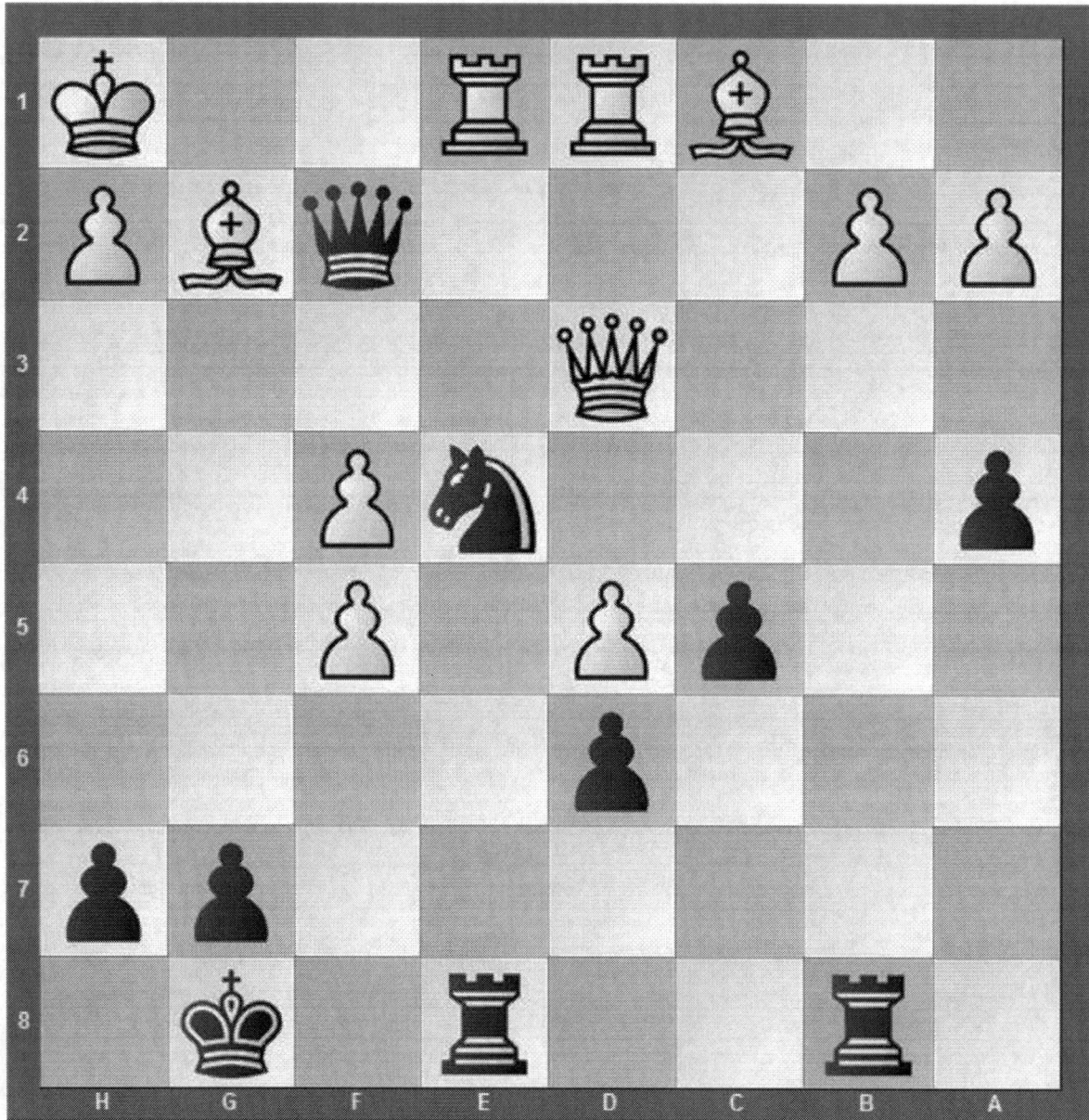

1		
2		

1		
2		

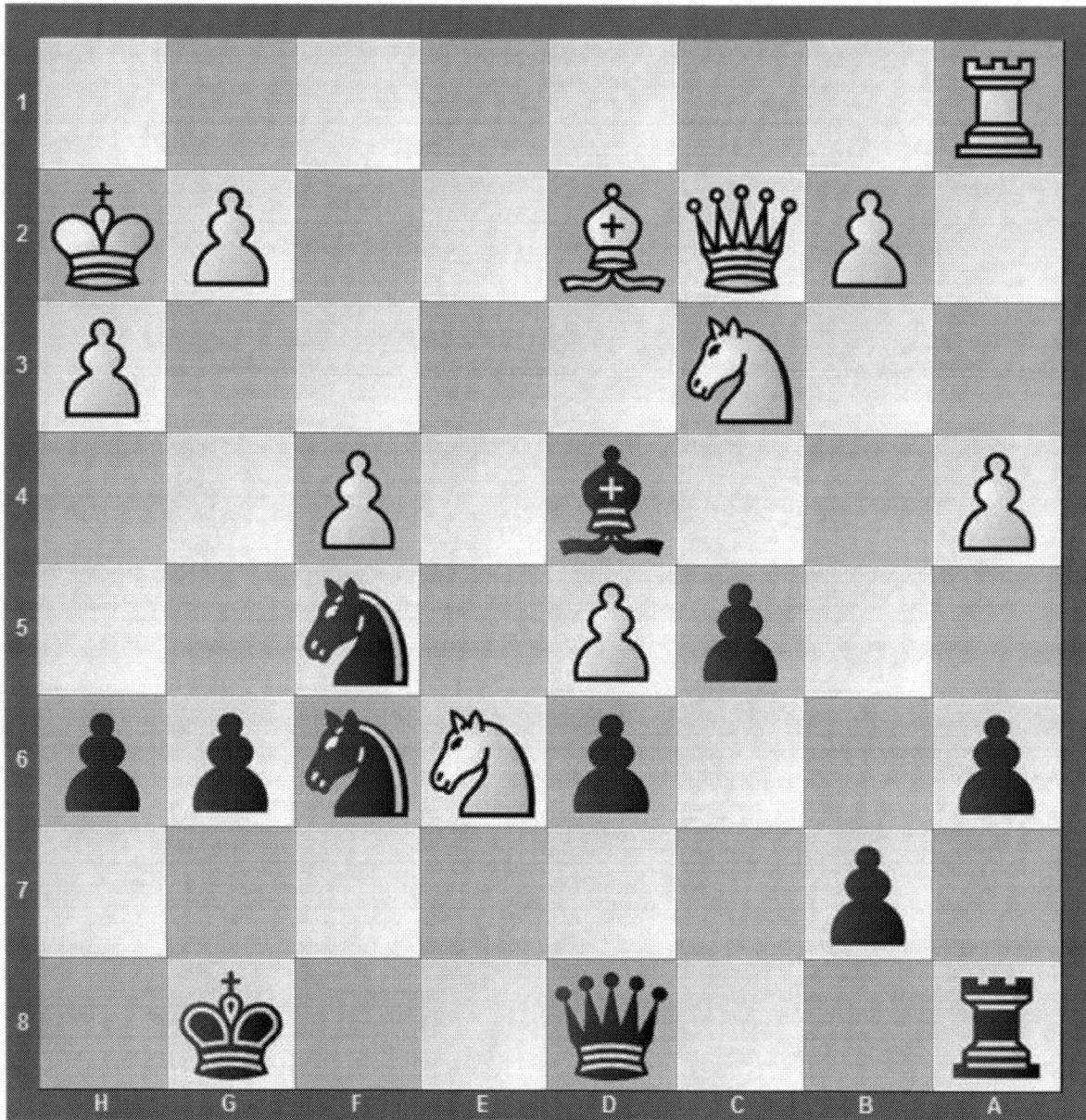

1		
2		

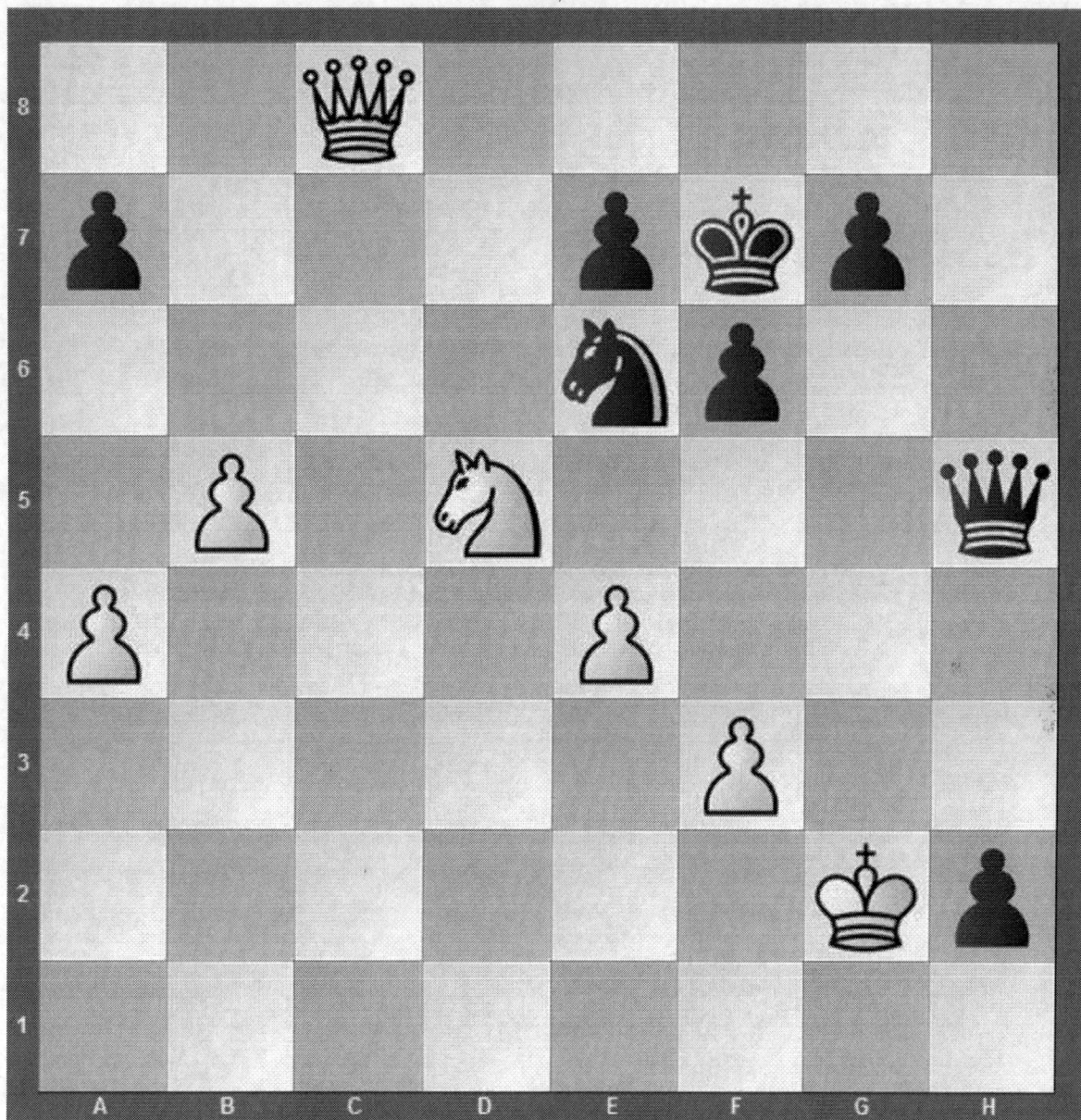

| 1 | | |
| 2 | | |

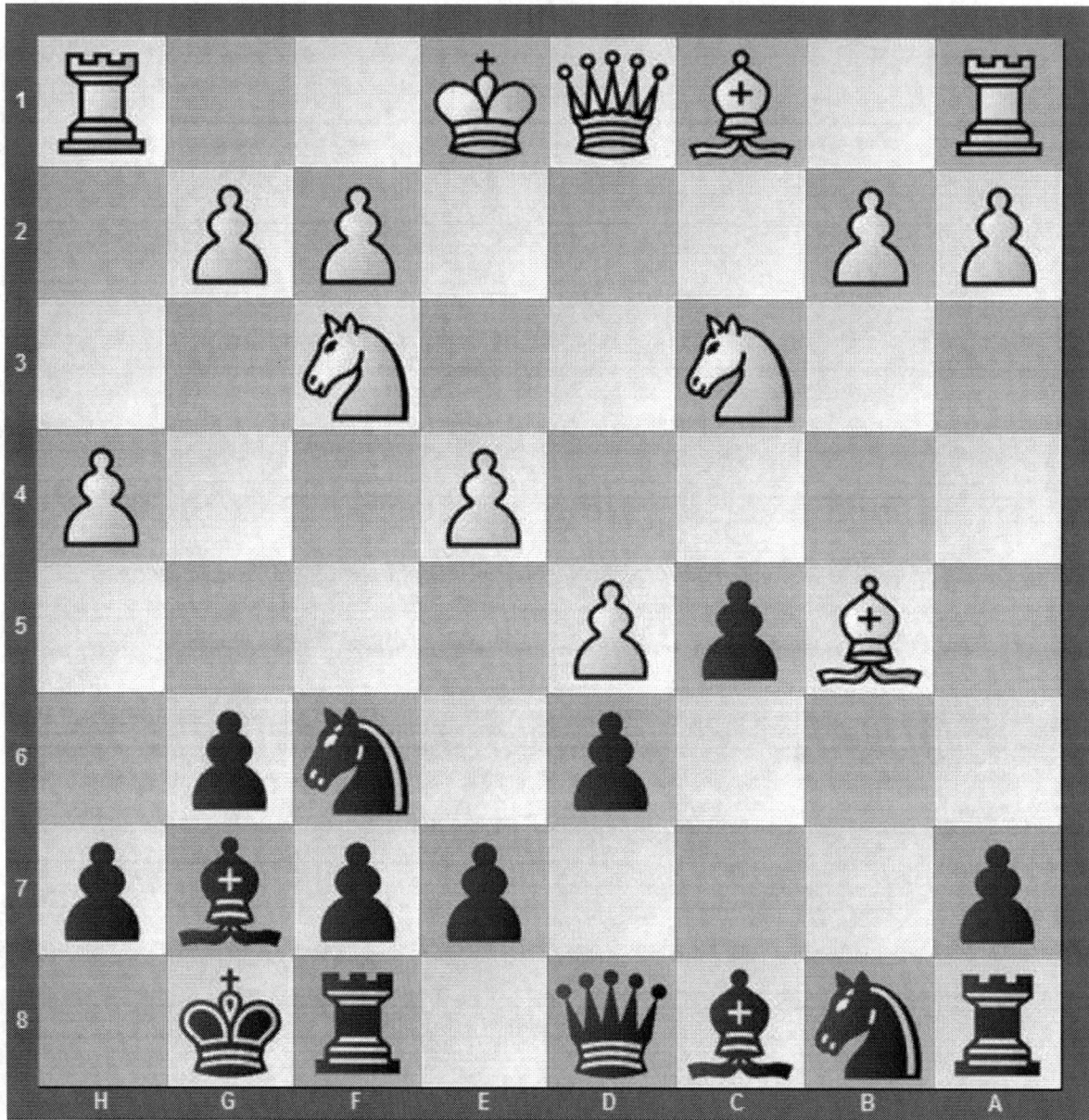

1		
2		

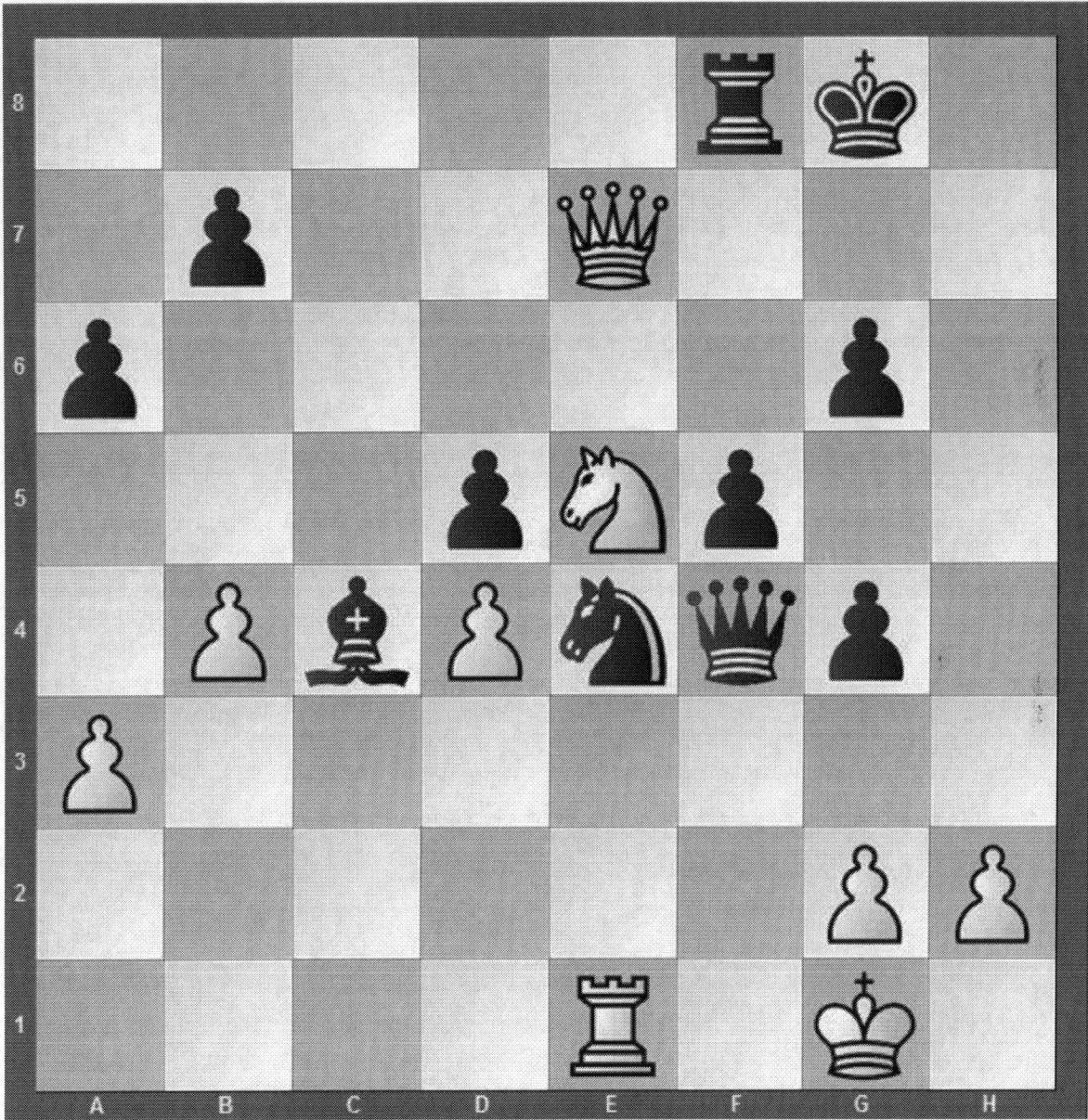

1		
2		

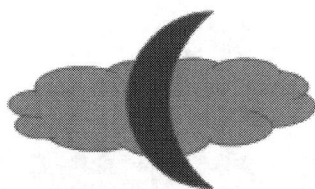

1		
2		

"The blunders are all there on the board, waiting to be made." – Savielly
Tartakover

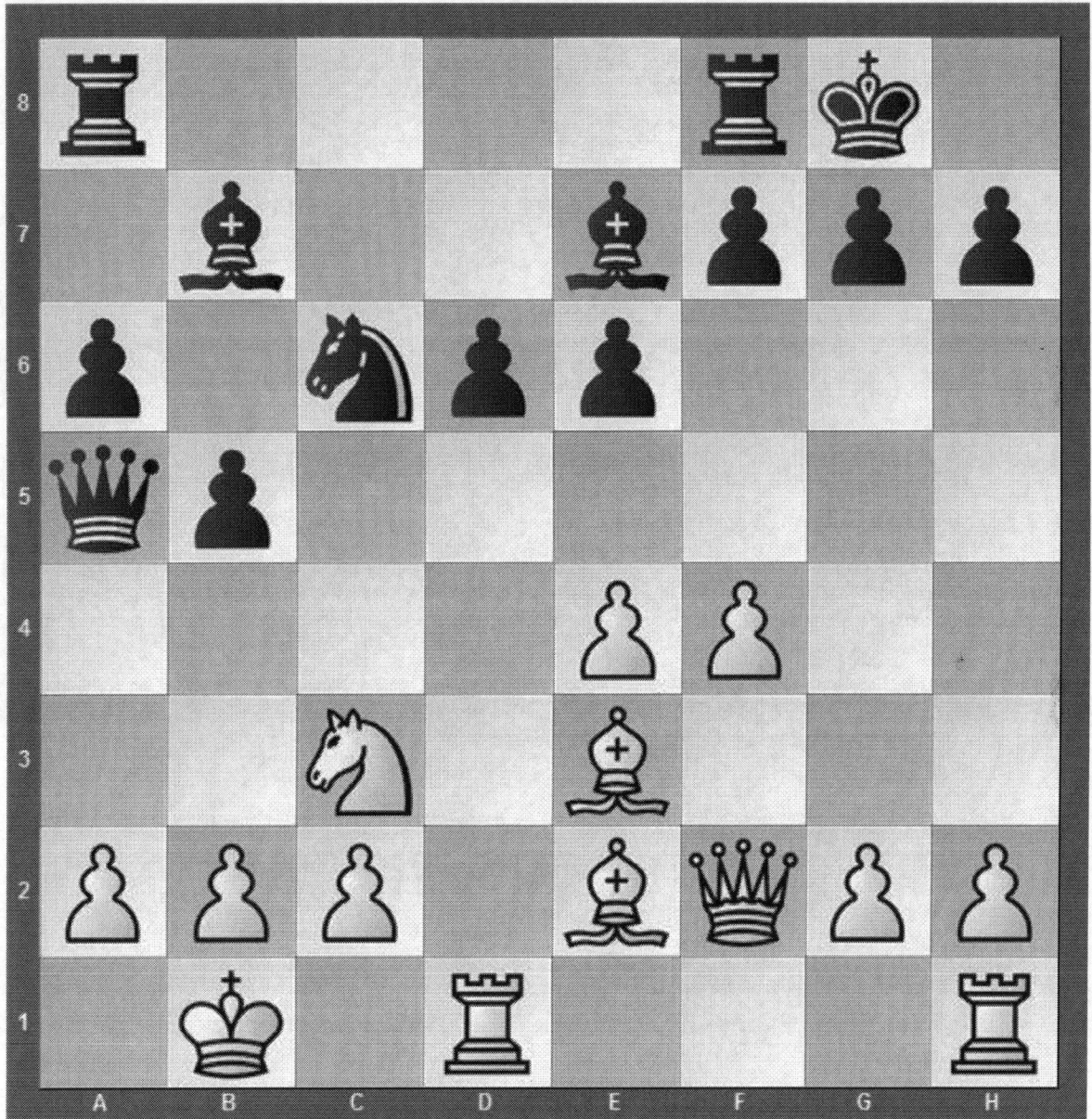

| 1 | | |
| 2 | | |

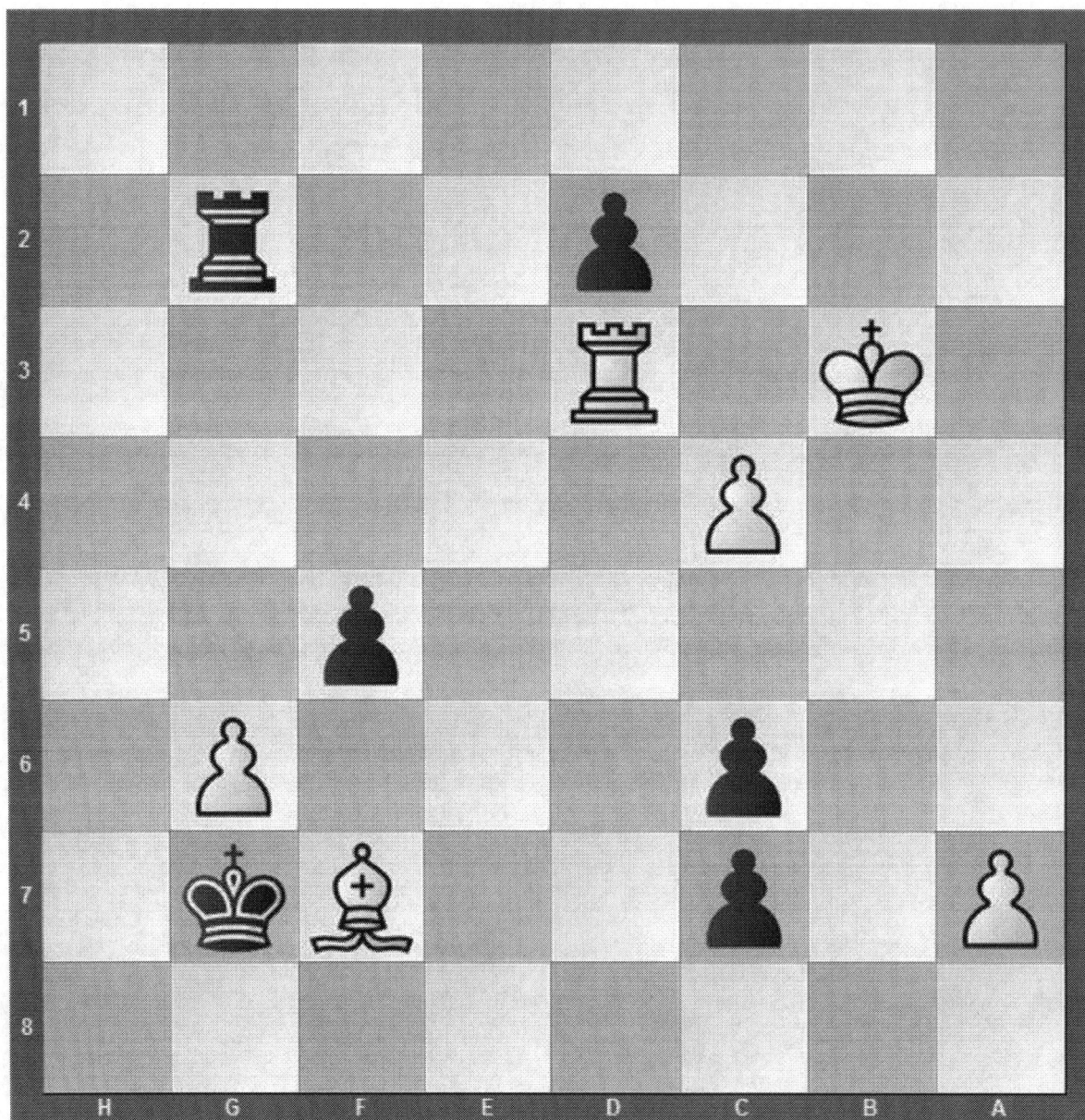

1		
2		

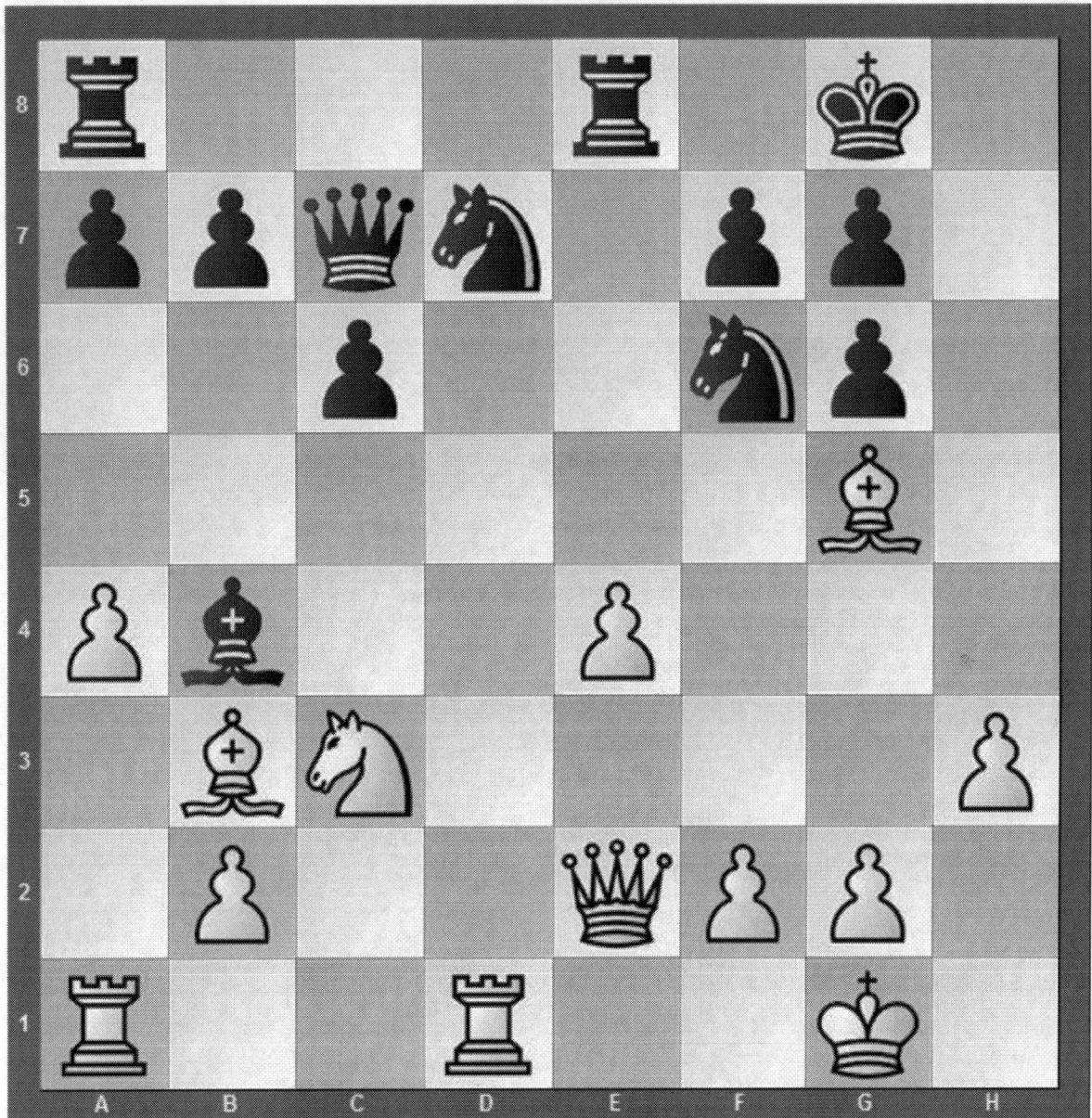

1		
2		

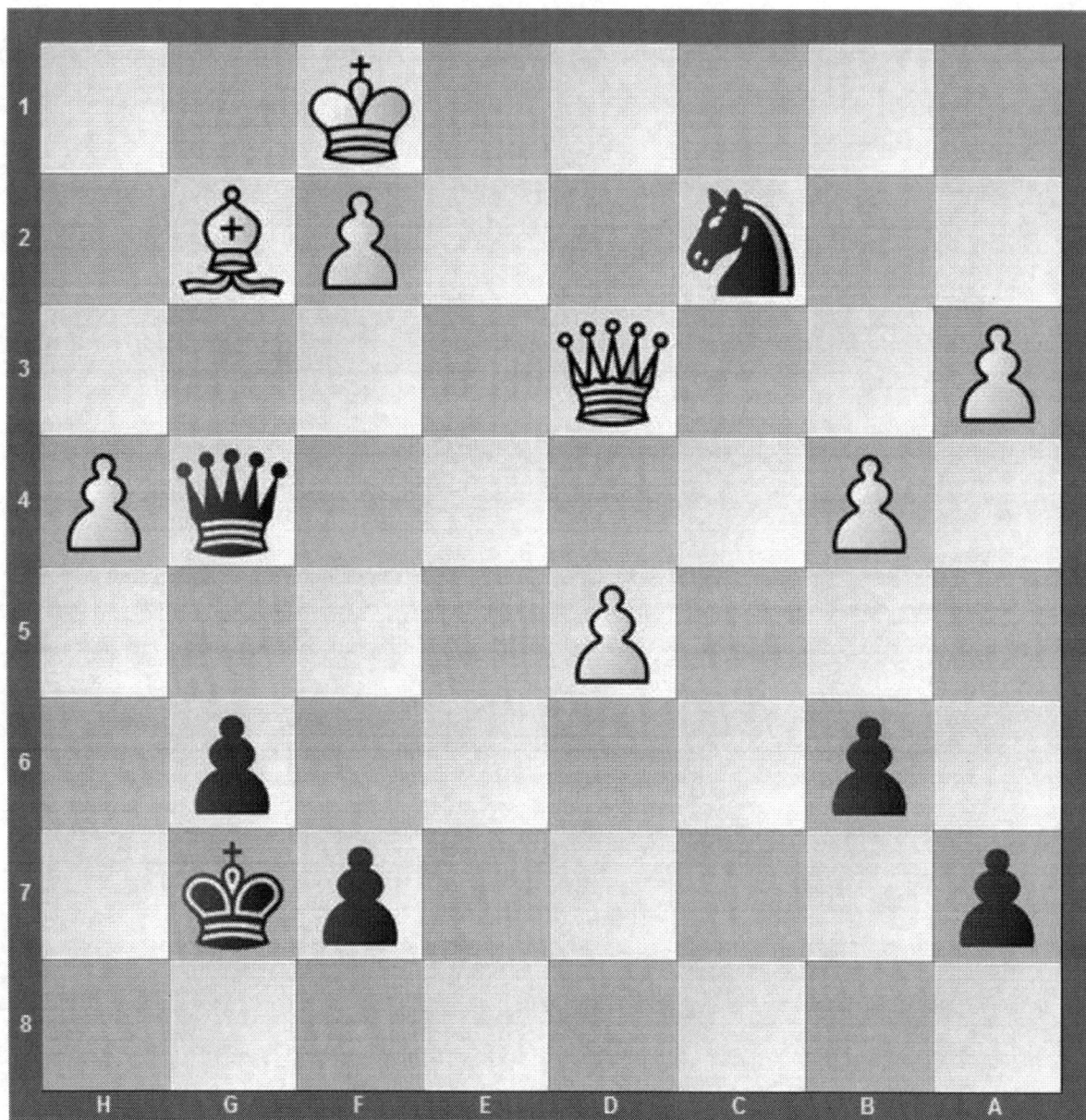

1		
2		

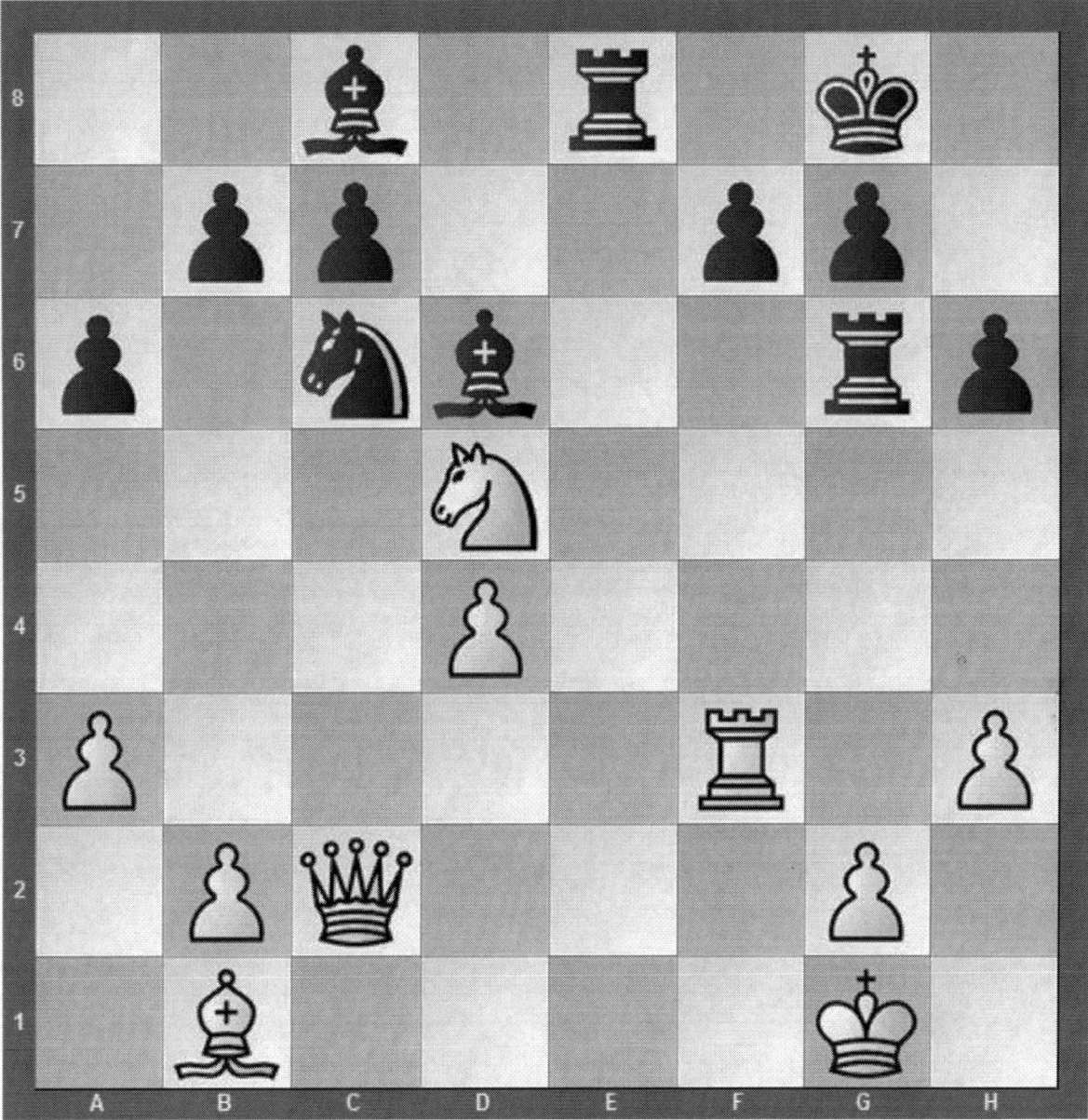

1		
2		

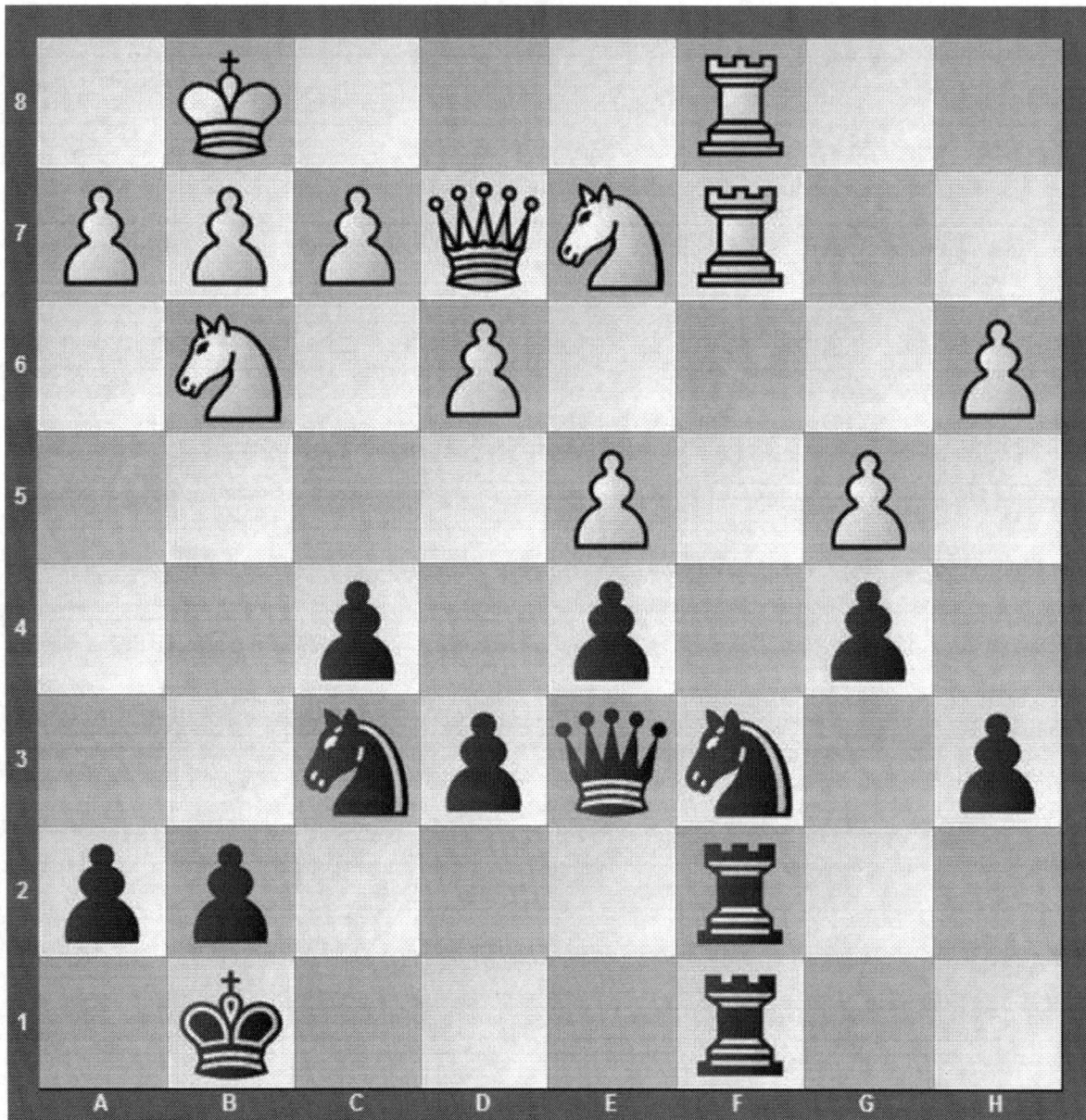

1		
2		

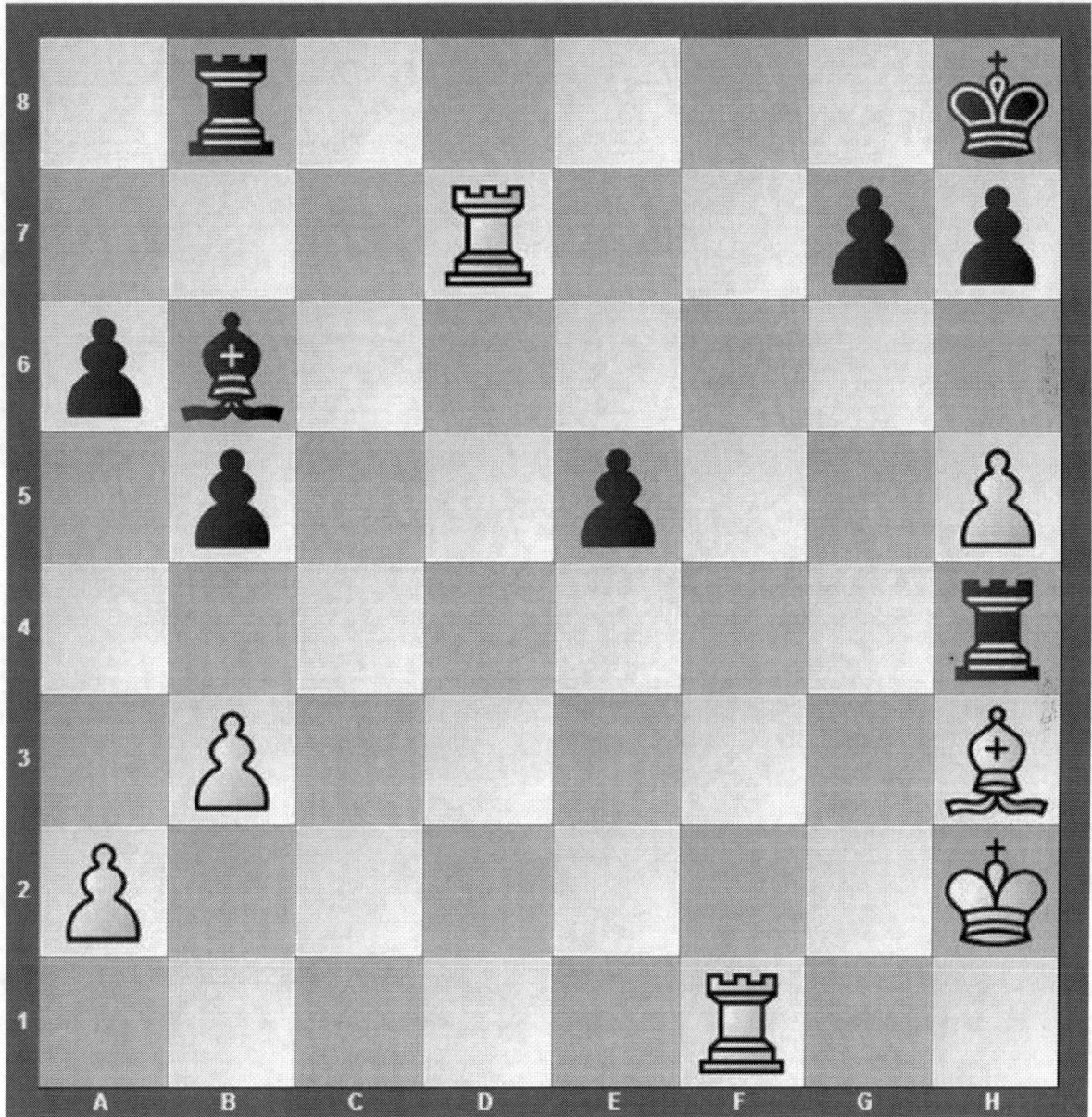

1		
2		

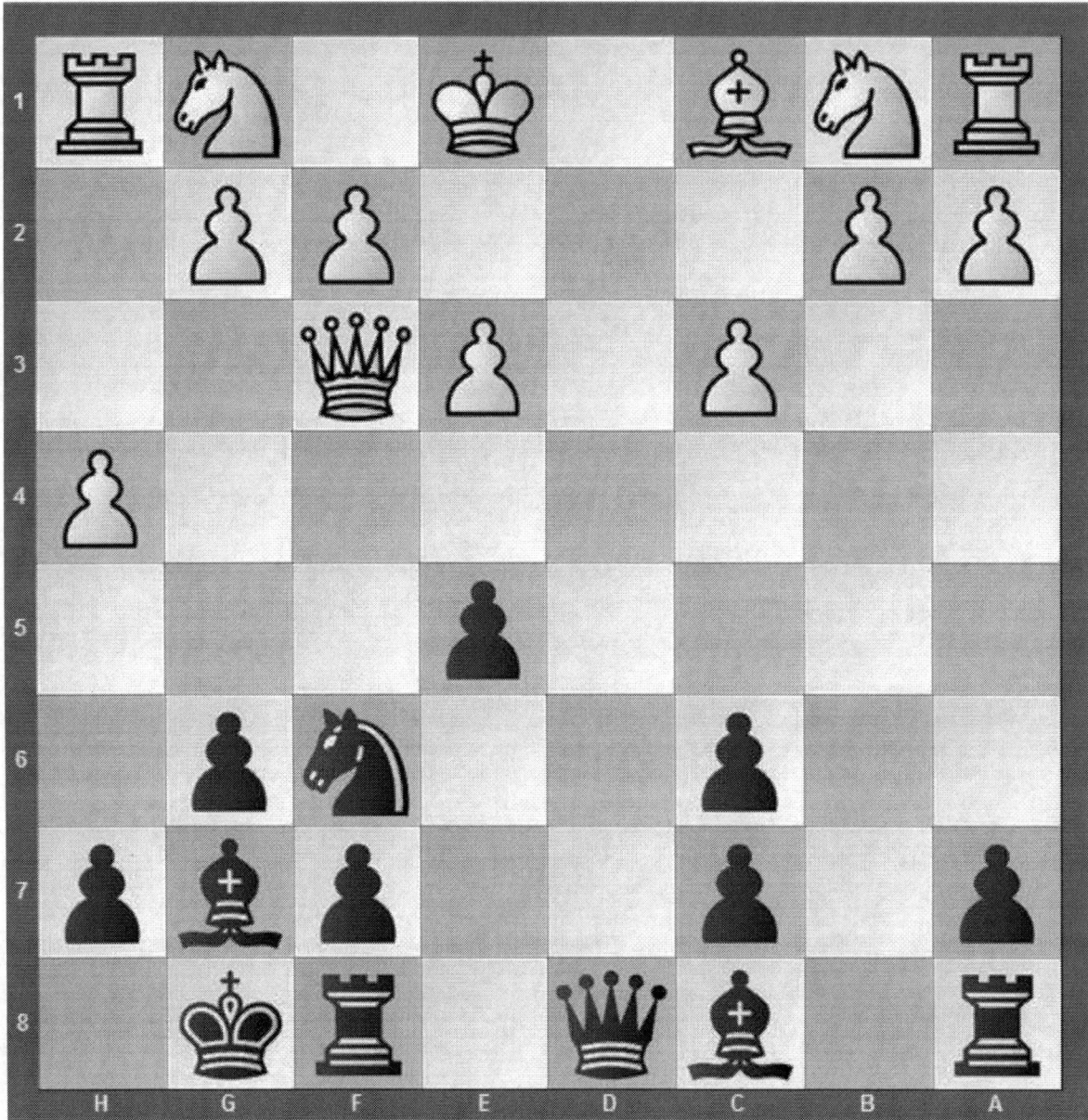

| 1 | | |
| 2 | | |

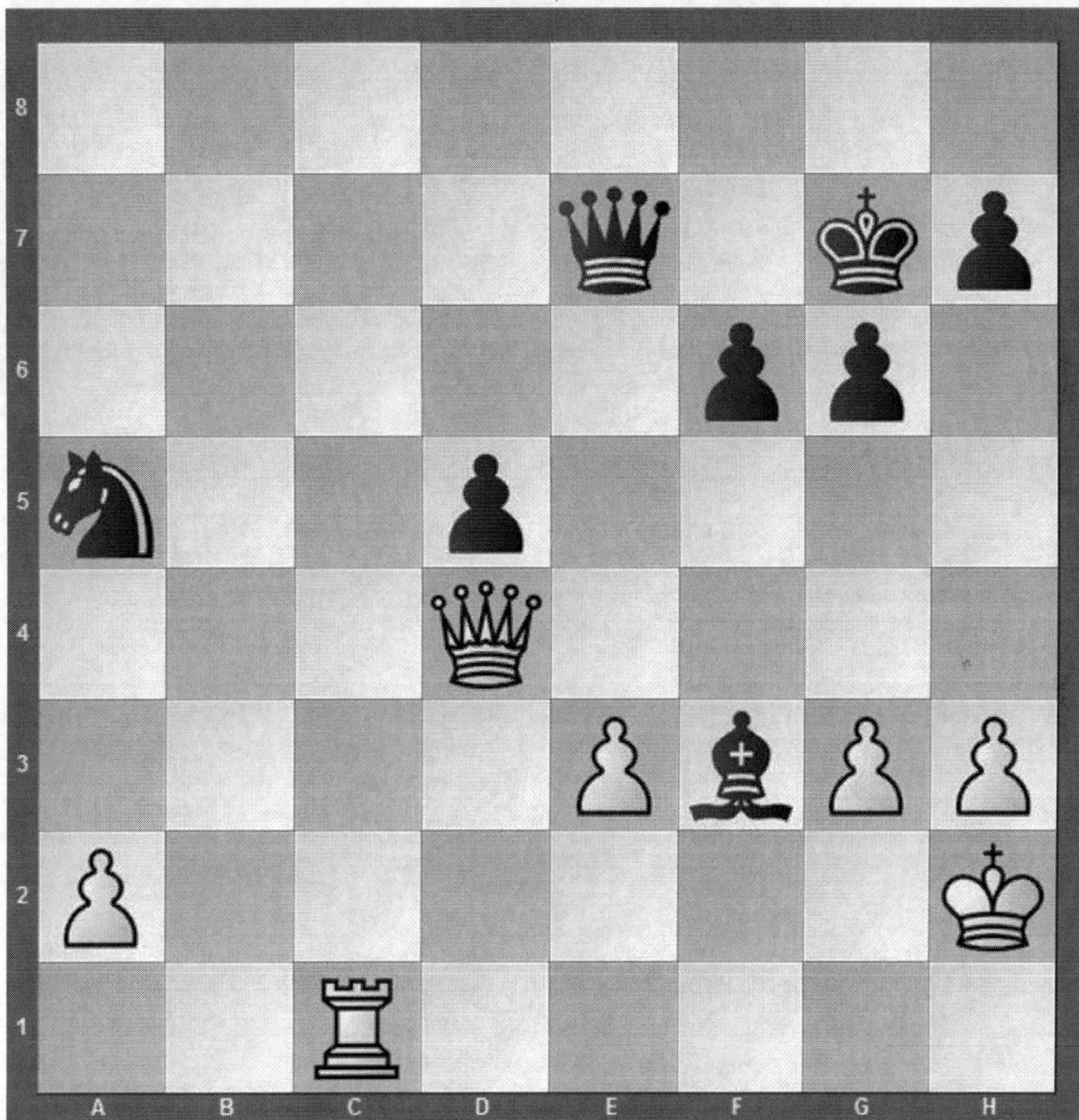

1		
2		

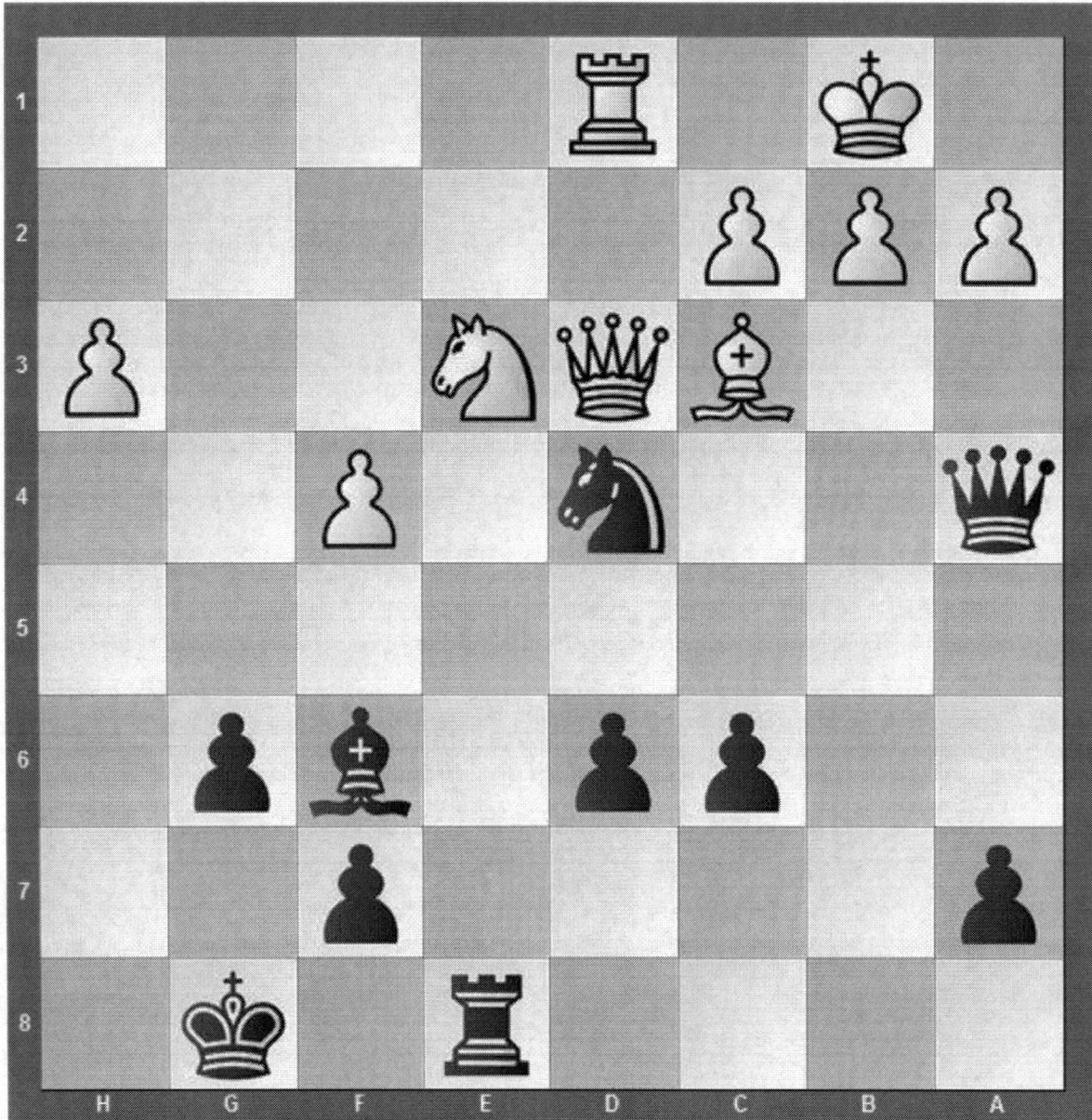

1		
2		

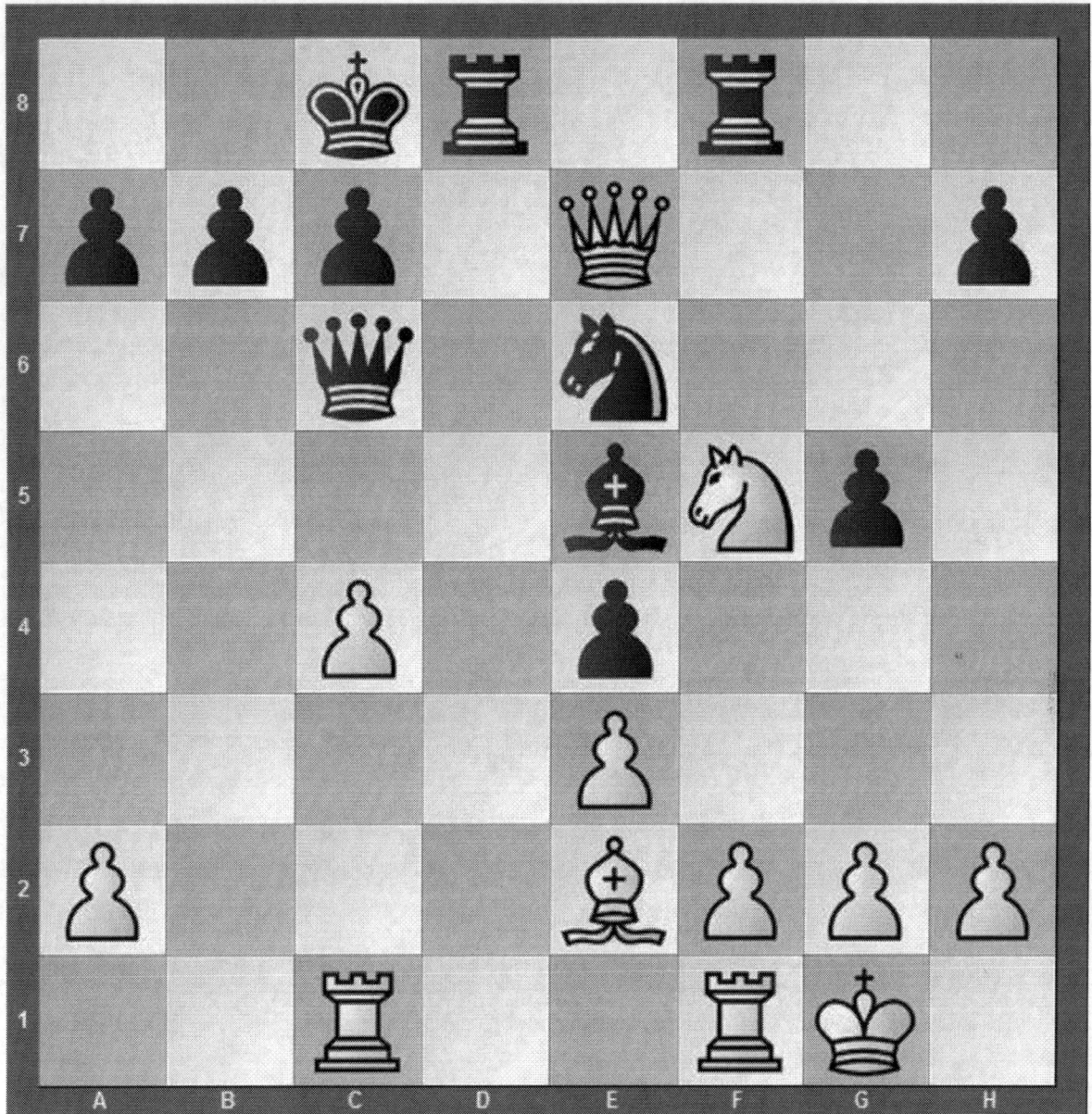

1		
2		

1		
2		

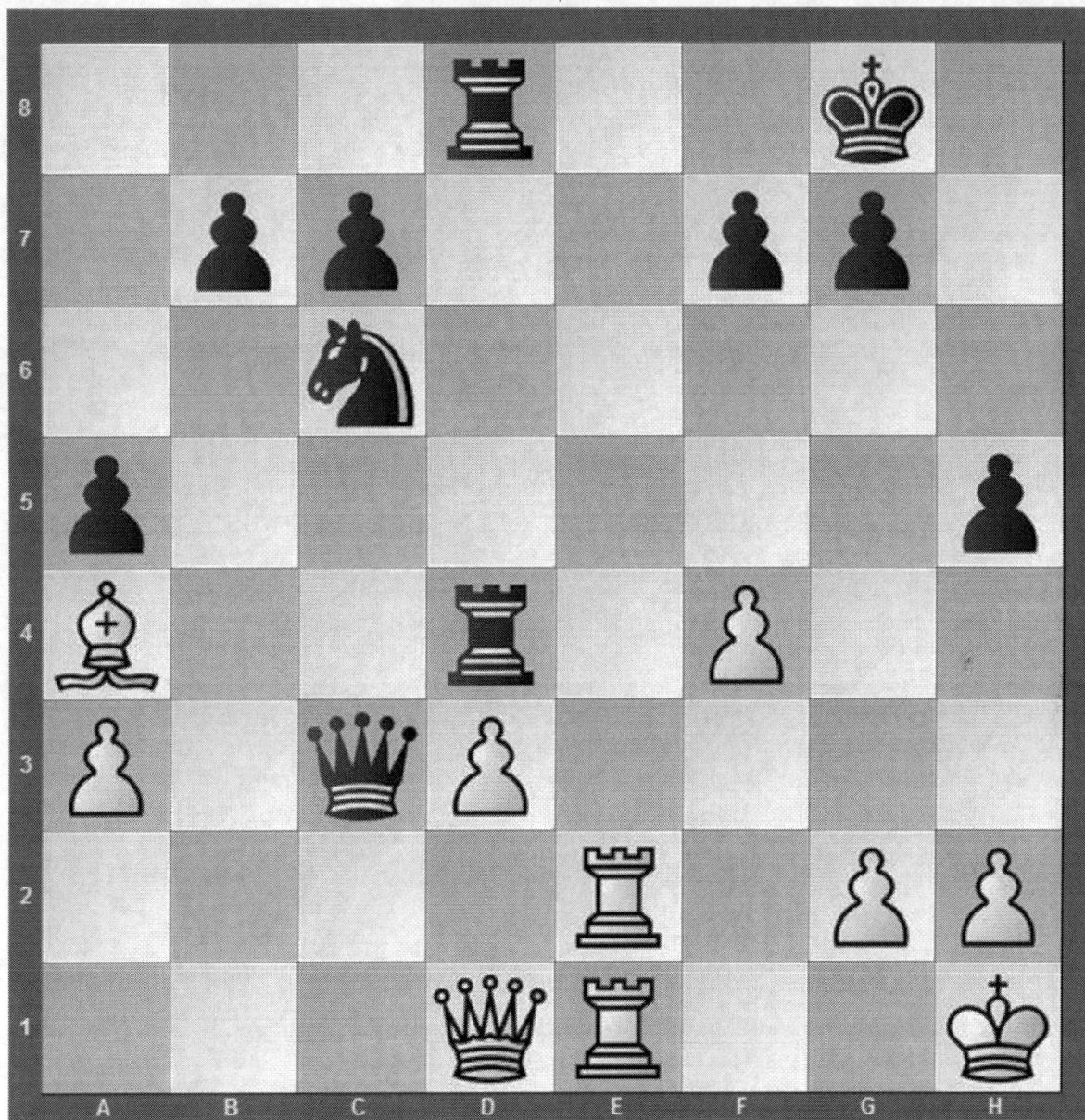

1		
2		

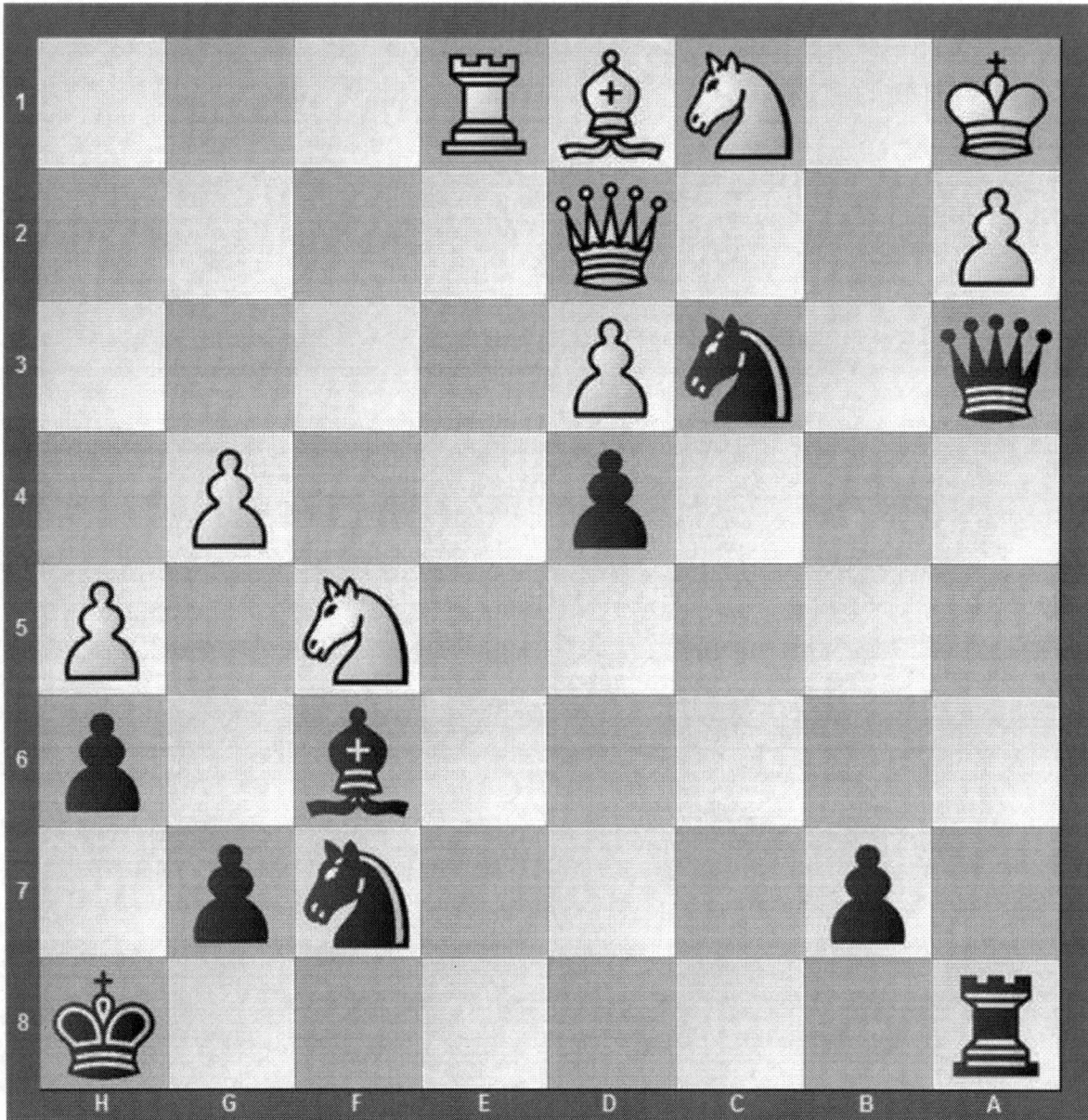

1		
2		

"Chess mastery essentially consists of analyzing chess positions accurately." – **Mikhail Botvinnik**

1		
2		

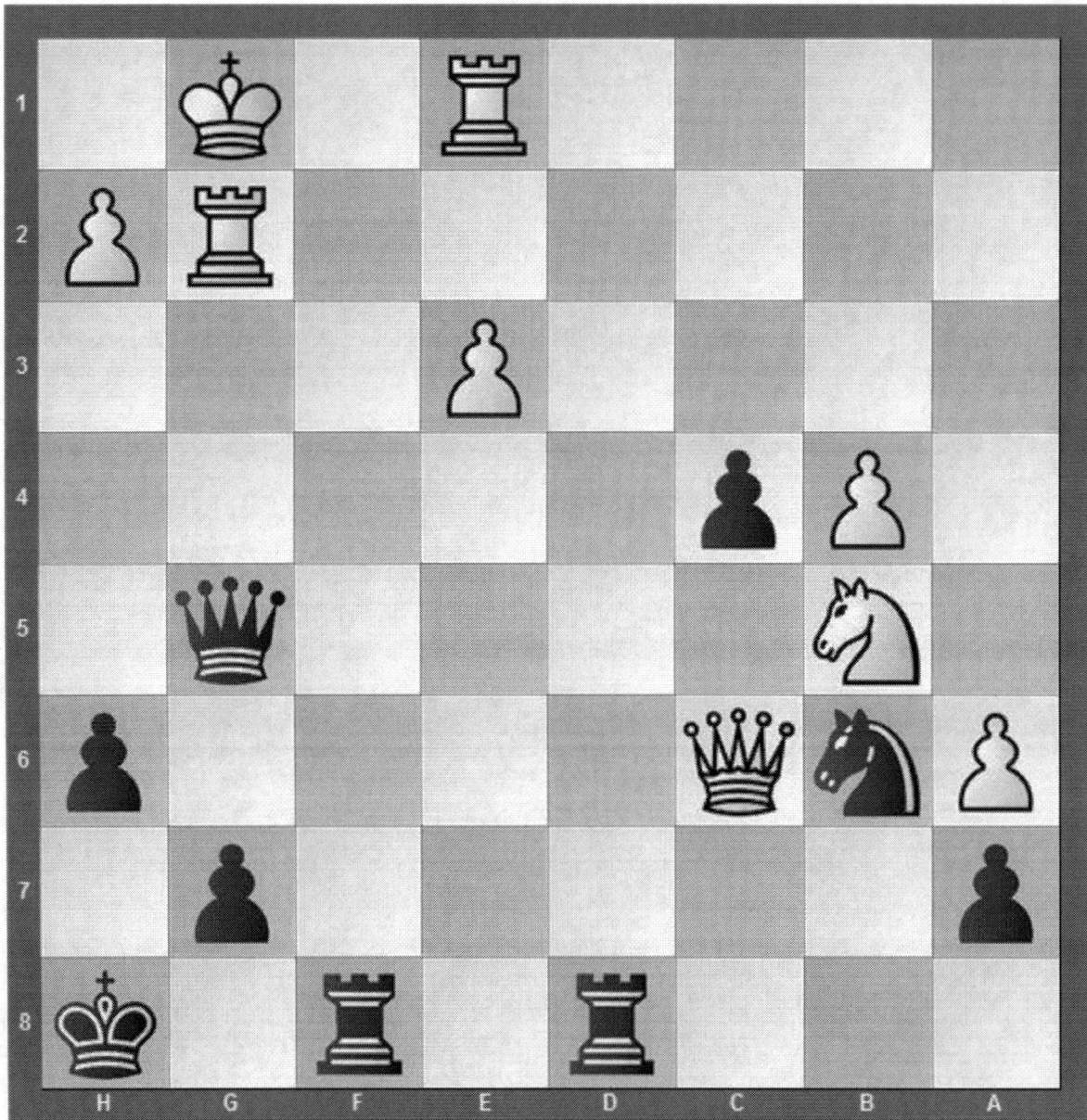

1		
2		

1		
2		

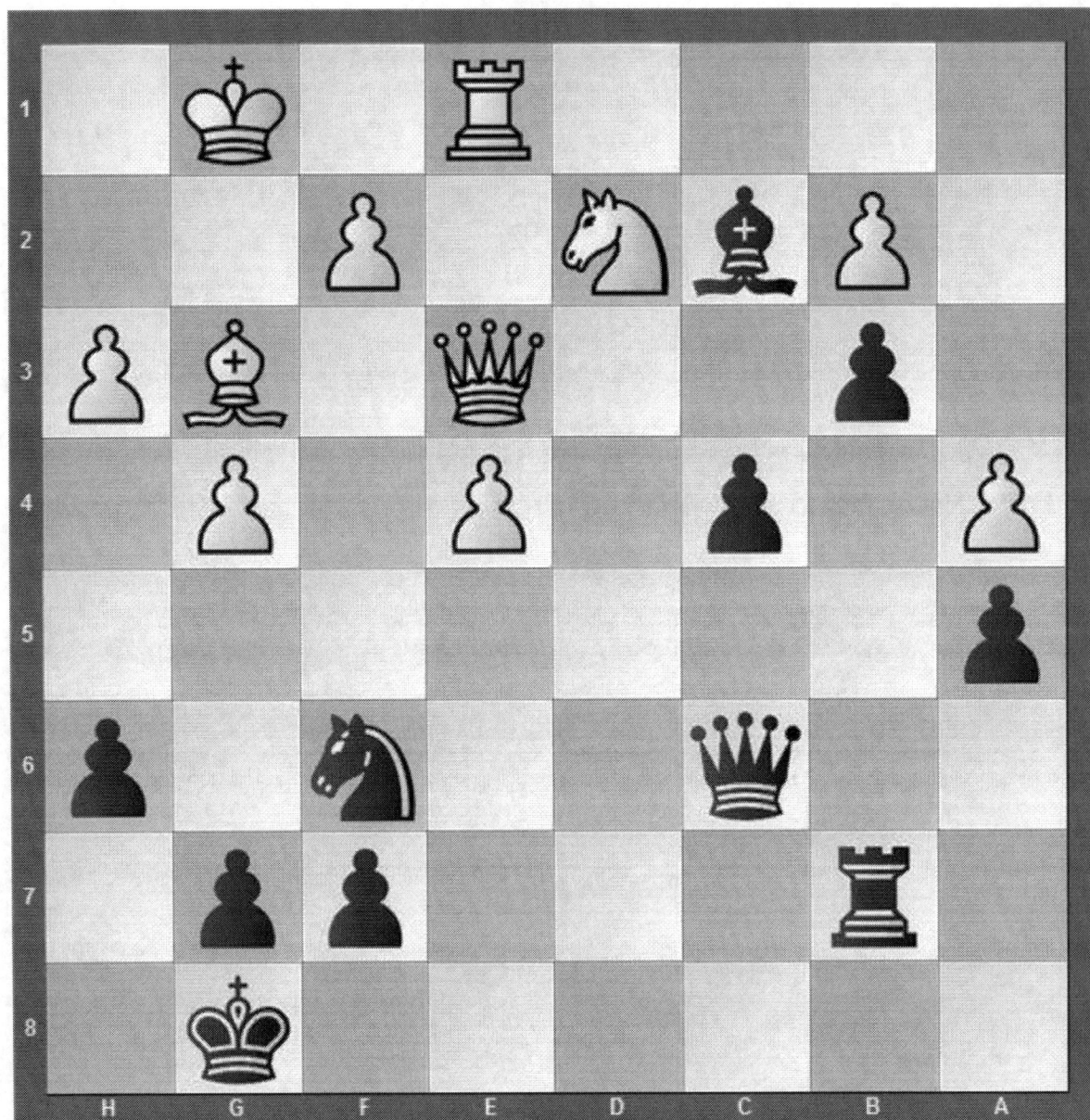

1		
2		

1		
2		

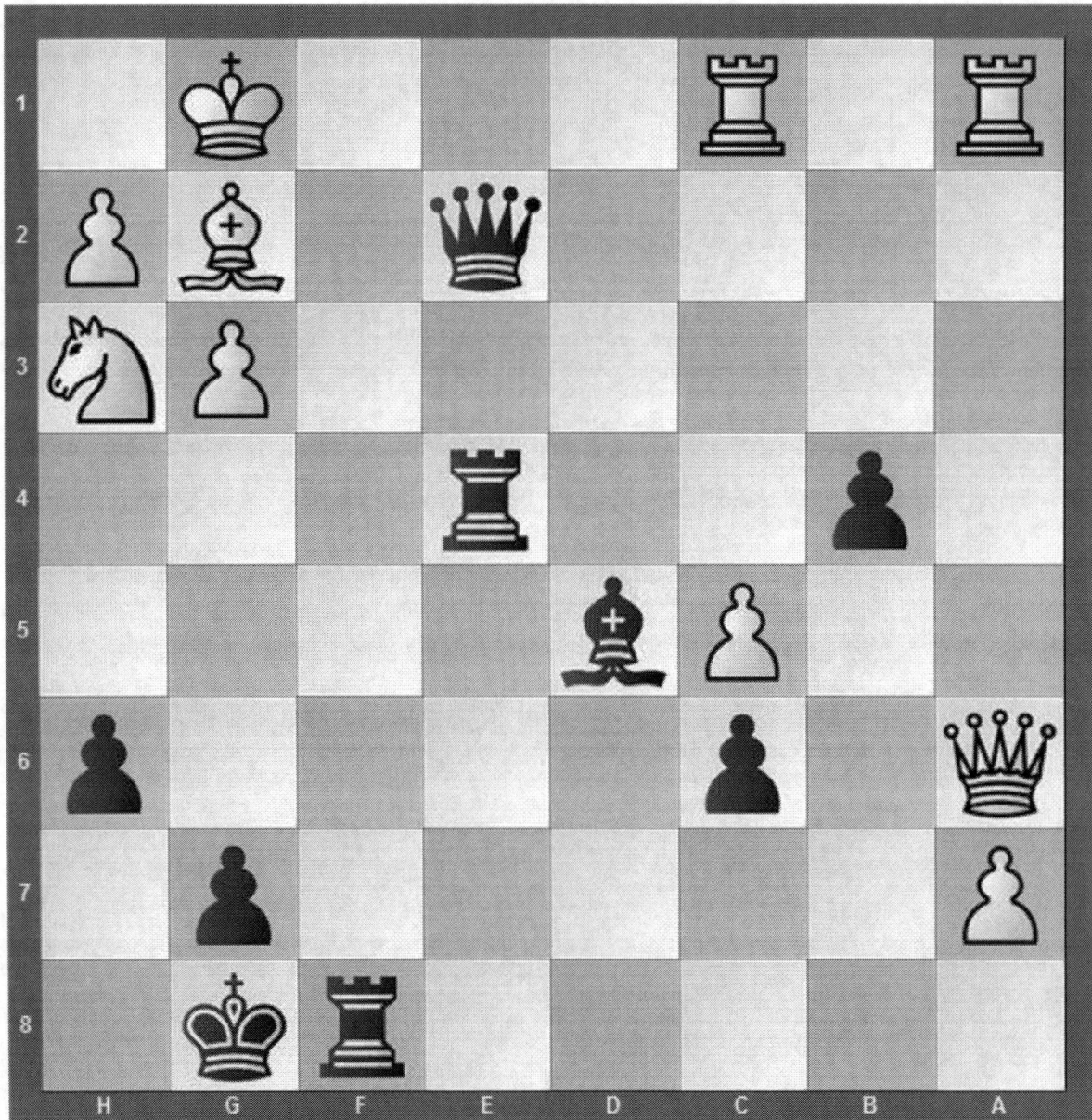

1		
2		

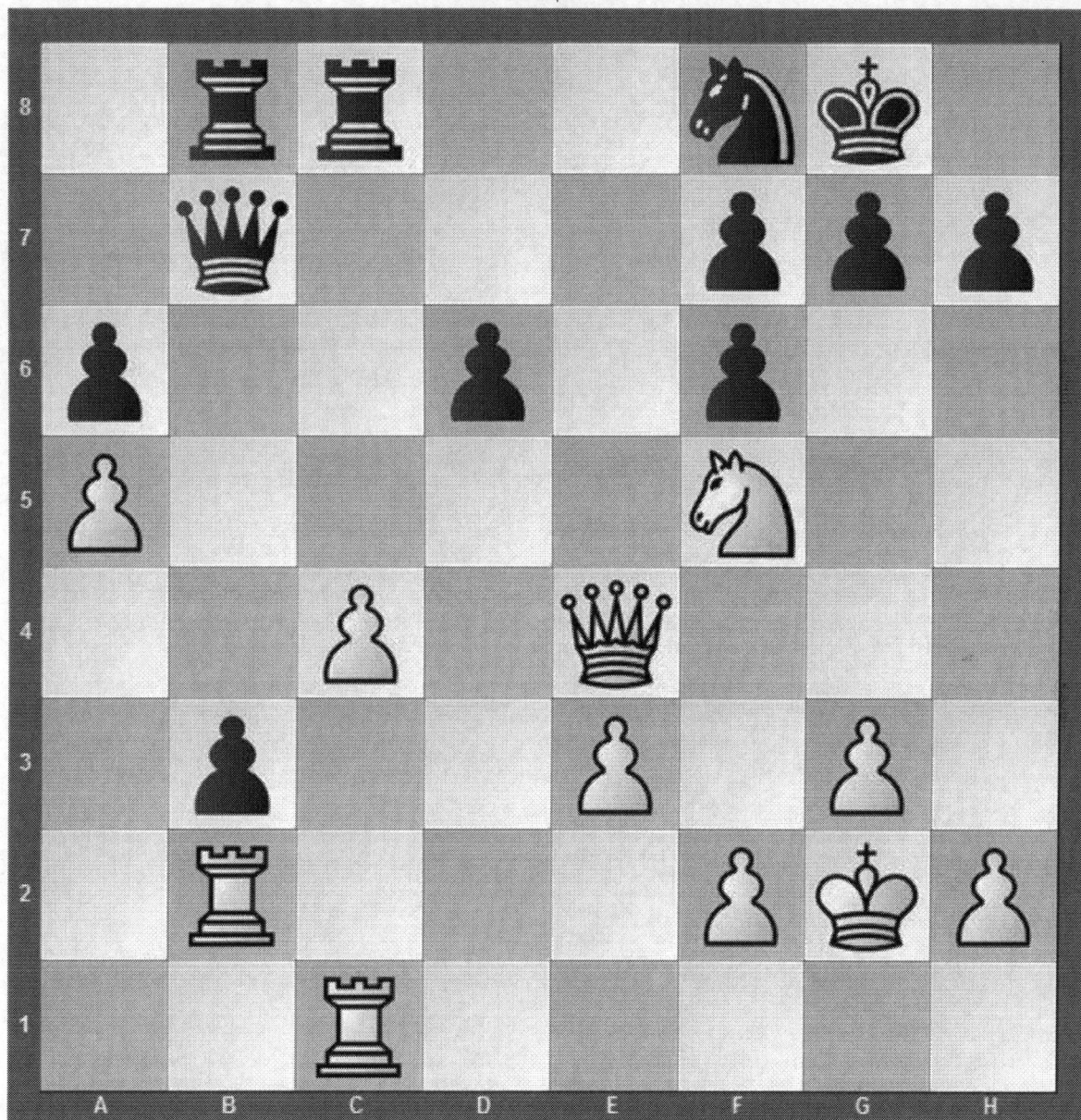

1		
2		

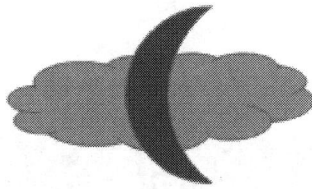

1		
2		

1		
2		

1		
2		

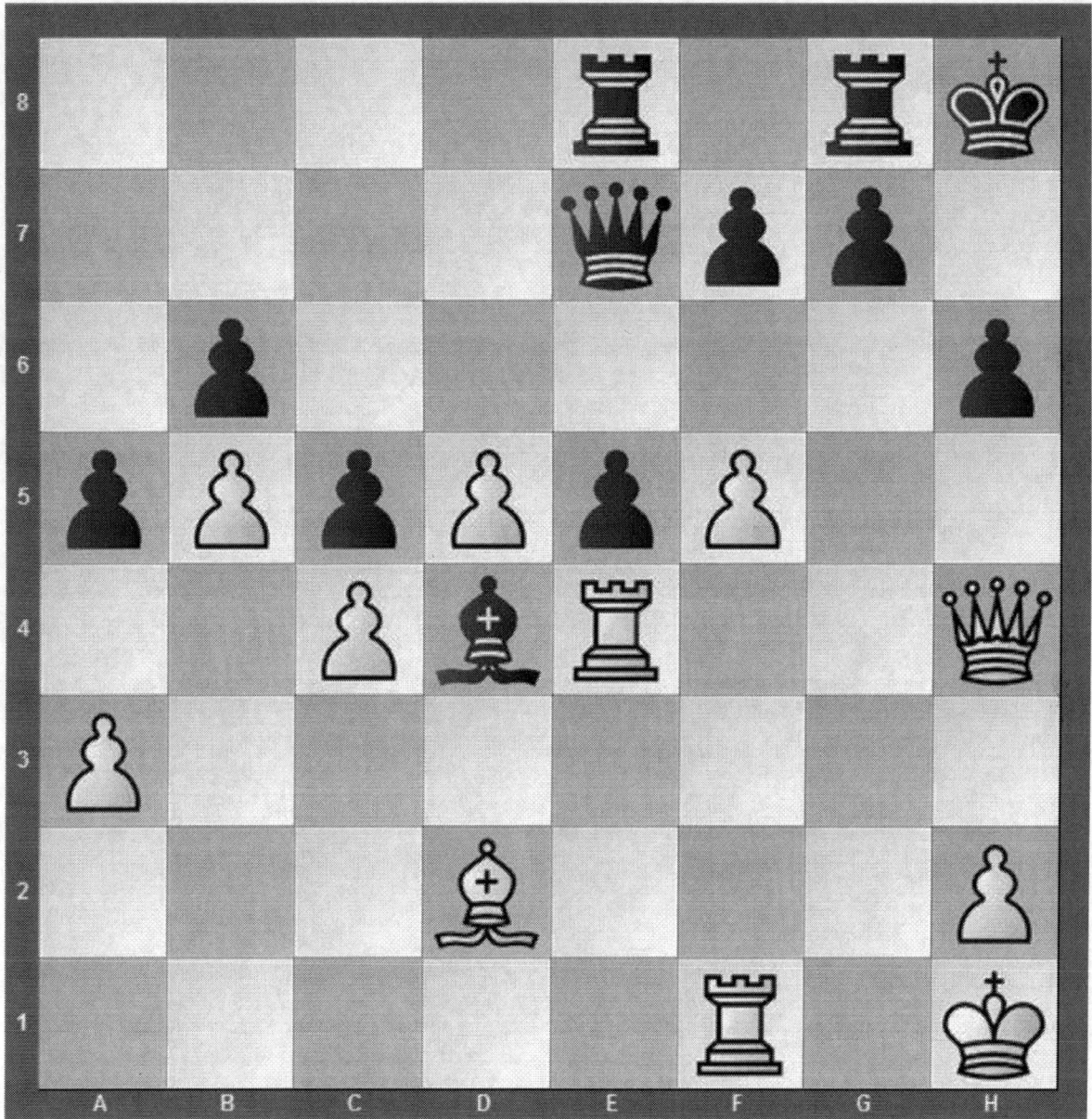

1		
2		

1		
2		

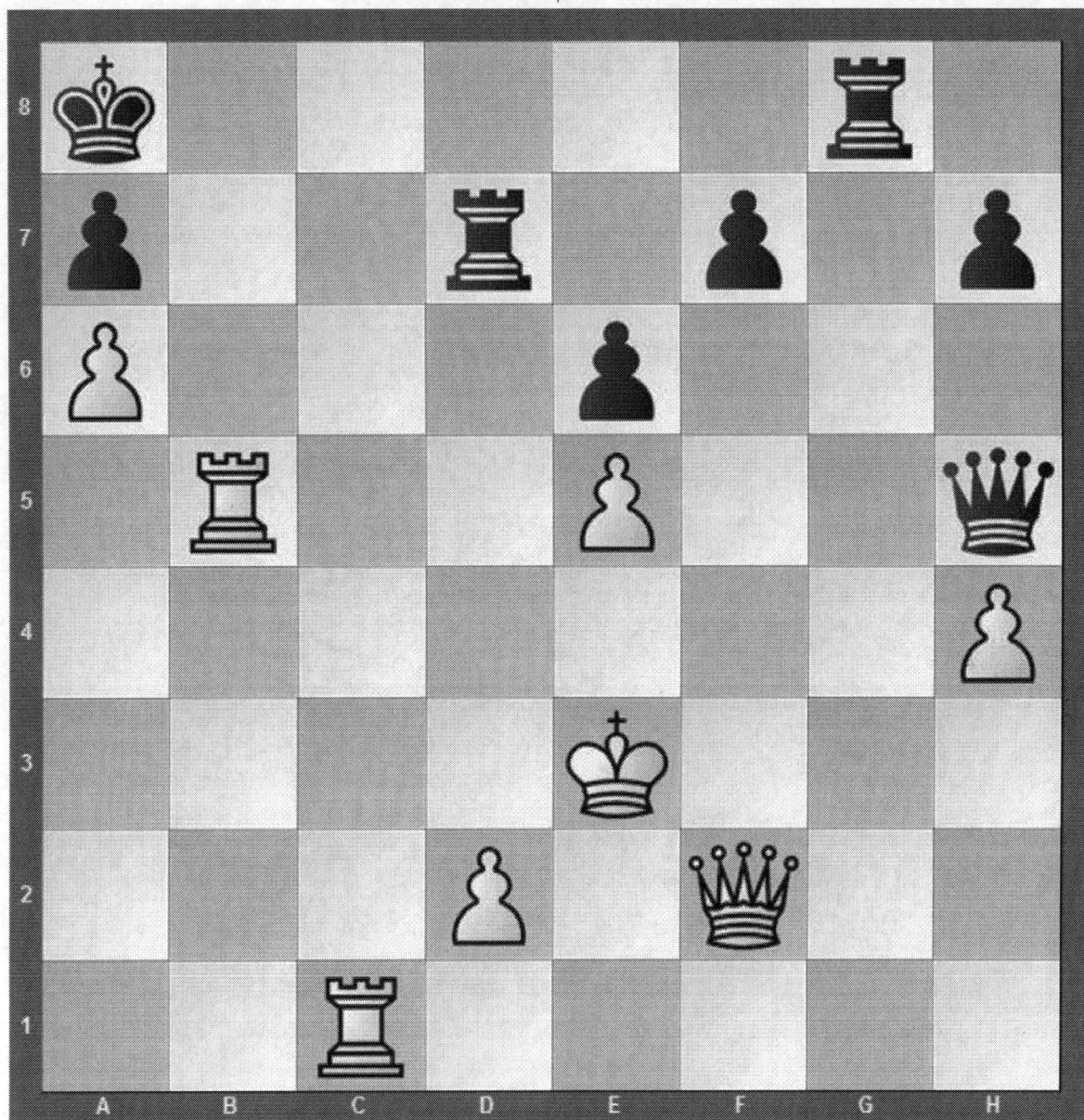

1		
2		

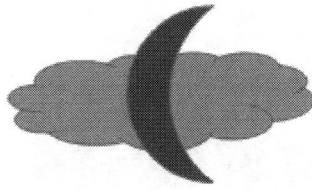

| 1 | | |
| 2 | | |

"You have to have the fighting spirit. You have to force moves and take chances." – **Bobby Fischer**

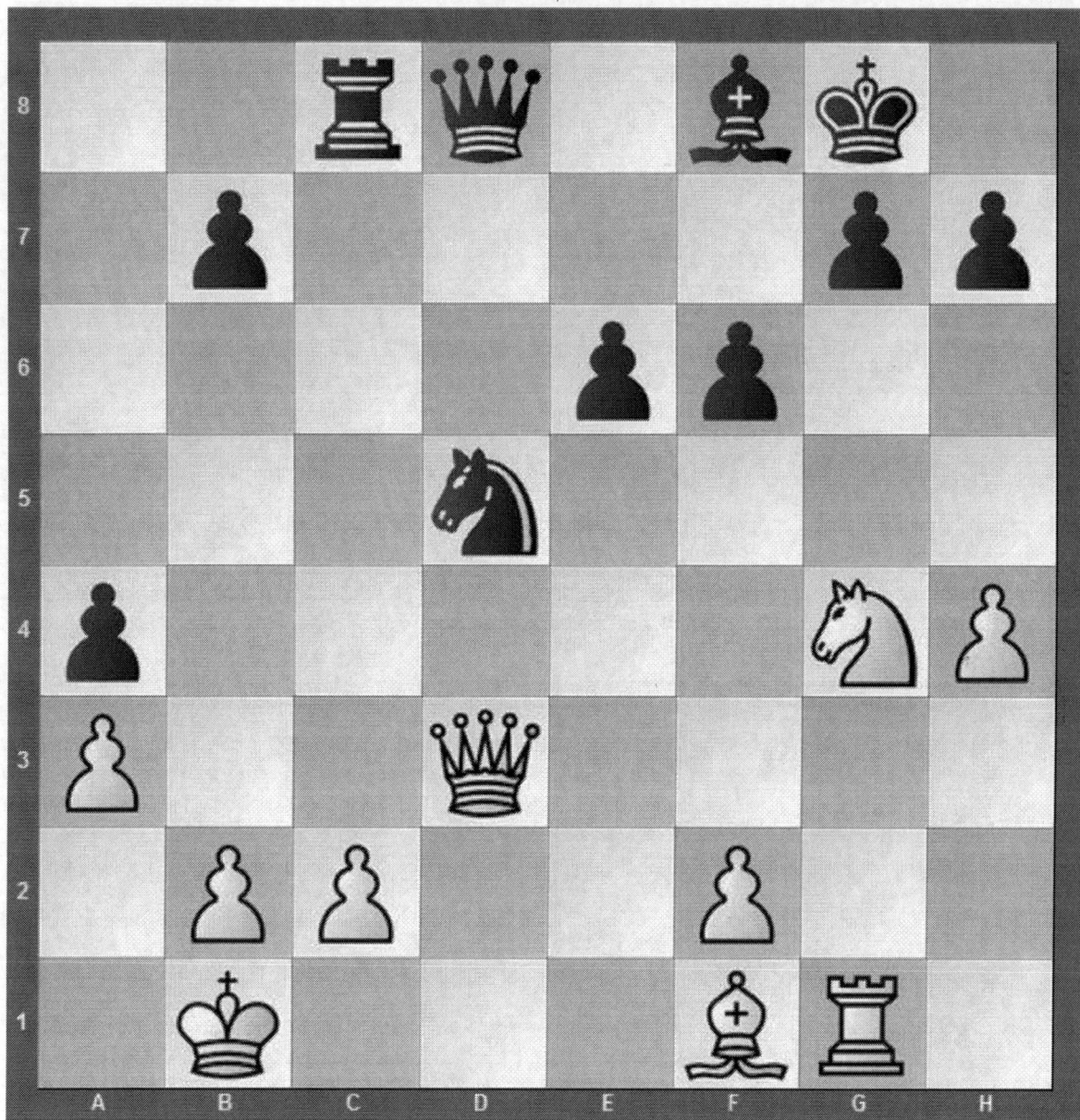

1		
2		

1		
2		

1		
2		

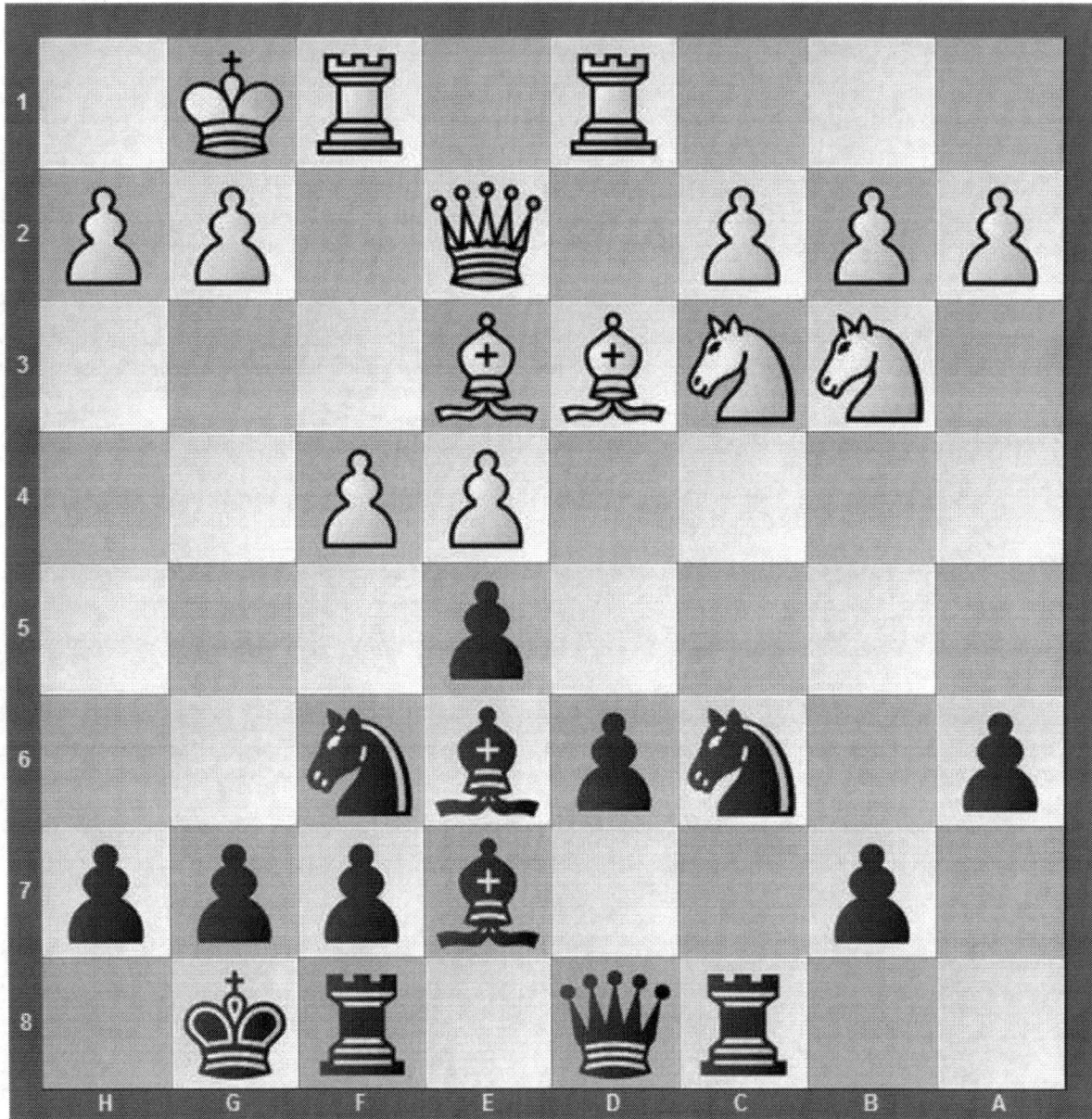

1		
2		

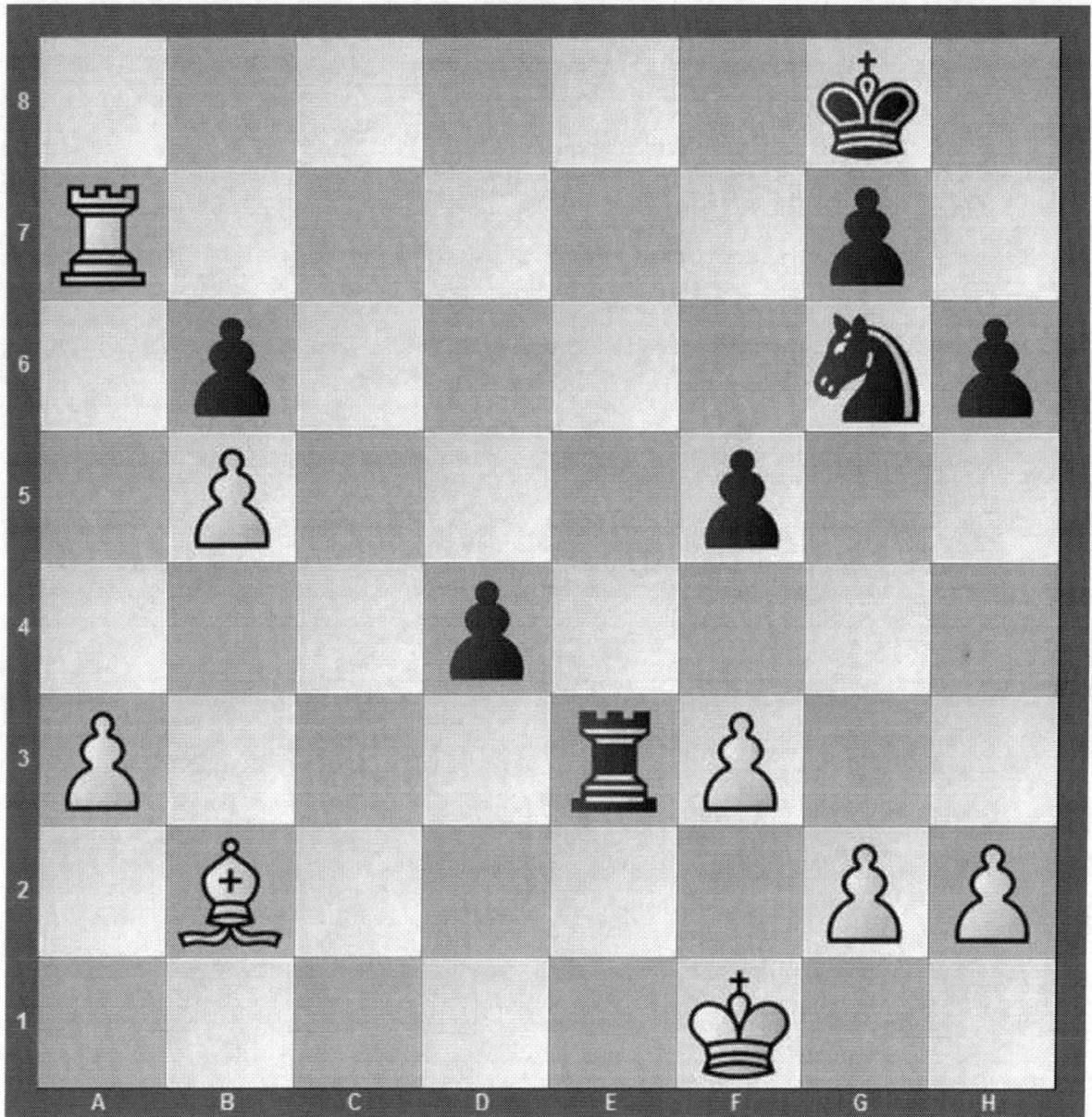

1		
2		

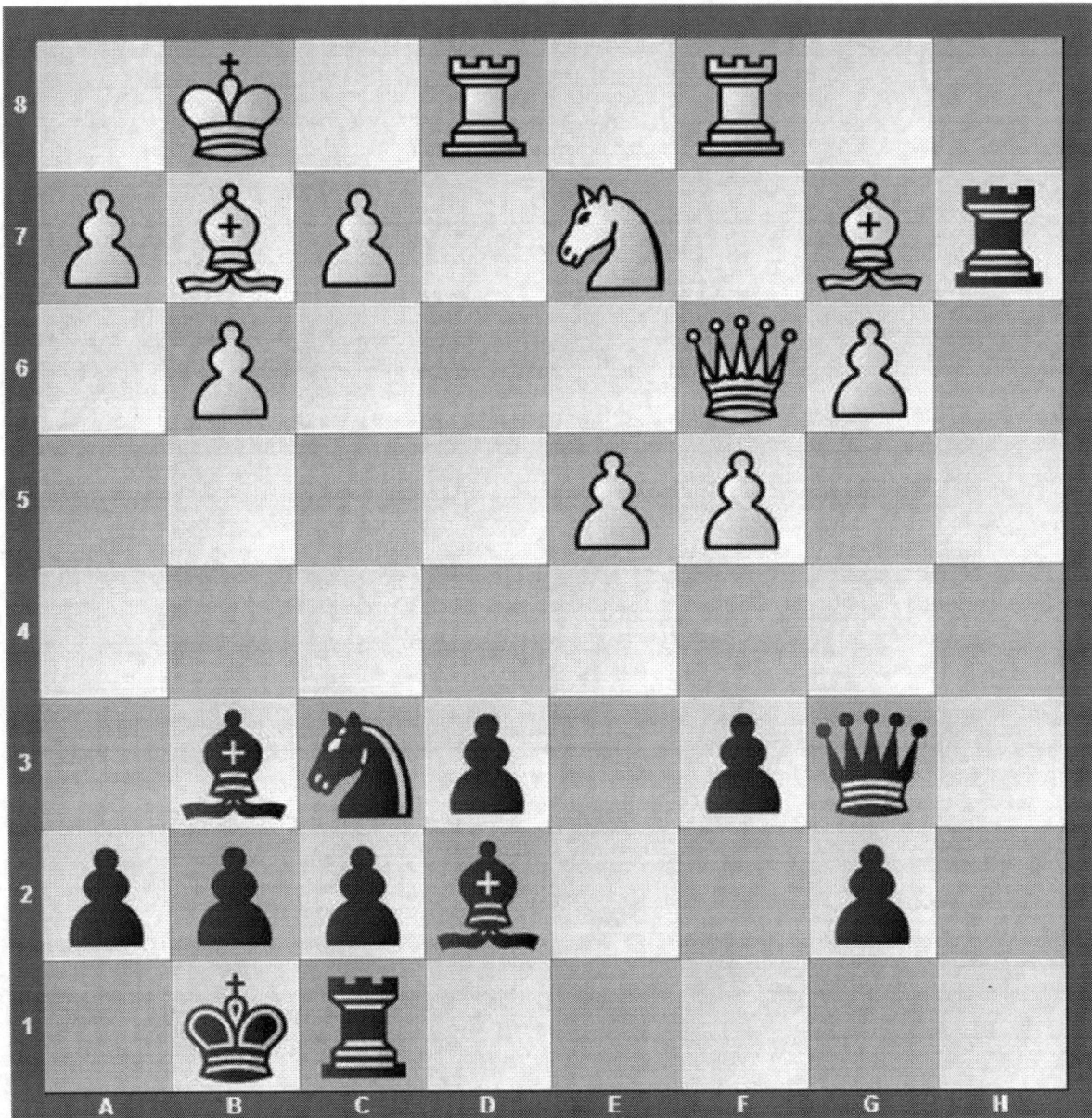

1		
2		

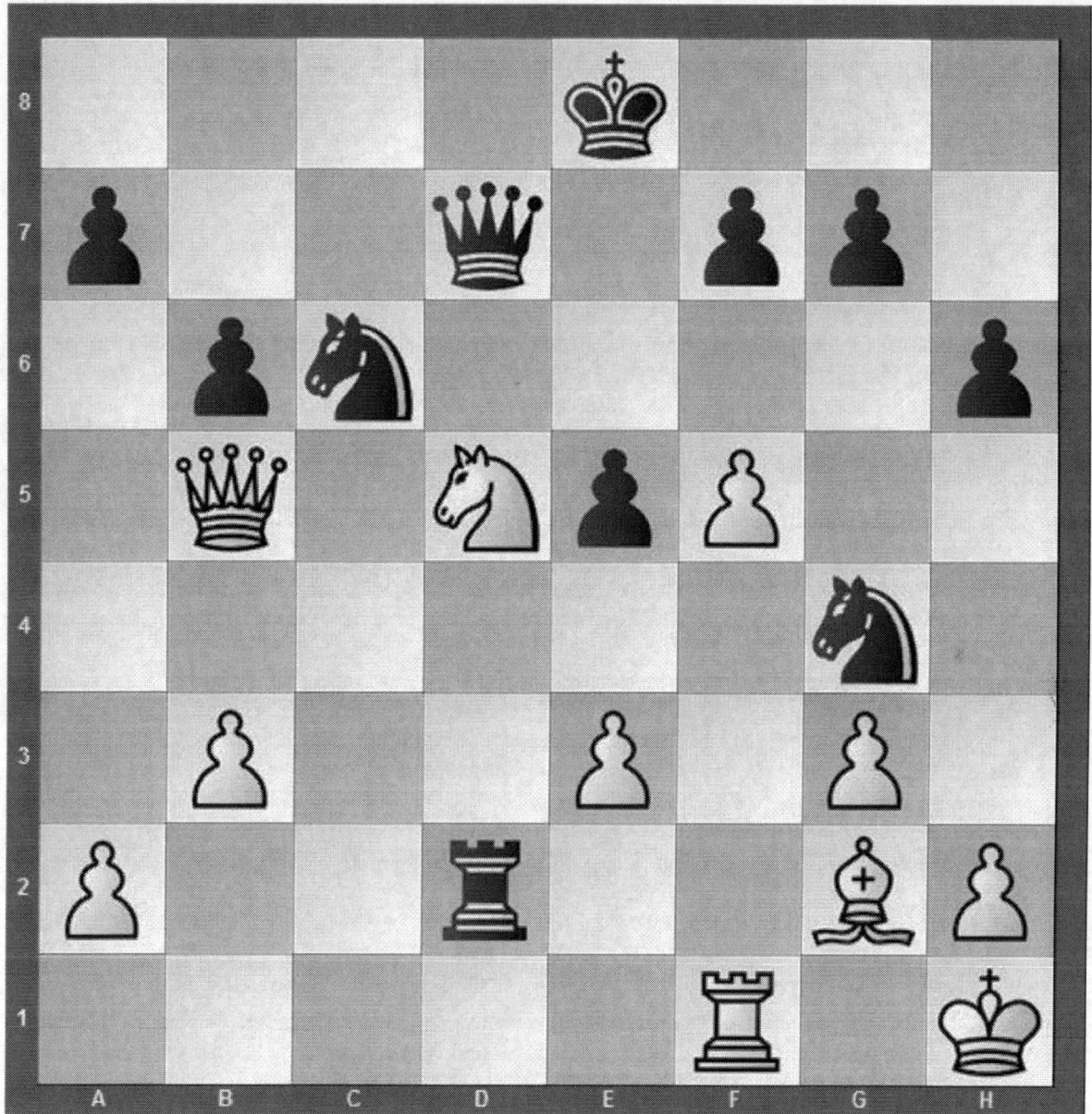

1		
2		

1		
2		

1		
2		

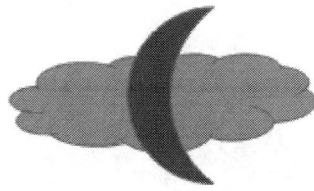

1		
2		

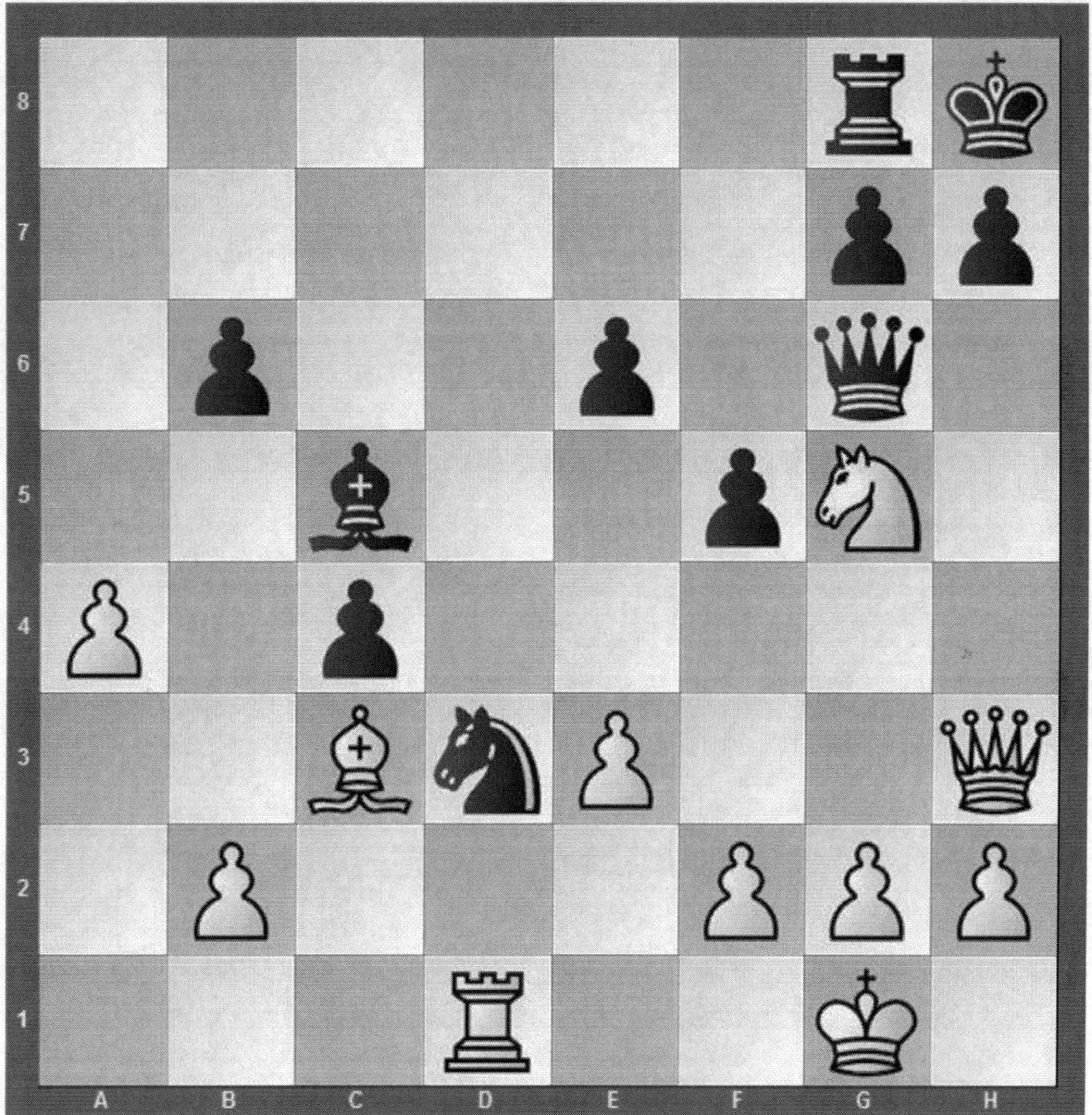

1		
2		

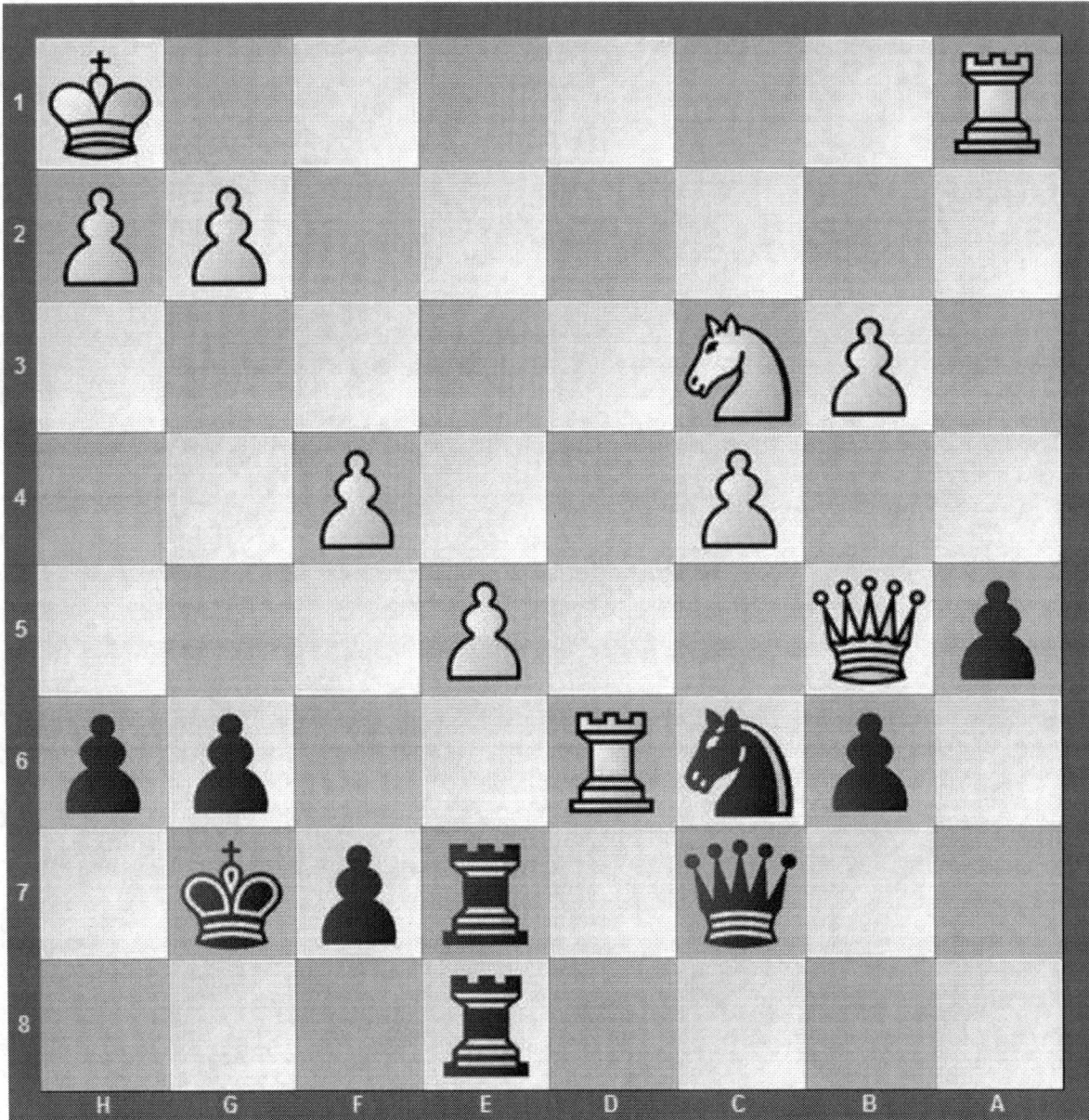

1		
2		

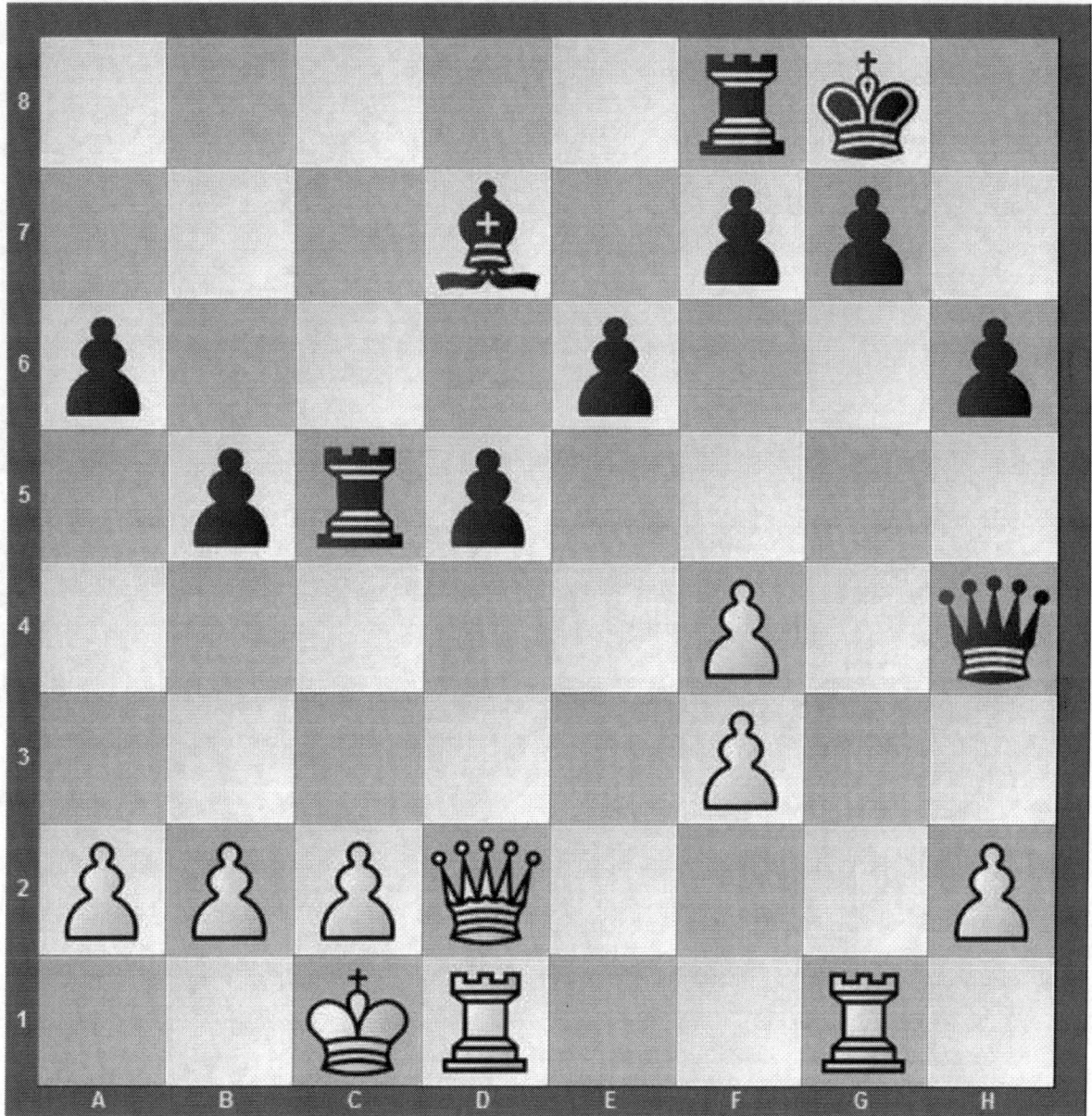

1		
2		

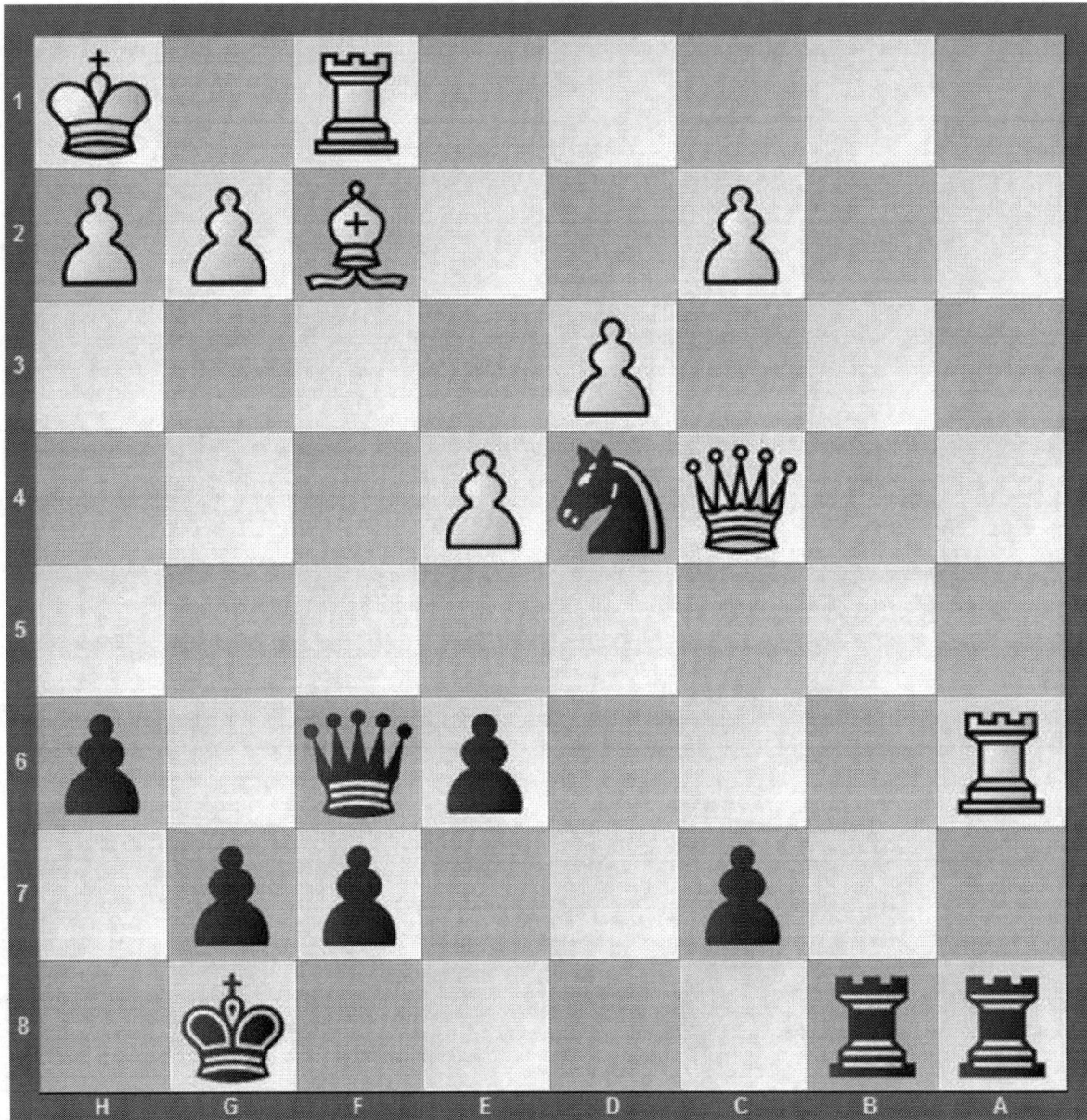

1		
2		

"Chess is mental torture." – **Garry Kasparov**

1		
2		

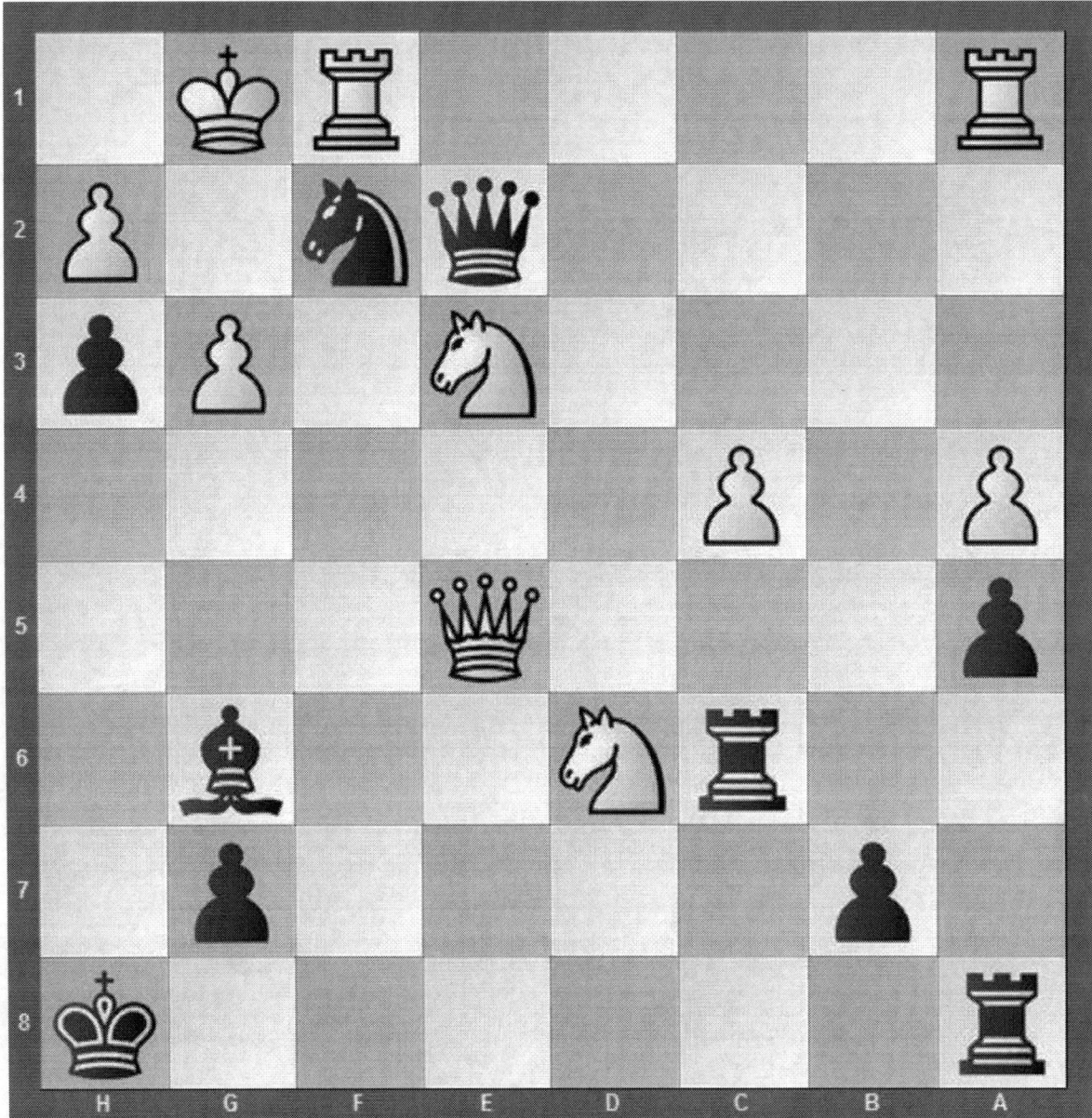

1		
2		

1		
2		

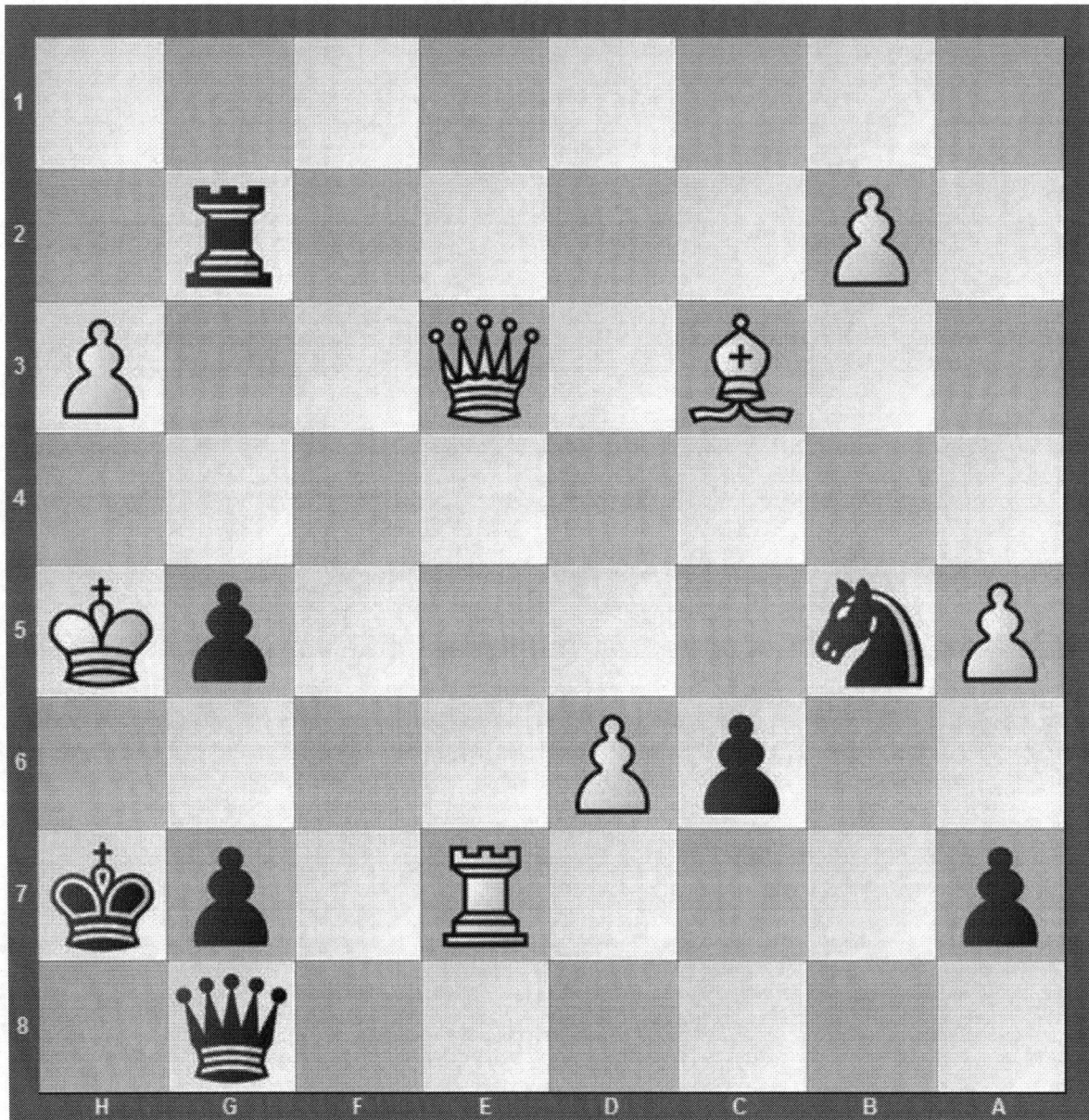

1		
2		

1		
2		

1		
2		

1		
2		

1		
2		

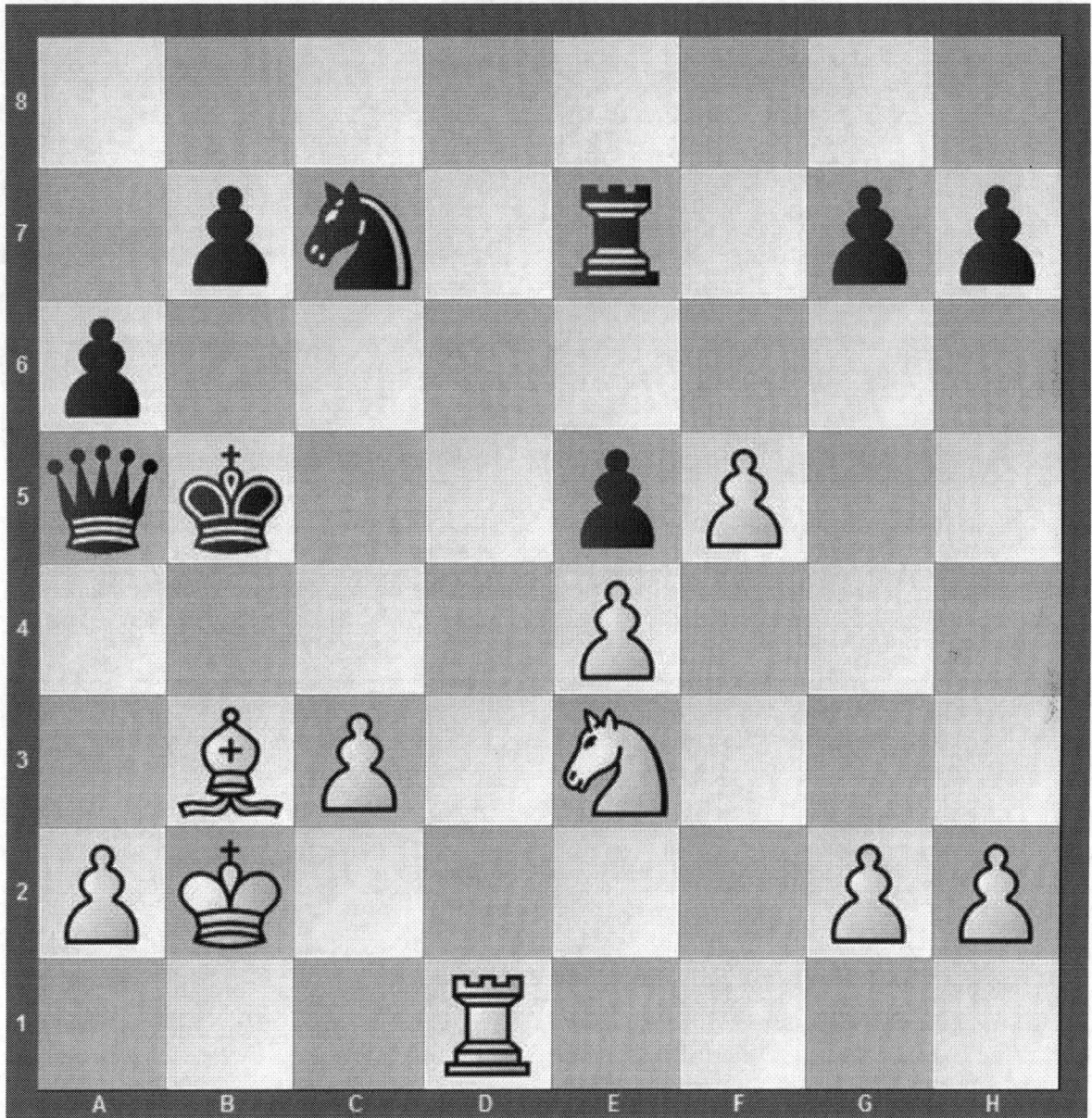

1		
2		

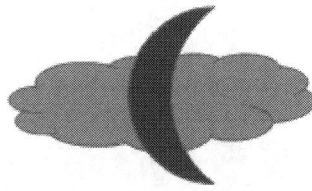

1		
2		

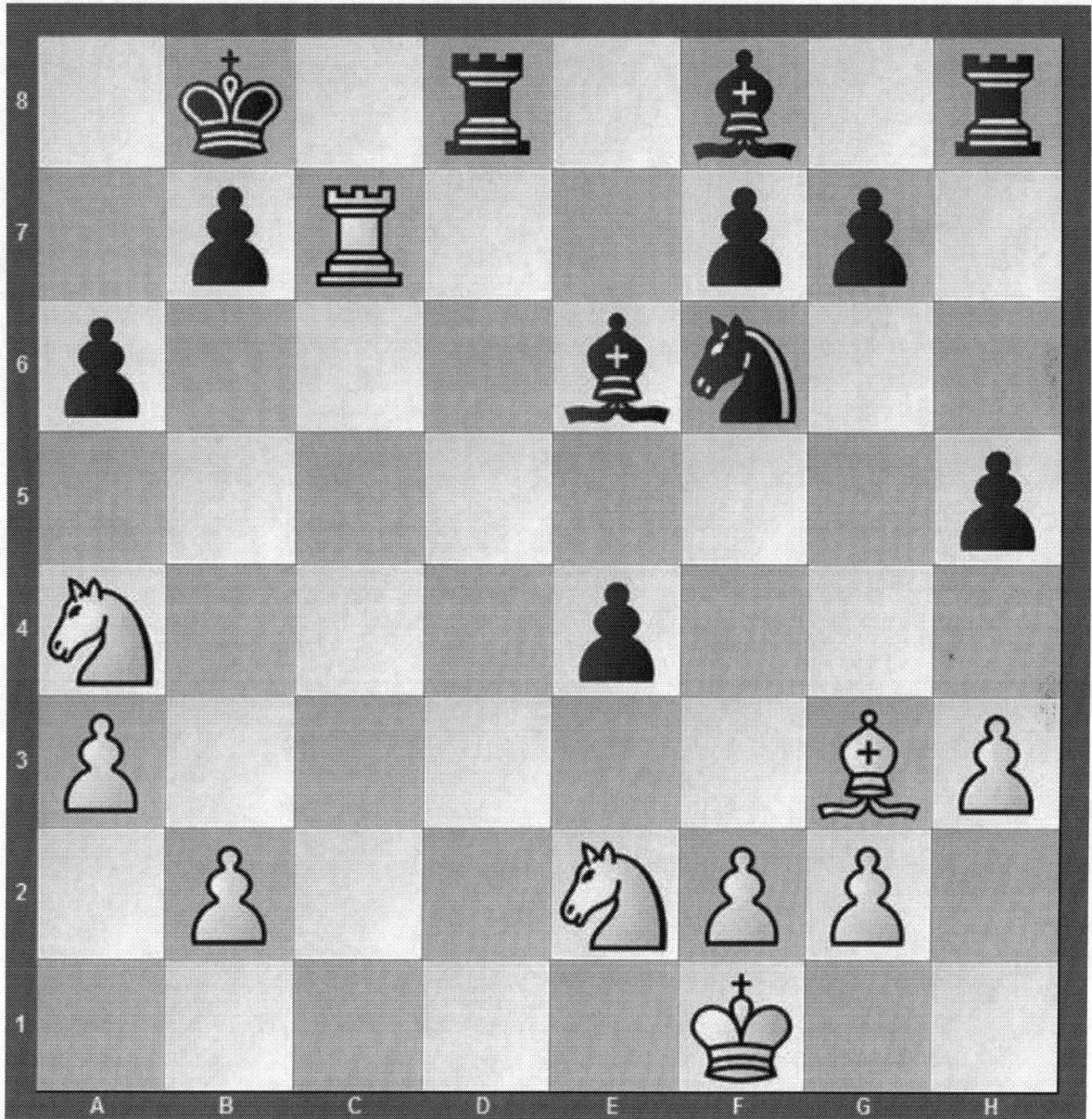

1		
2		

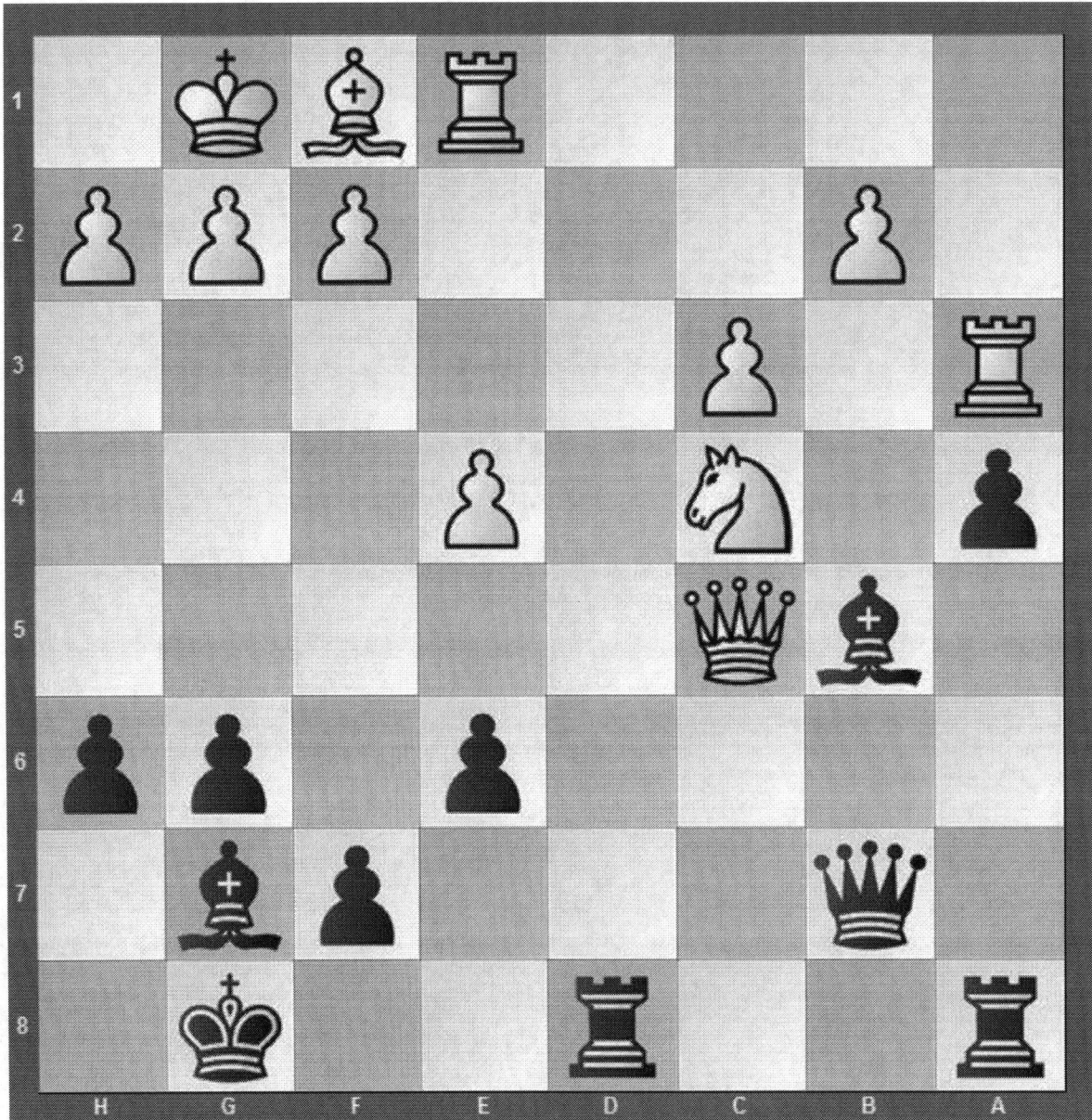

1		
2		

1		
2		

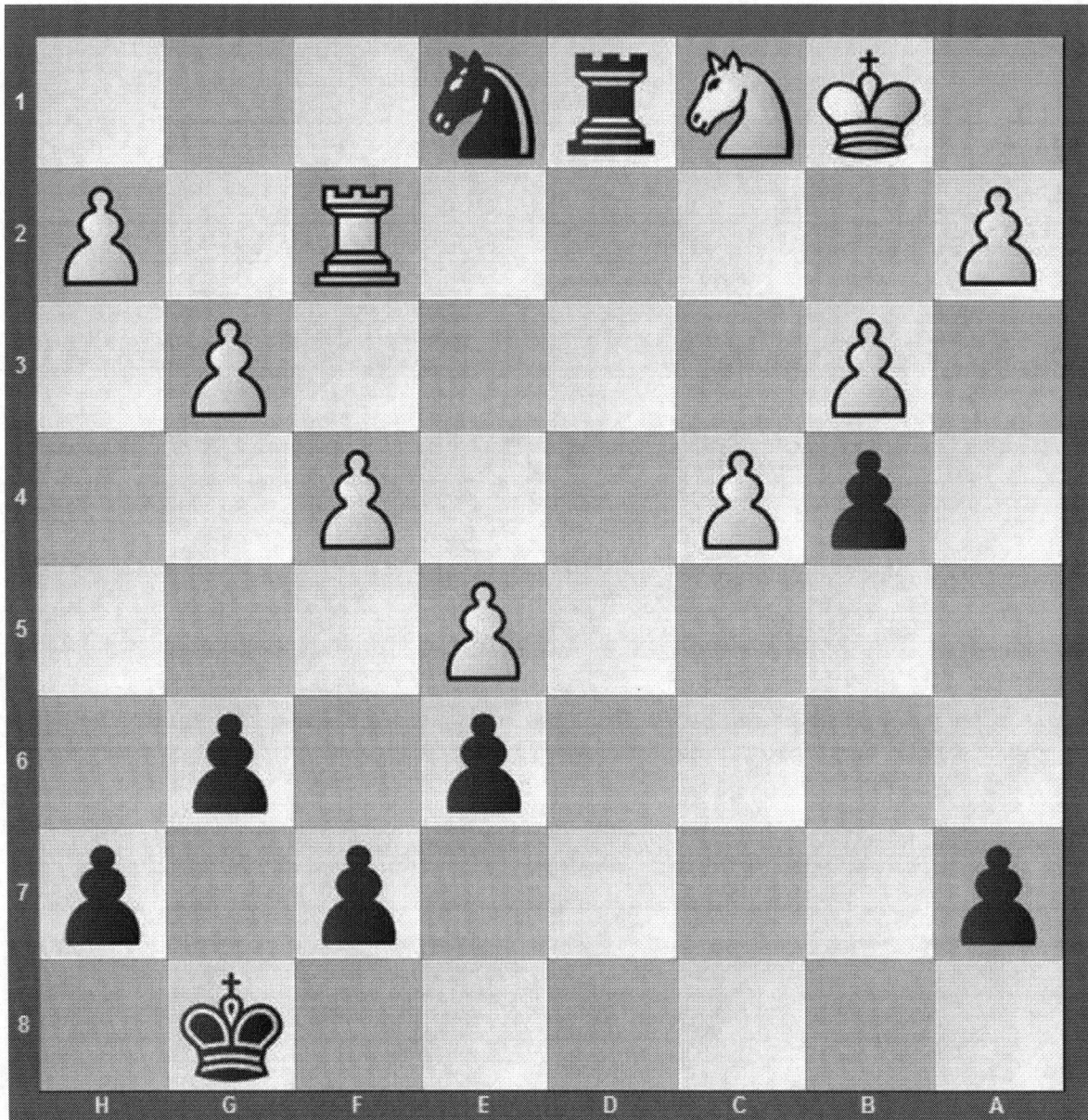

1		
2		

"Chess is a sport. The main object in the game of chess remains the achievement of victory." – **Max Euwe**

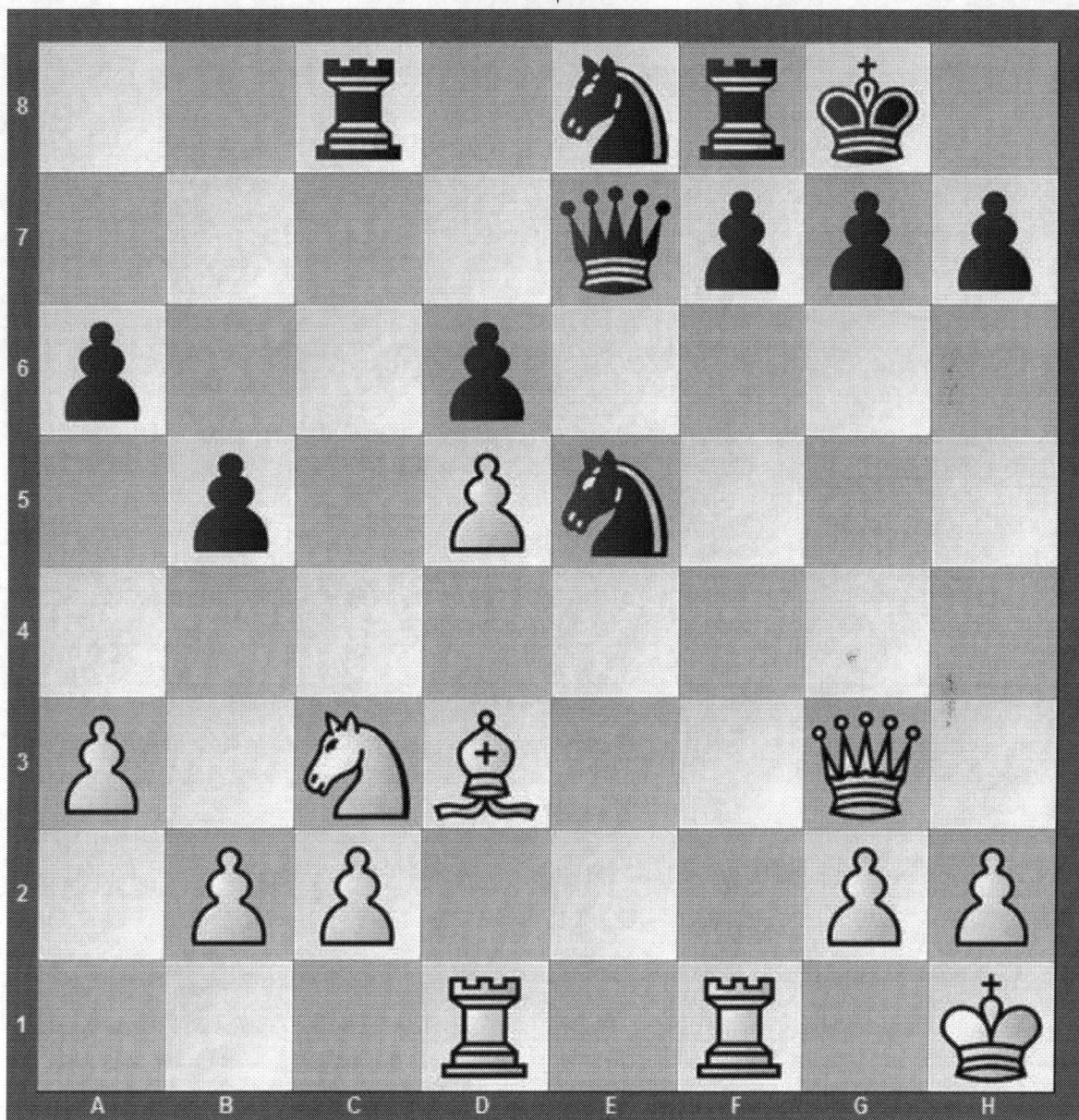

1		
2		

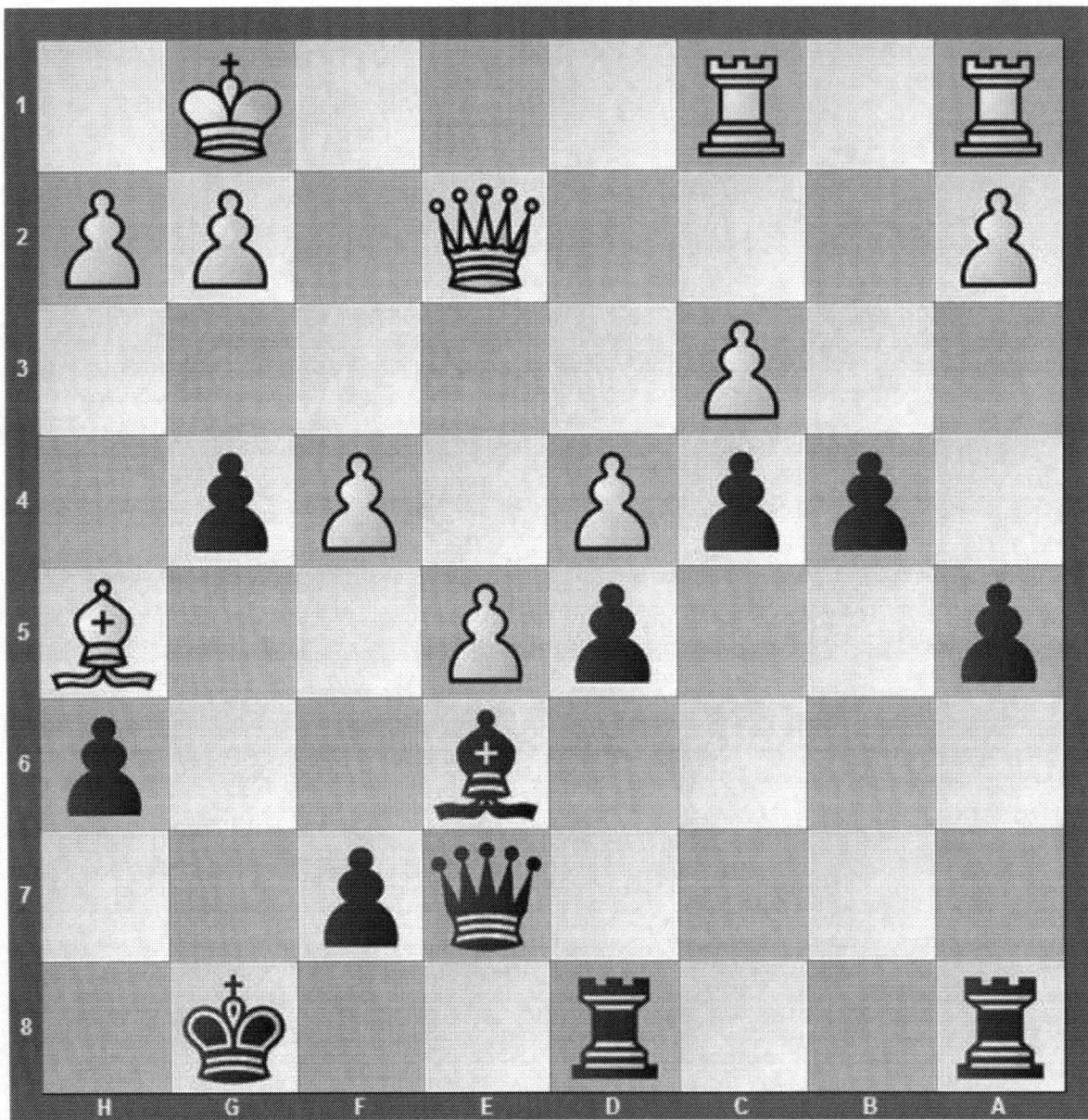

1		
2		

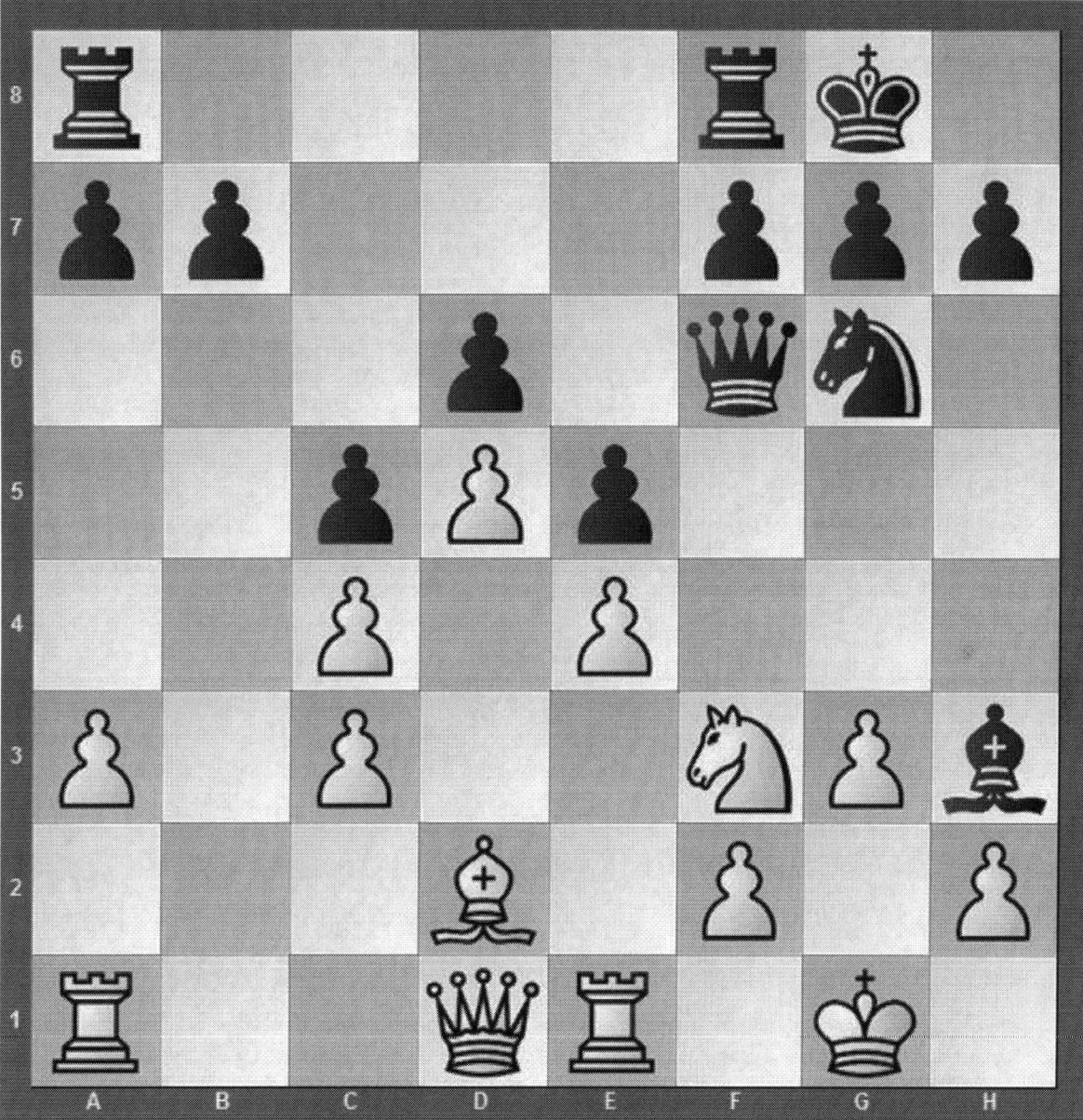

1		
2		

1		
2		

1		
2		

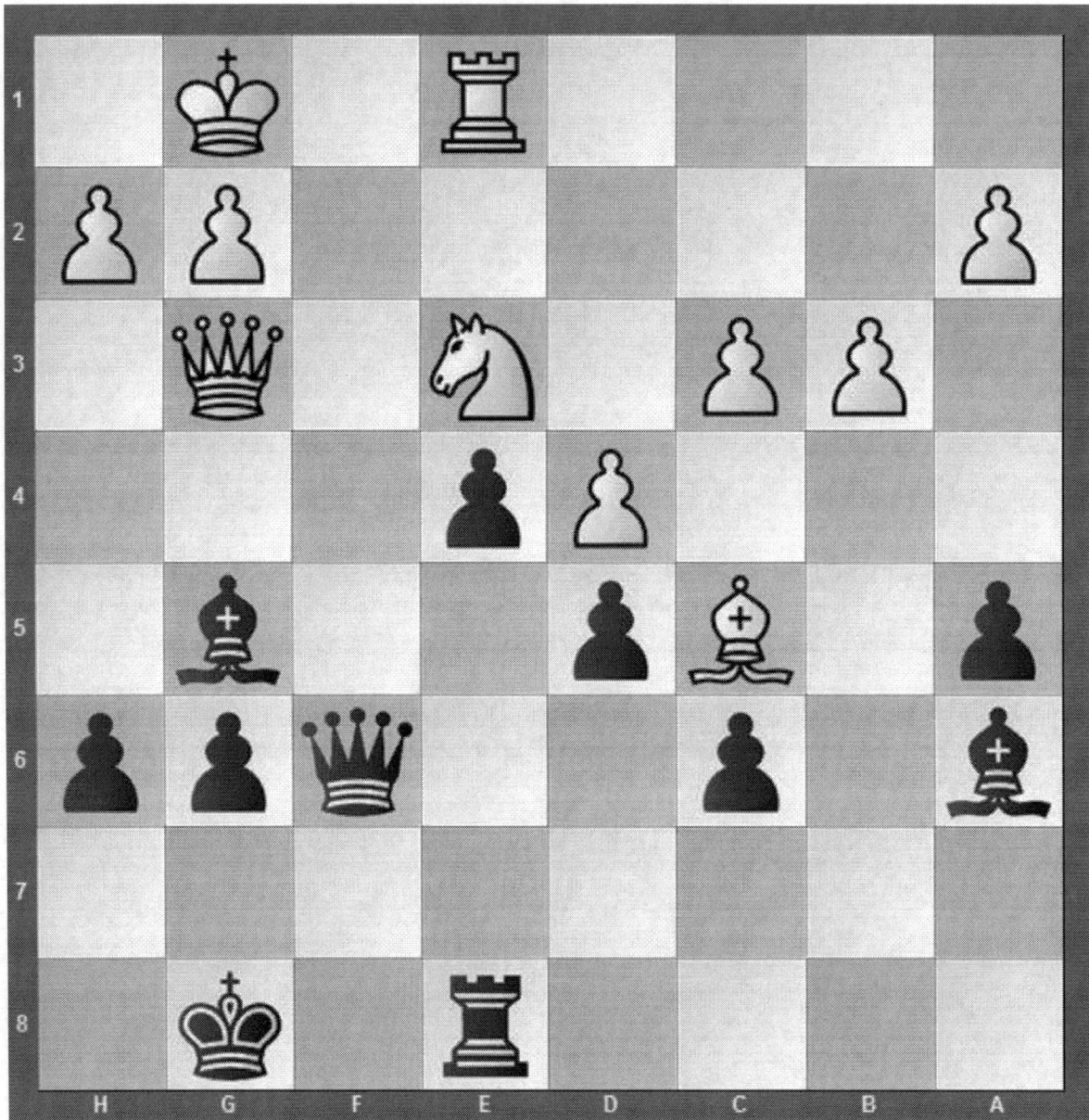

1		
2		

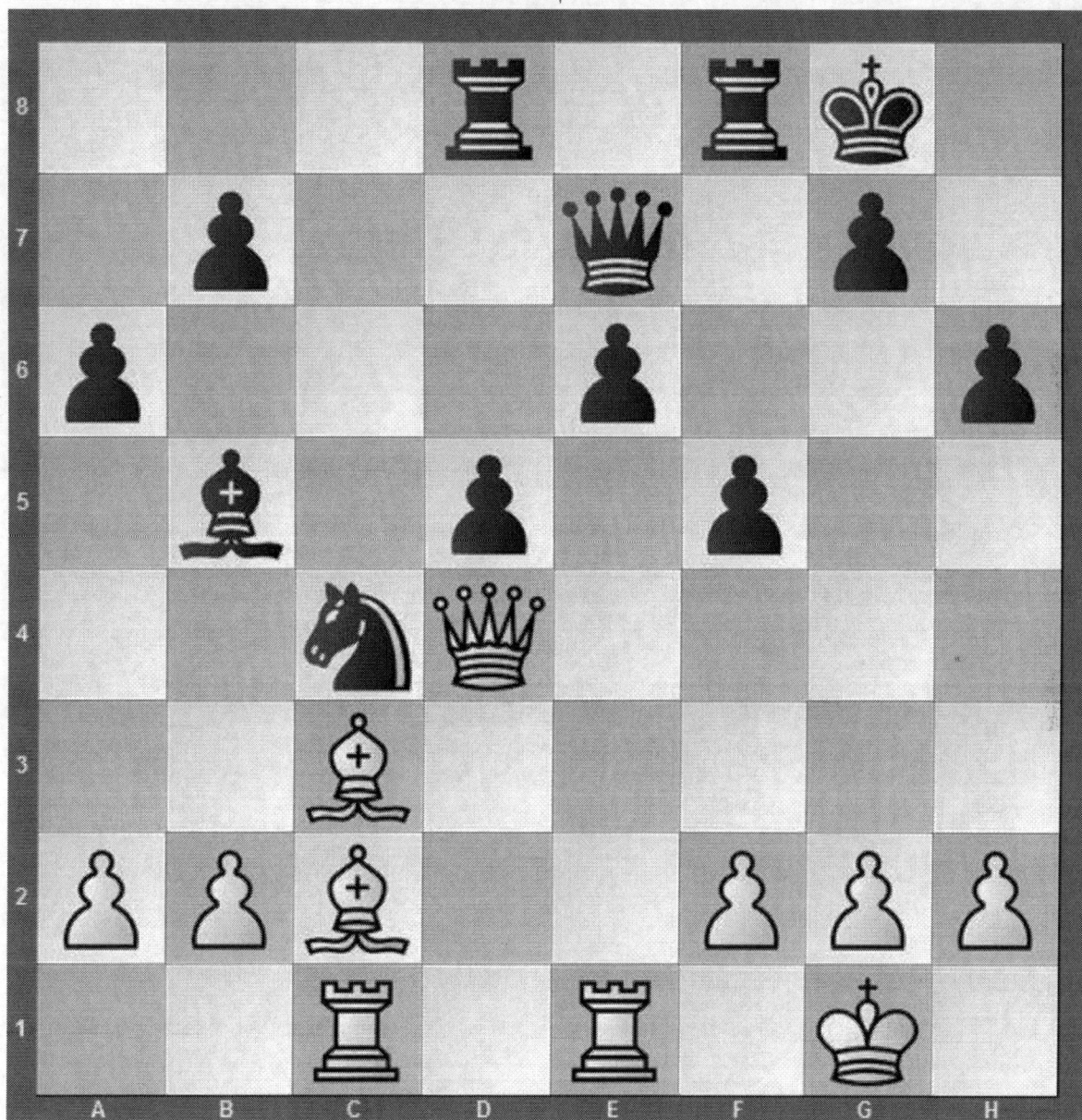

1		
2		

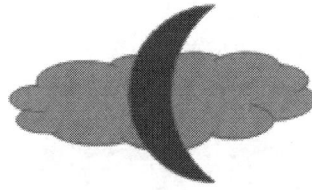

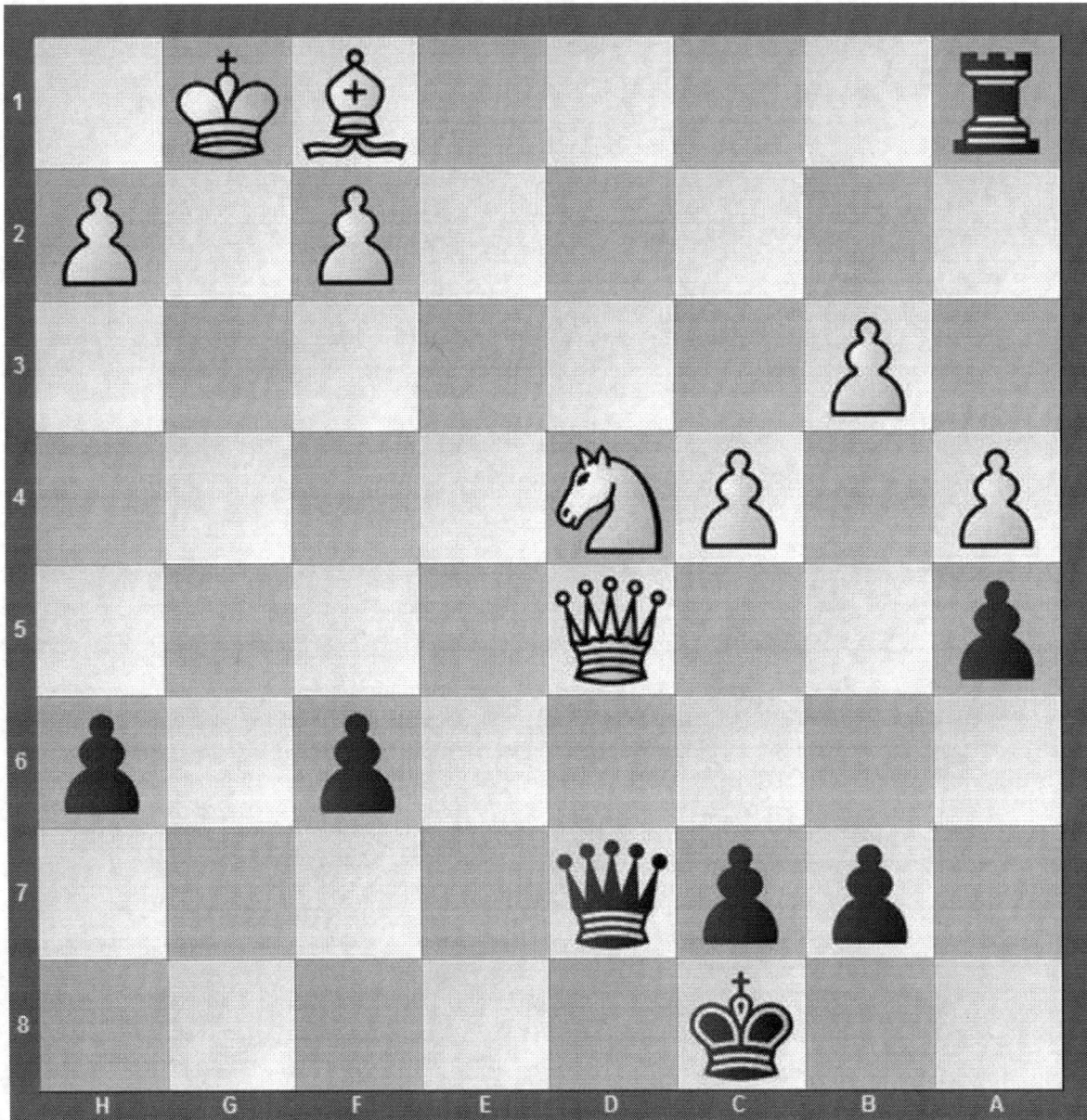

1		
2		

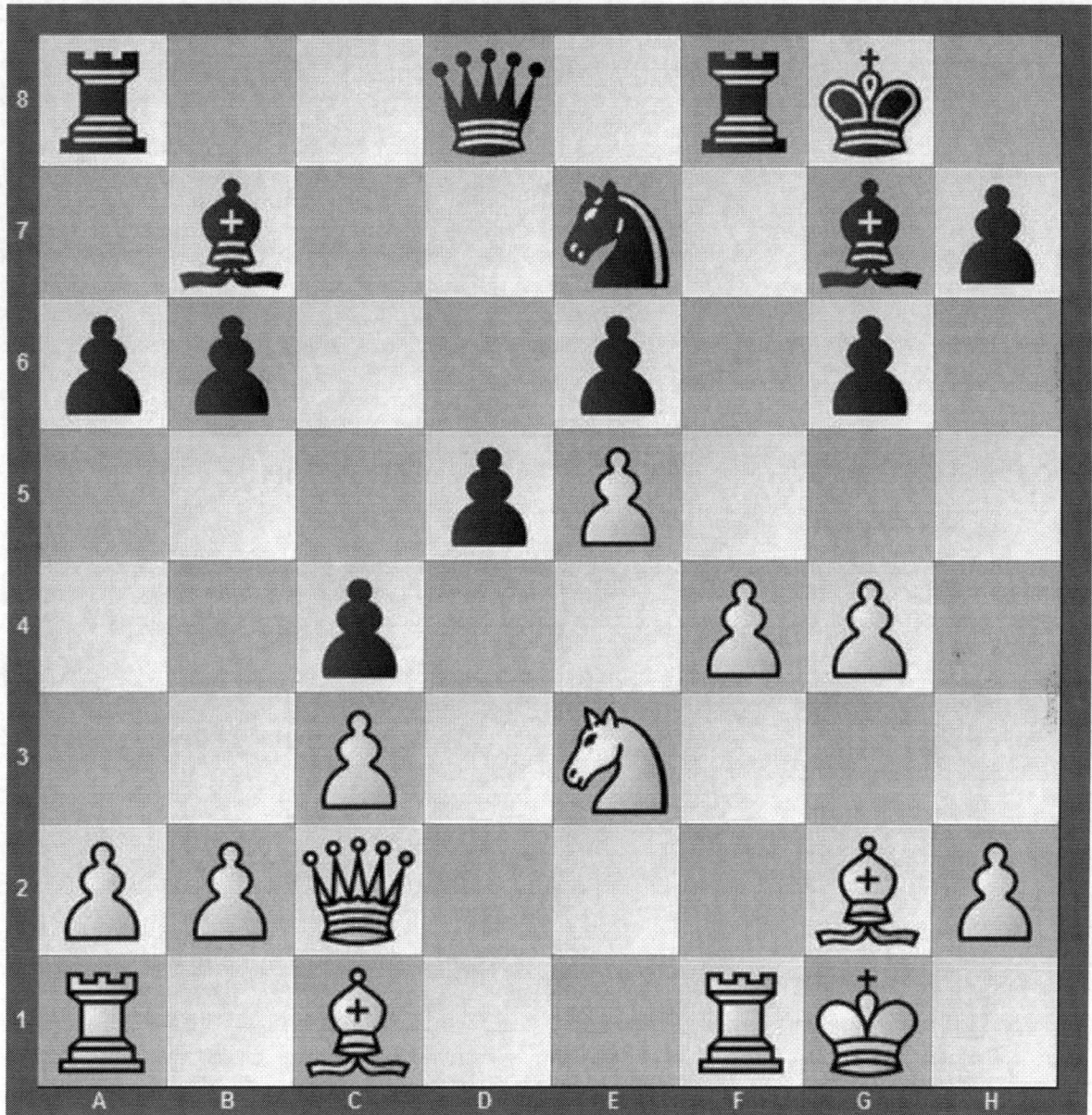

1		
2		

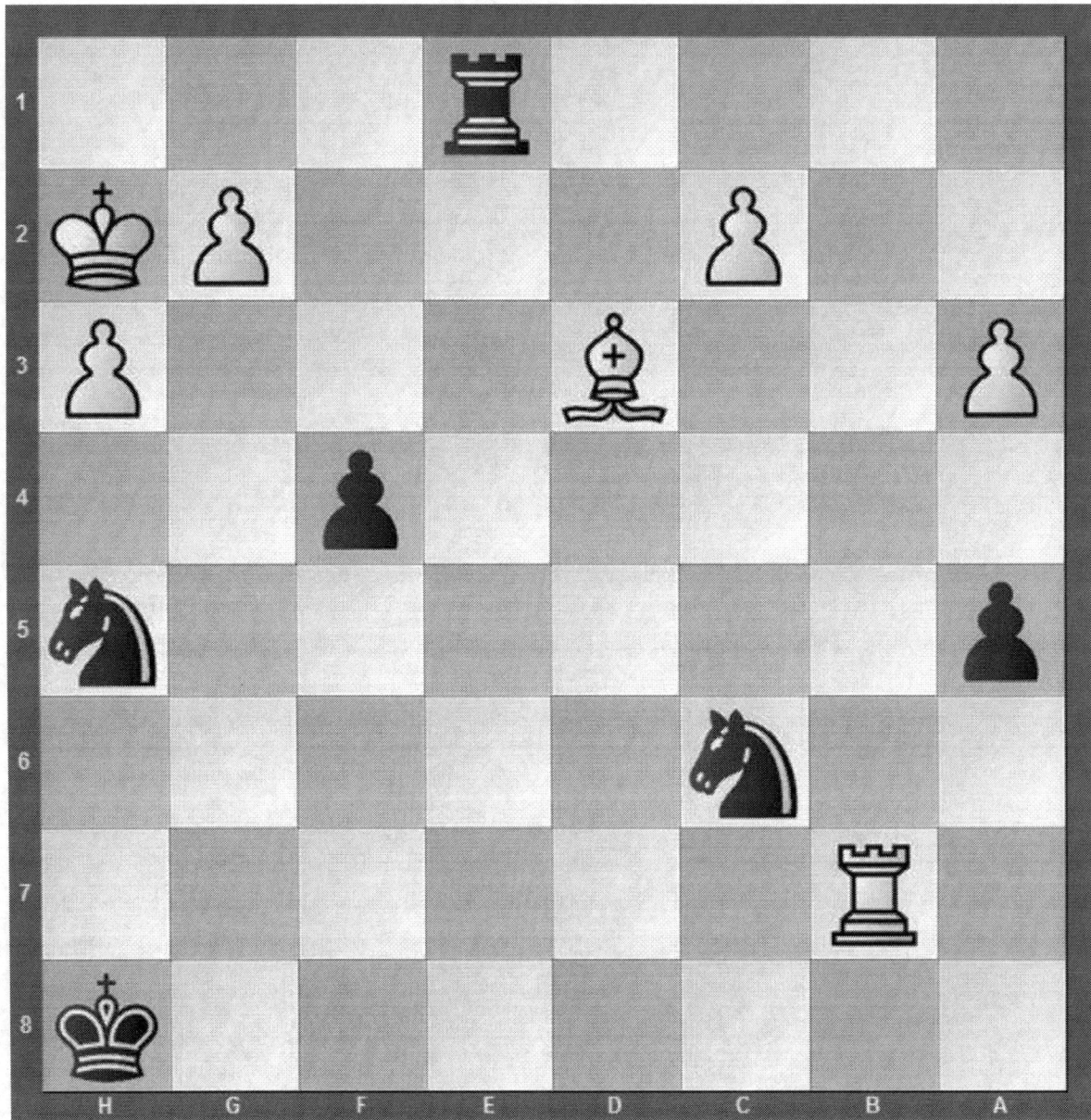

1		
2		

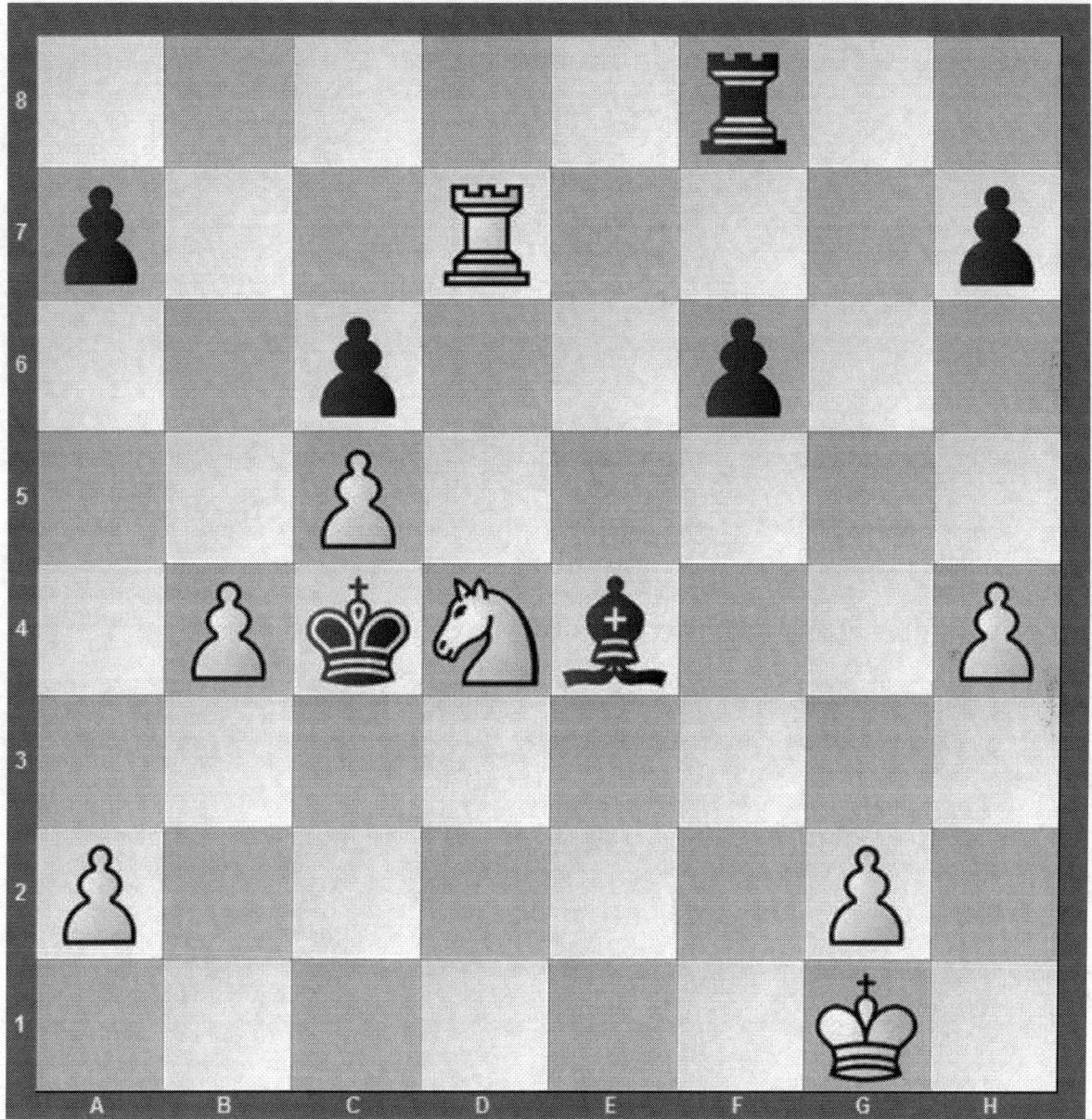

1		
2		

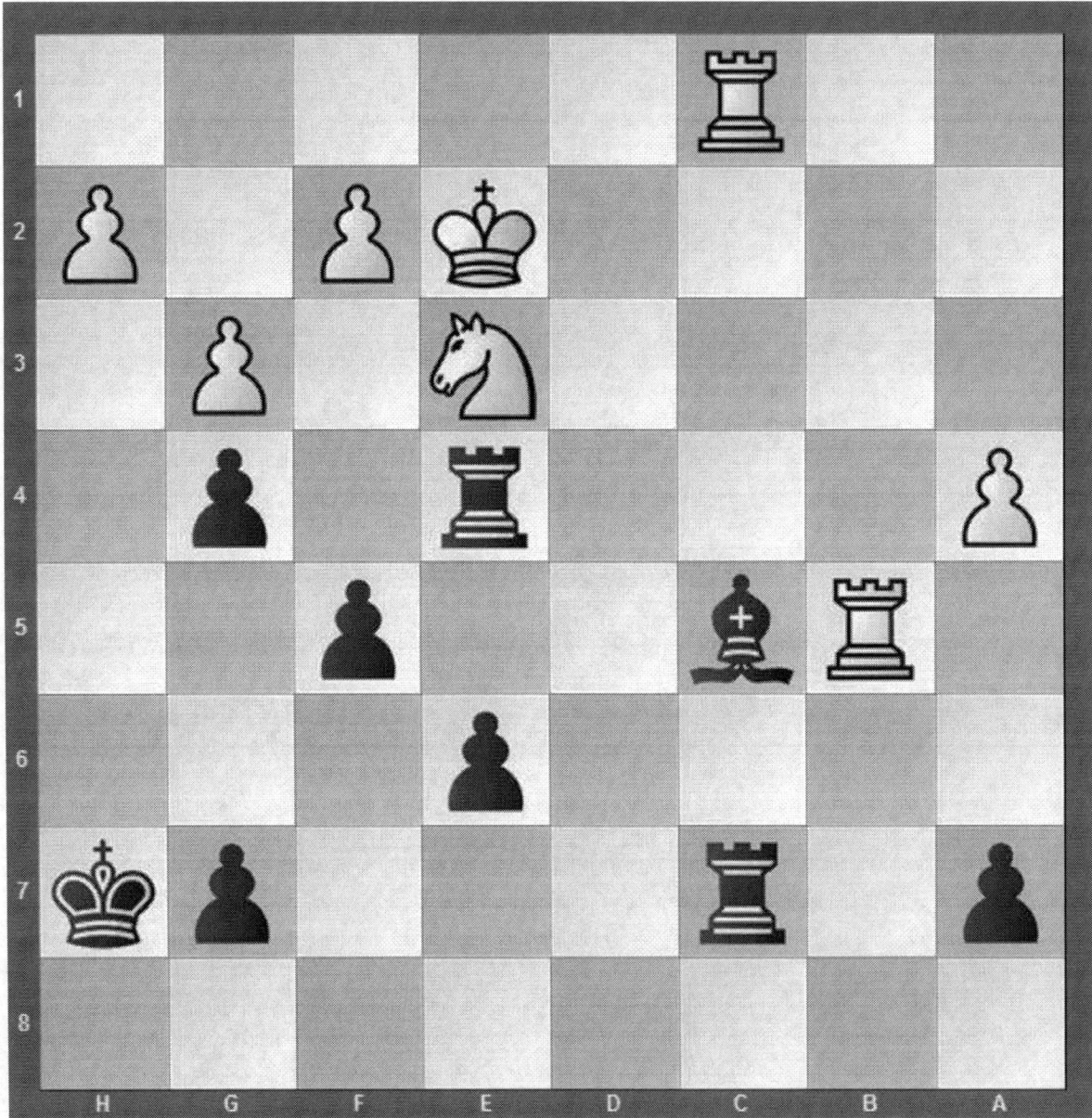

1		
2		

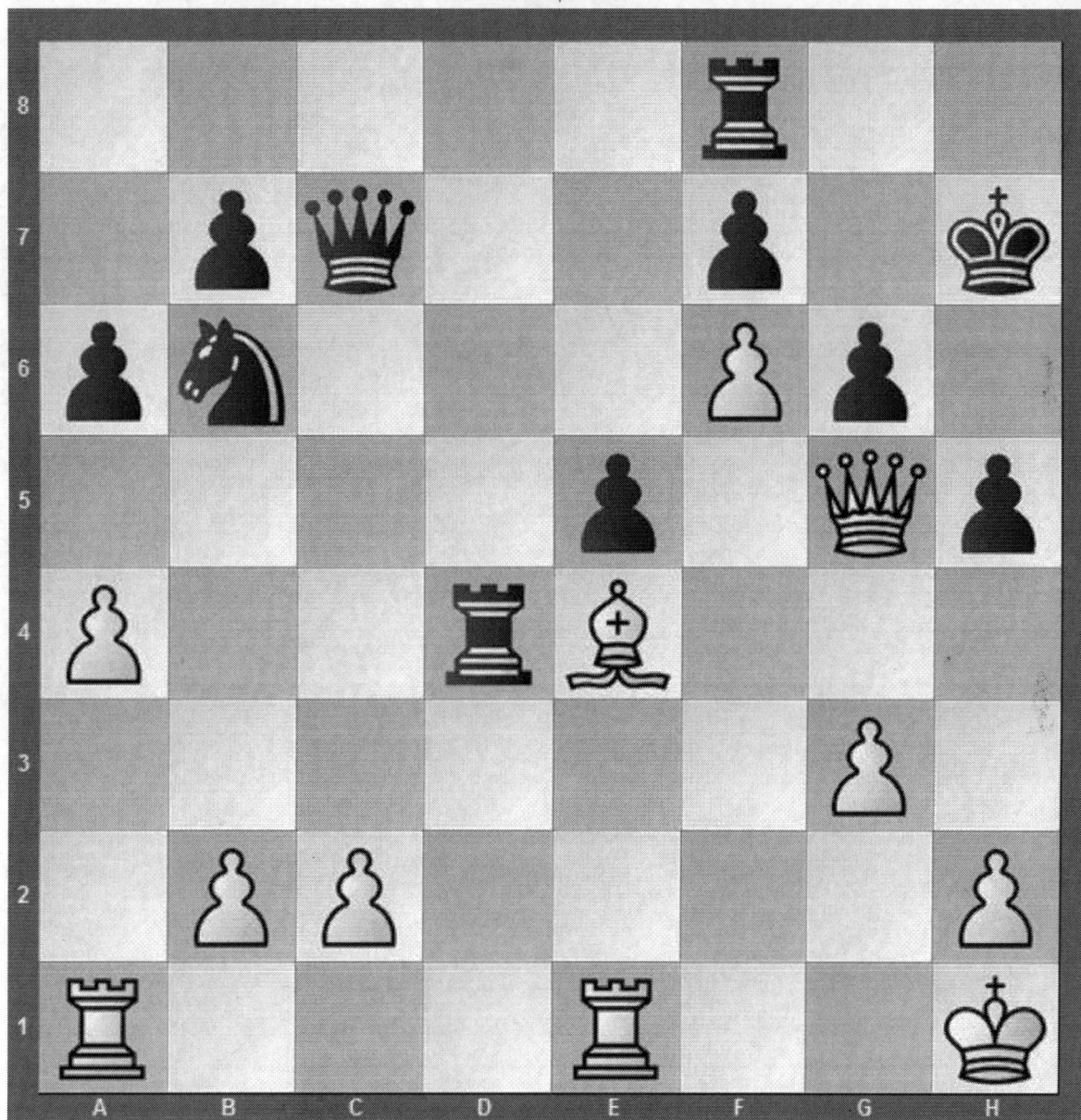

1		
2		

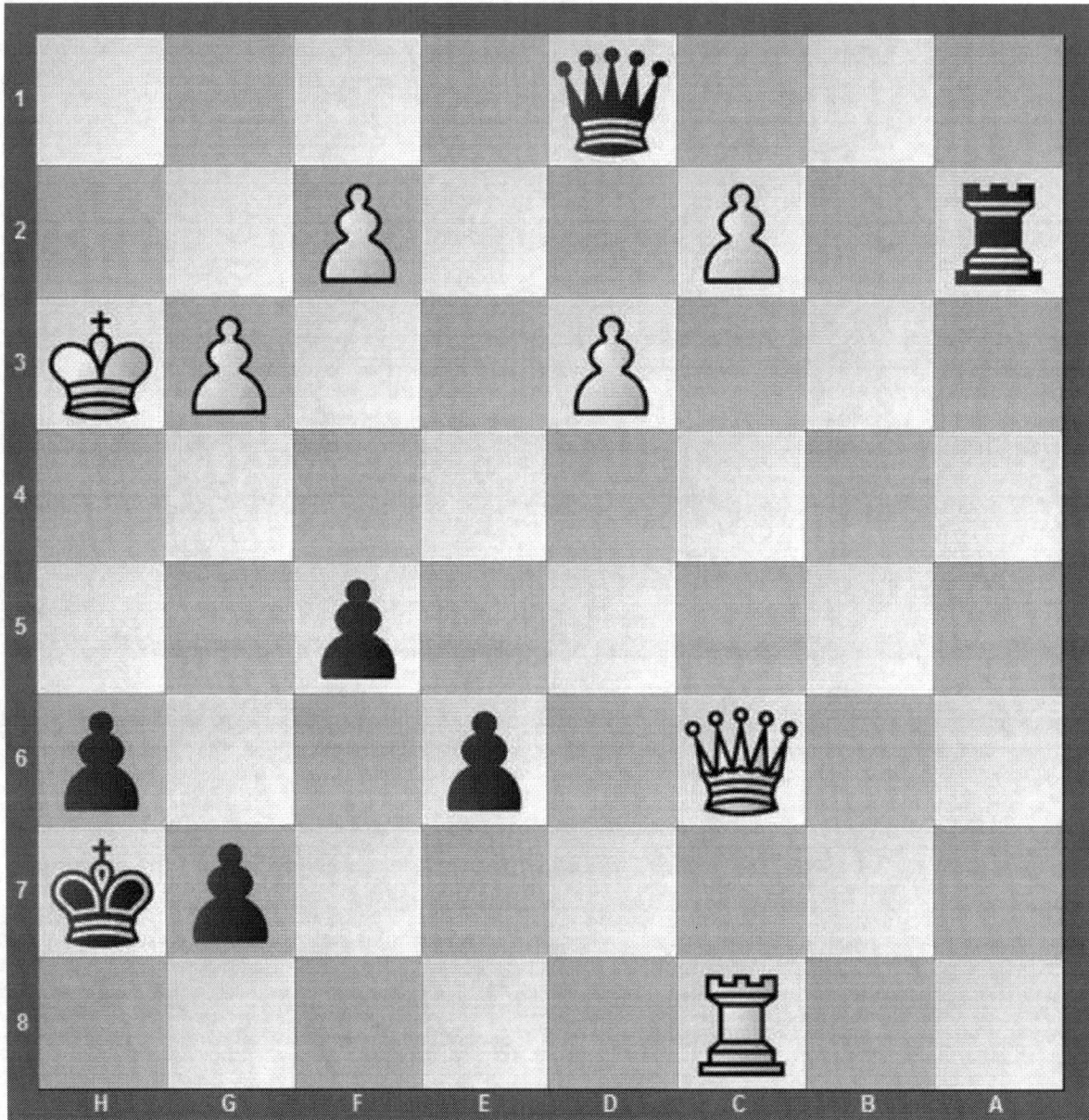

1		
2		

"The pawns are the soul of chess." – **Francois Andre Danican Philidor**

1		
2		

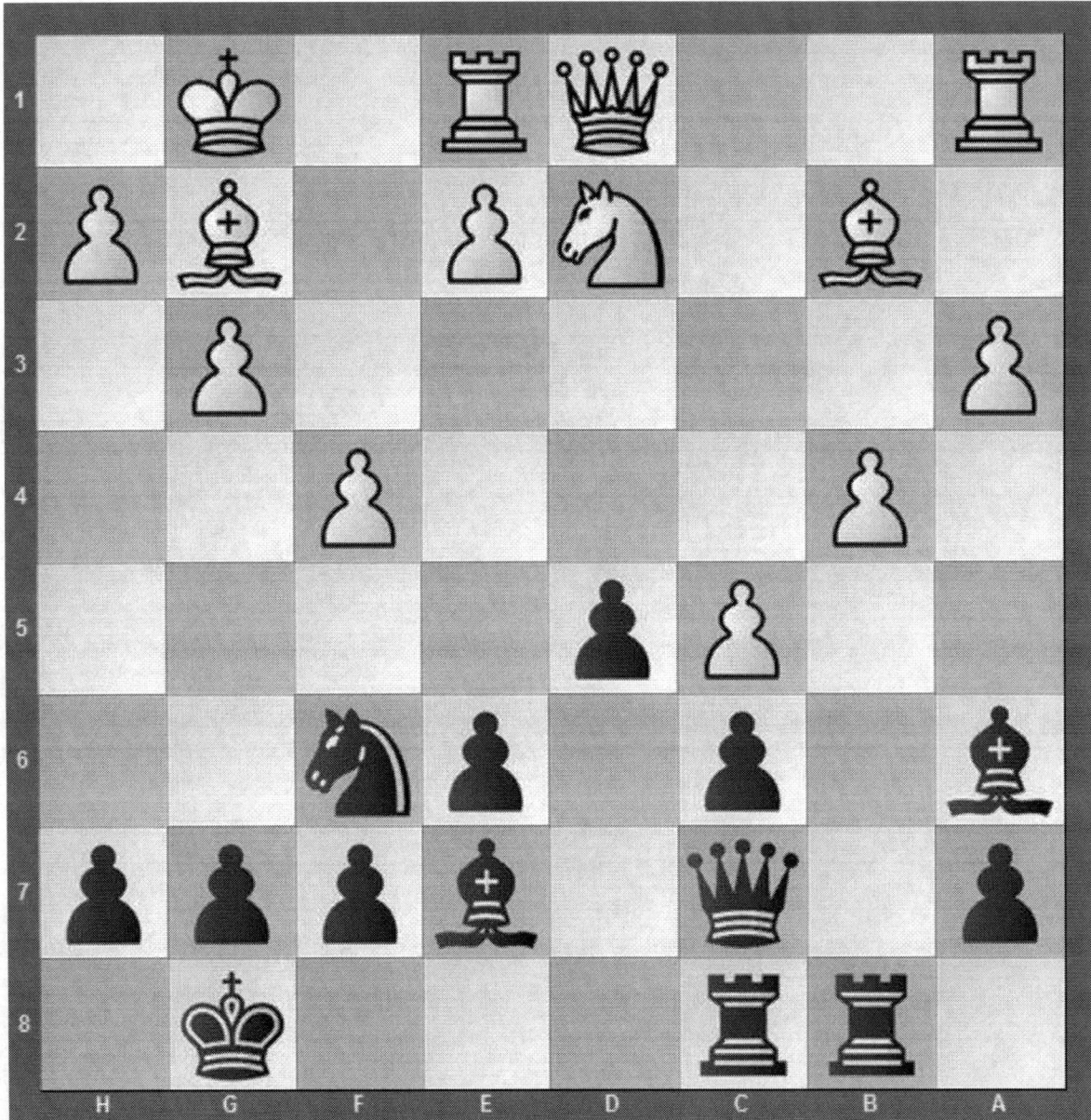

1		
2		

1		
2		

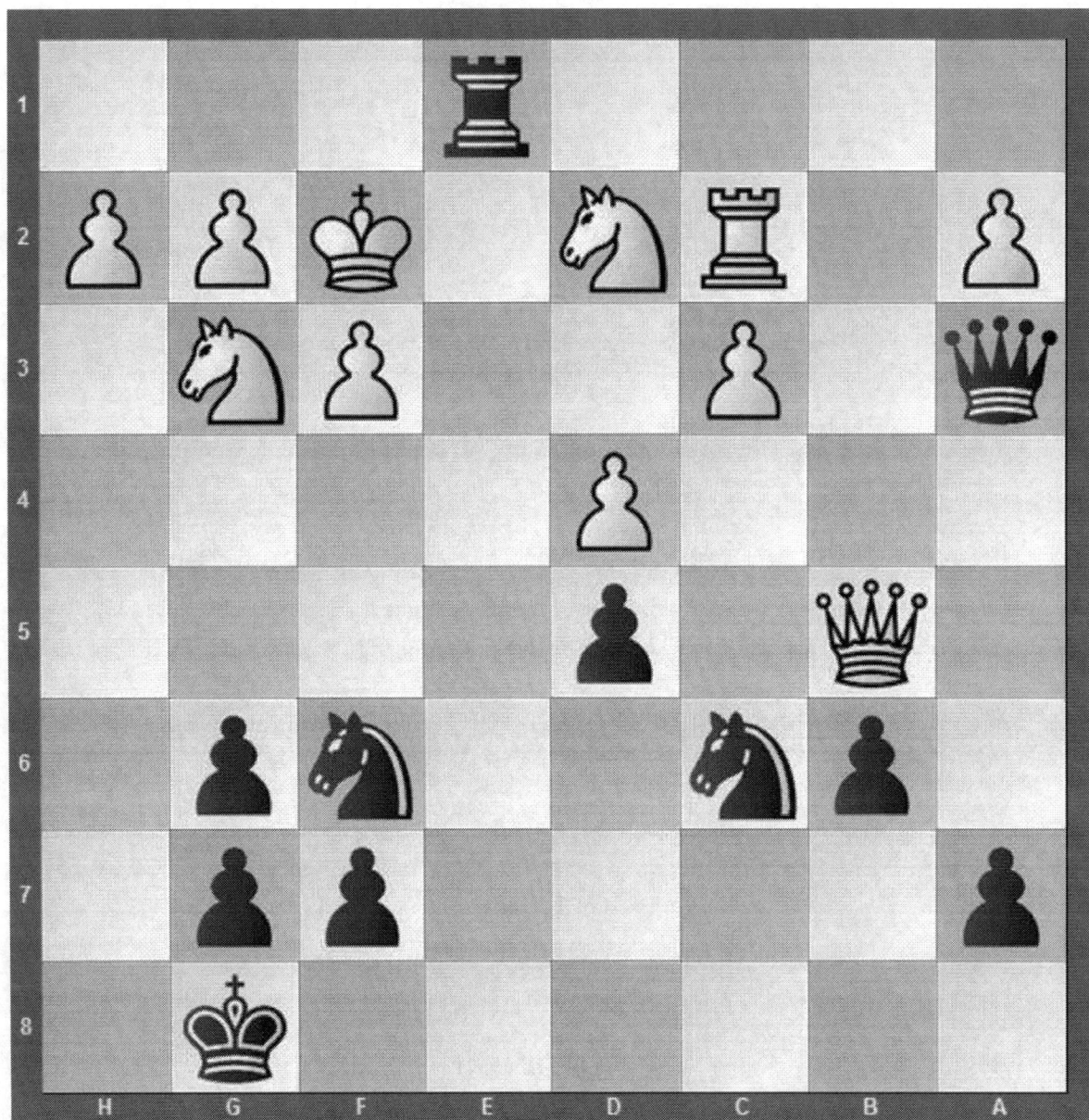

1		
2		

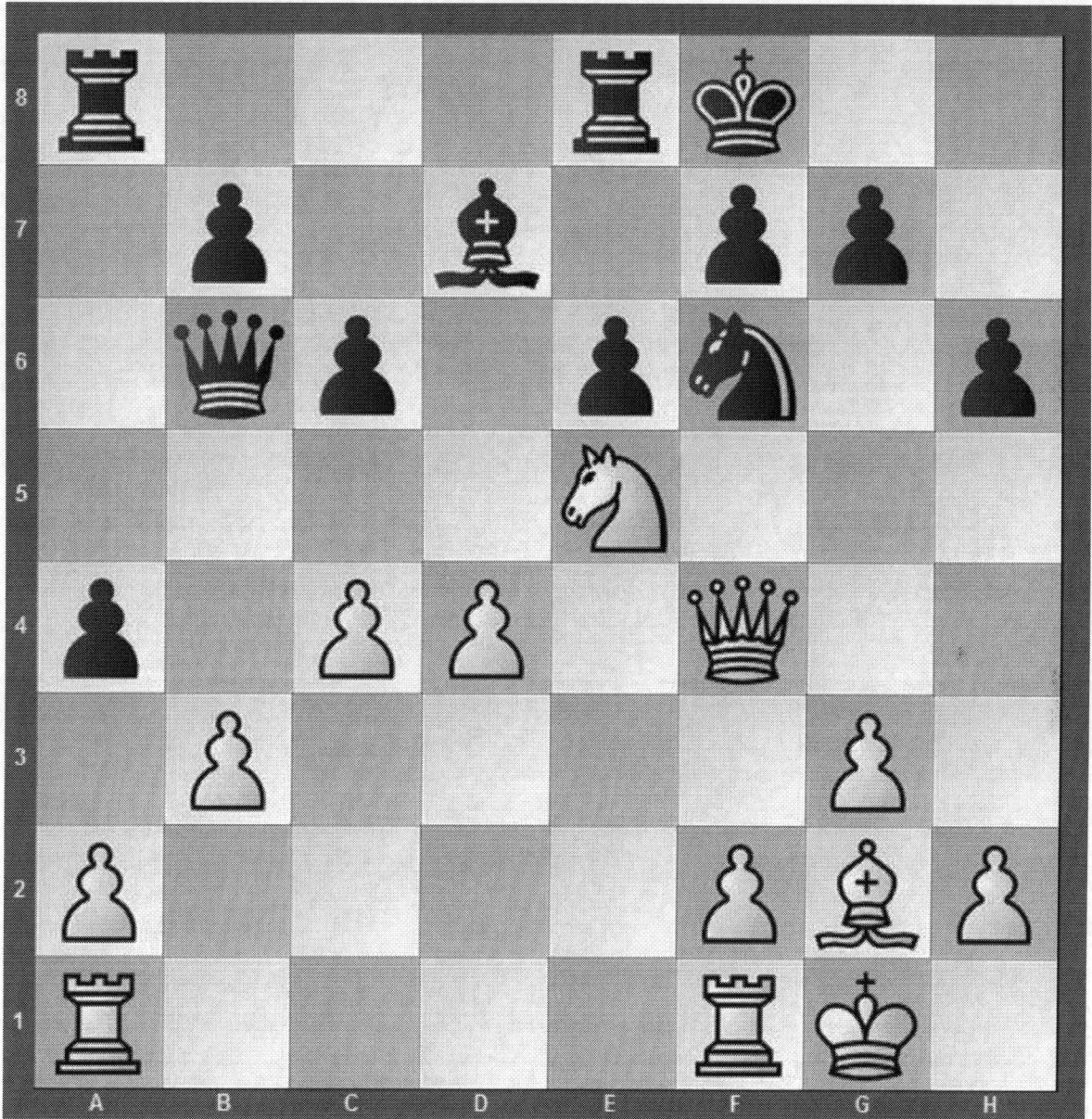

1		
2		

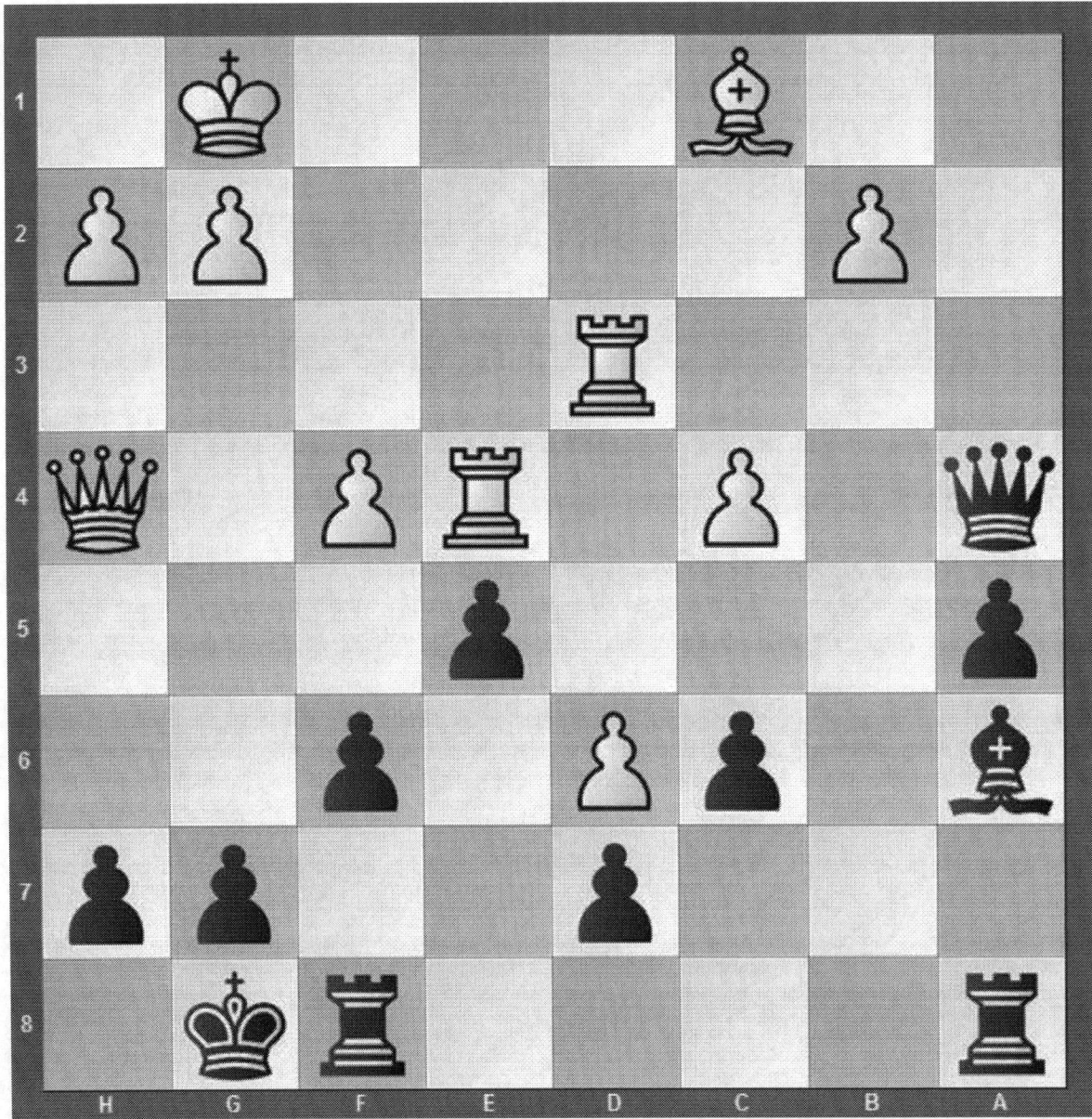

1		
2		

1		
2		

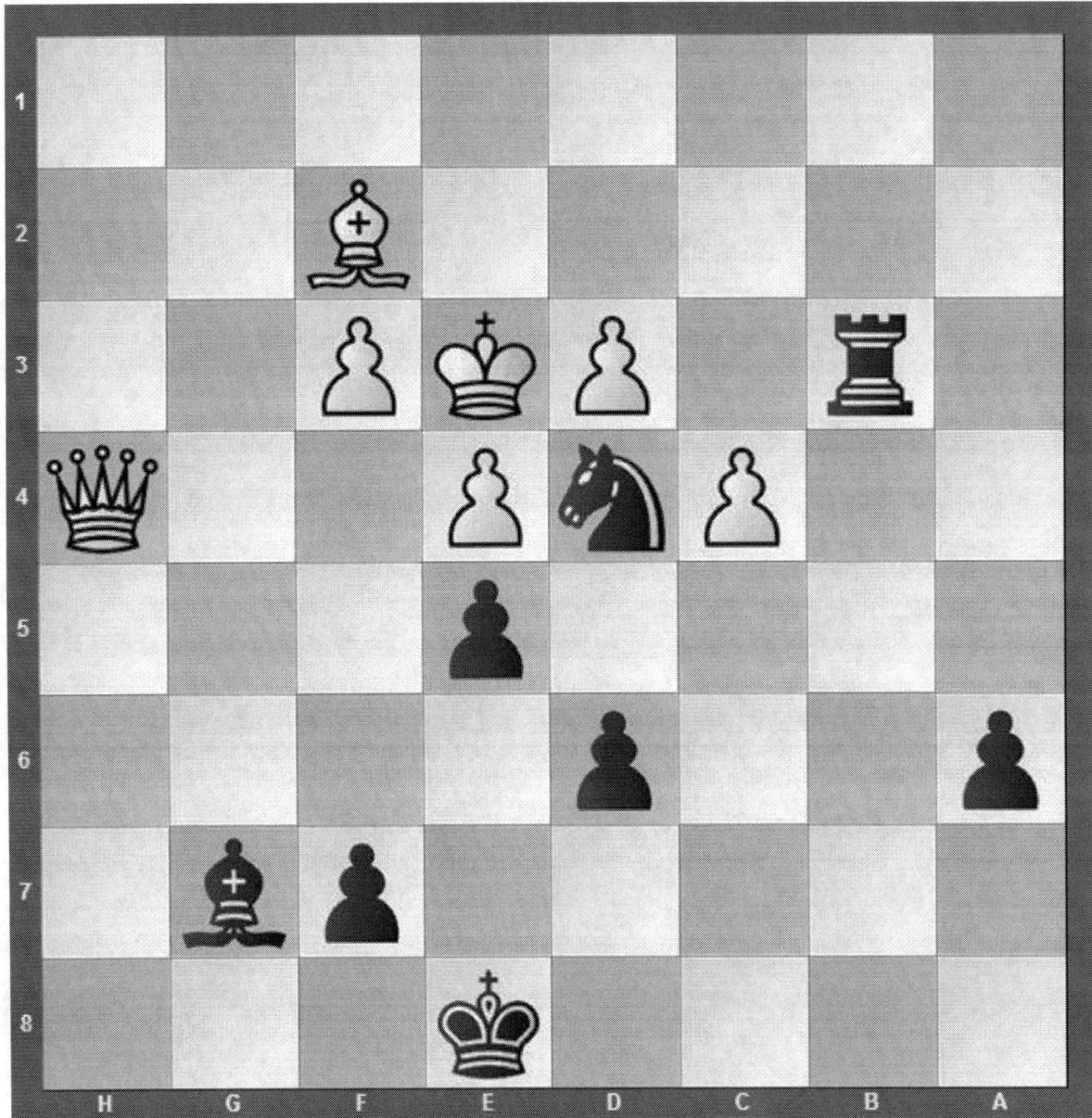

1		
2		

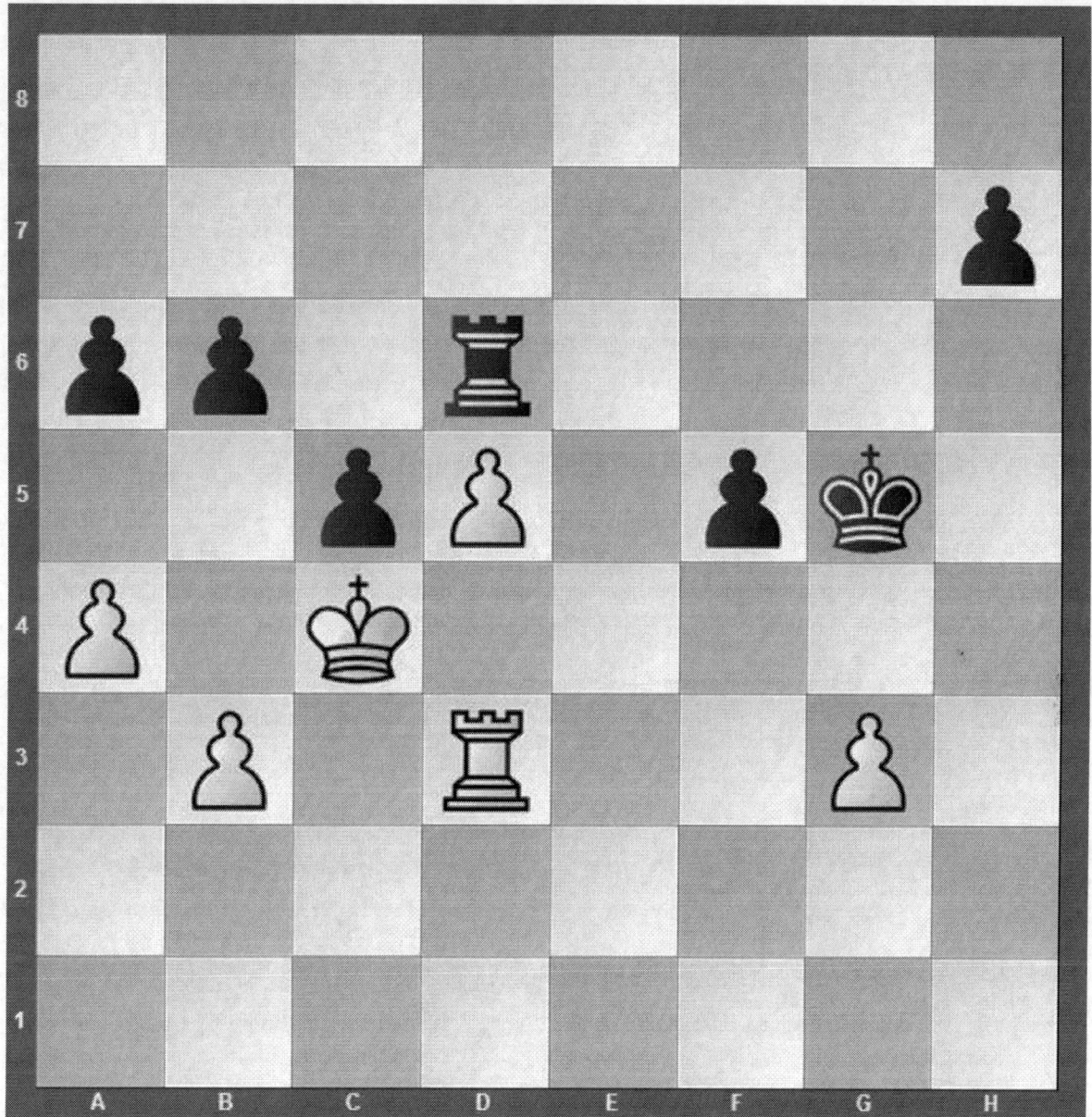

1		
2		

1		
2		

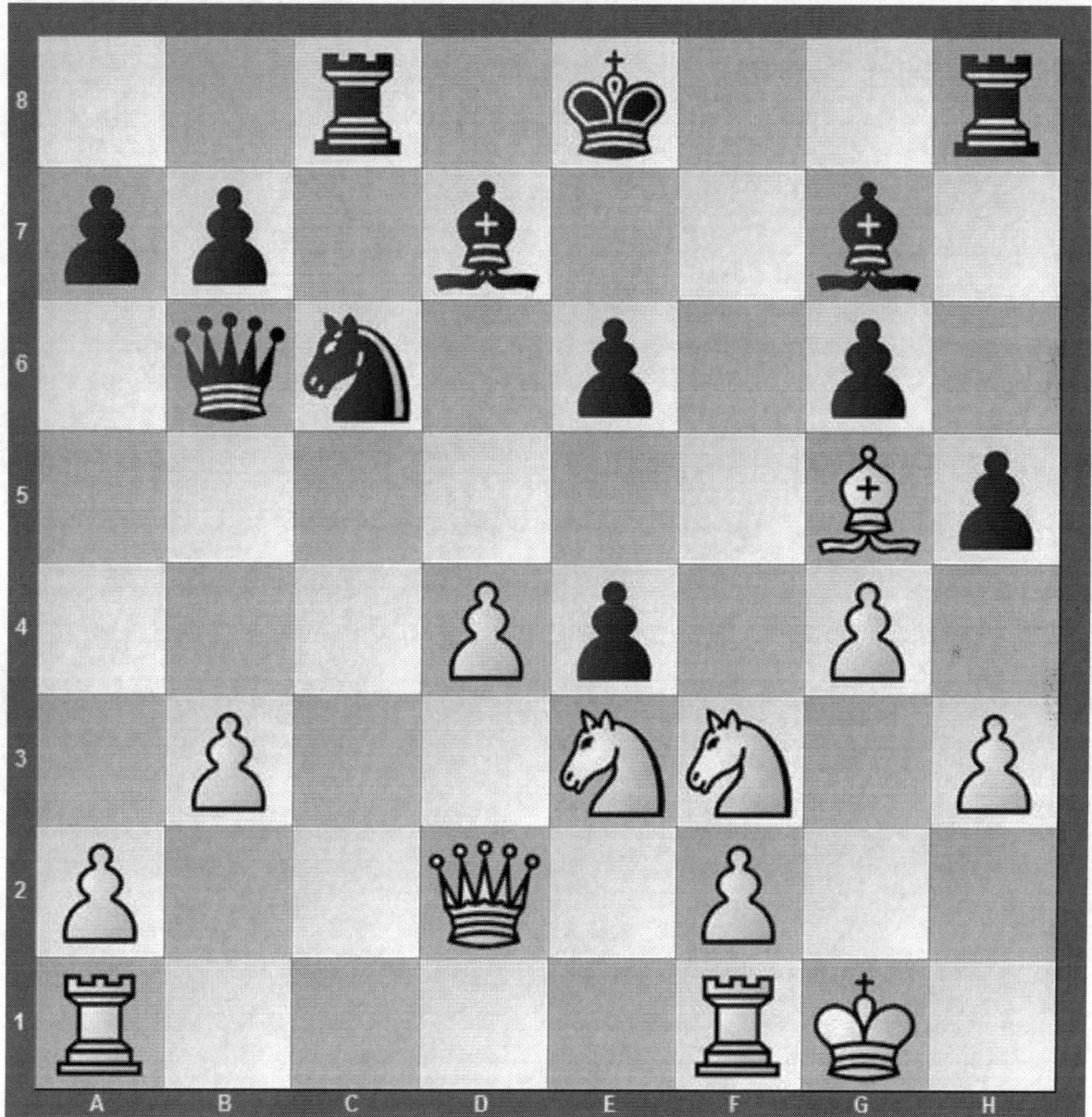

1		
2		

1		
2		

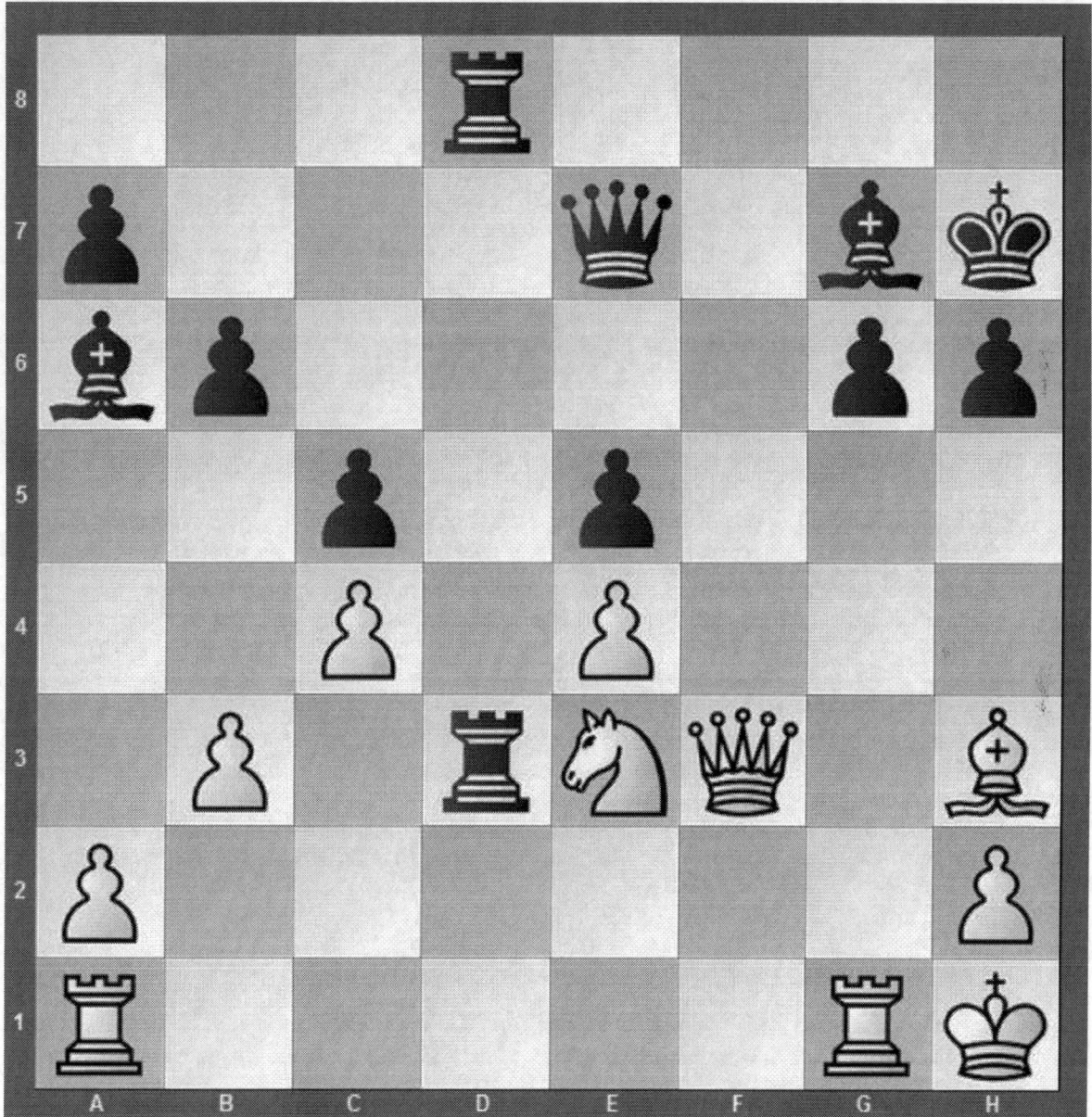

1		
2		

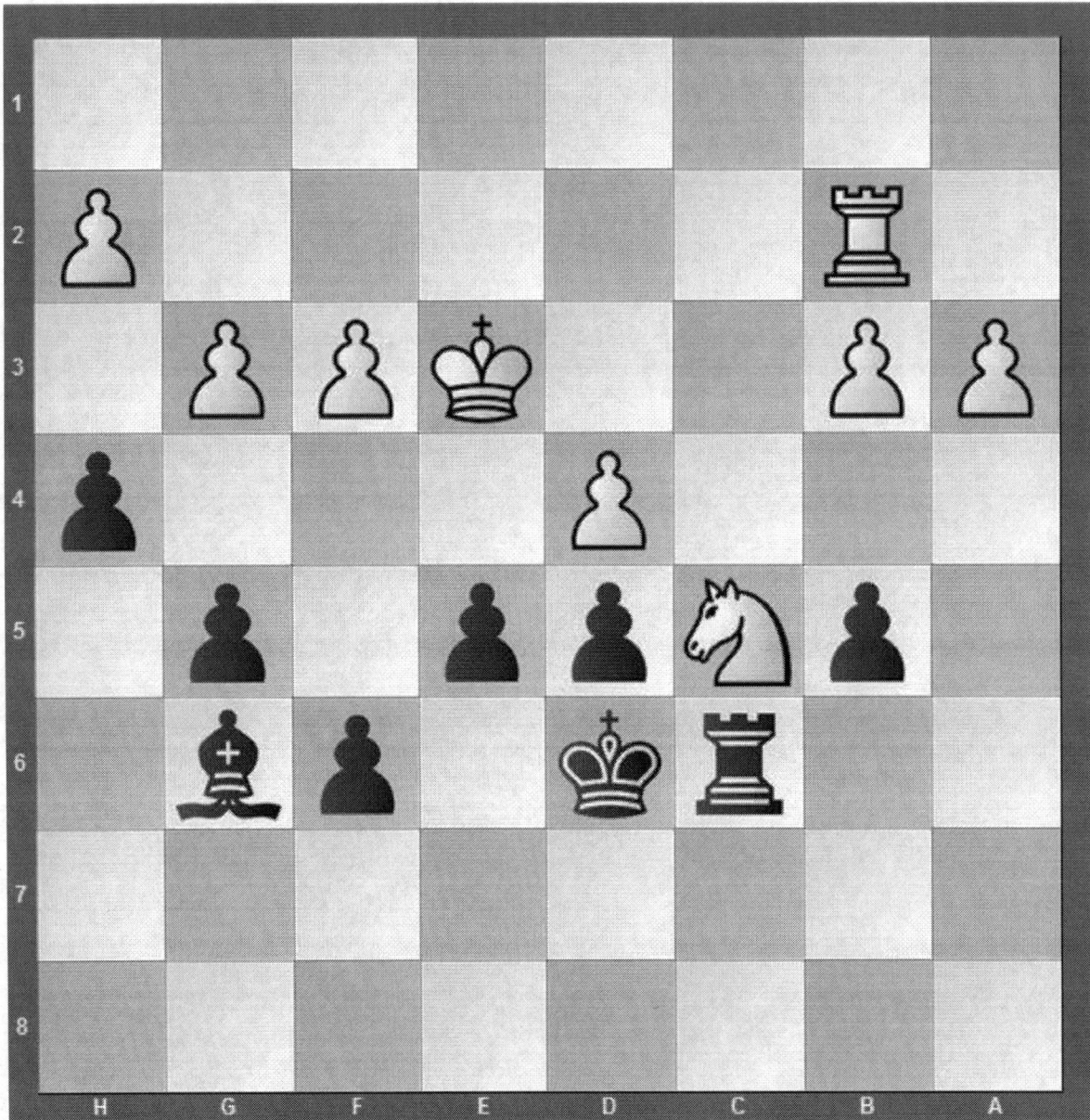

1		
2		

"*Play the opening like a book, and play the middle game like a magician, and play the endgame like a machine.*" – **Rudolf Spielmann**

1		
2		

1		
2		

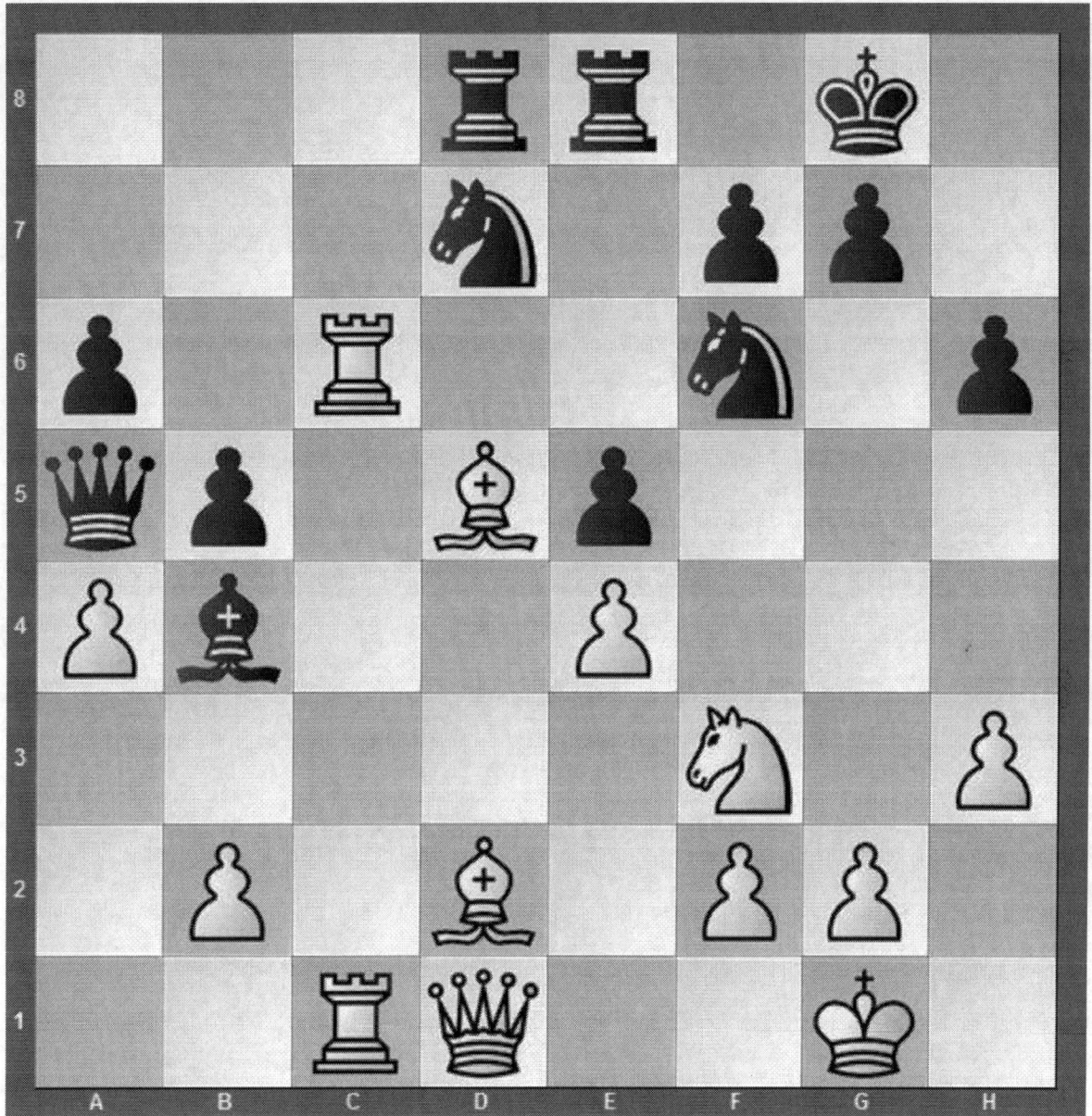

1		
2		

1		
2		

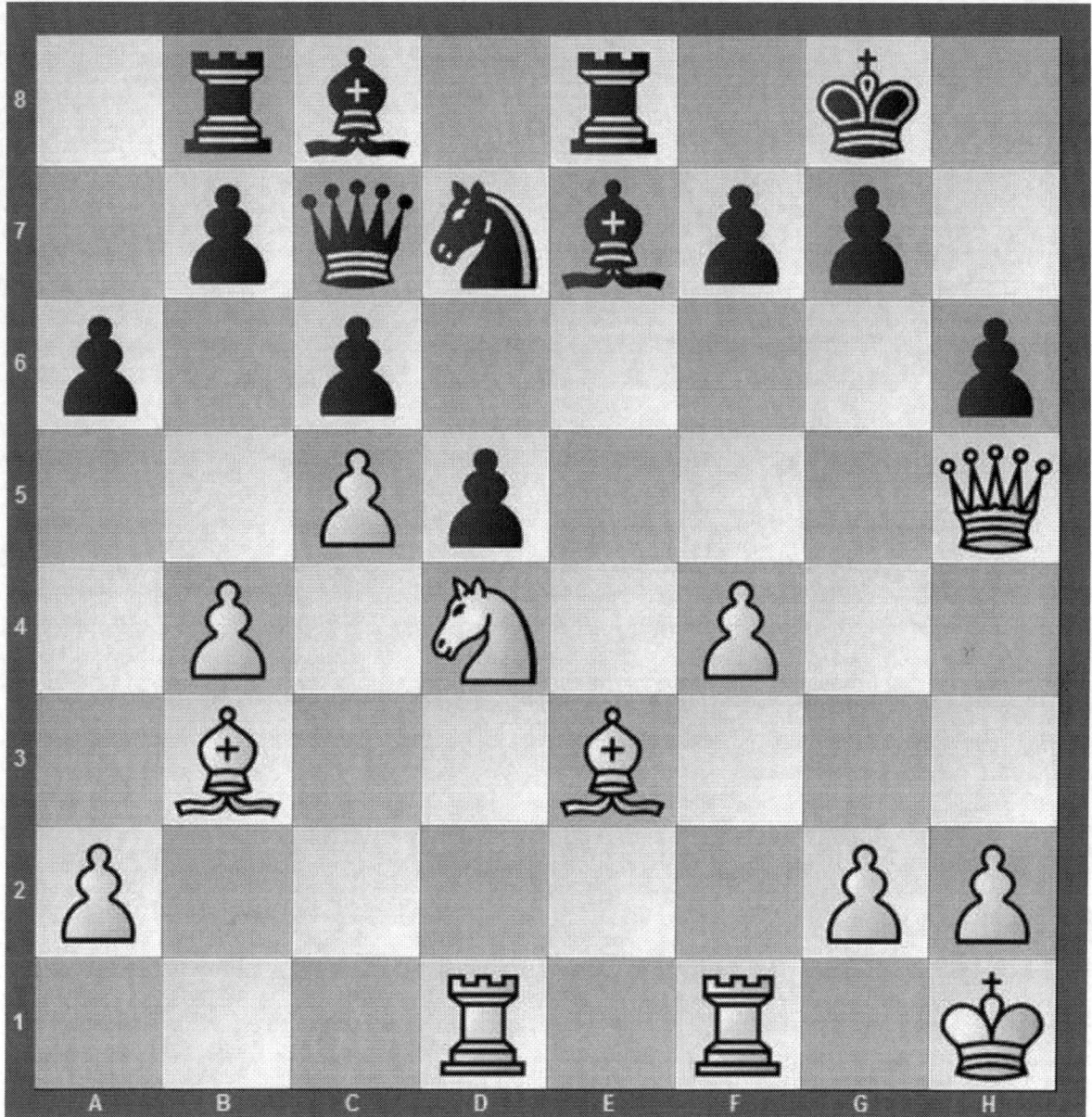

1		
2		

1		
2		

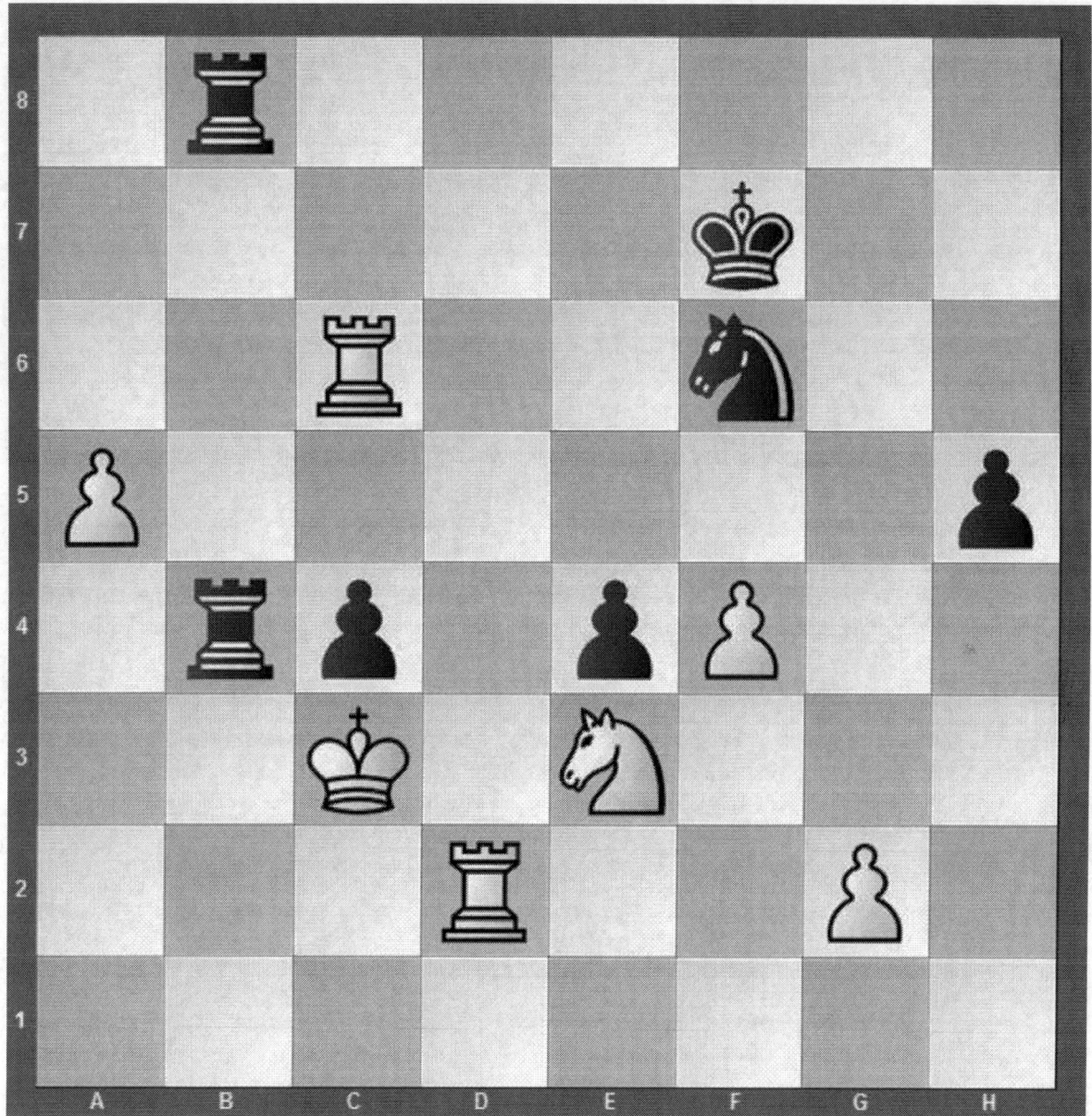

1		
2		

1		
2		

1		
2		

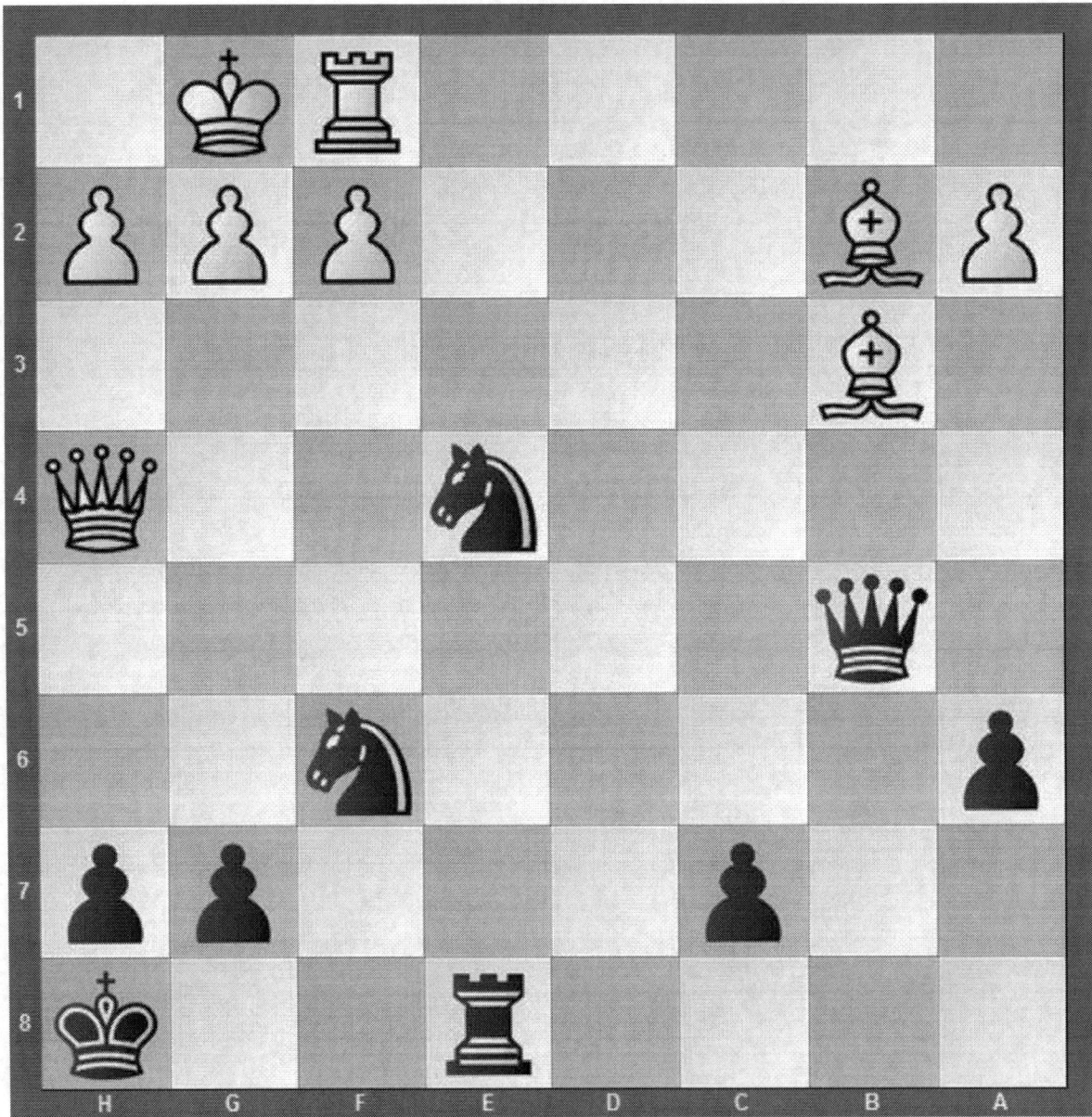

1		
2		

| 1 | | |
| 2 | | |

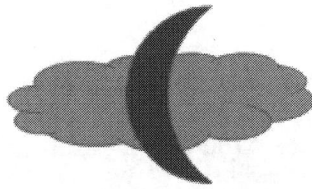

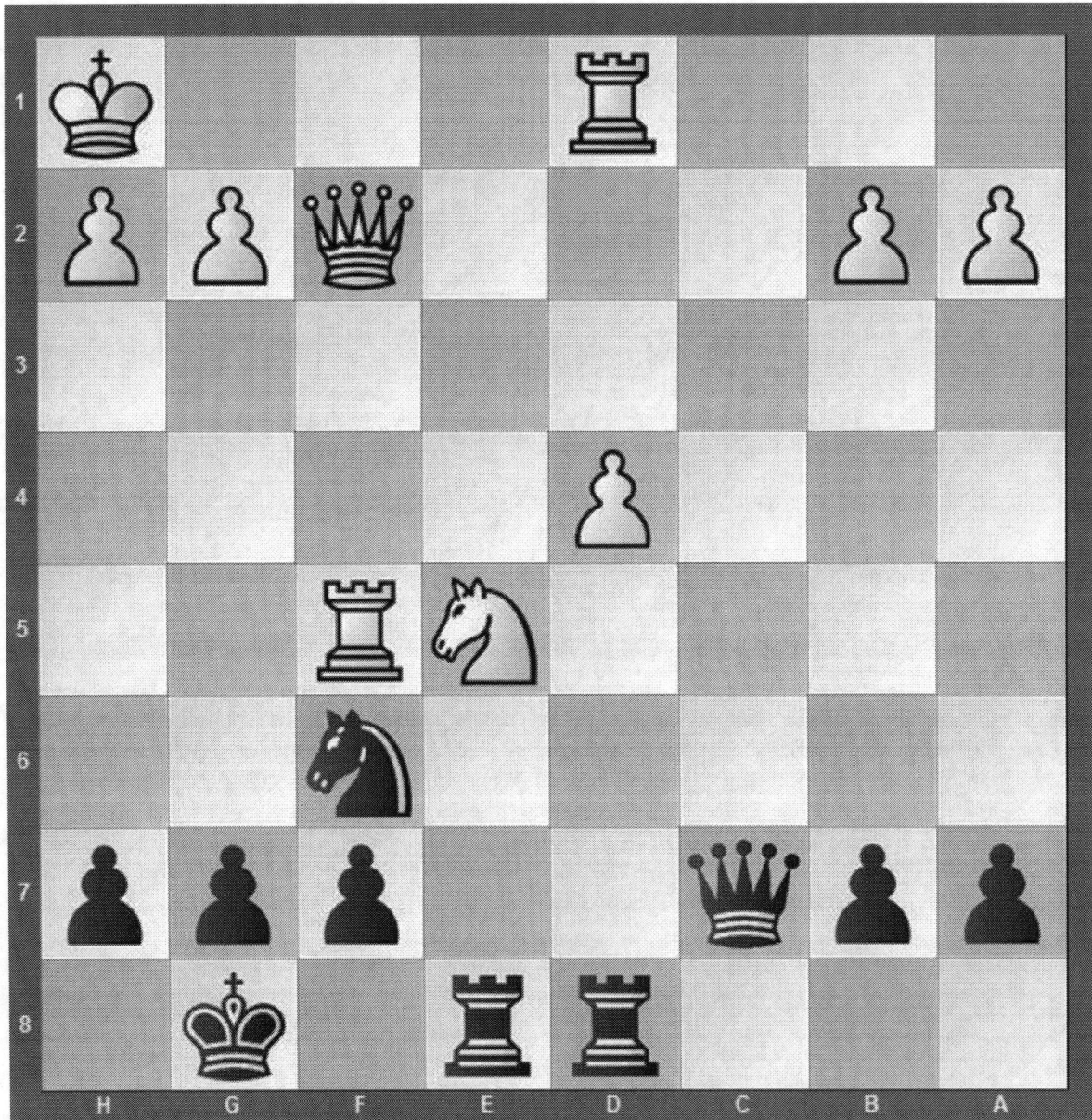

1		
2		

1		
2		

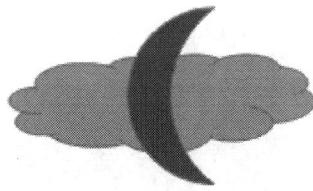

1		
2		

"Chess is like body-building. If you train every day, you stay in top shape. It is the same with your brain – chess is a matter of daily training." – **Vladimir Kramnik**

1		
2		

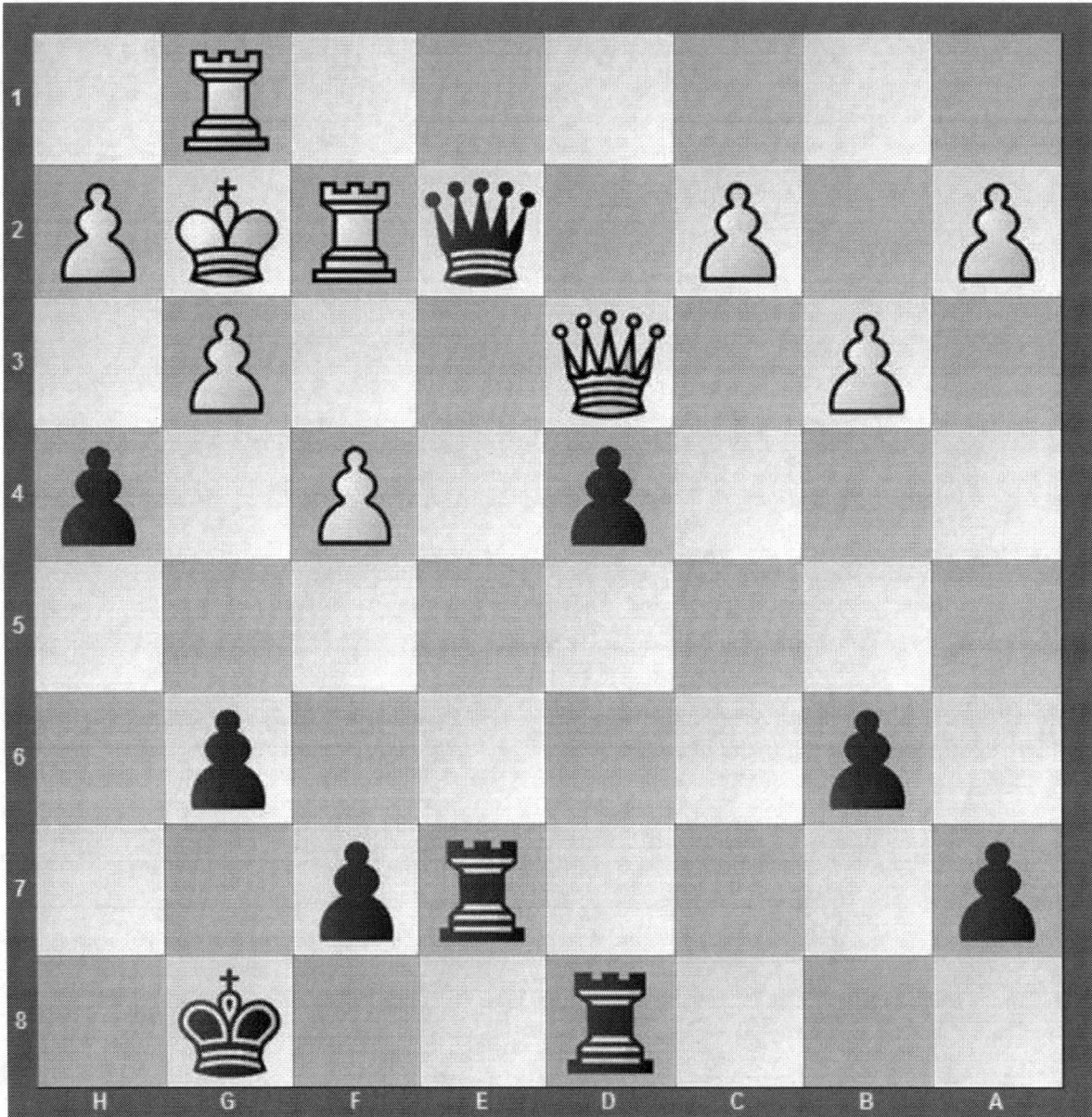

1		
2		

1		
2		

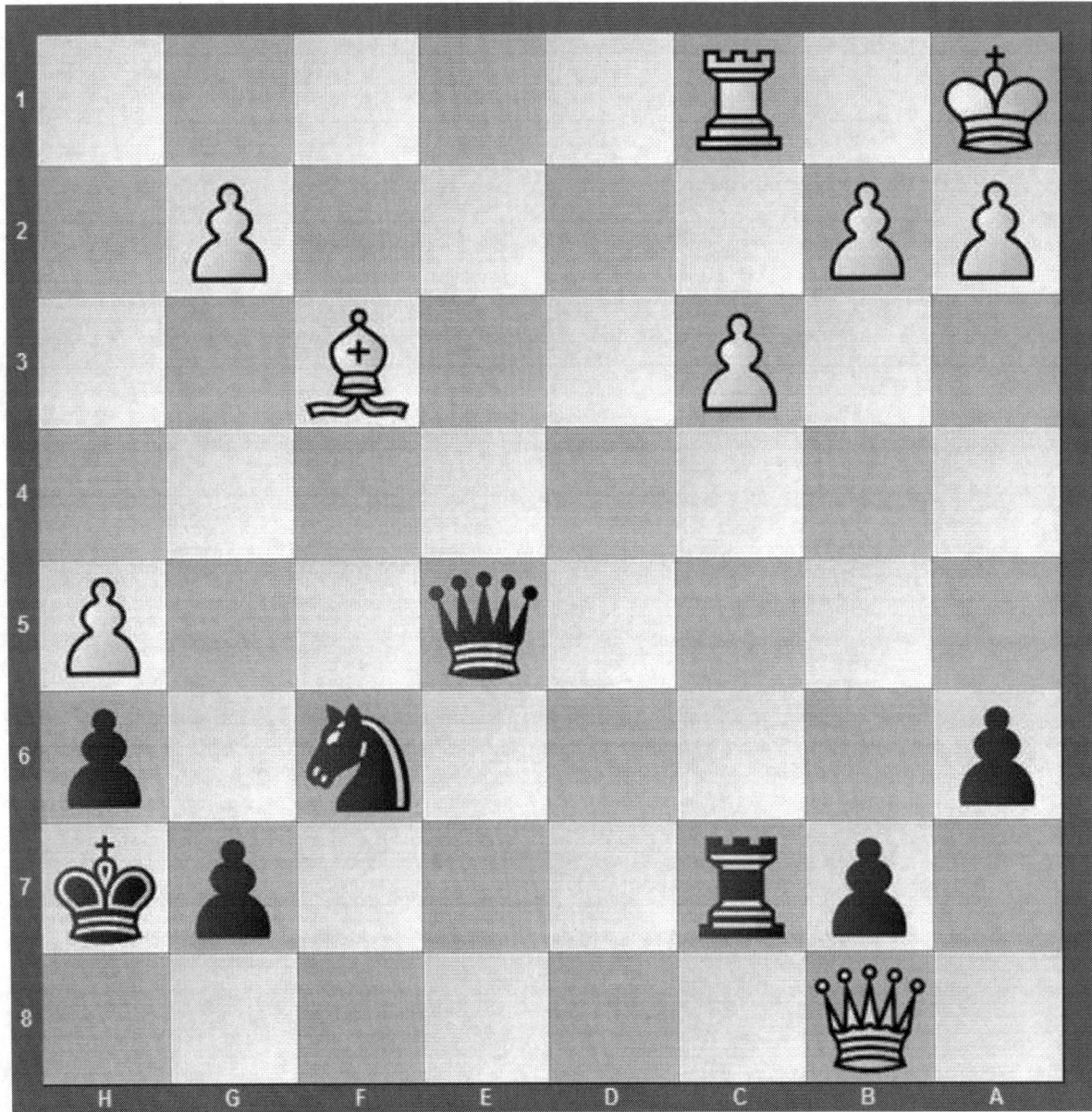

1		
2		

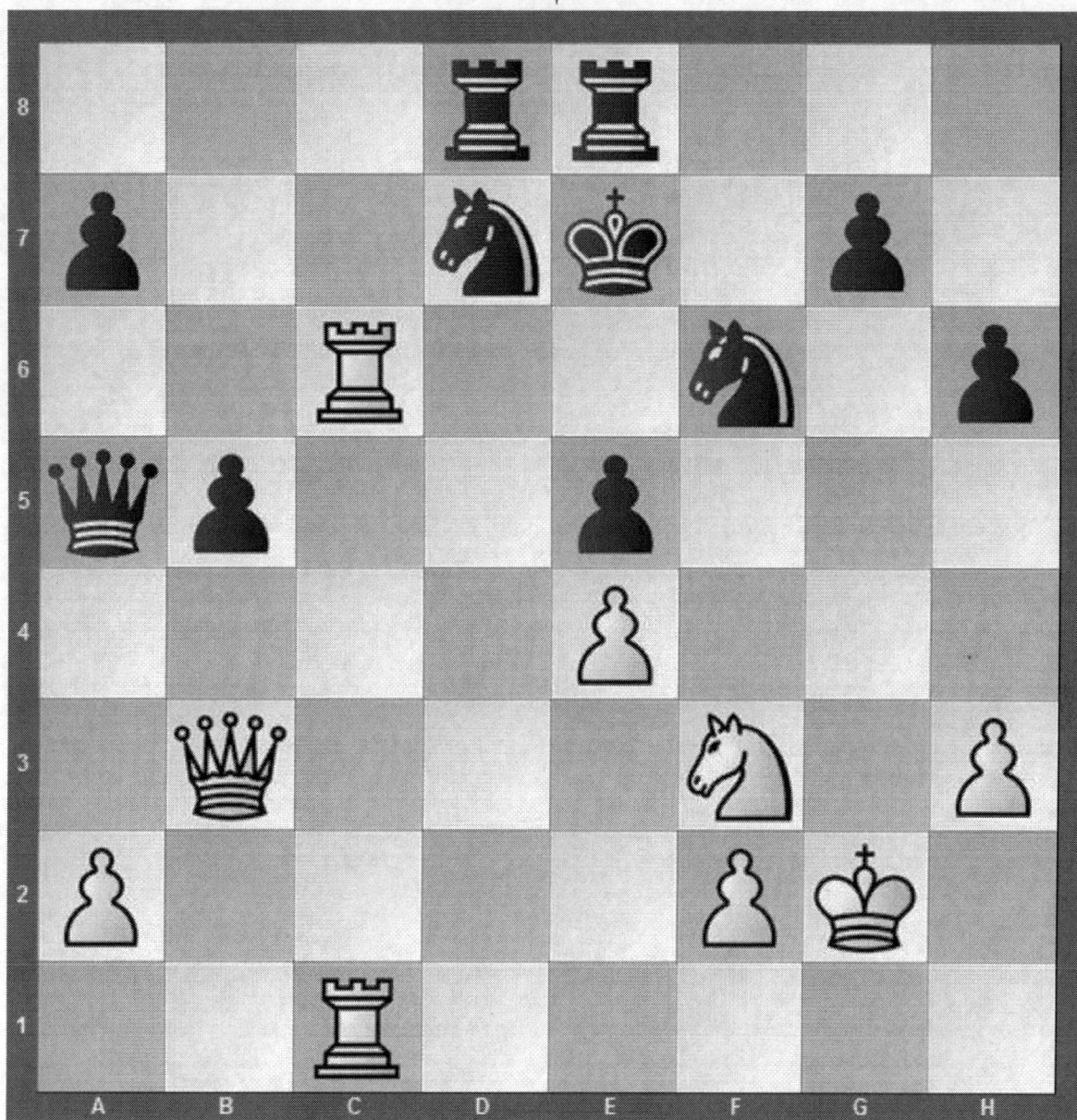

1		
2		

1		
2		

1		
2		

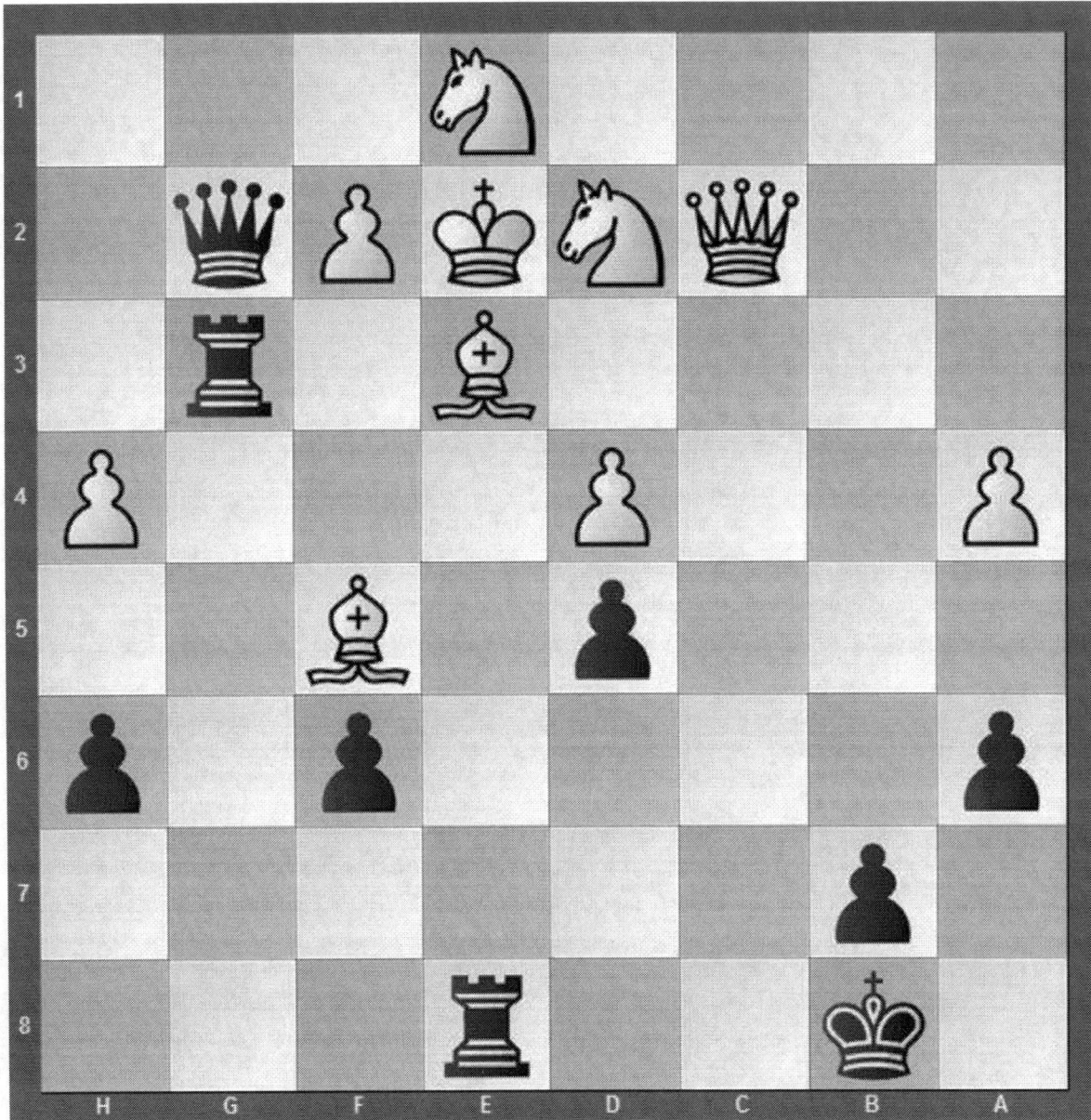

1		
2		

1		
2		

1		
2		

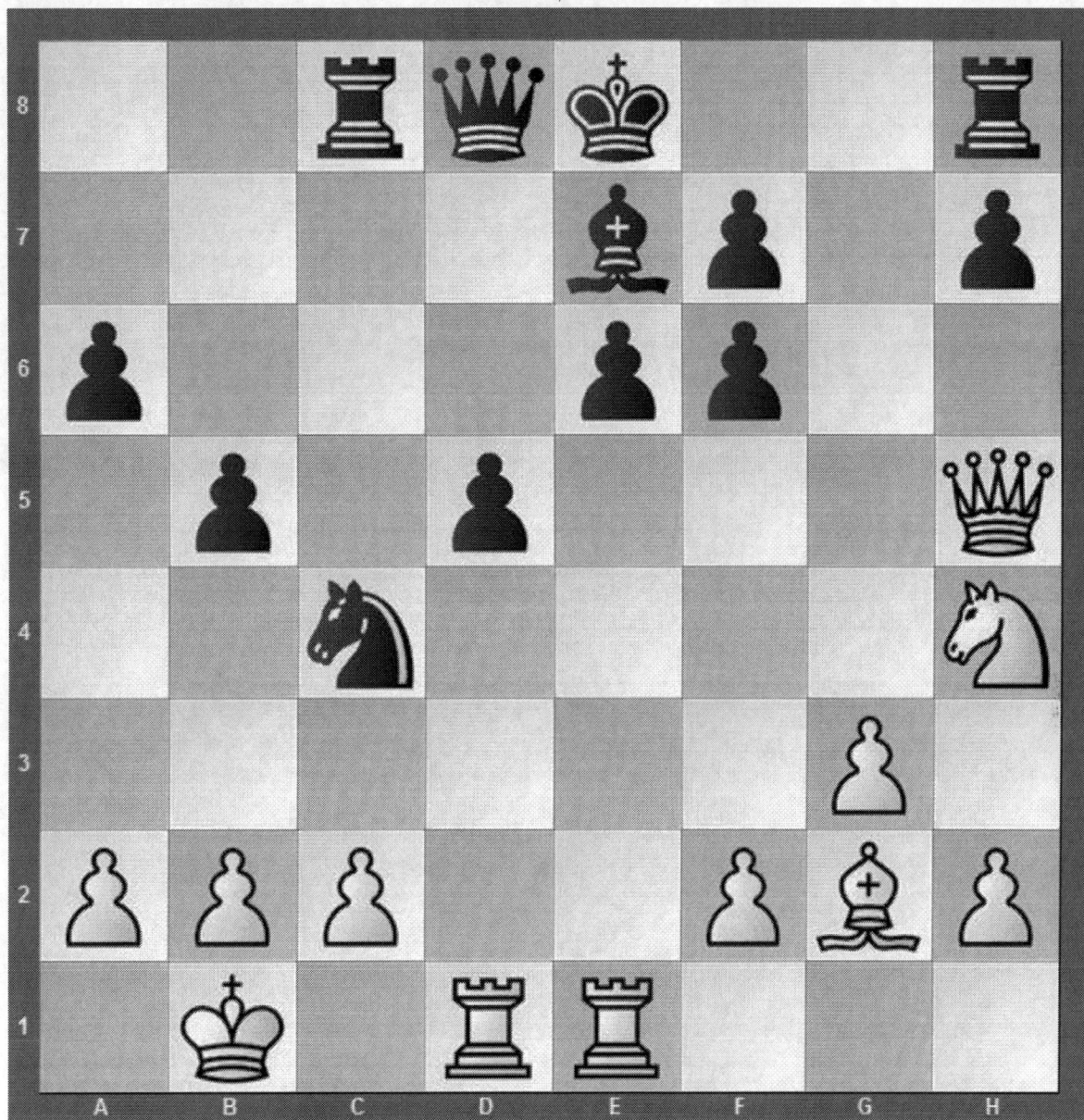

1		
2		

1		
2		

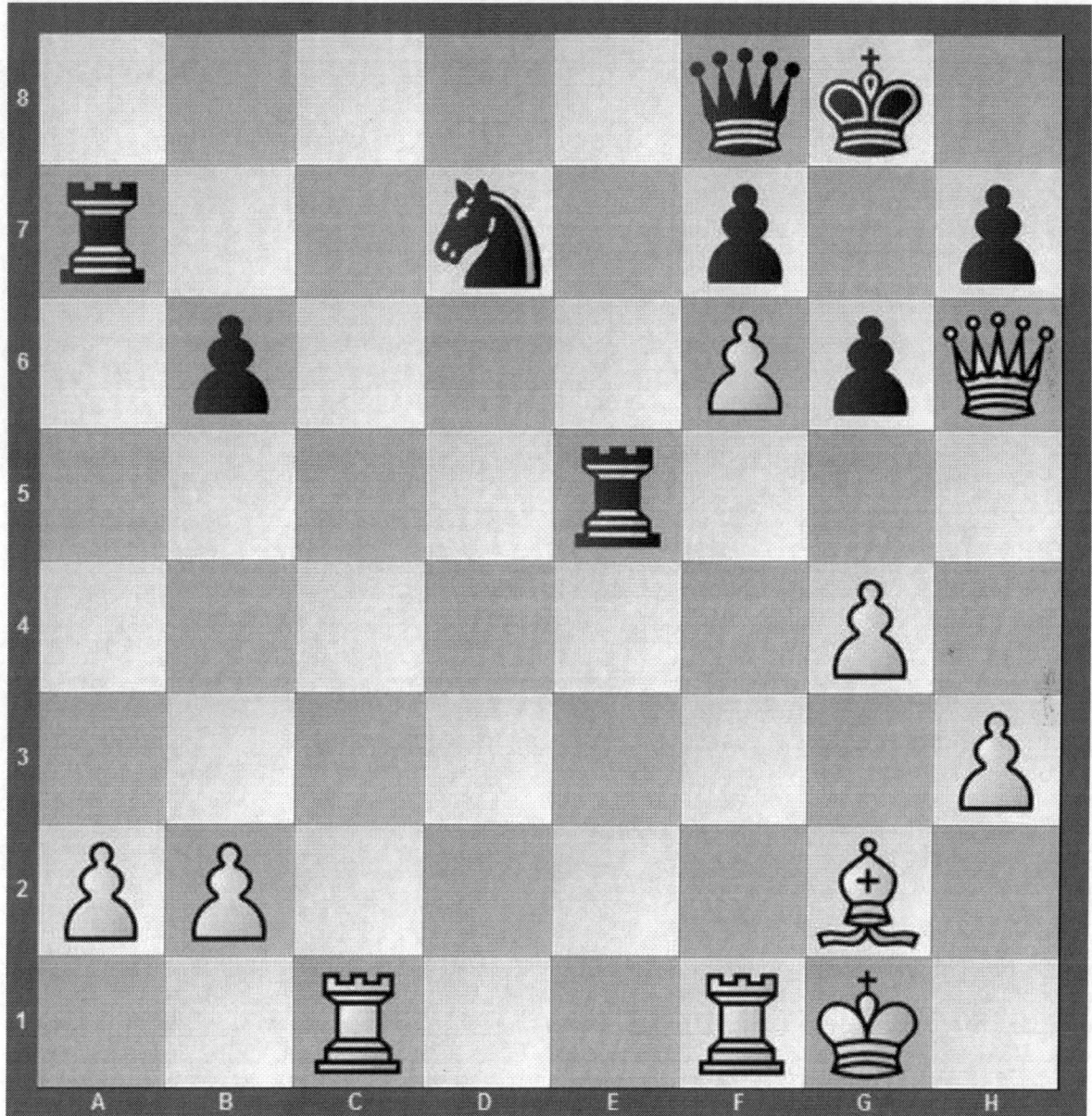

1		
2		

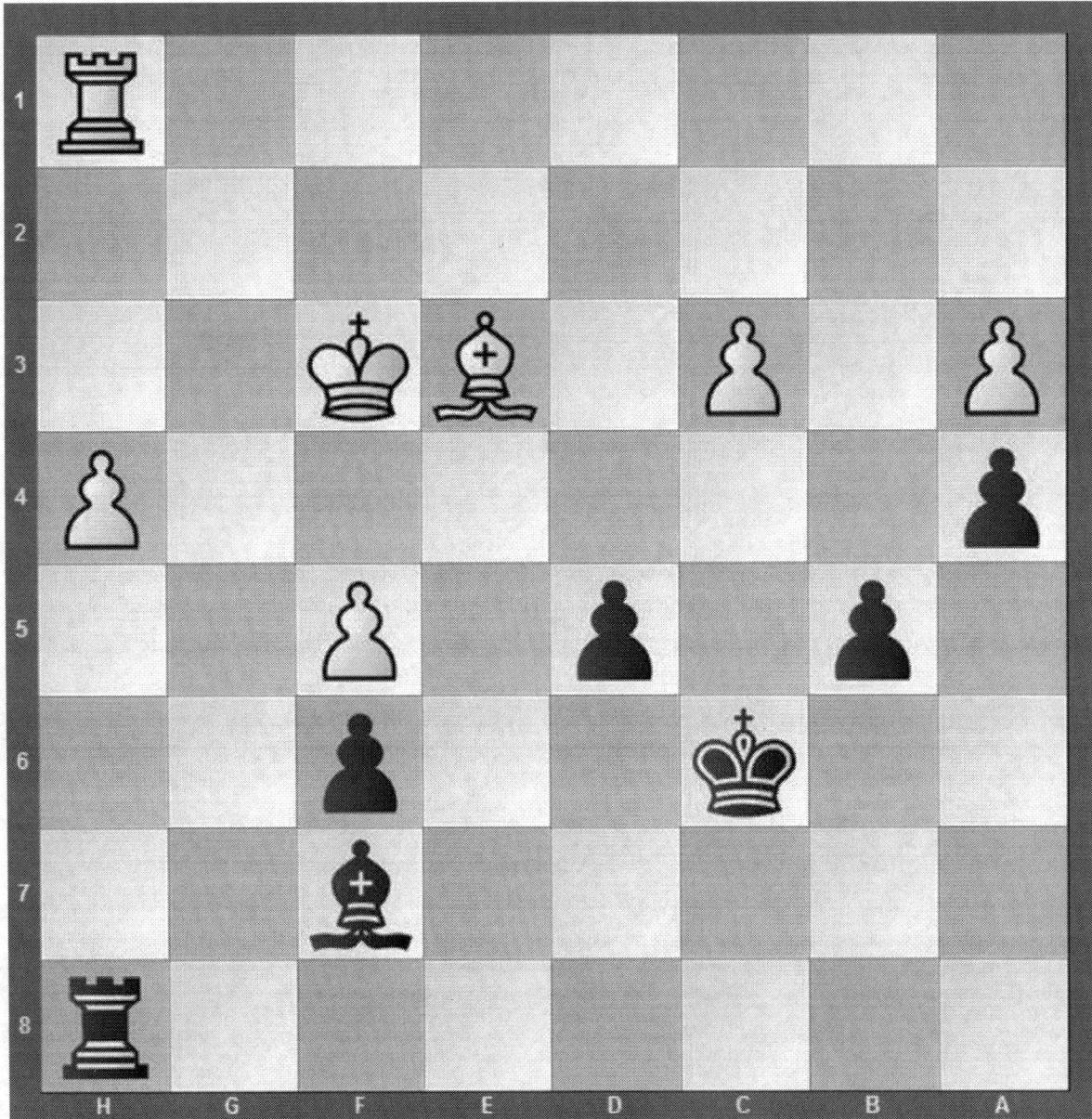

1		
2		

"Chess is a cold bath for the mind" – **Sir John Simon**

1		
2		

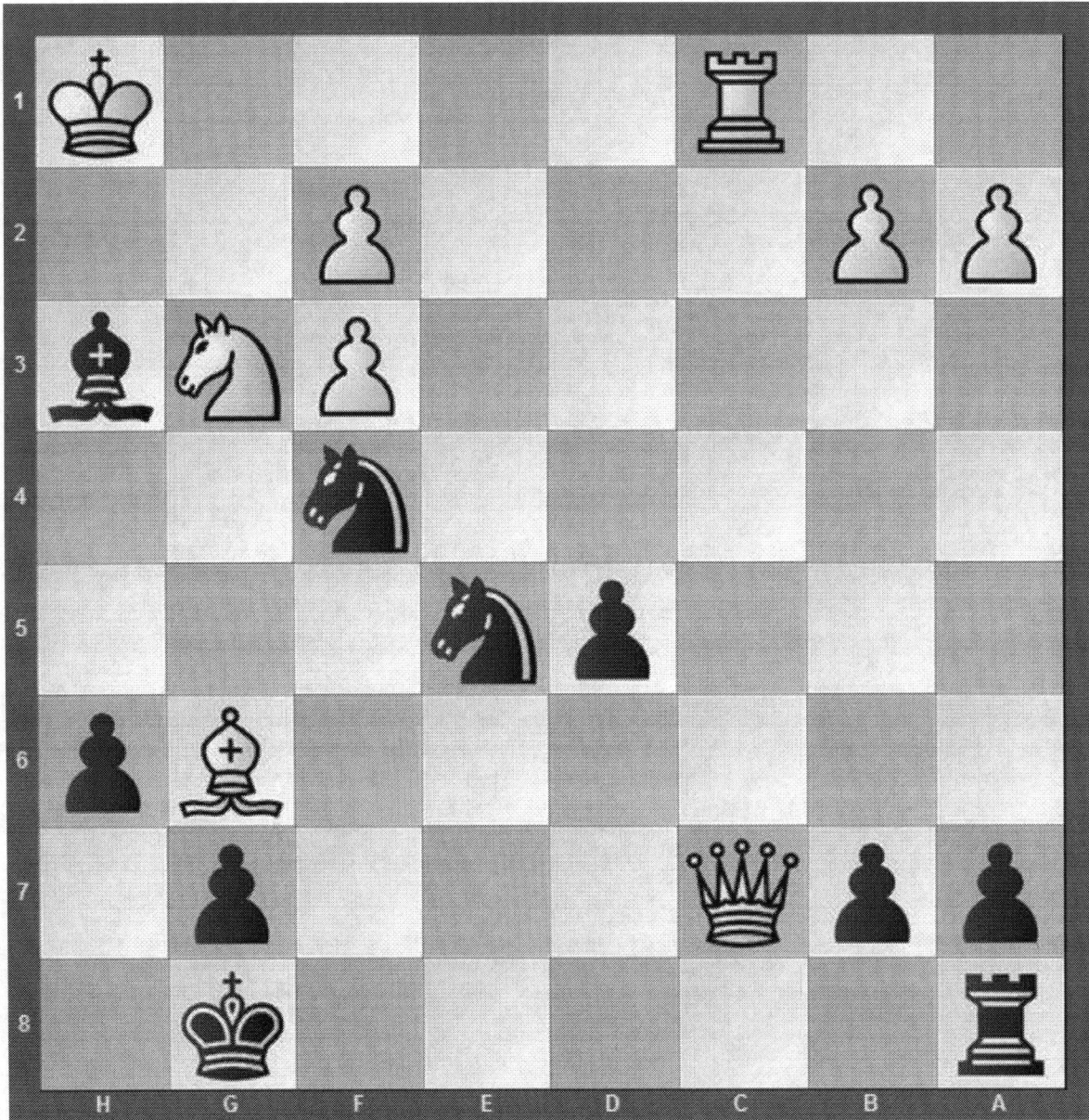

1		
2		

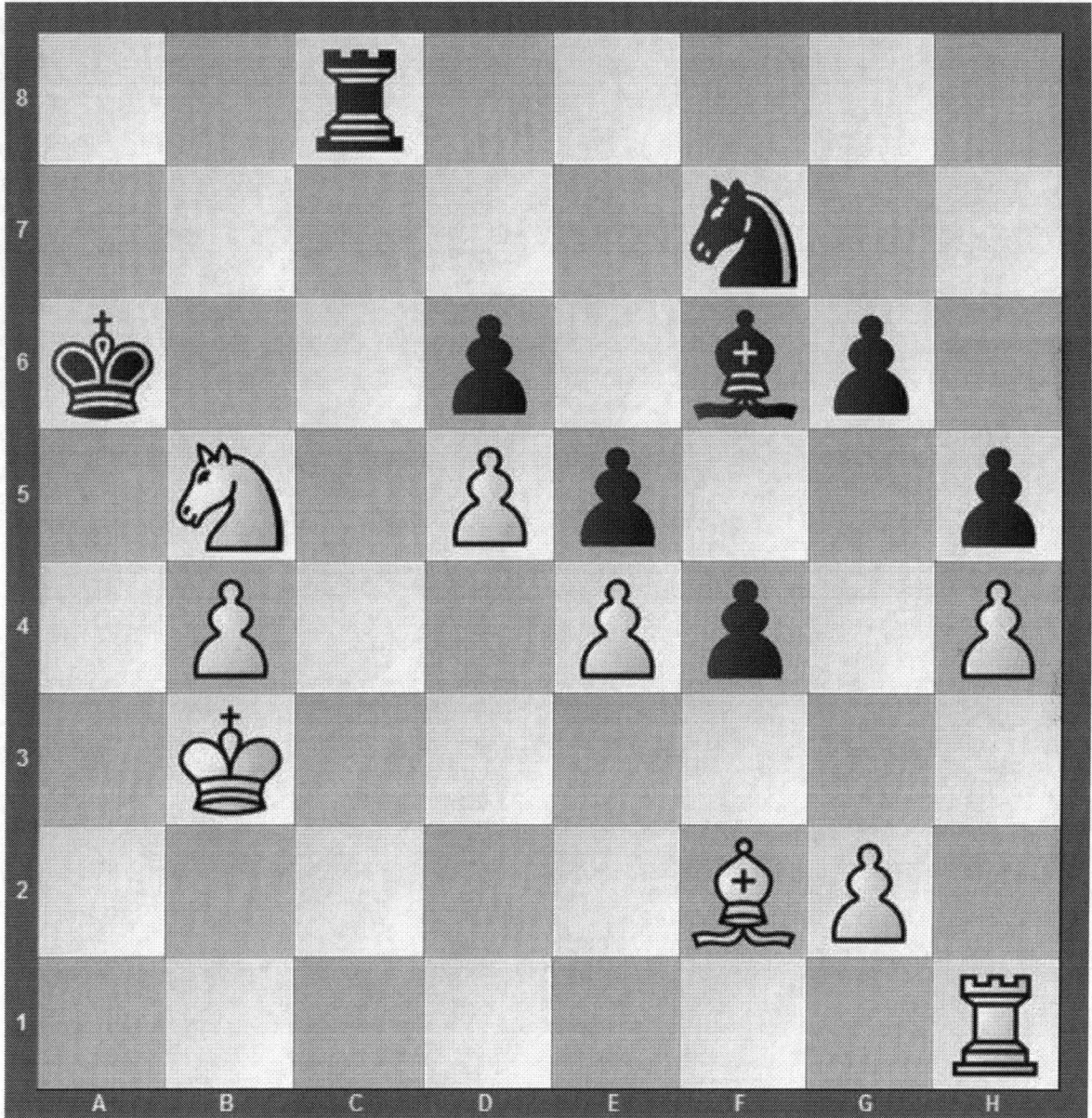

1		
2		

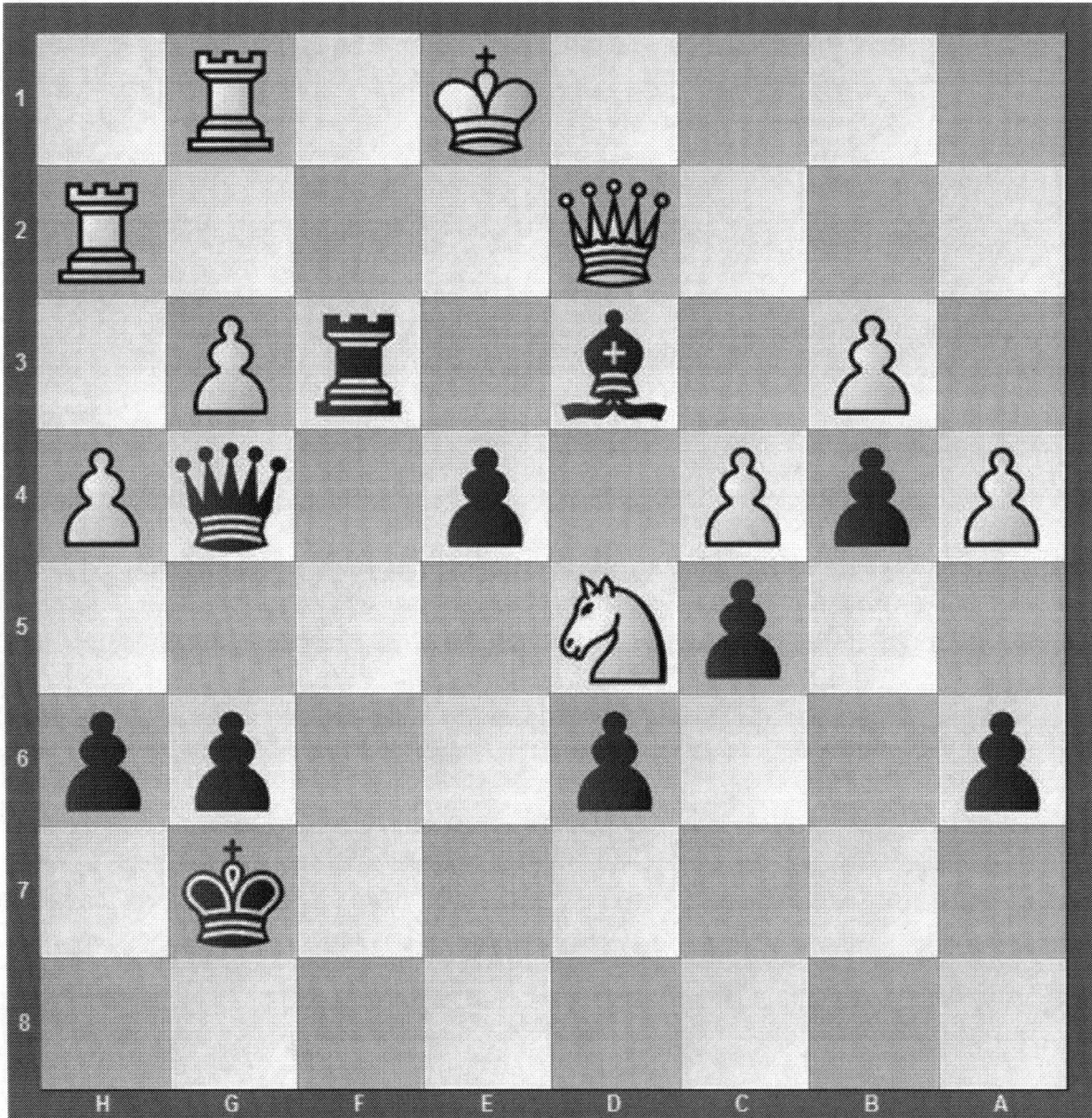

1		
2		

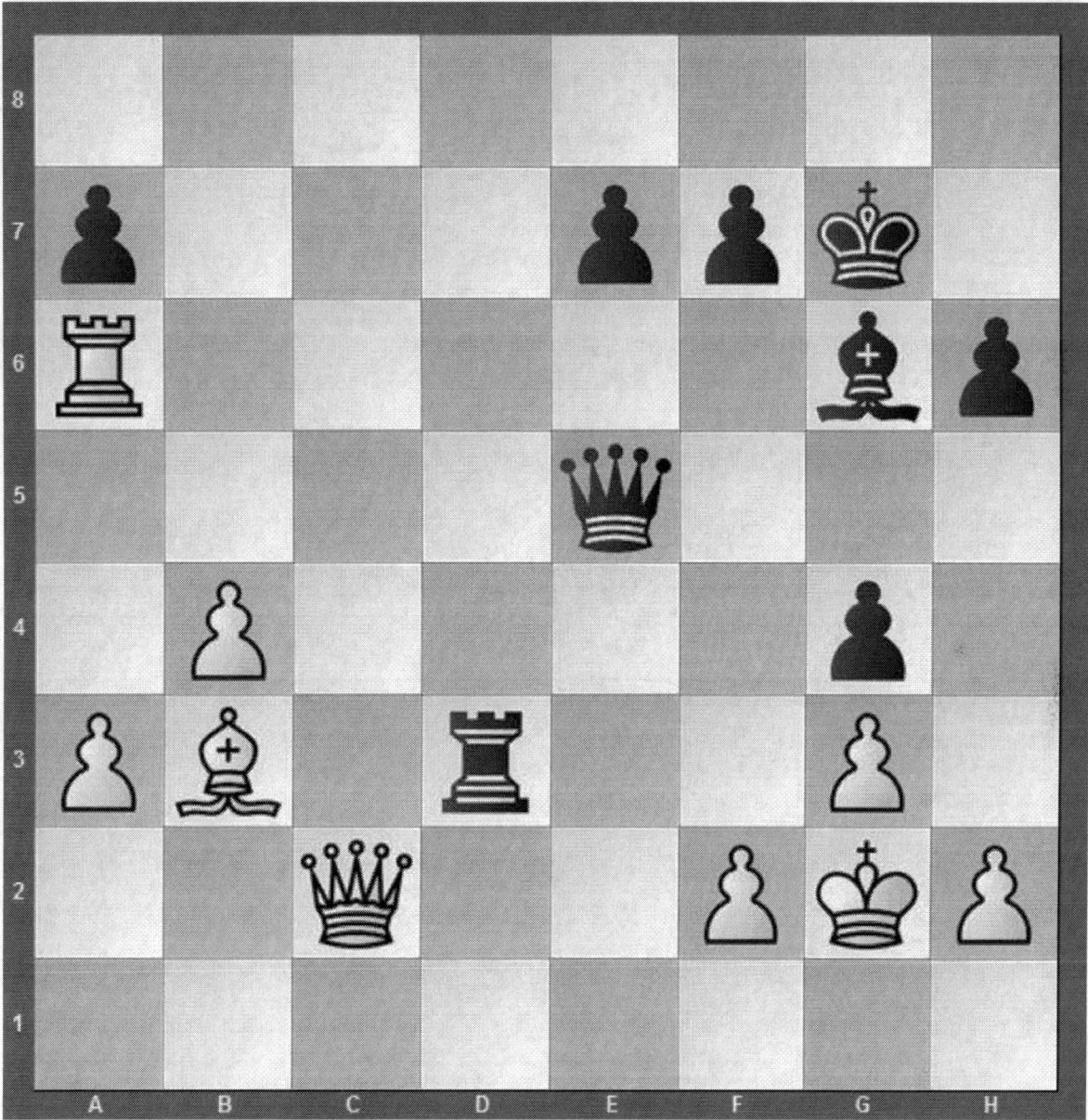

1		
2		

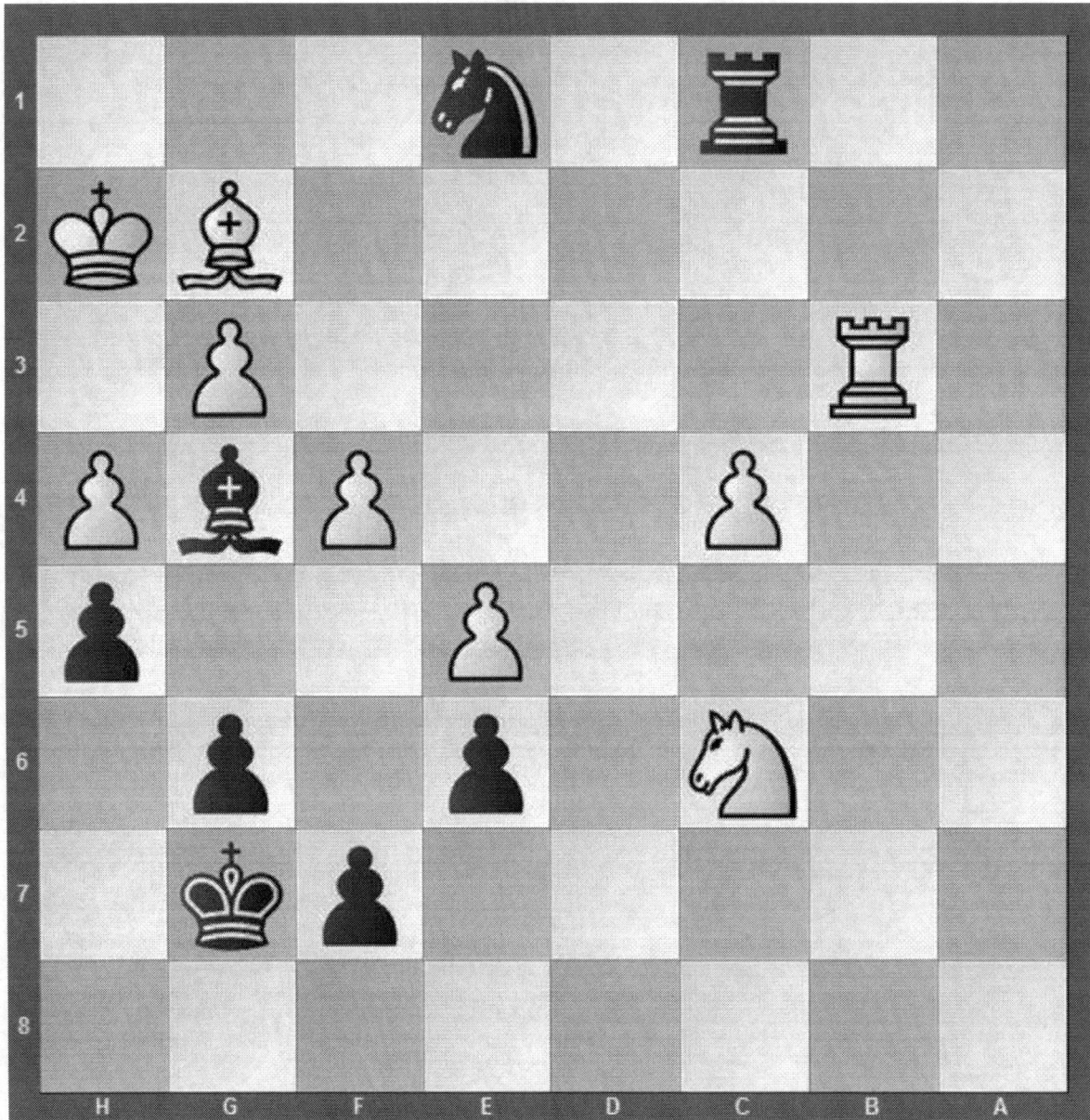

1		
2		

136

1		
2		

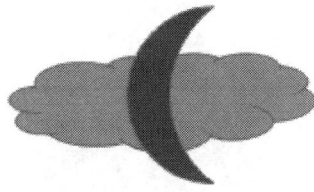

1		
2		

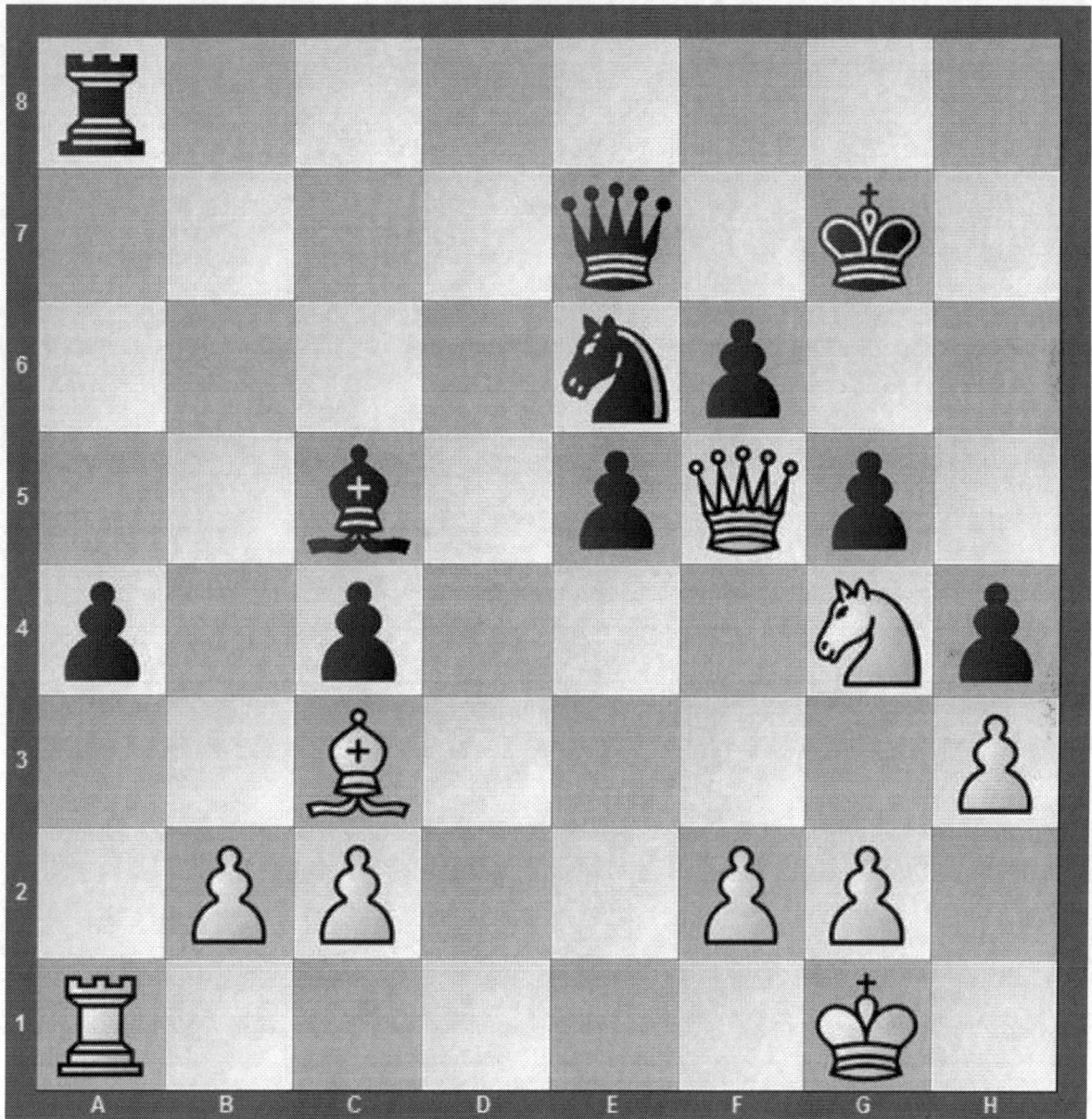

1		
2		

1		
2		

1		
2		

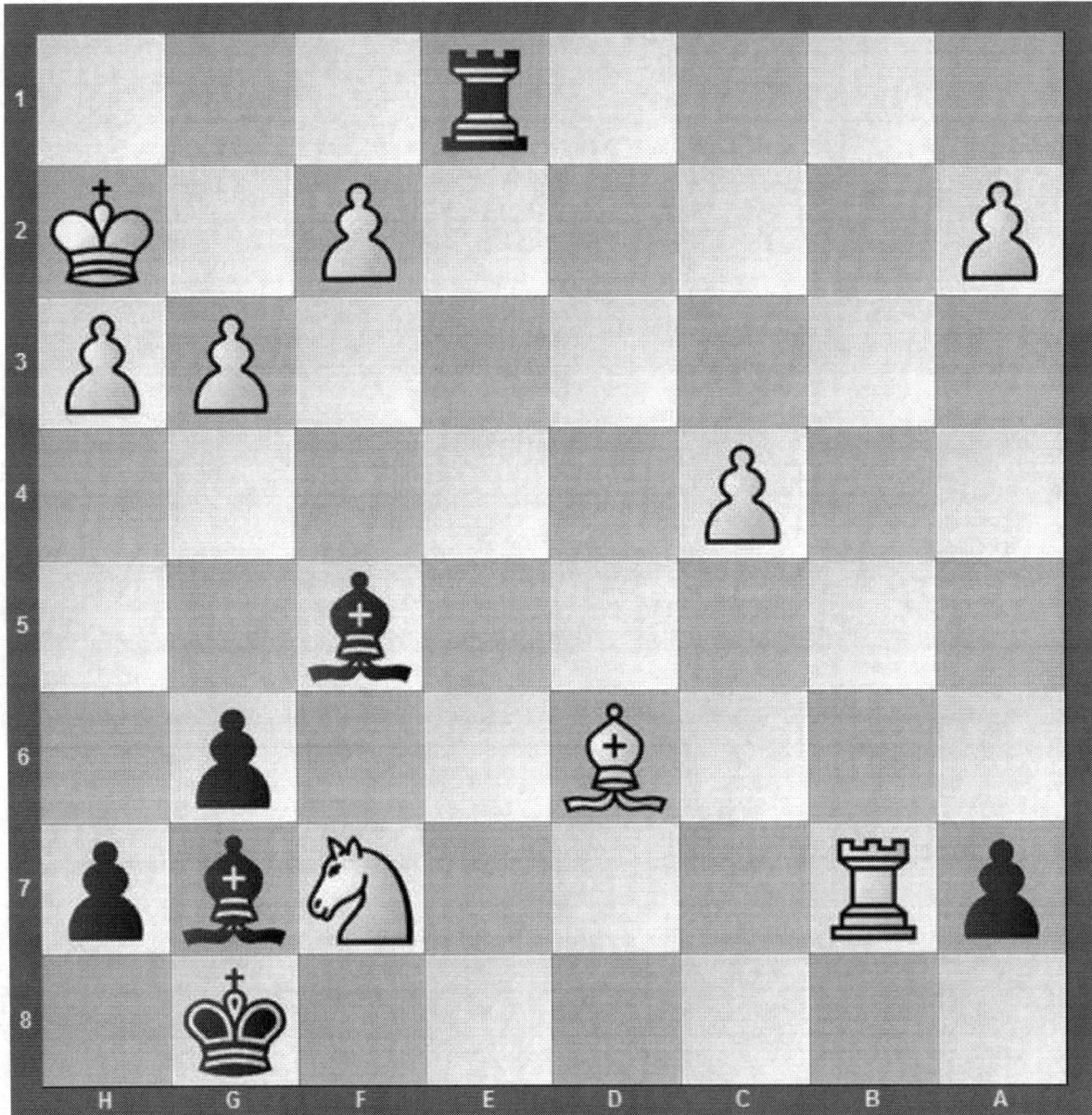

1		
2		

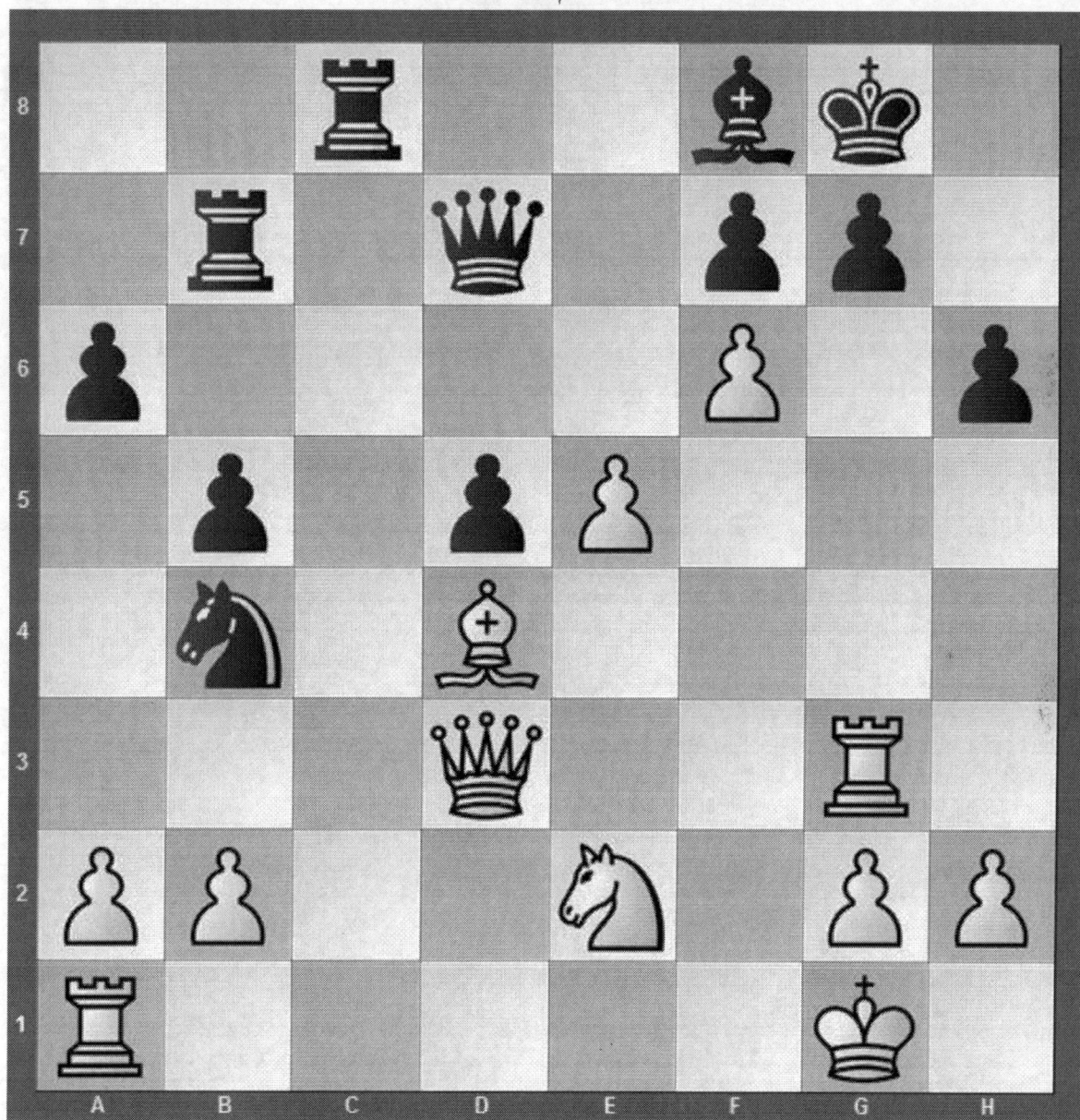

1		
2		

1		
2		

"Weak points or holes in the opponent's position must be occupied by pieces not Pawns." – **Siegbert Tarrasch**

1		
2		

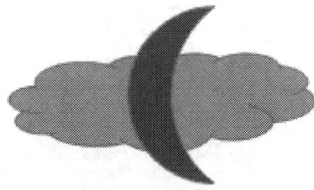

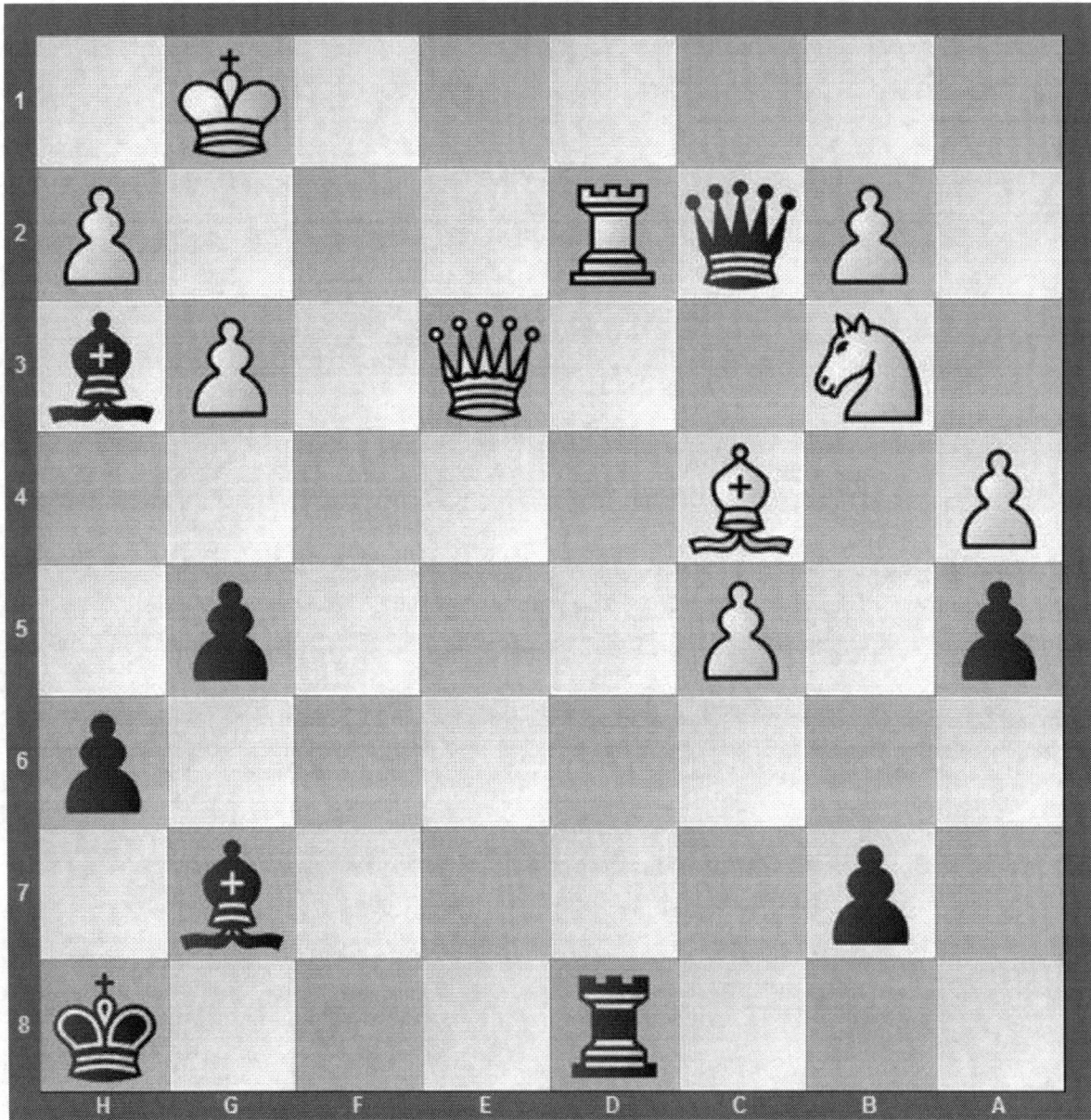

1		
2		

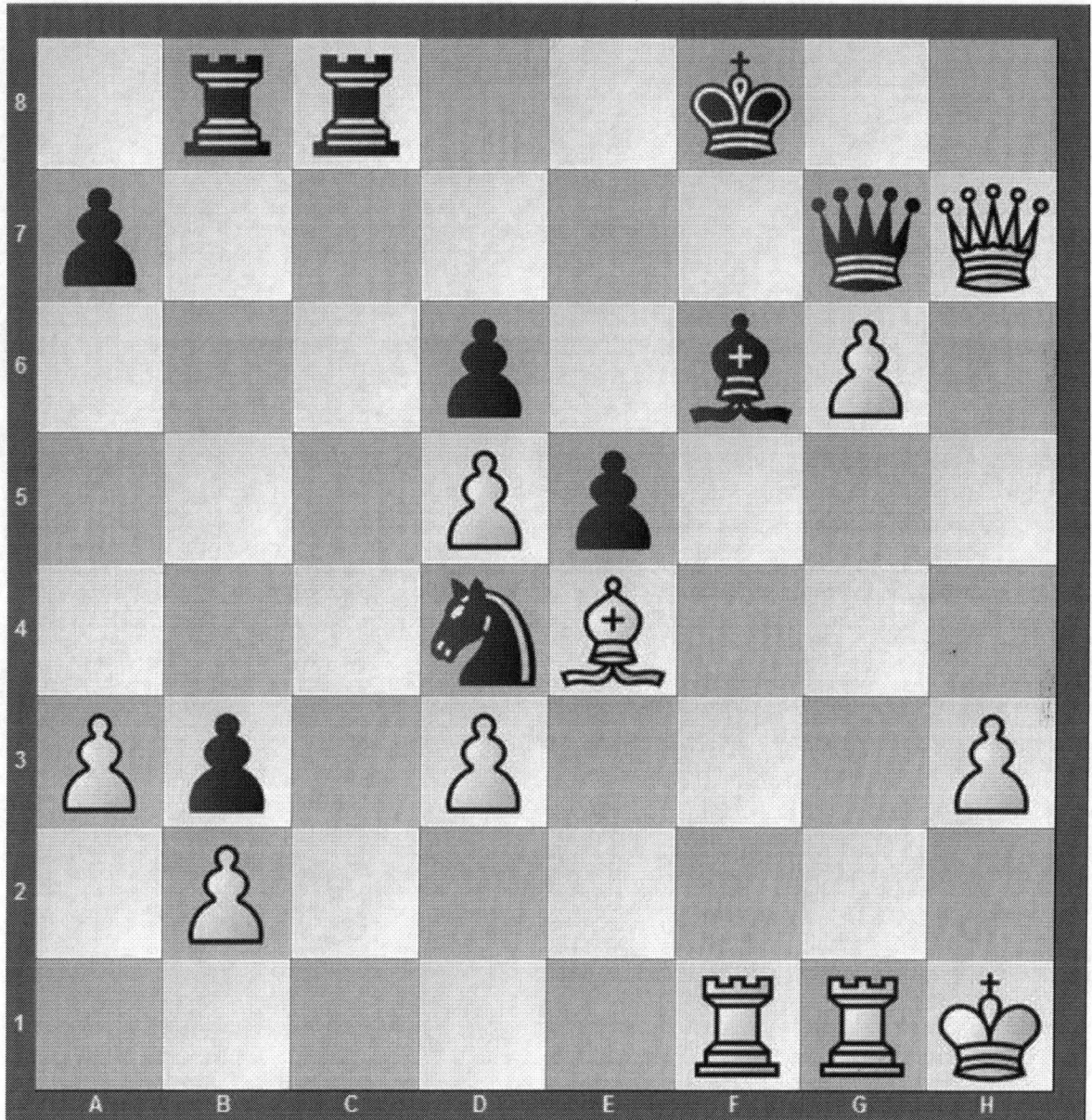

1		
2		

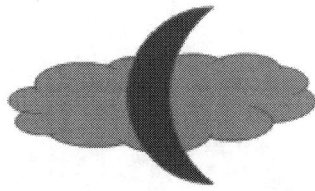

1		
2		

1		
2		

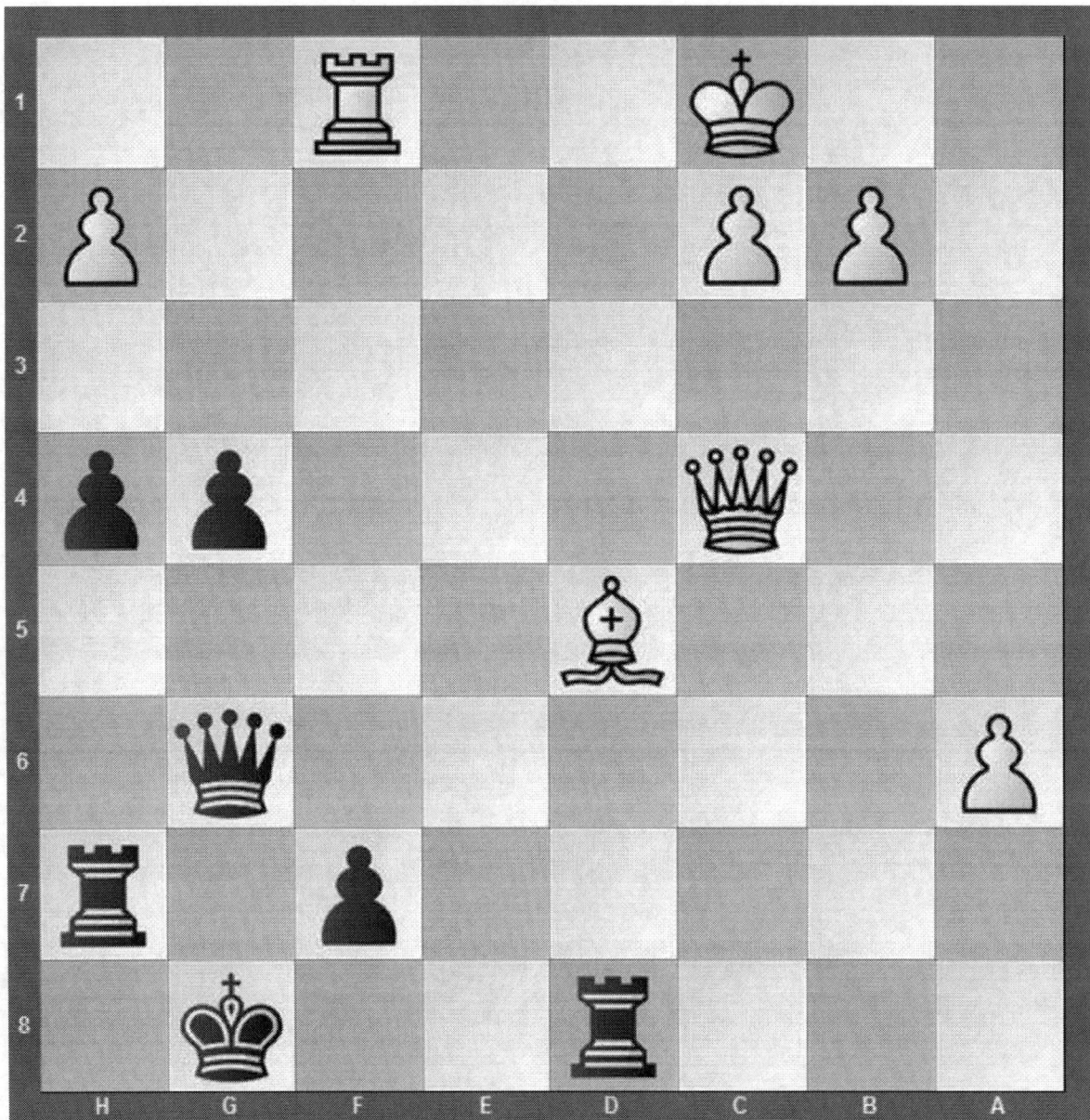

1		
2		

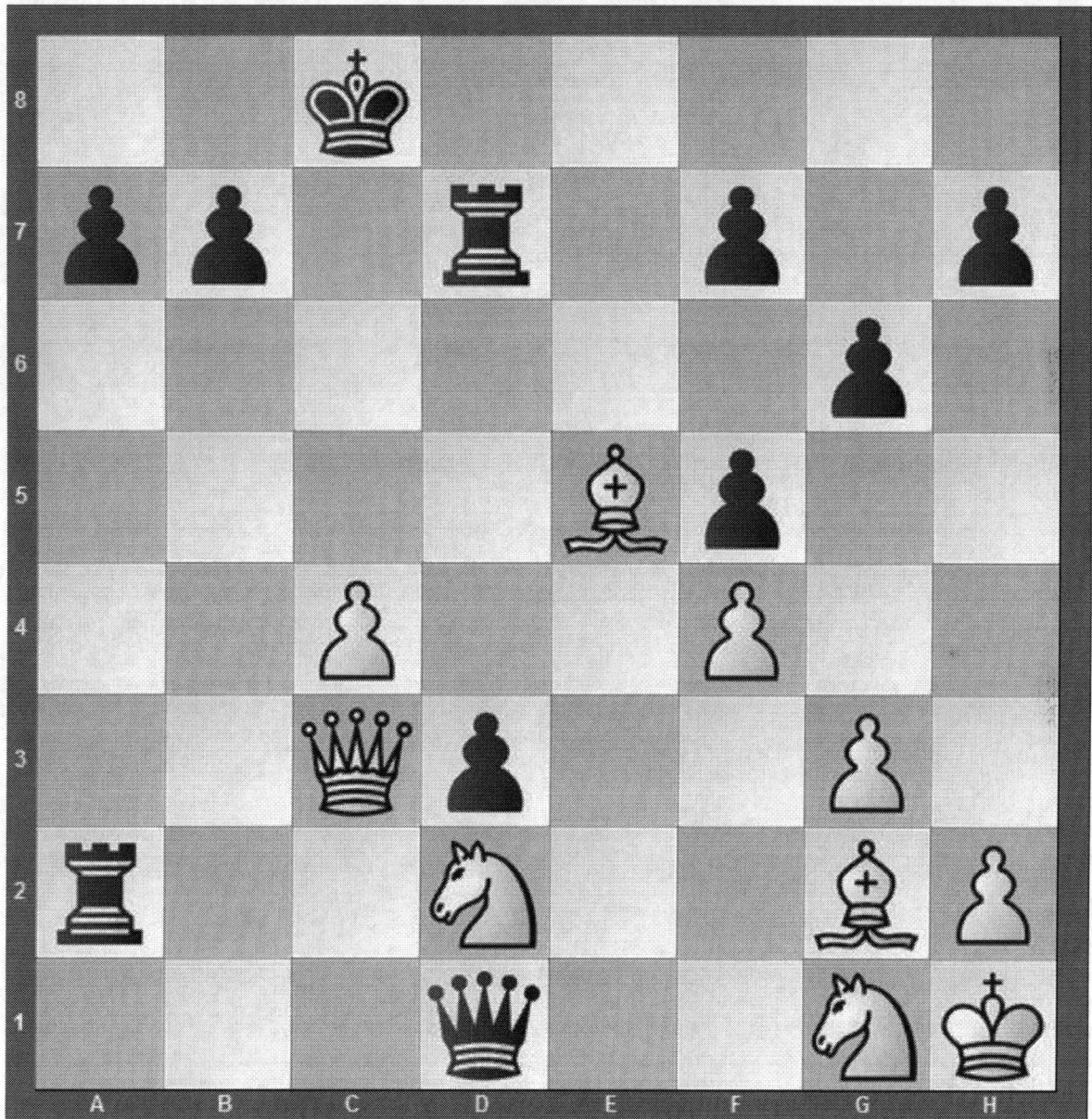

1		
2		

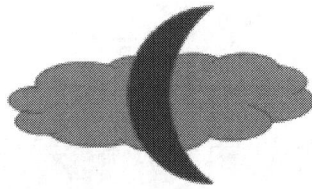

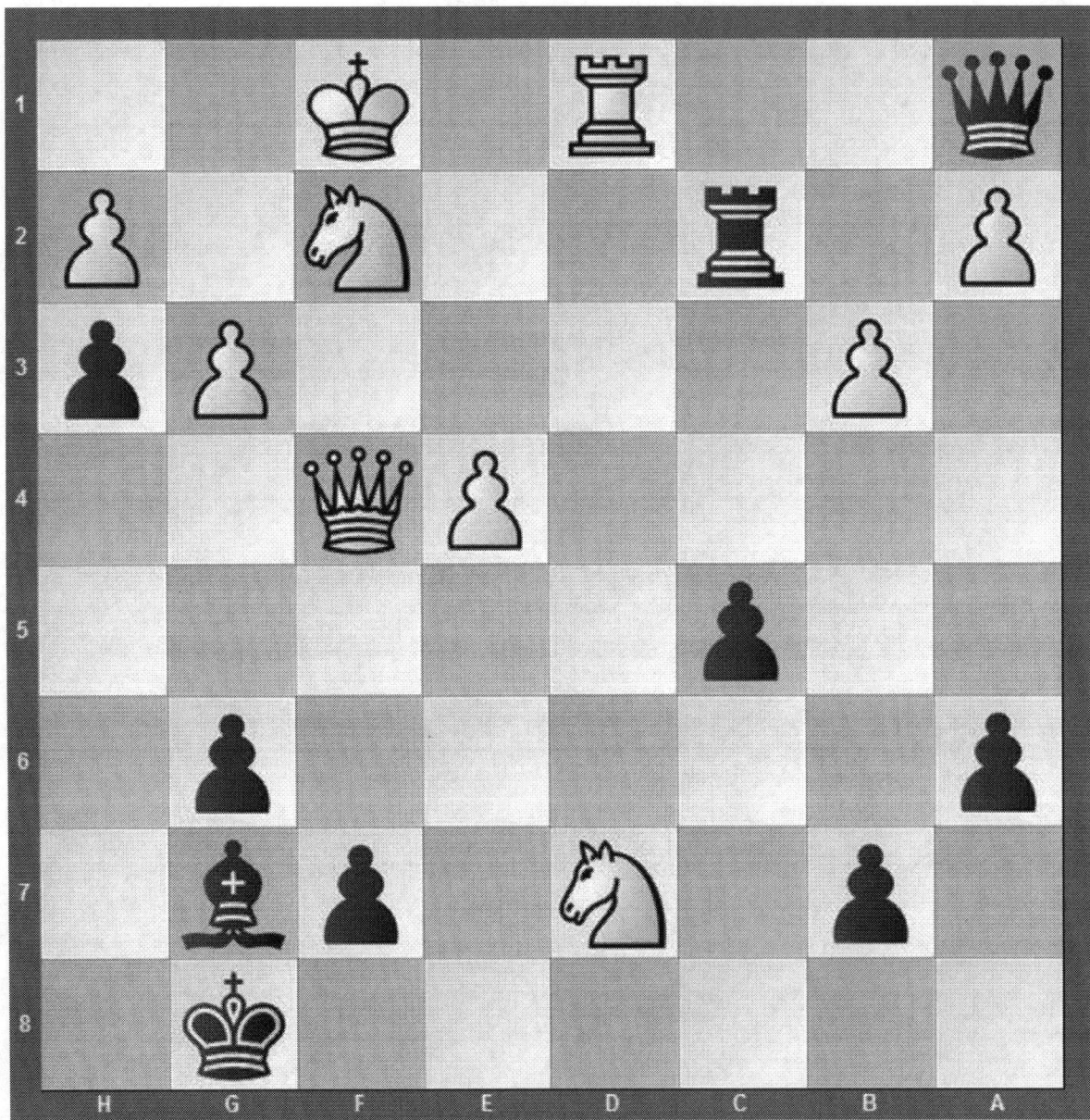

1		
2		

1		
2		

1		
2		

1		
2		

1		
2		

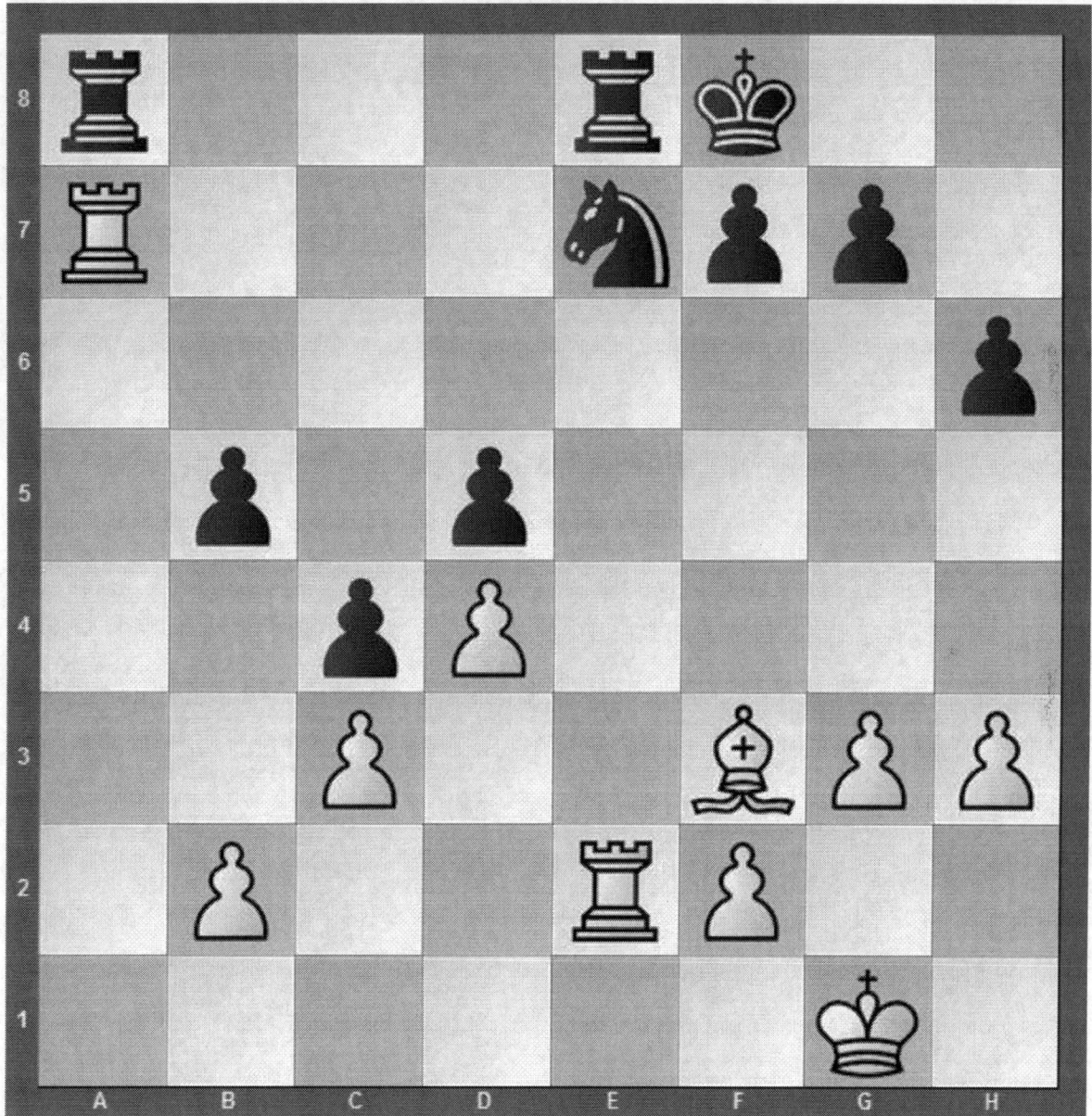

1		
2		

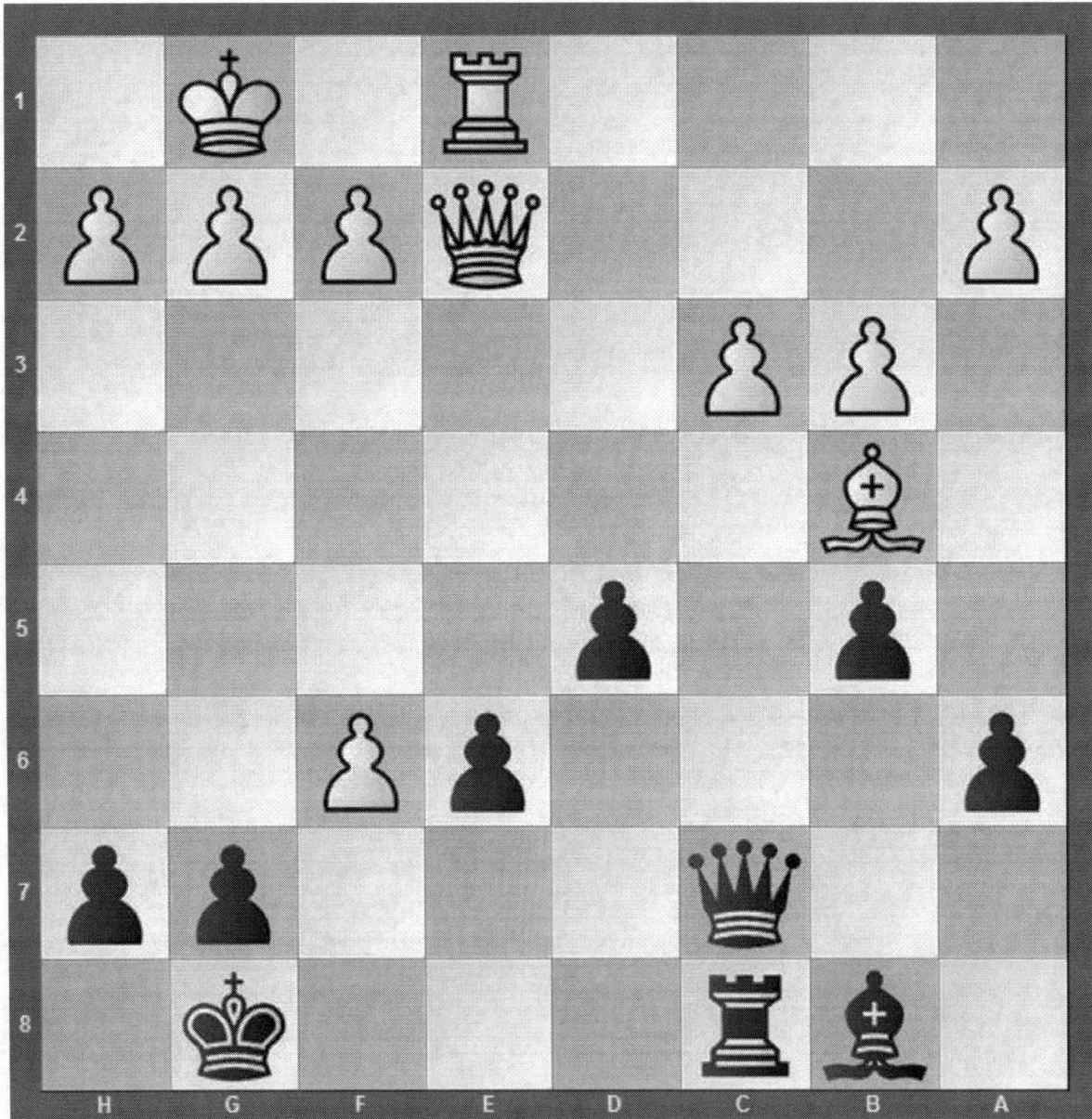

1		
2		

"Psychology is the most important factor in chess." – **Alexander Alekhine**

1		
2		

1		
2		

1		
2		

1		
2		

1		
2		

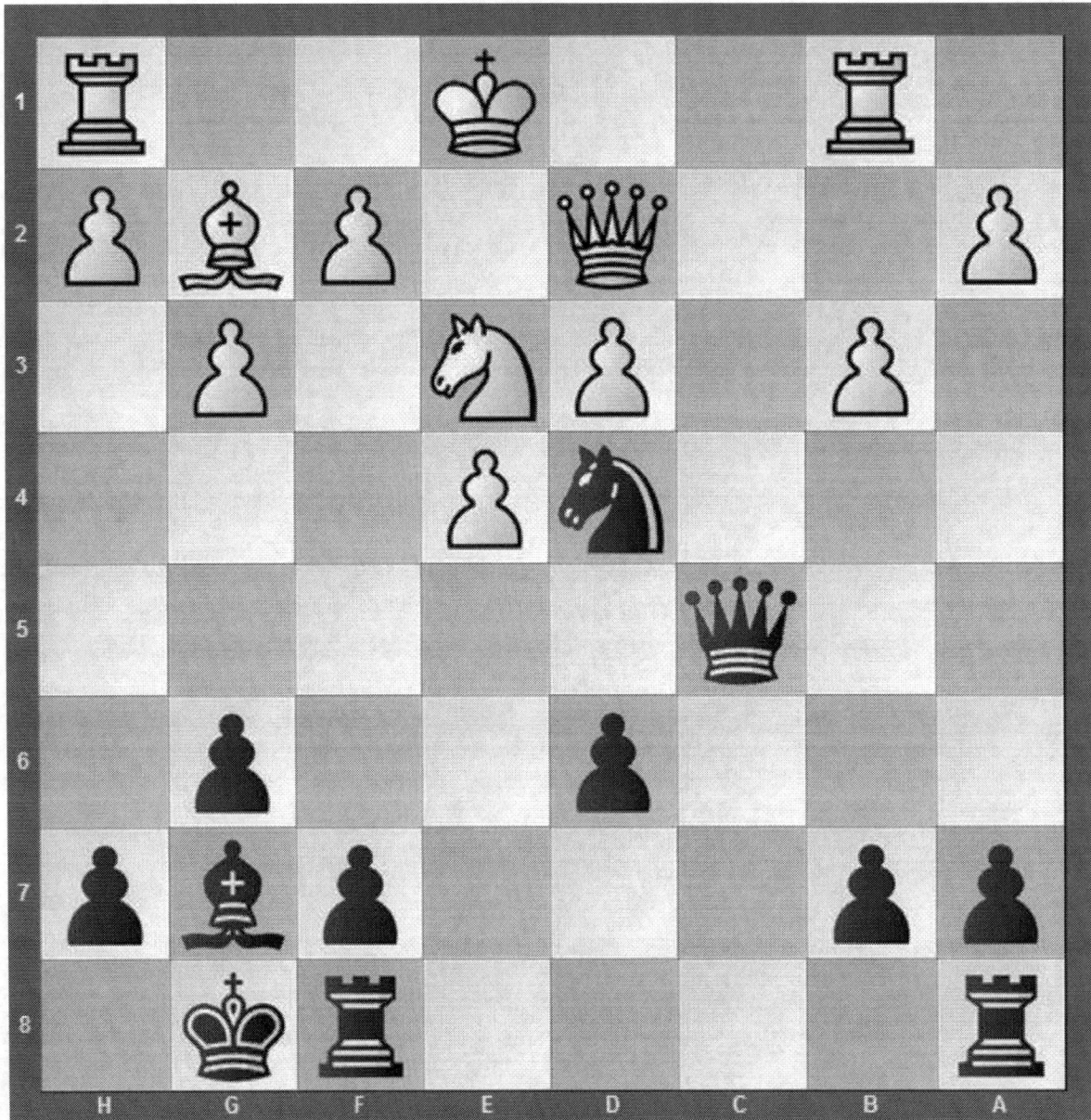

1		
2		

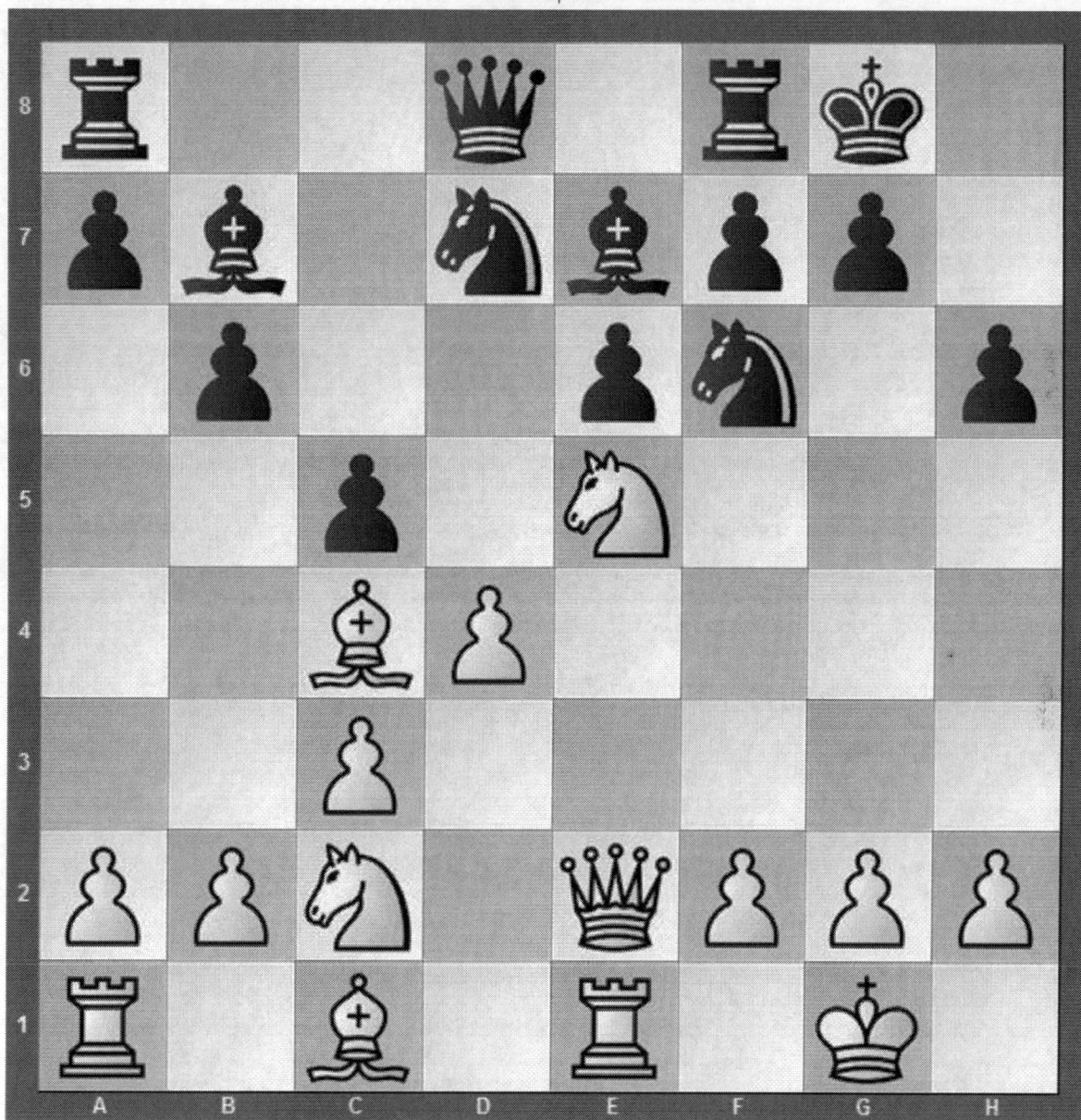

1		
2		

1		
2		

1		
2		

1		
2		

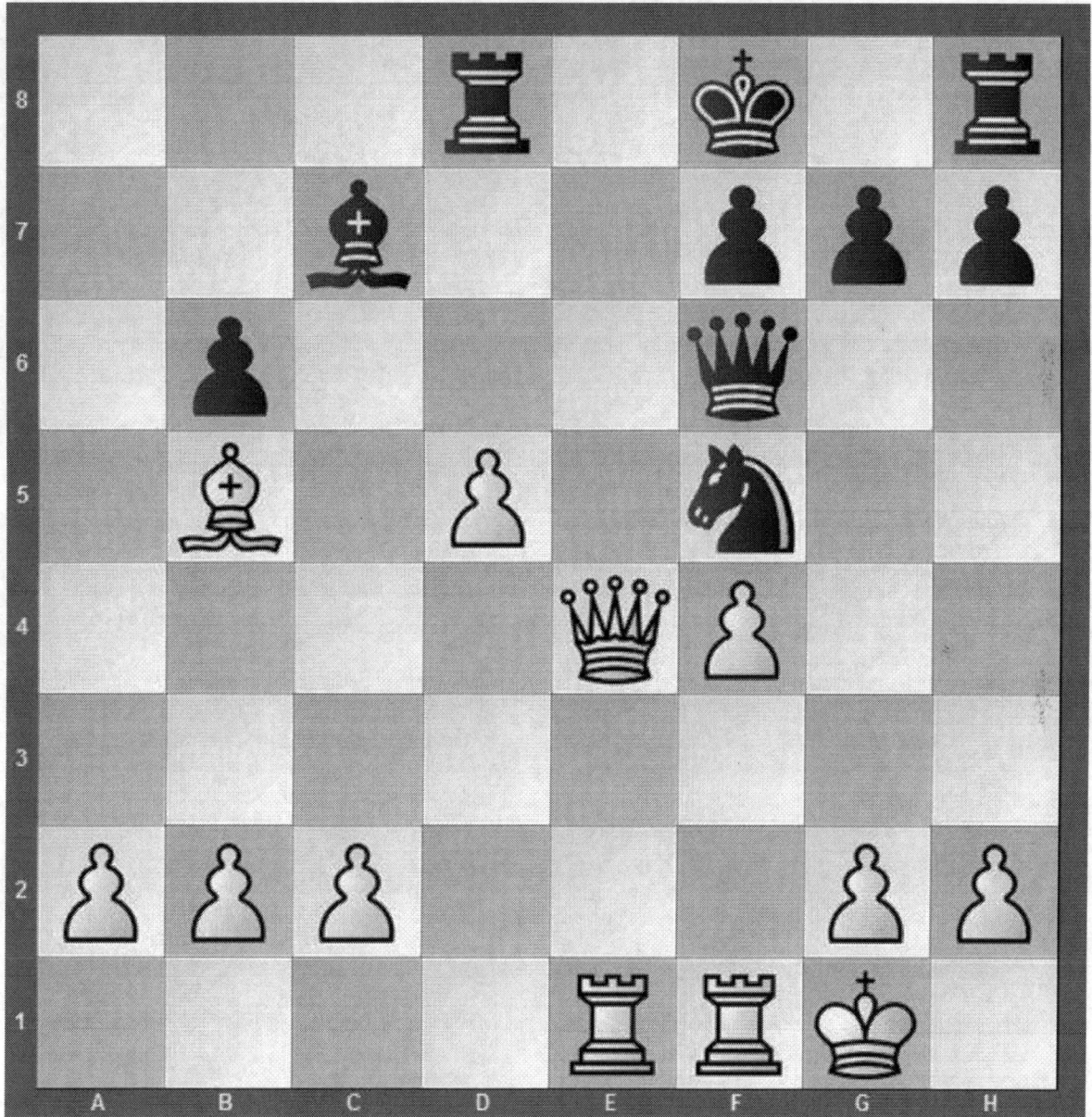

1		
2		

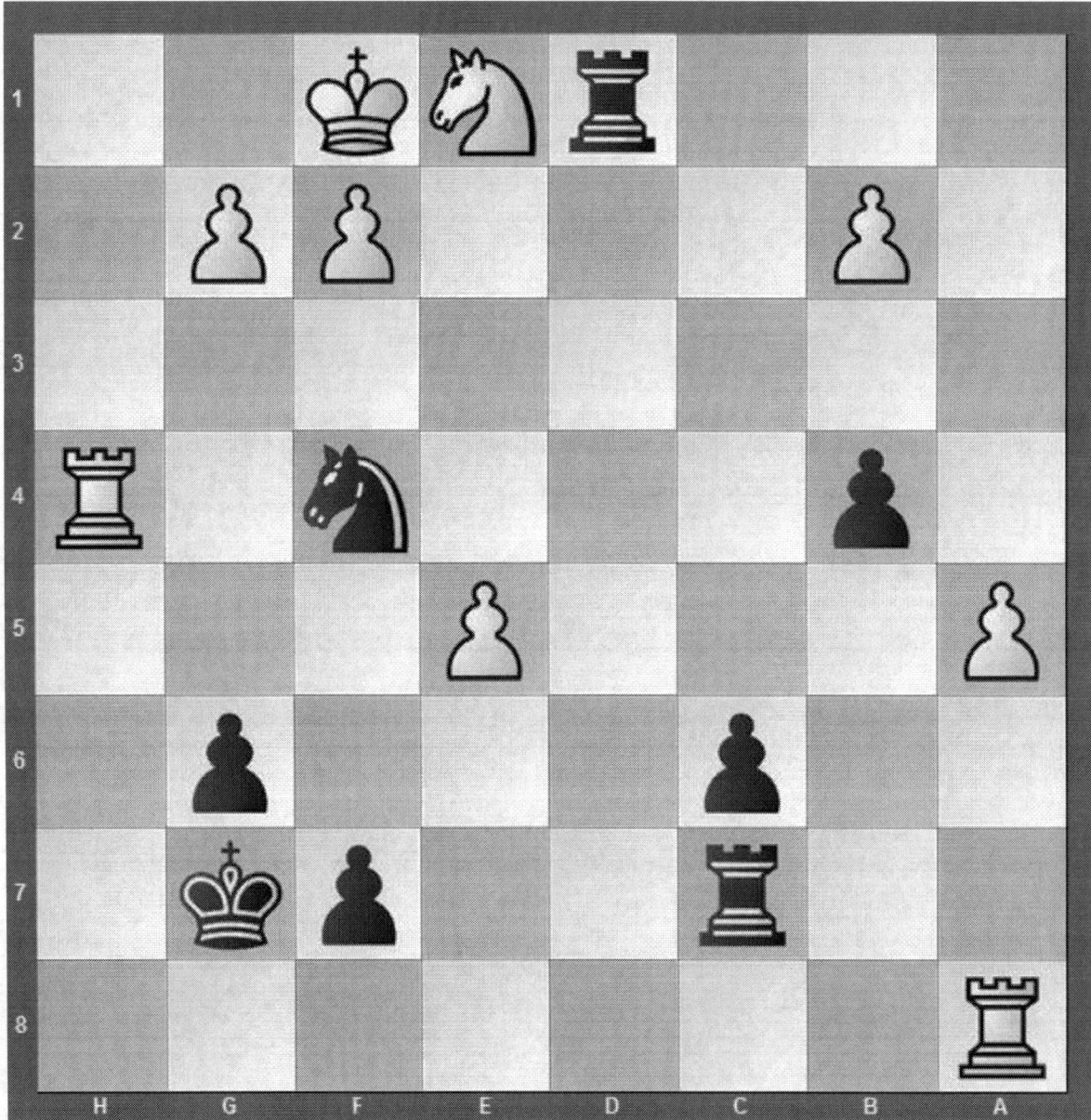

1		
2		

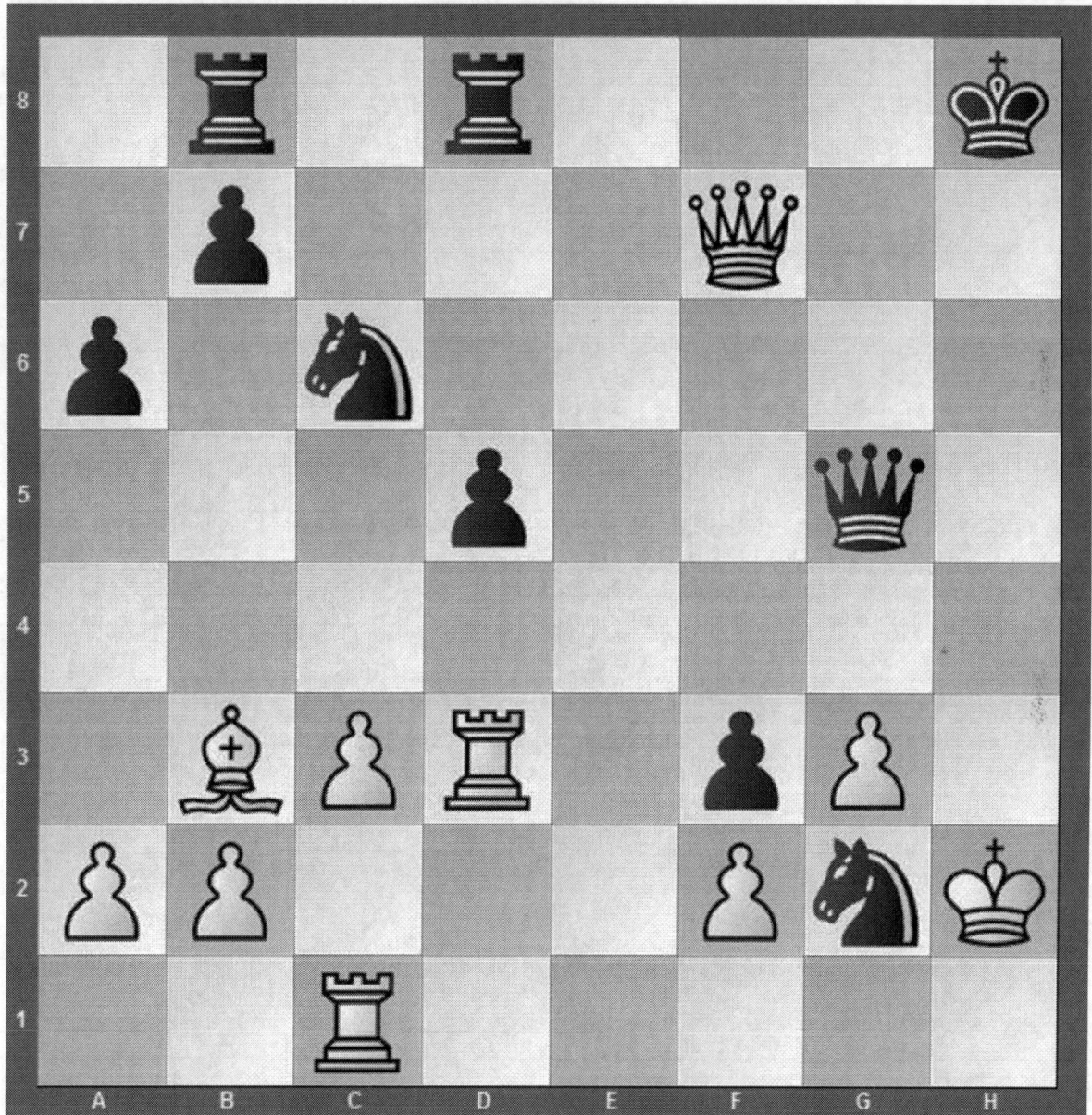

1		
2		

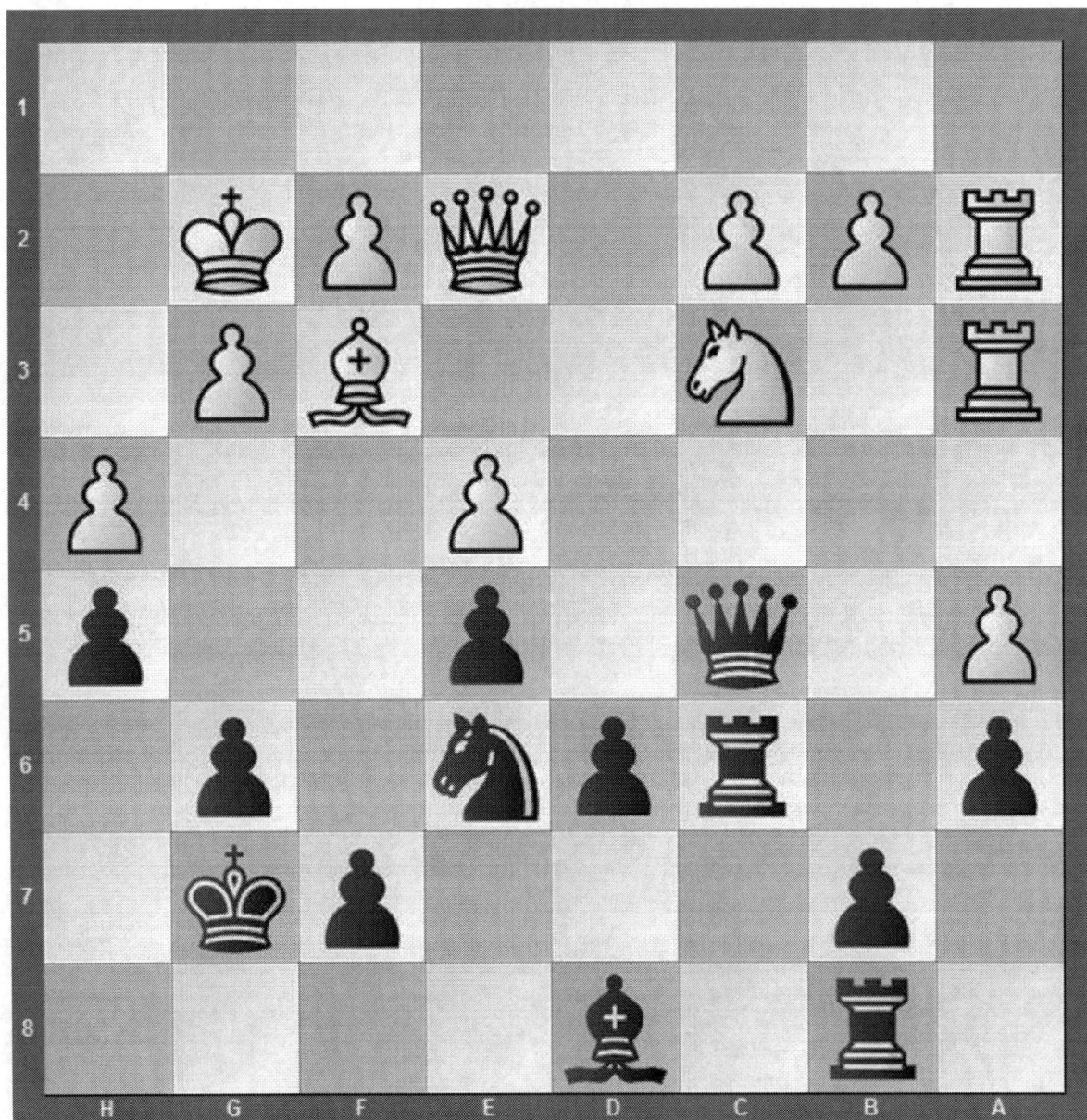

1		
2		

"Chess improves strategic thinking, attention span, patience, camaraderie and sportsmanship." – **Wynton Marsalis**

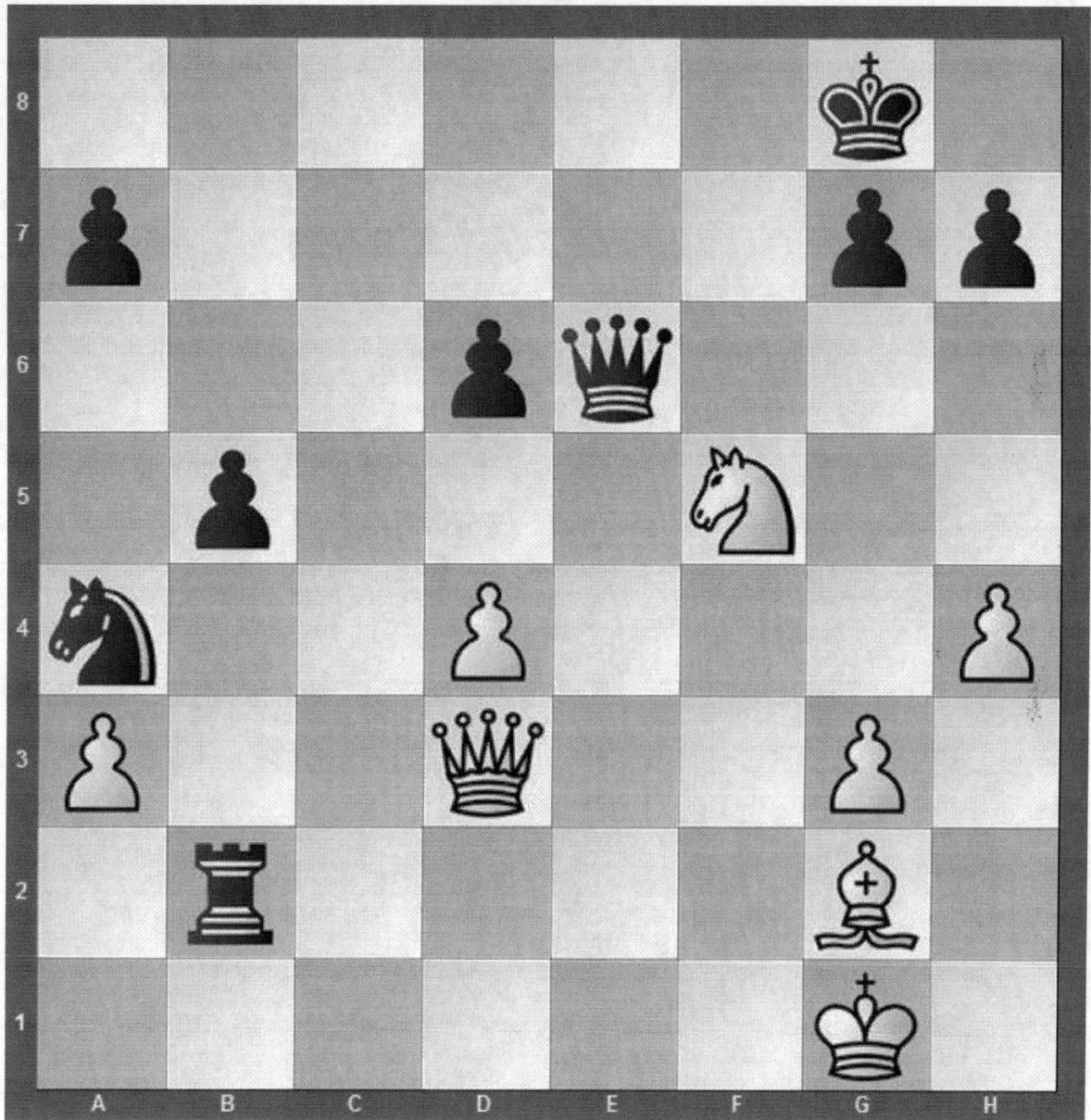

1		
2		

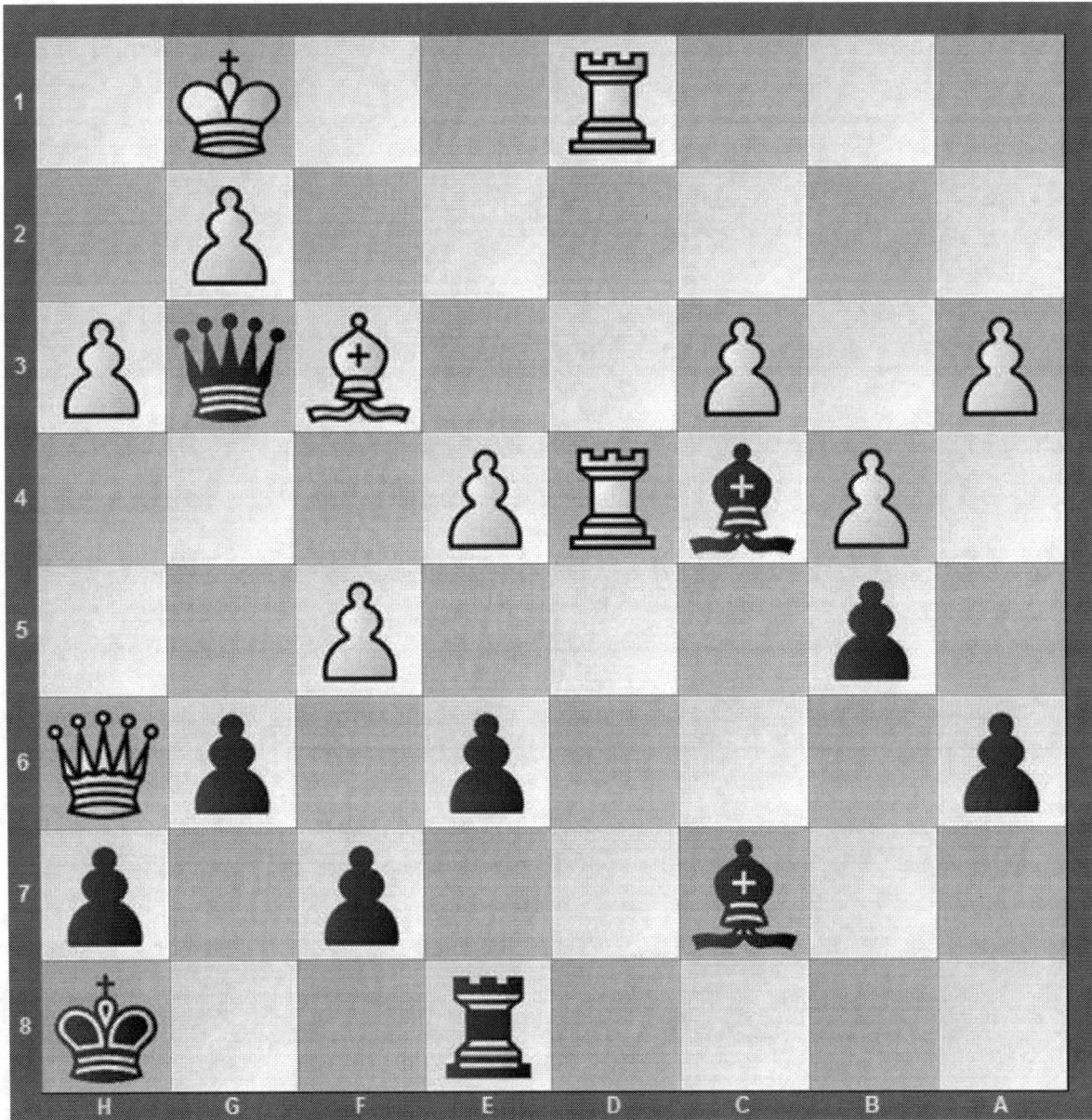

1		
2		

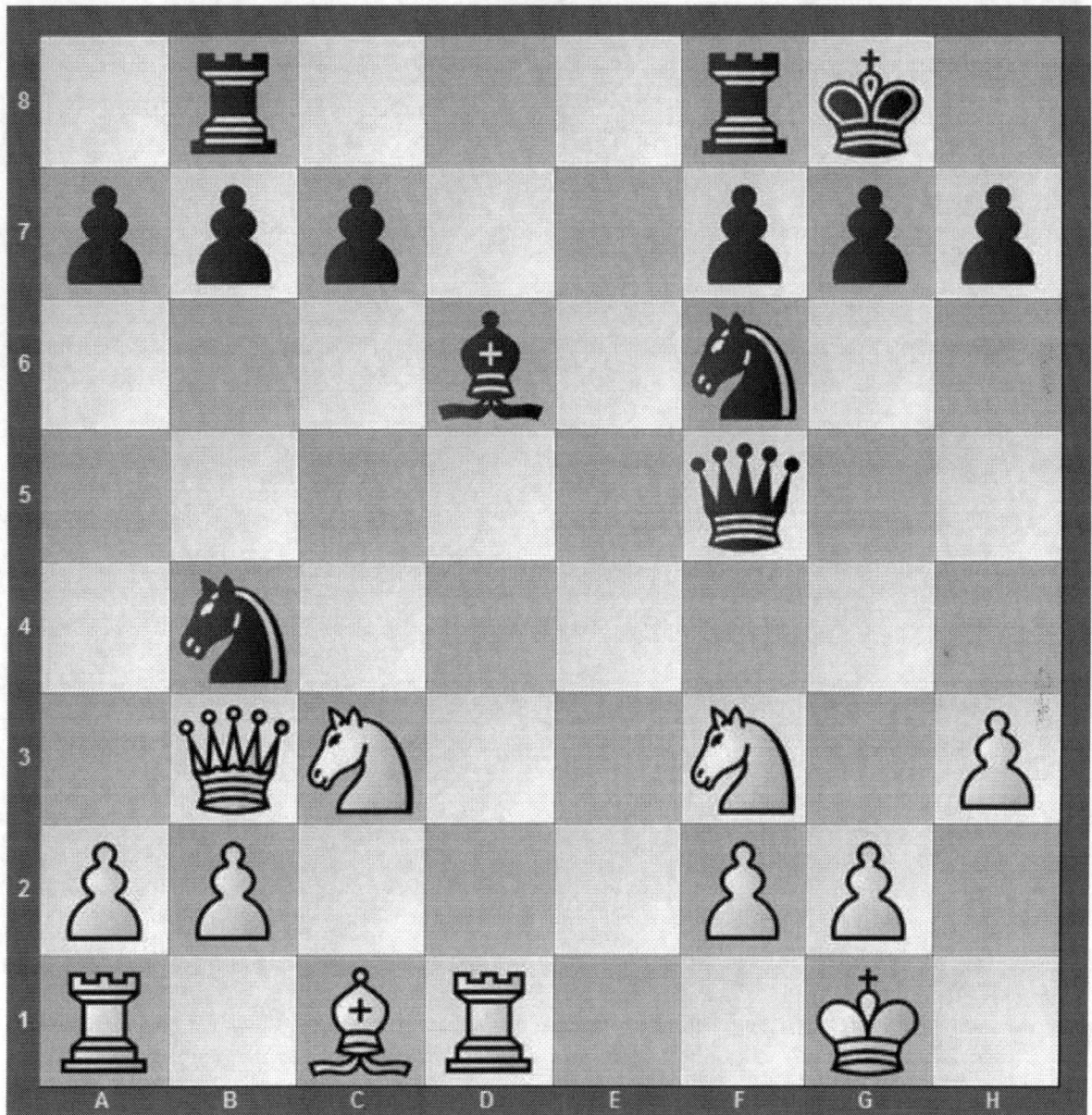

1		
2		

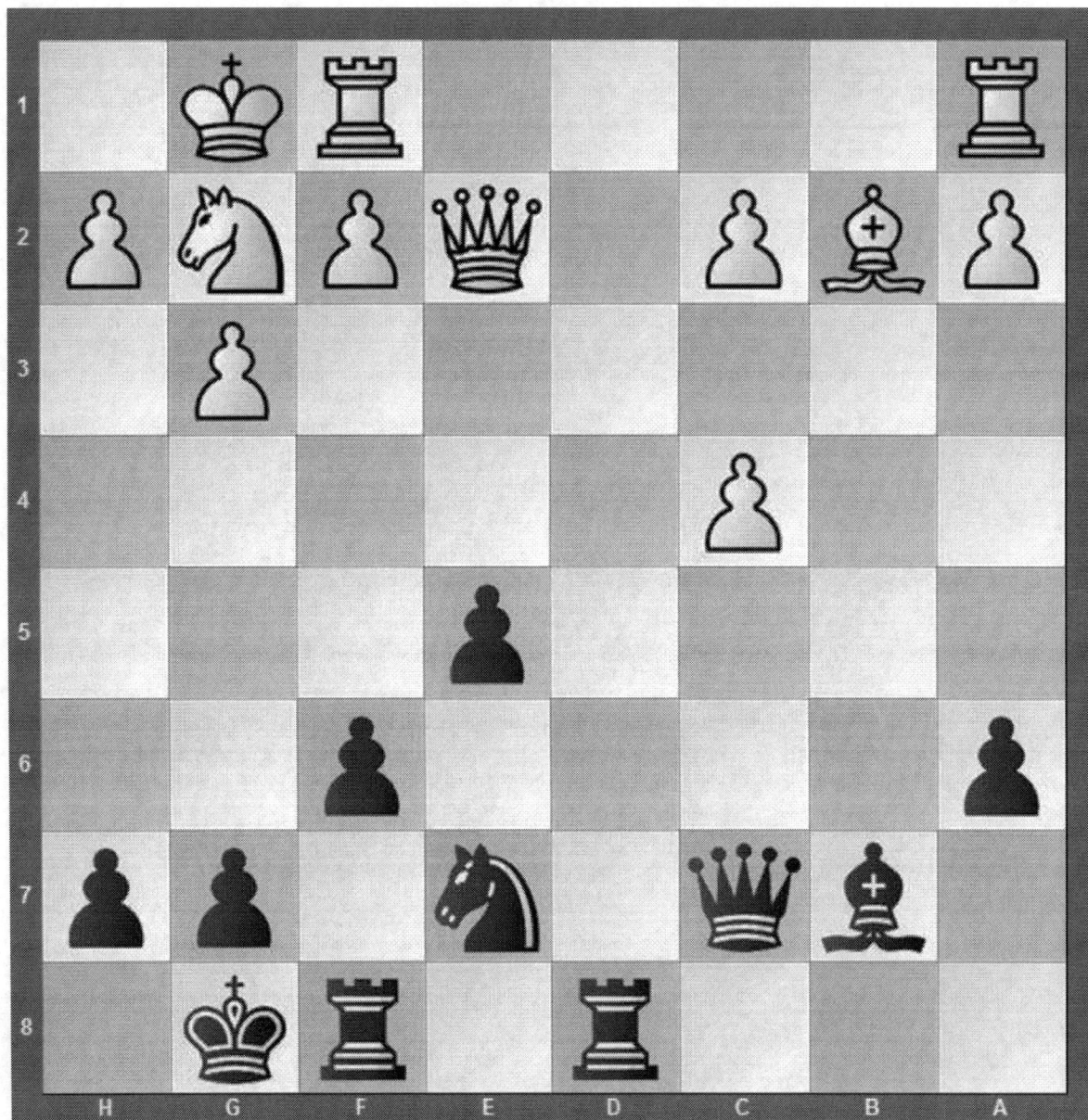

1		
2		

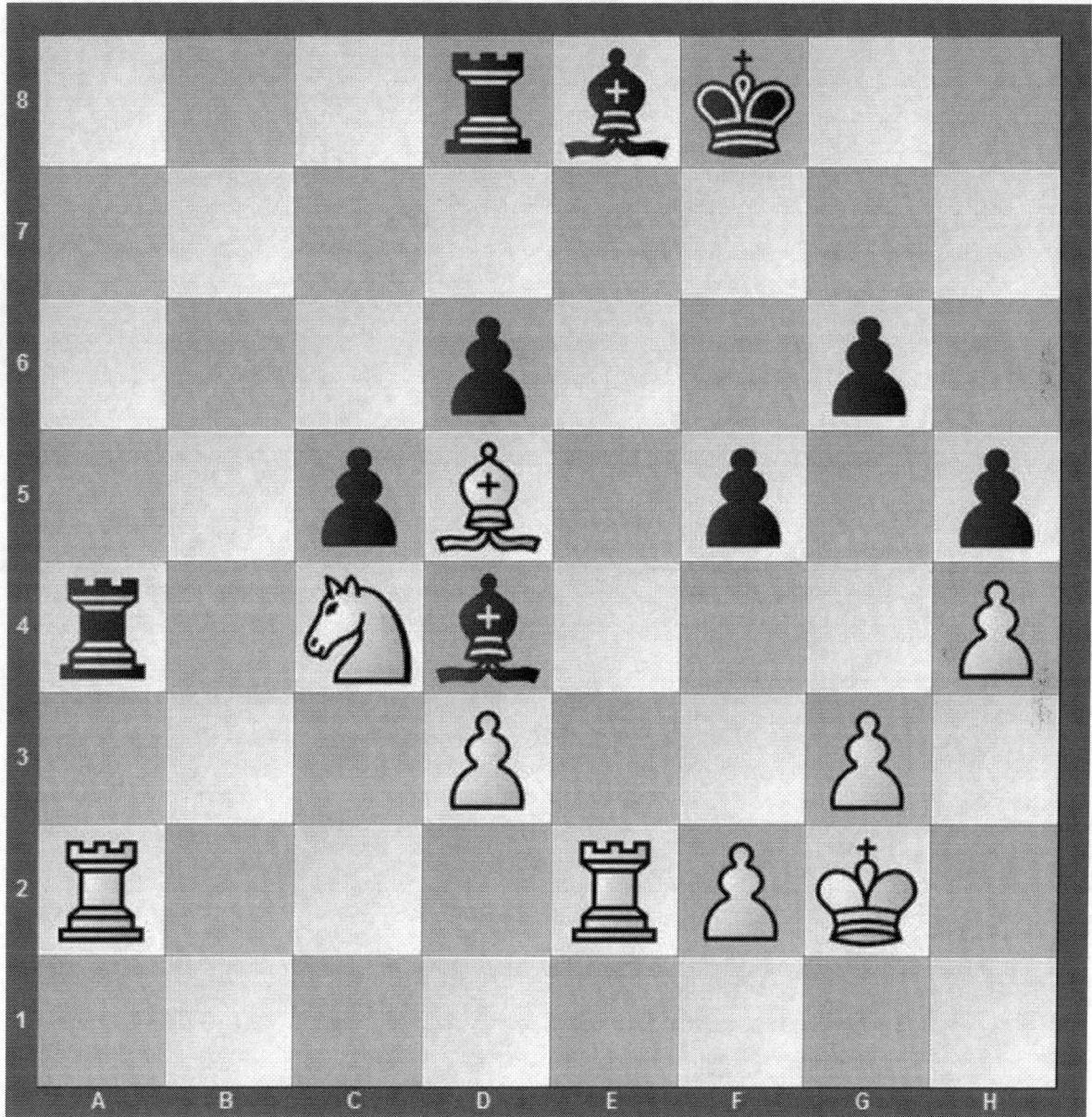

1		
2		

1		
2		

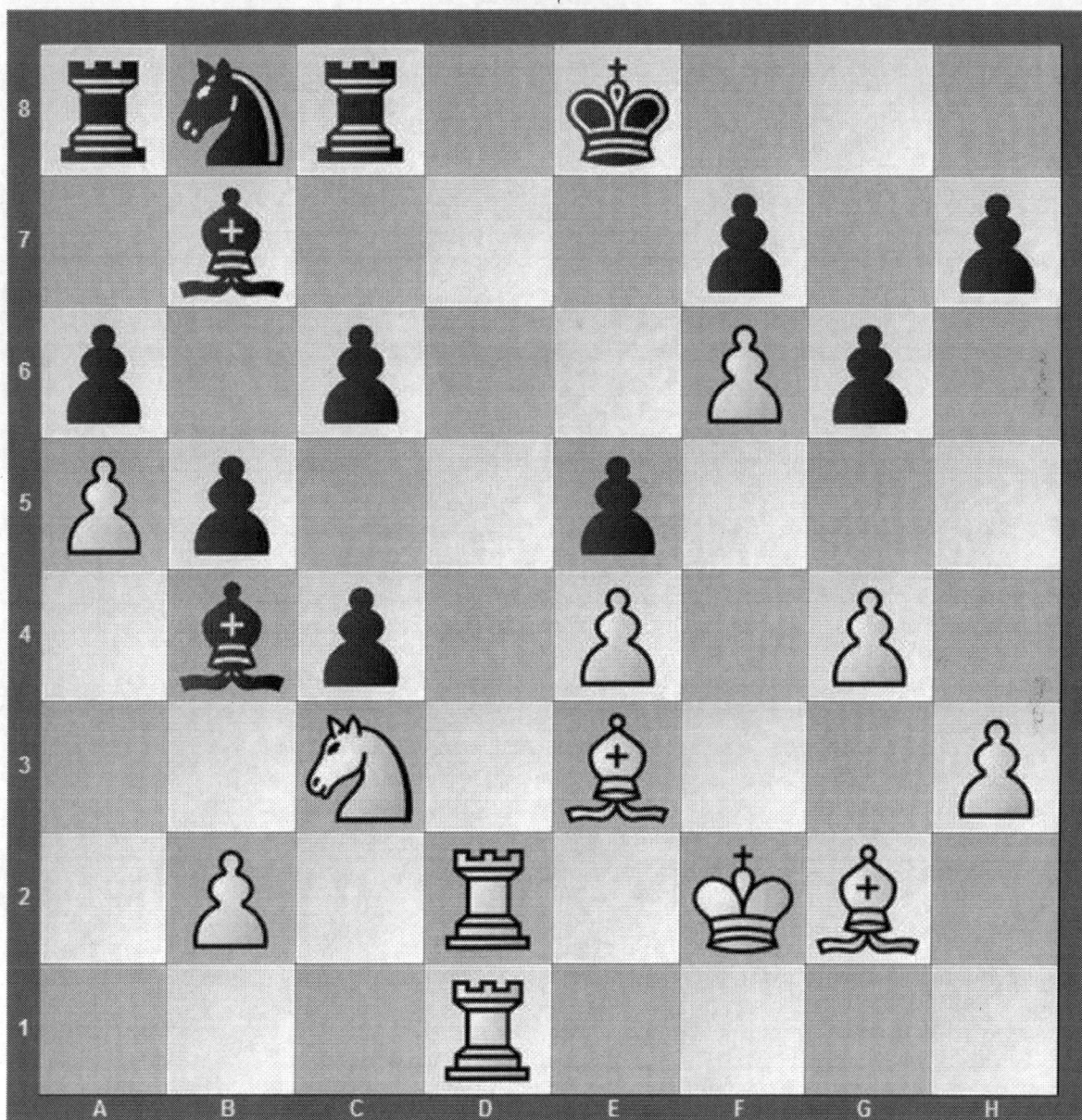

1		
2		

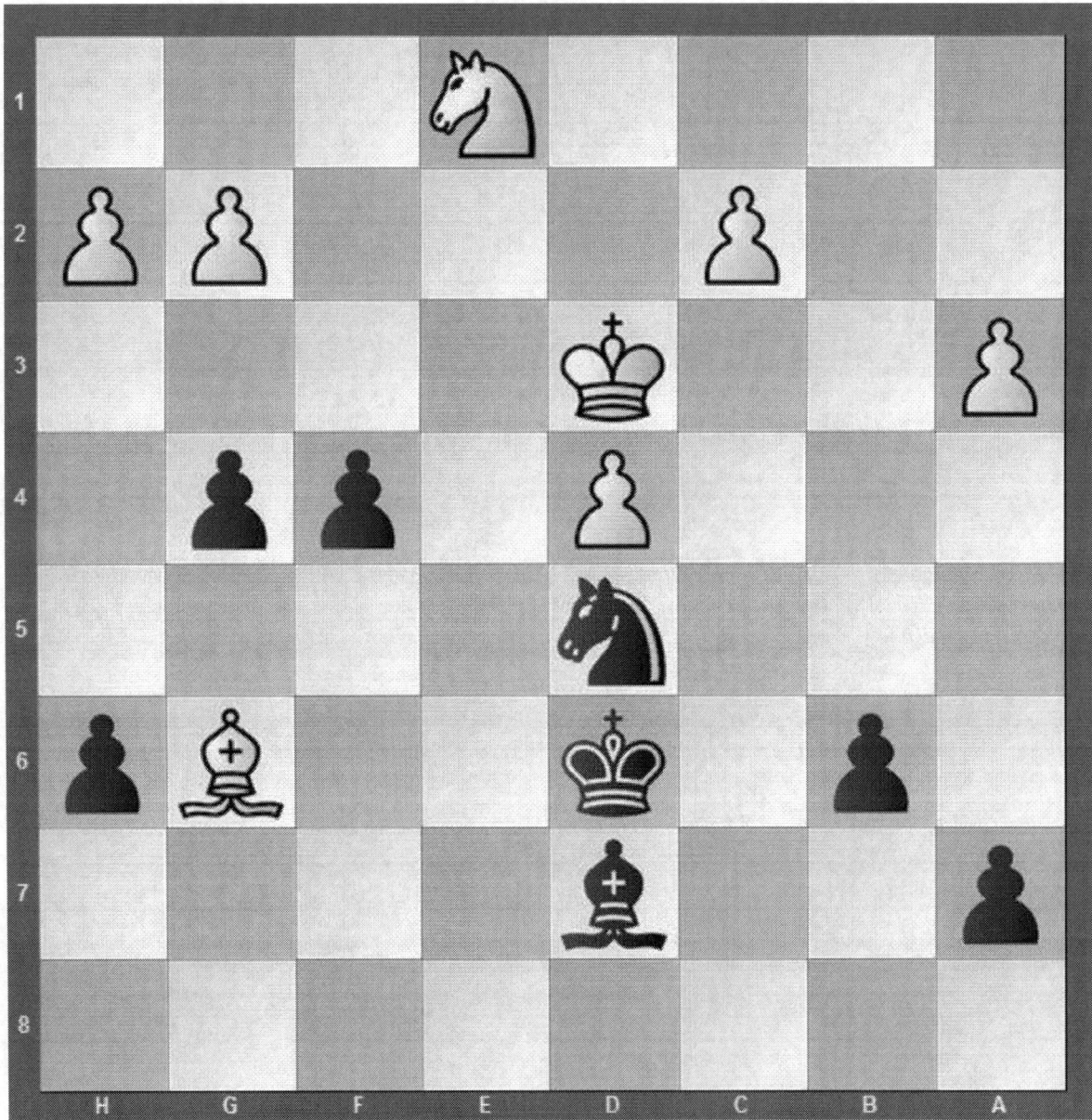

1		
2		

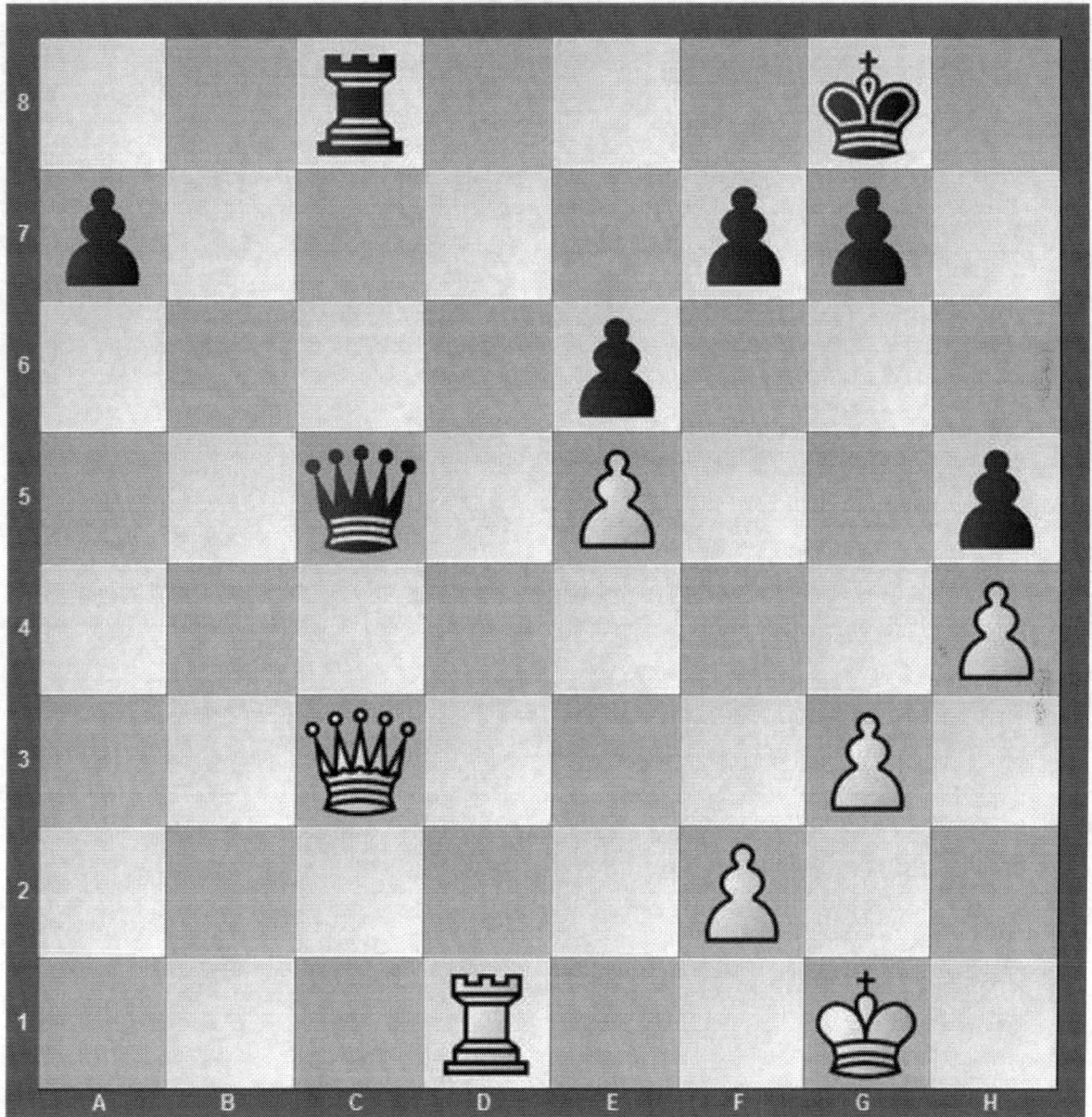

1		
2		

1		
2		

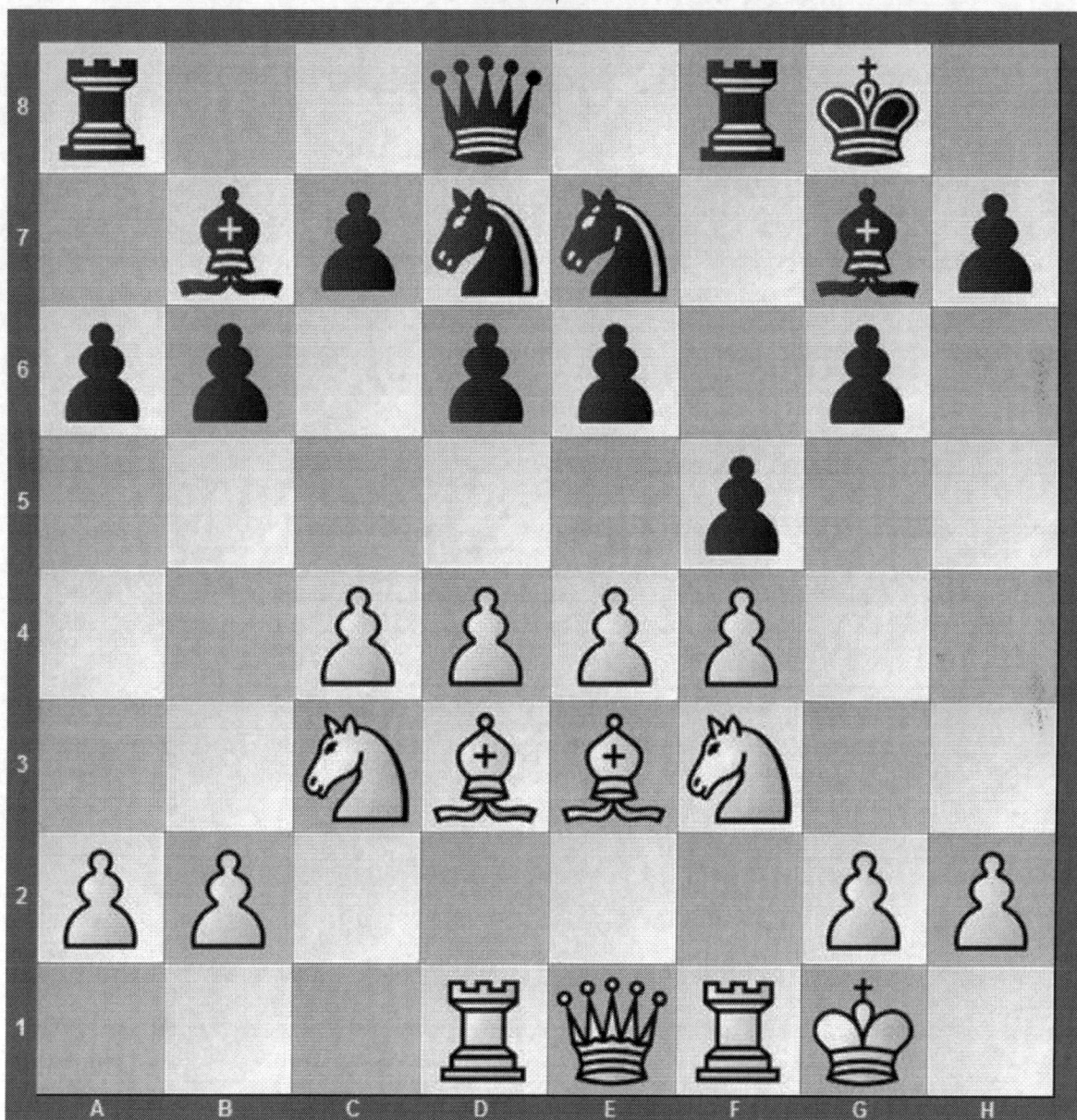

1		
2		

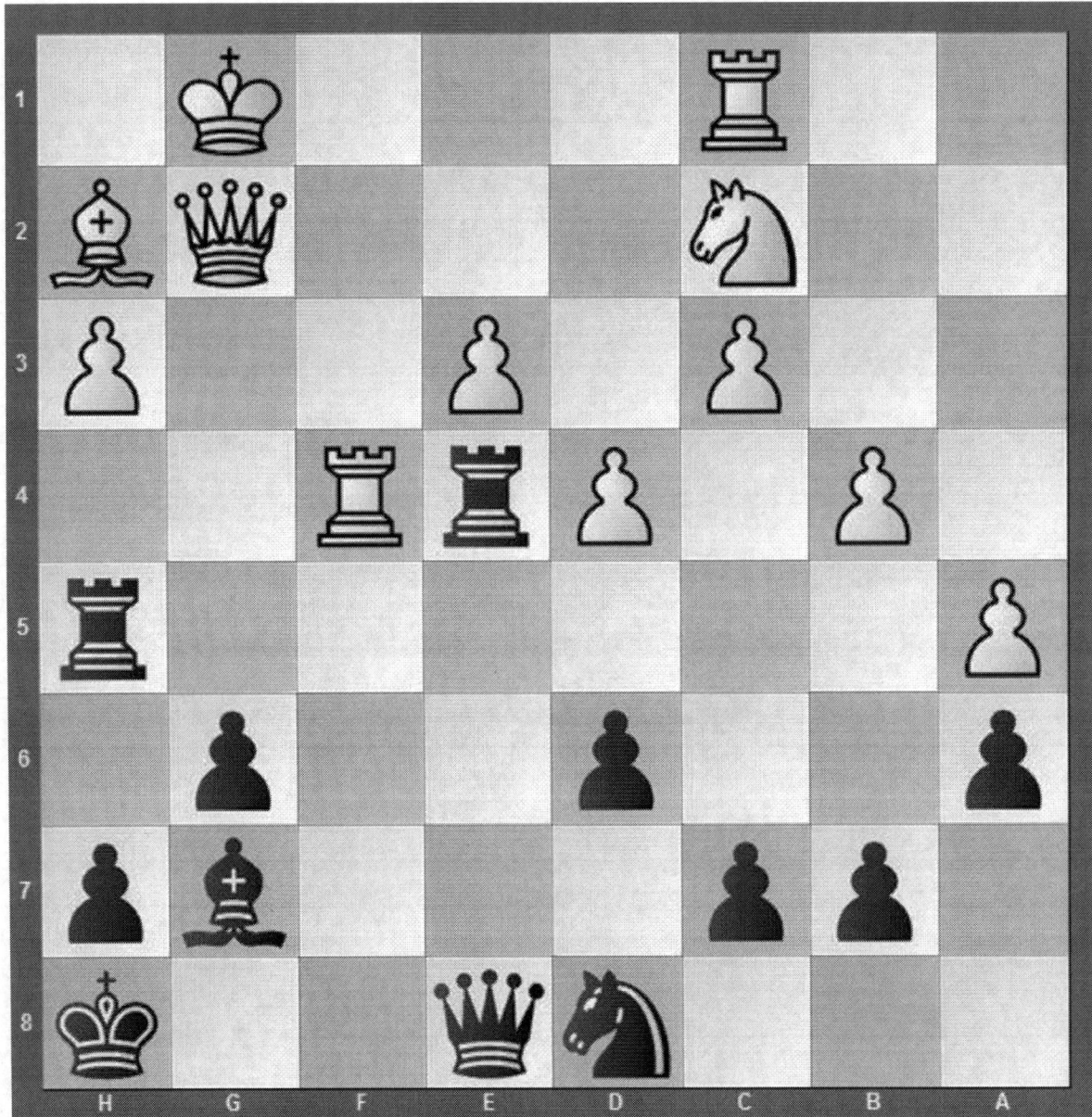

1		
2		

1		
2		

1		
2		

"Later, I began to succeed in decisive games. Perhaps because I realized a very simple truth: not only was I worried, but also my opponent." **– Mikhail Tal**

1		
2		

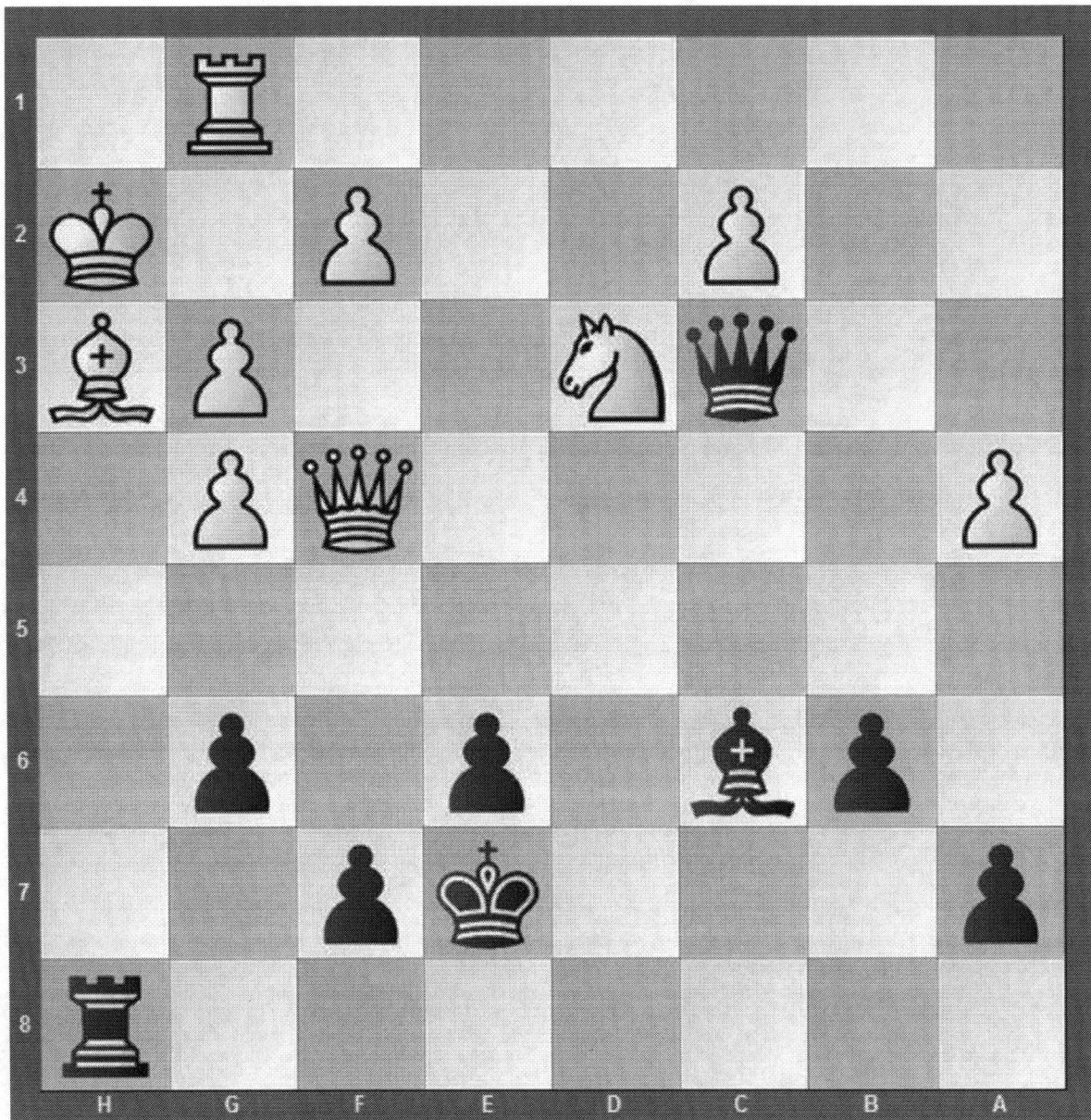

1		
2		

1		
2		

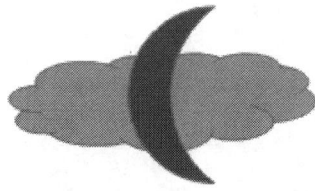

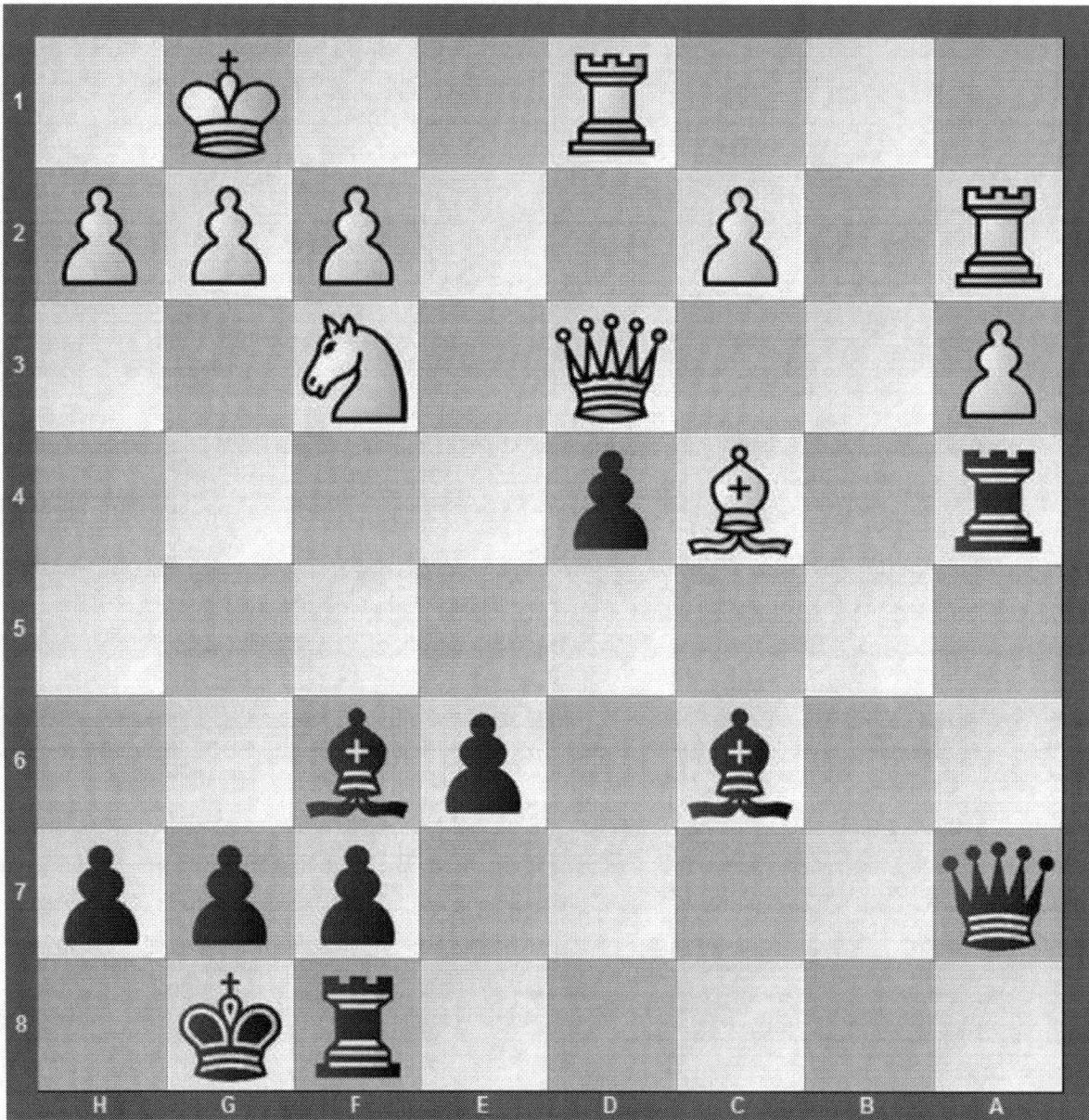

1		
2		

1		
2		

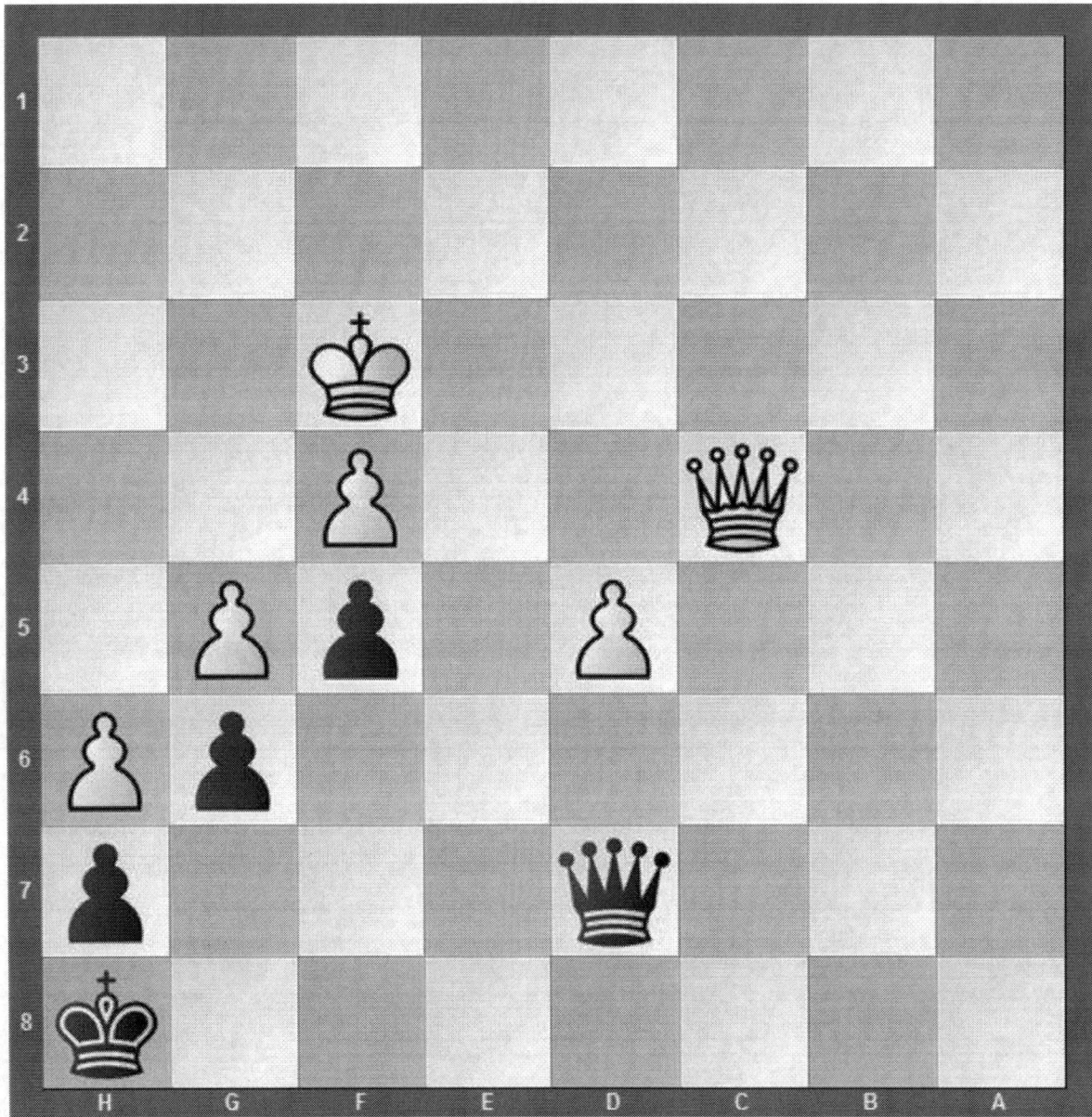

1		
2		

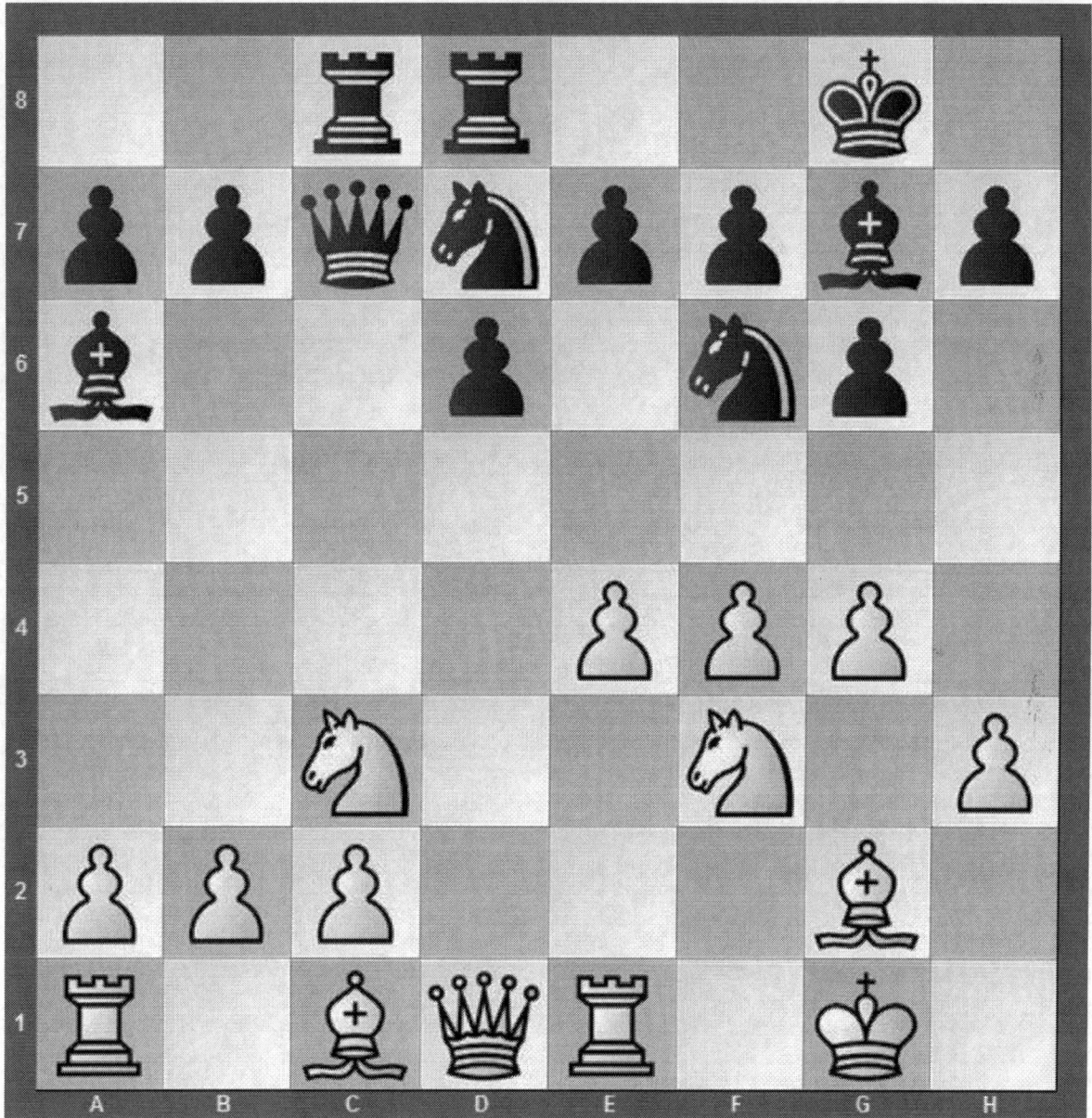

1		
2		

1		
2		

1		
2		

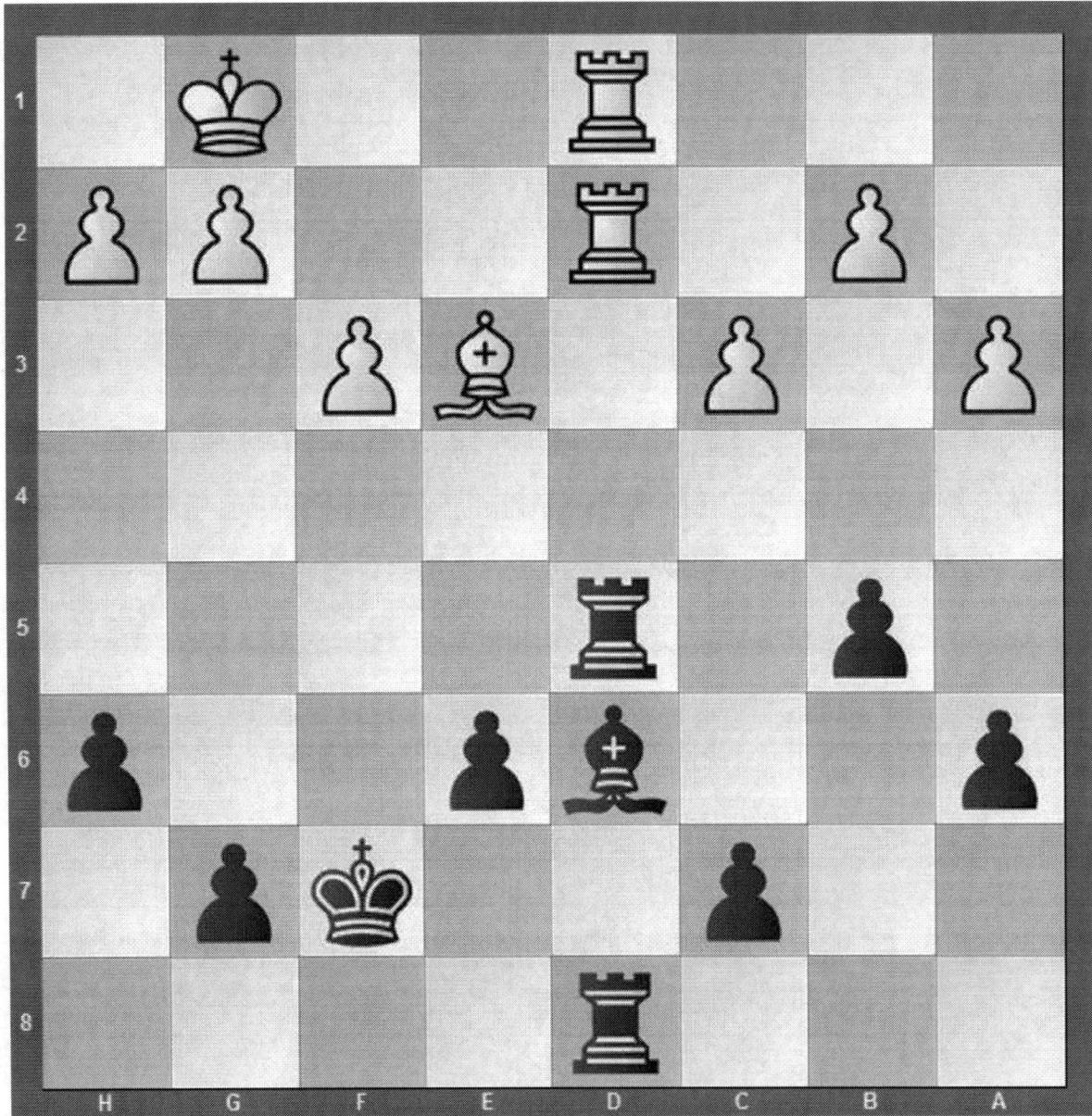

1		
2		

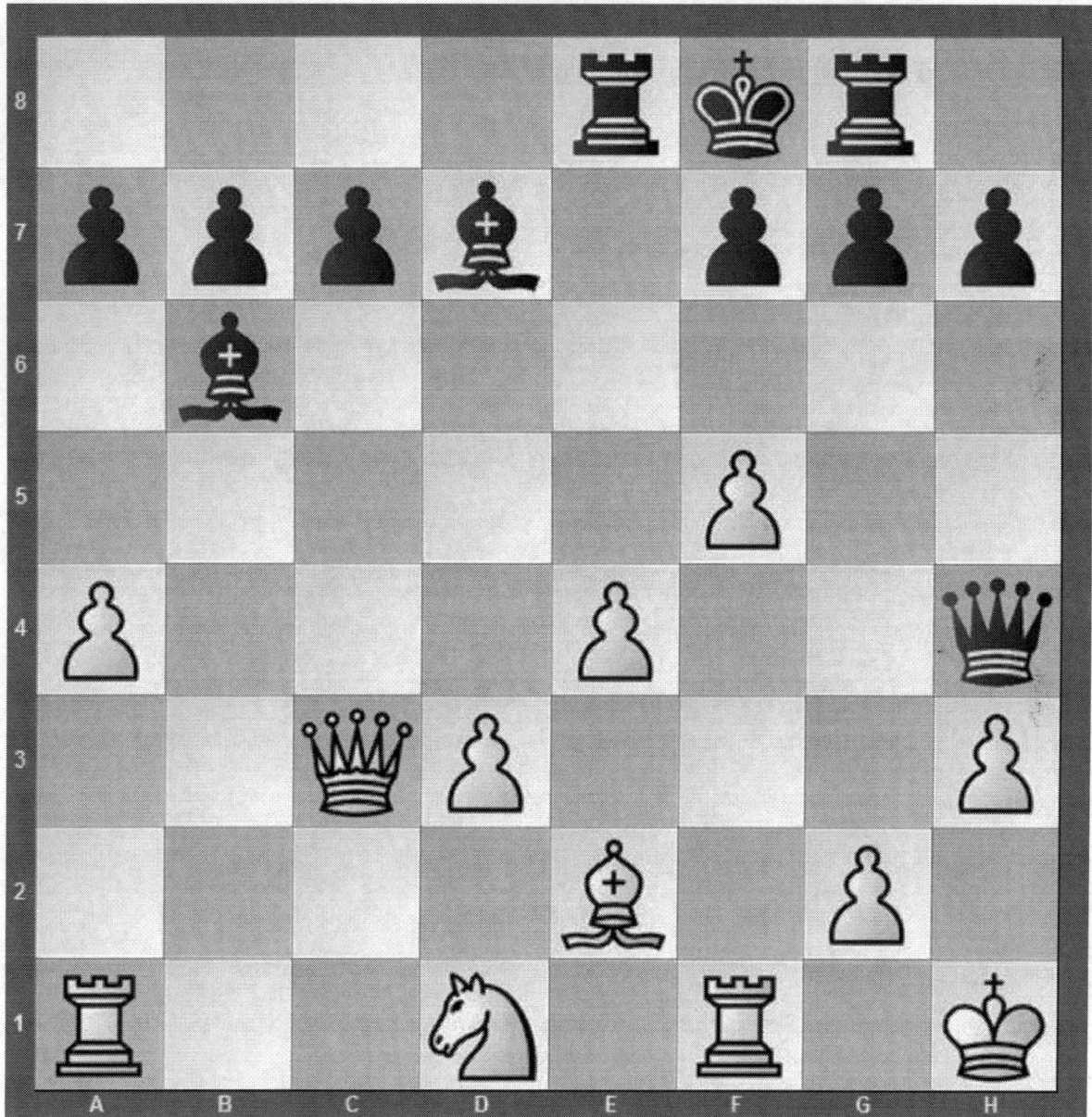

1		
2		

1		
2		

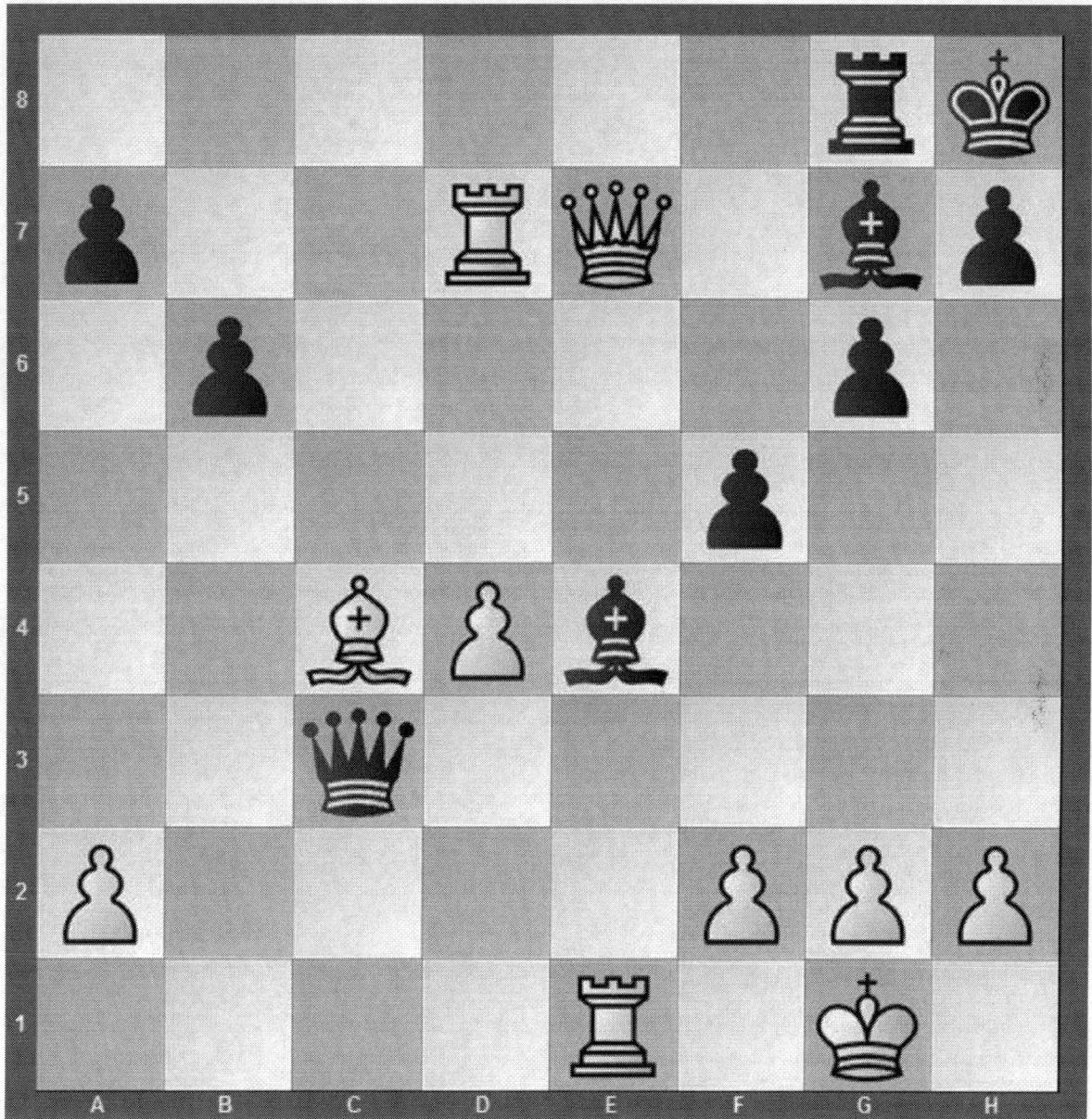

1		
2		

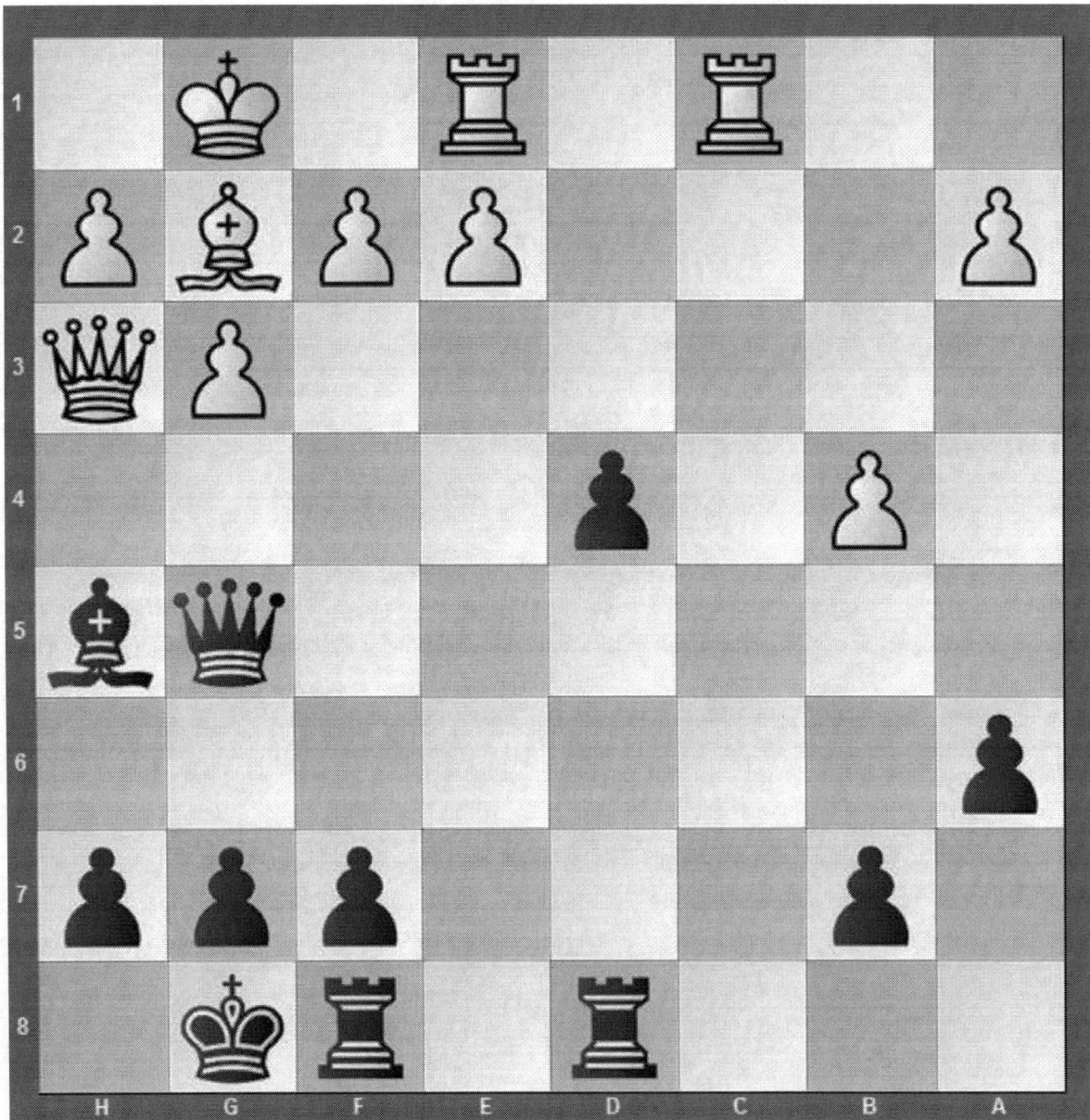

1		
2		

"I would never suggest to anyone that they drop school for chess. First of all even if you can make it in chess, your social skills need to be developed there." – **Viswanathan Anand**

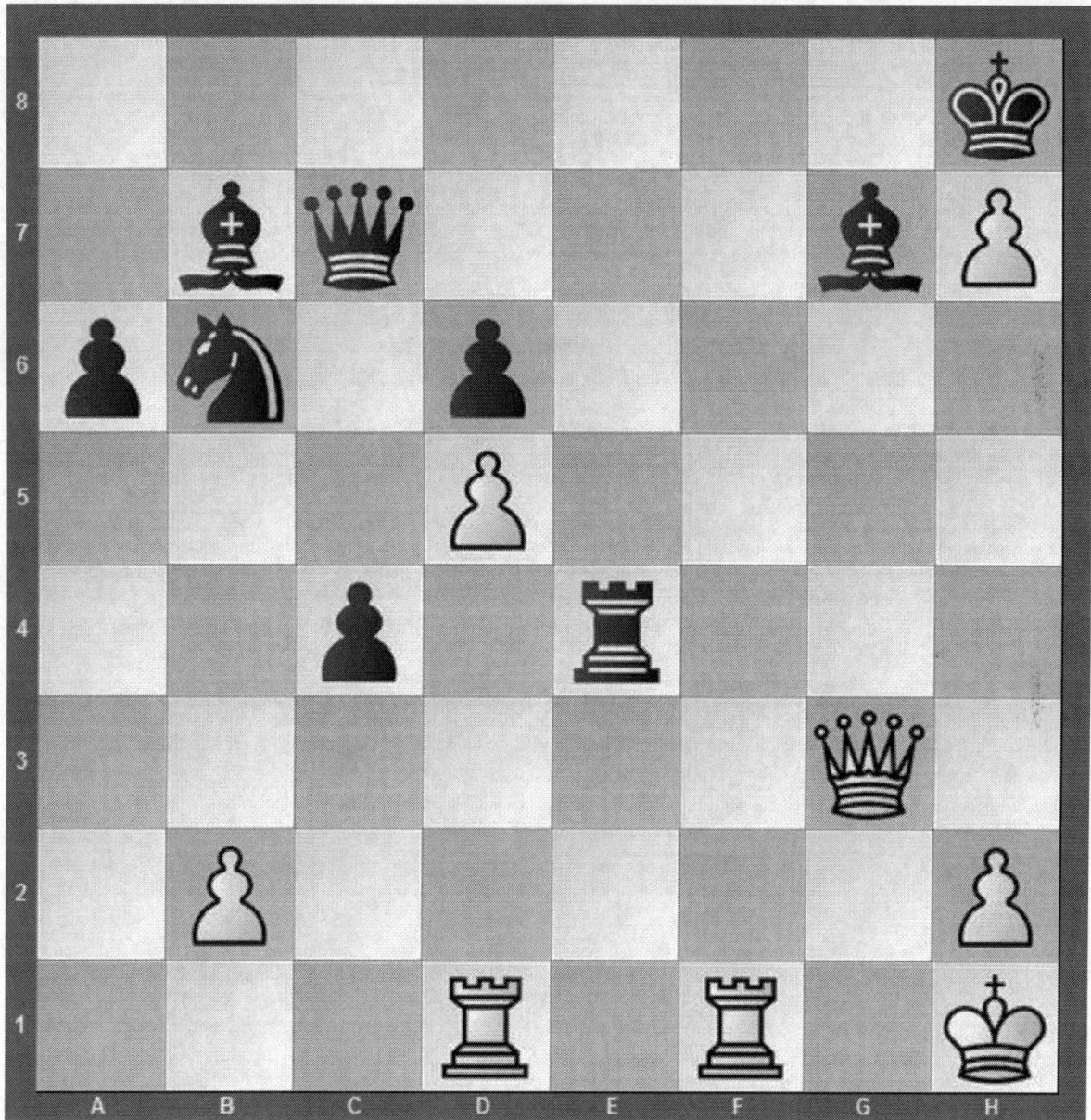

1		
2		

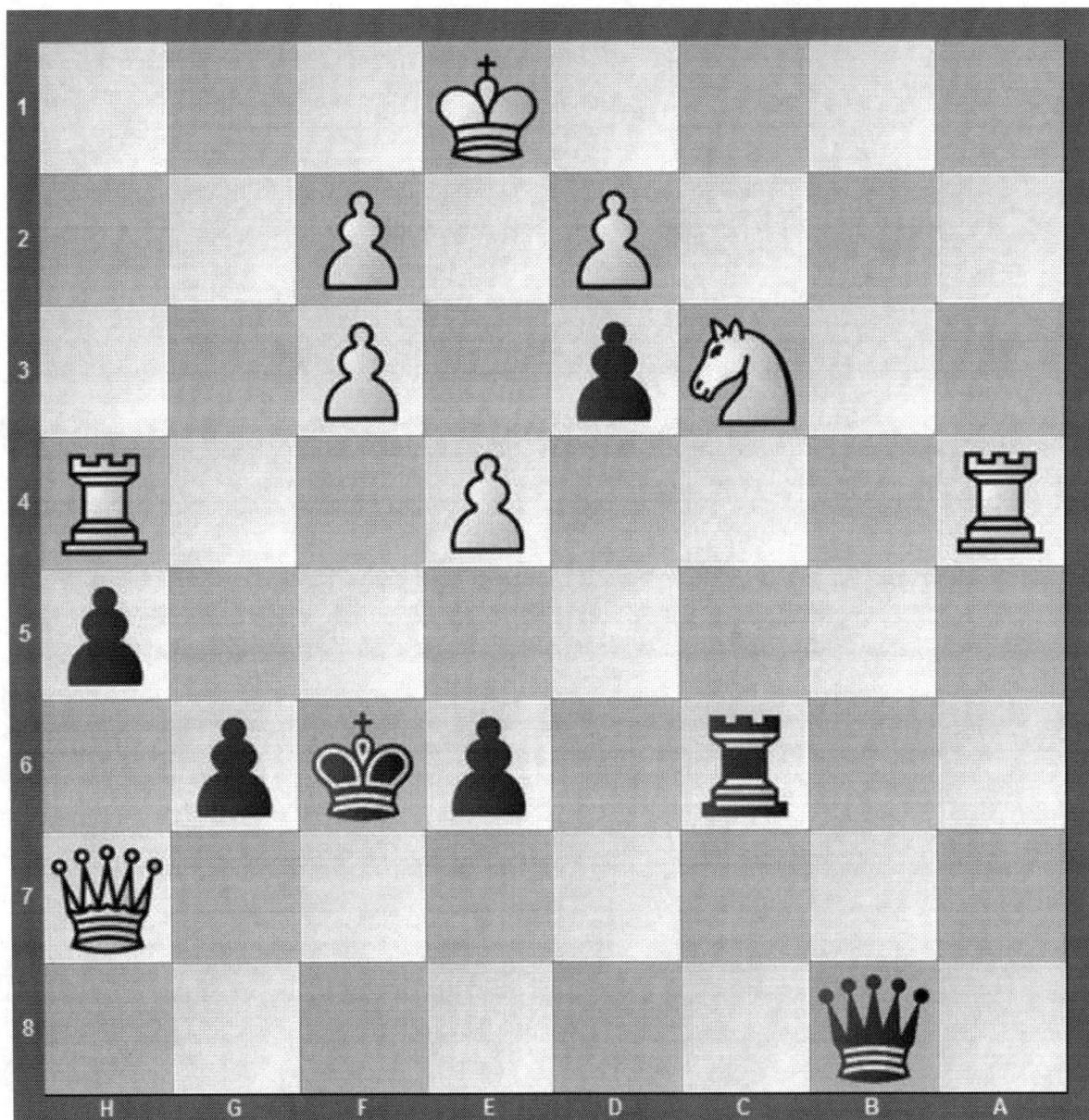

1		
2		

1		
2		

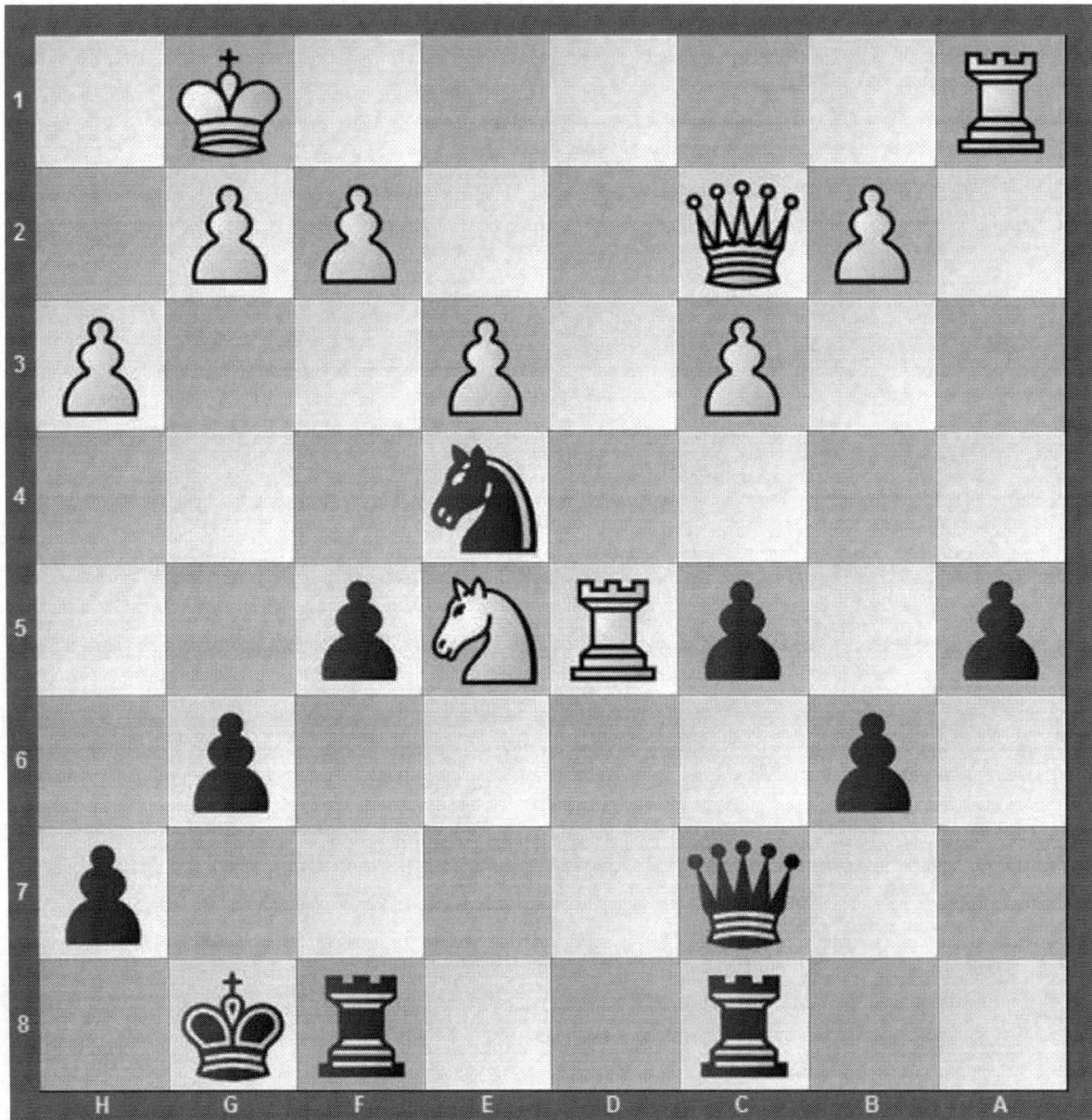

1		
2		

1		
2		

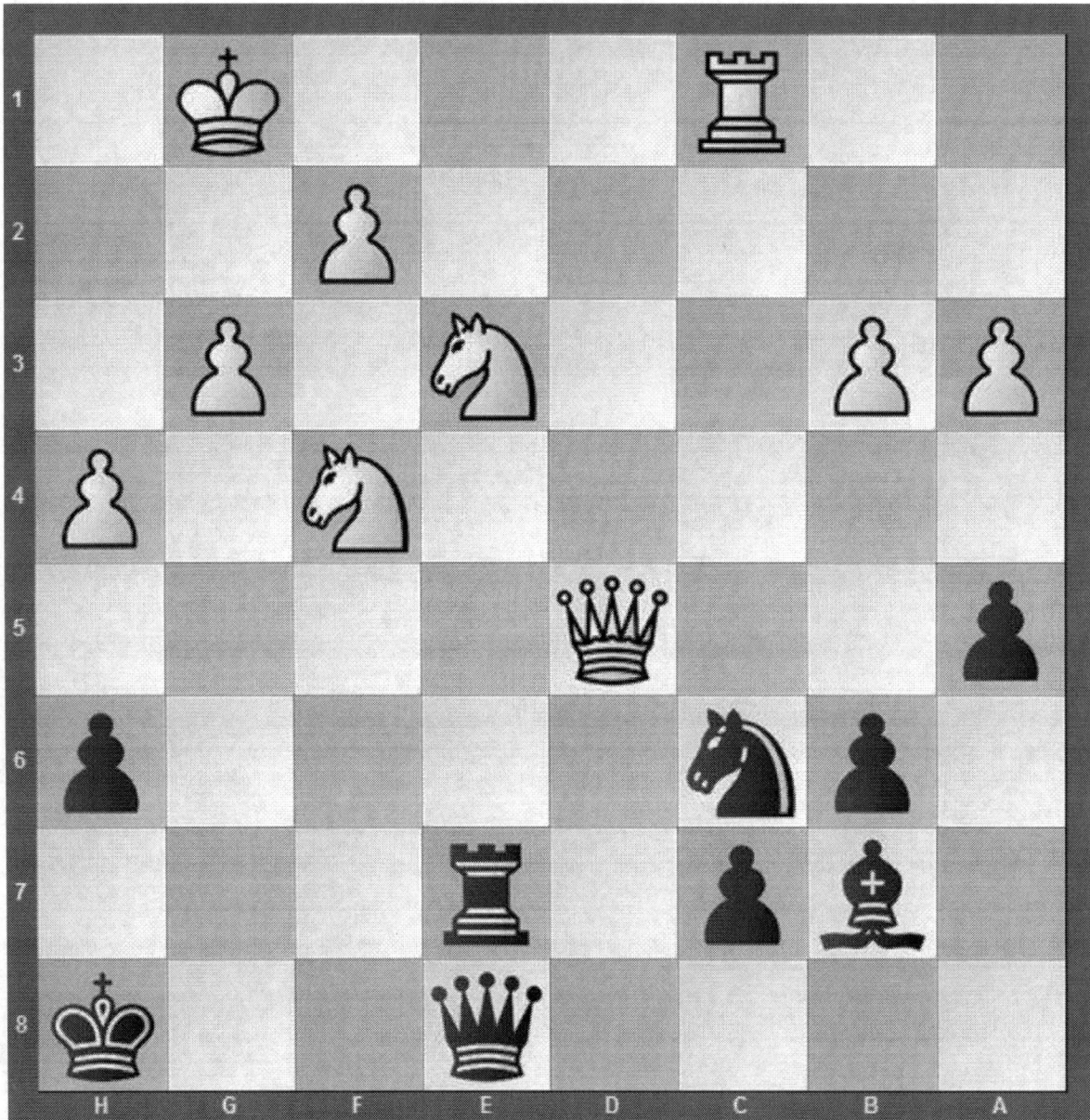

1		
2		

1		
2		

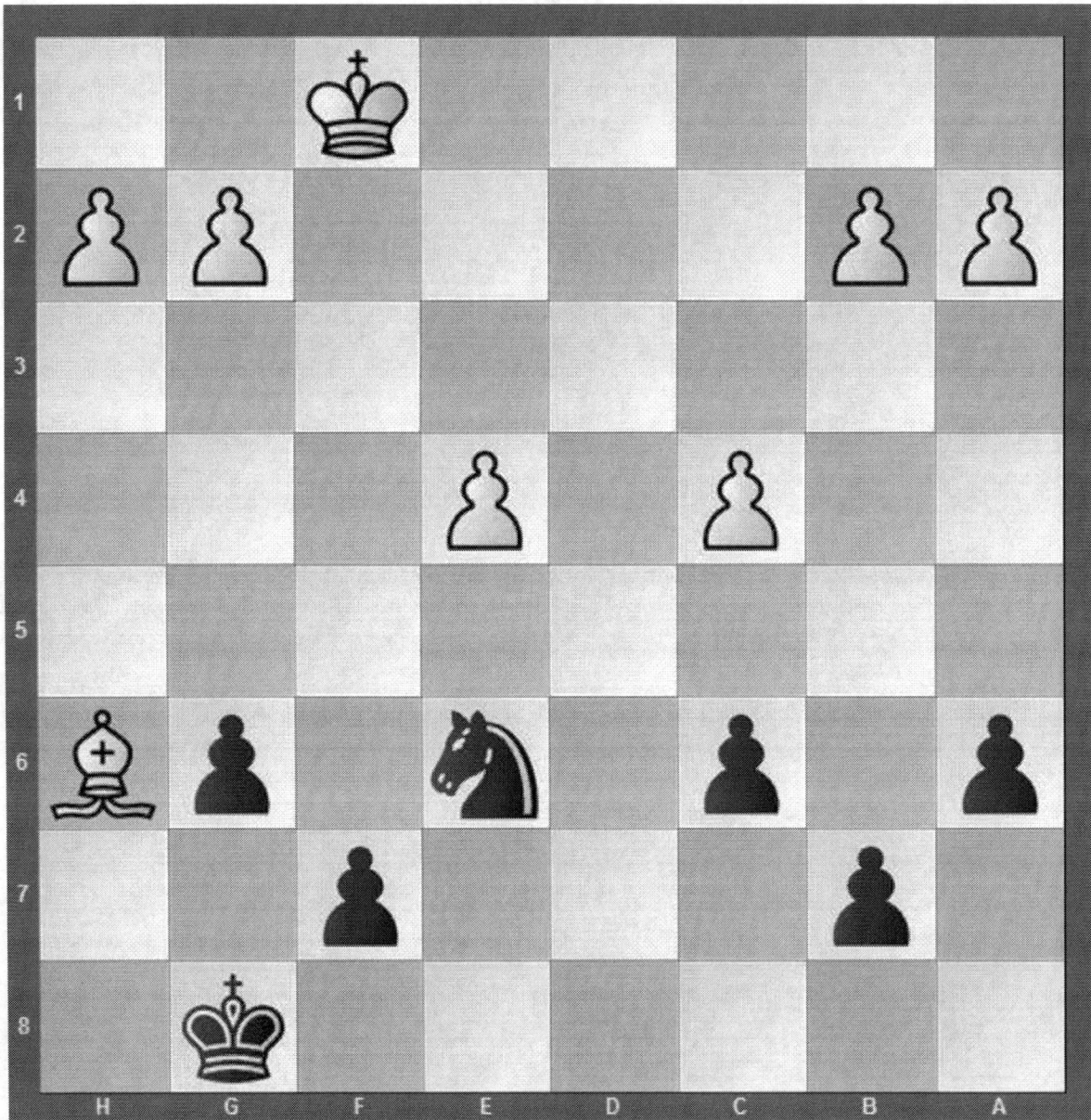

1		
2		

1		
2		

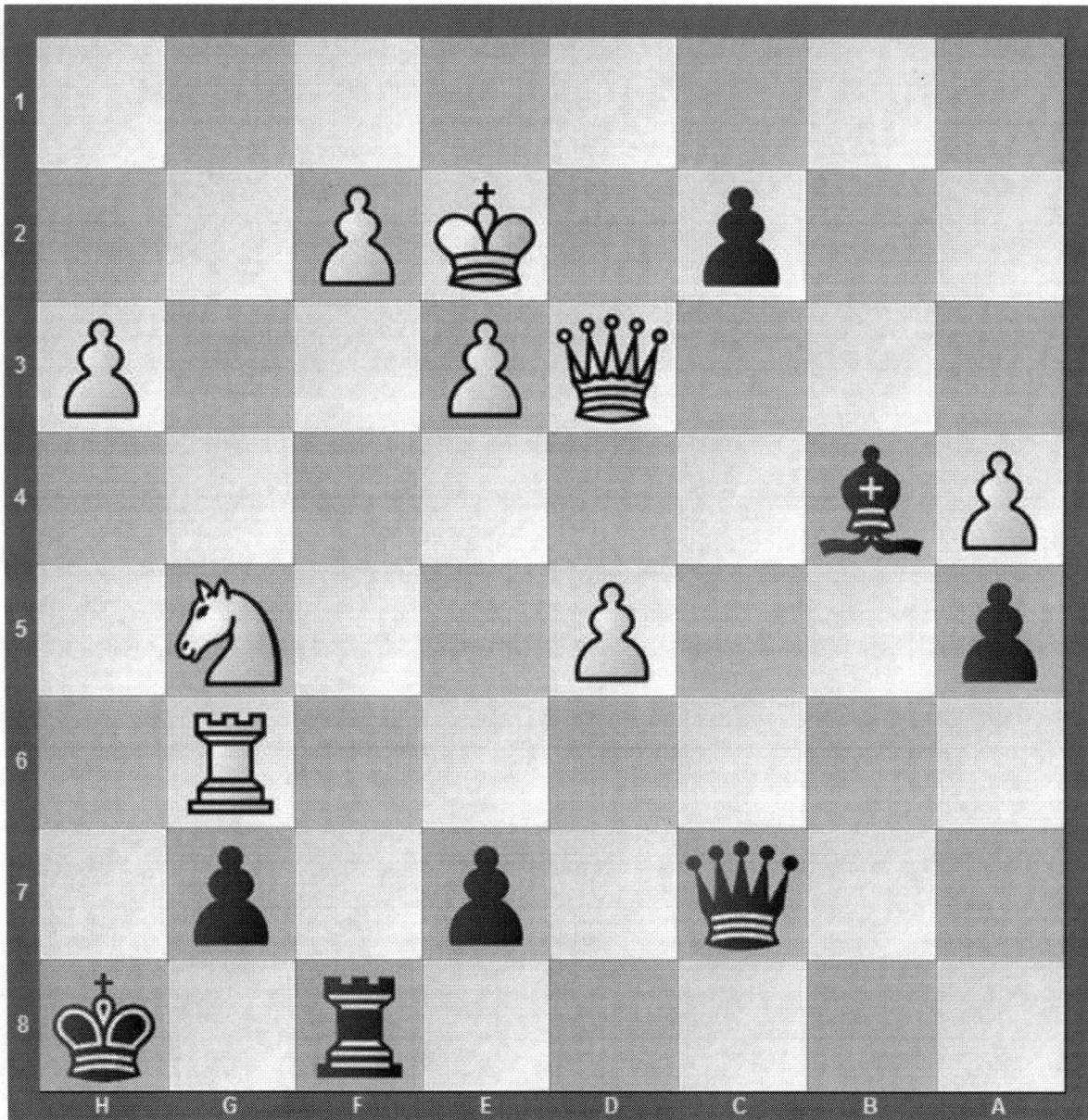

1		
2		

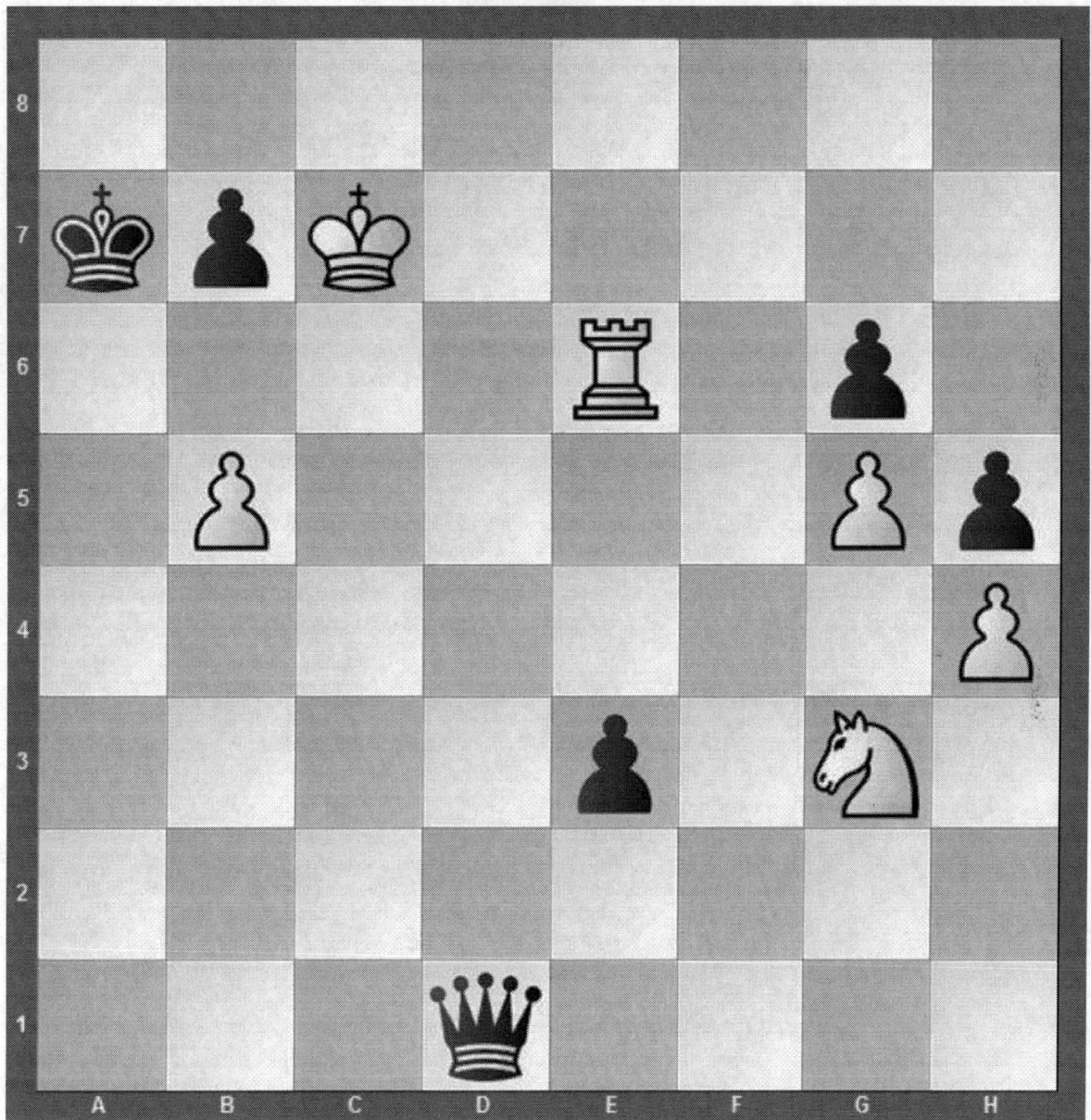

1		
2		

1		
2		

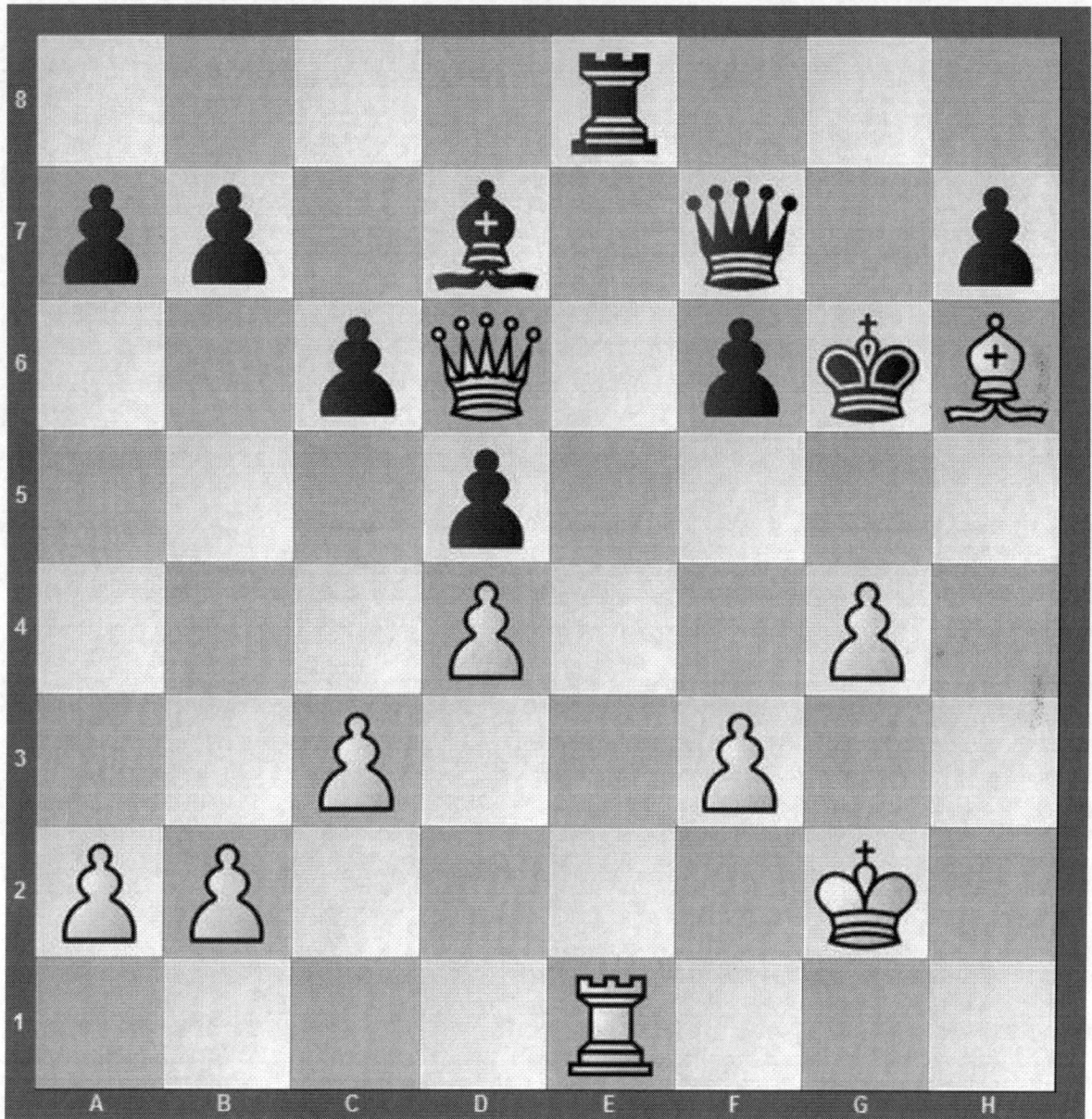

1		
2		

1		
2		

"If you make a mistake and do not correct it, this is called a mistake." – **Proverb**

1		
2		

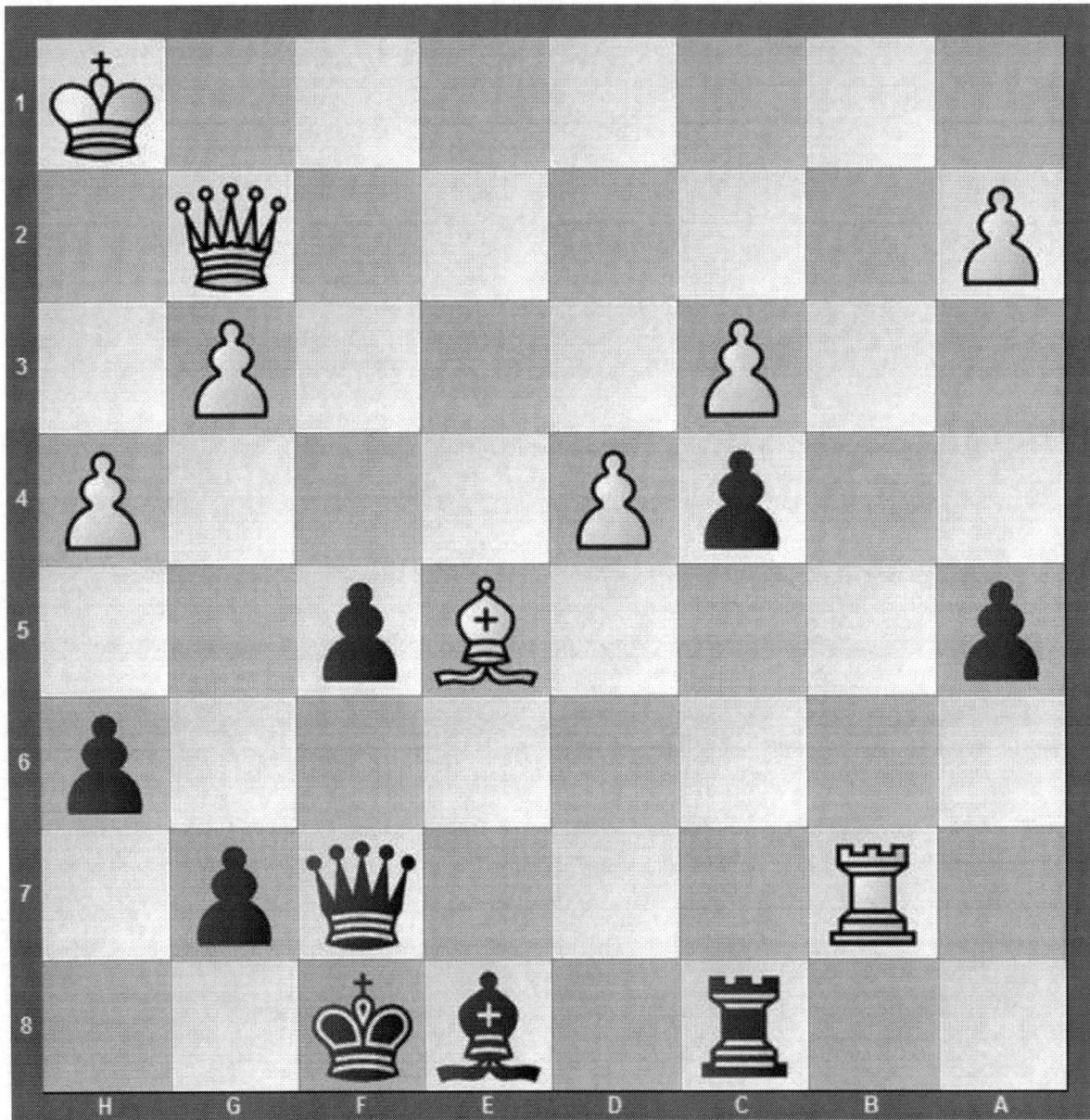

1		
2		

1		
2		

2 Mastering chess sight

1		
2		

1		
2		

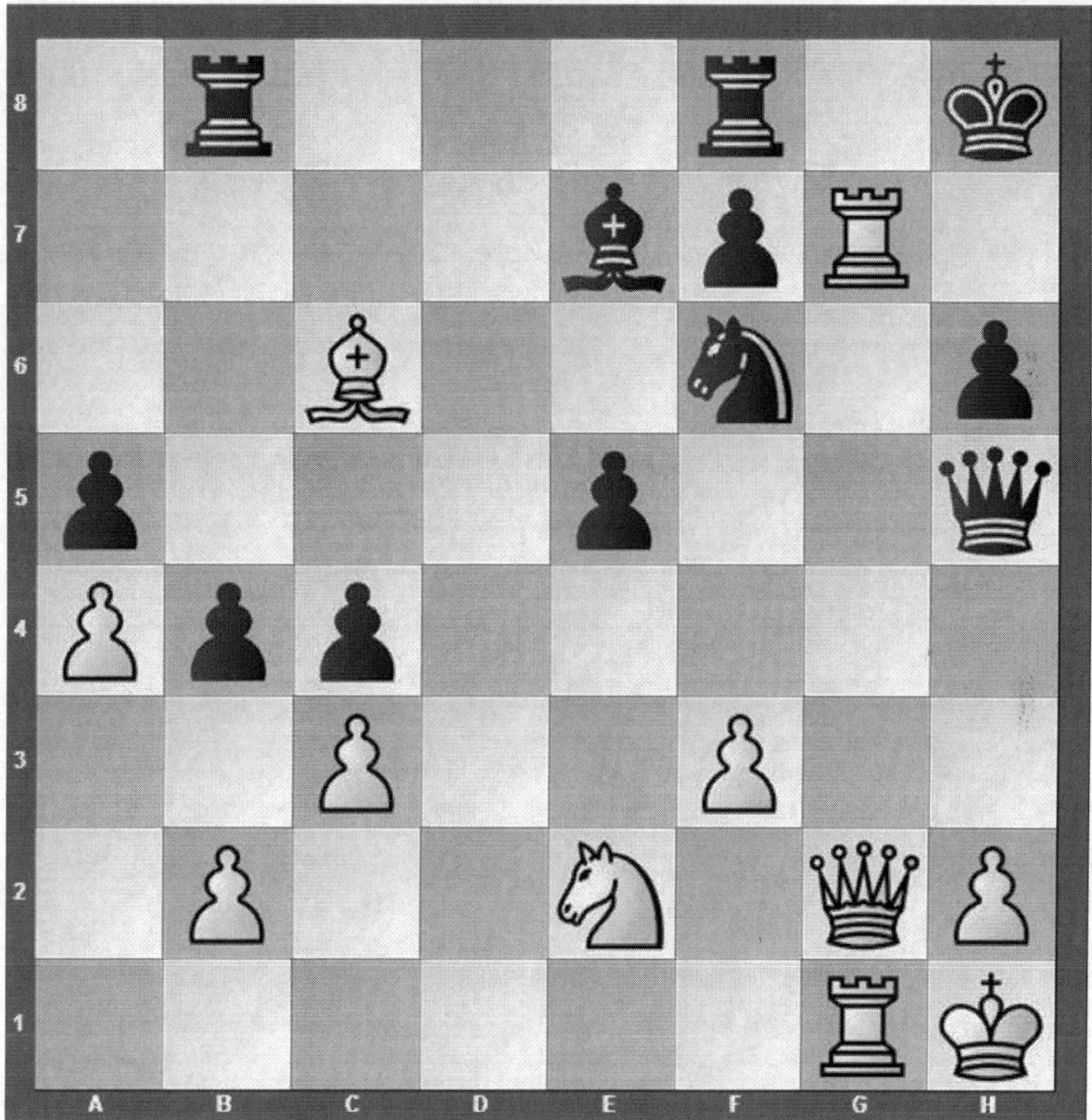

1		
2		

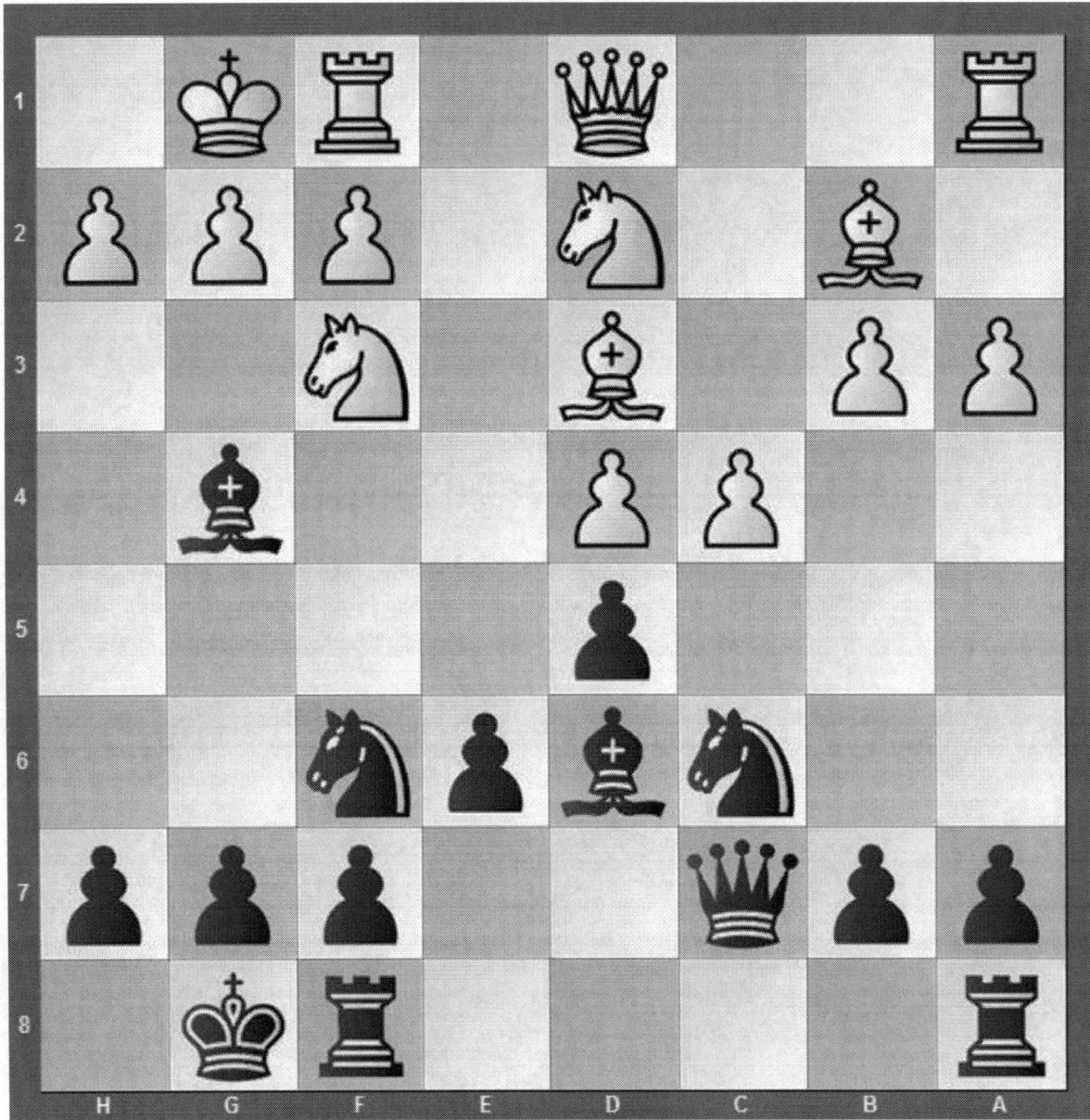

1		
2		

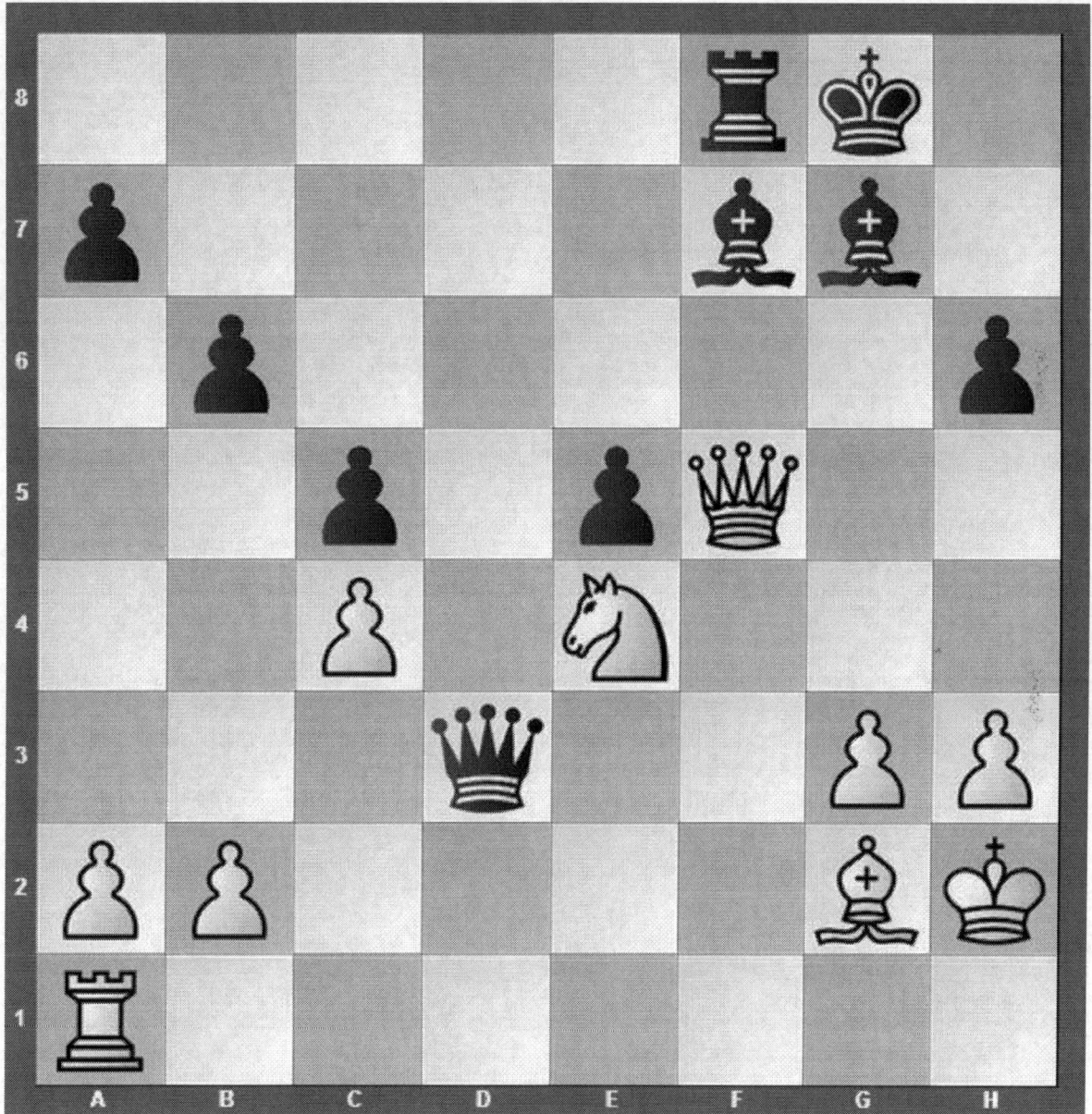

1		
2		

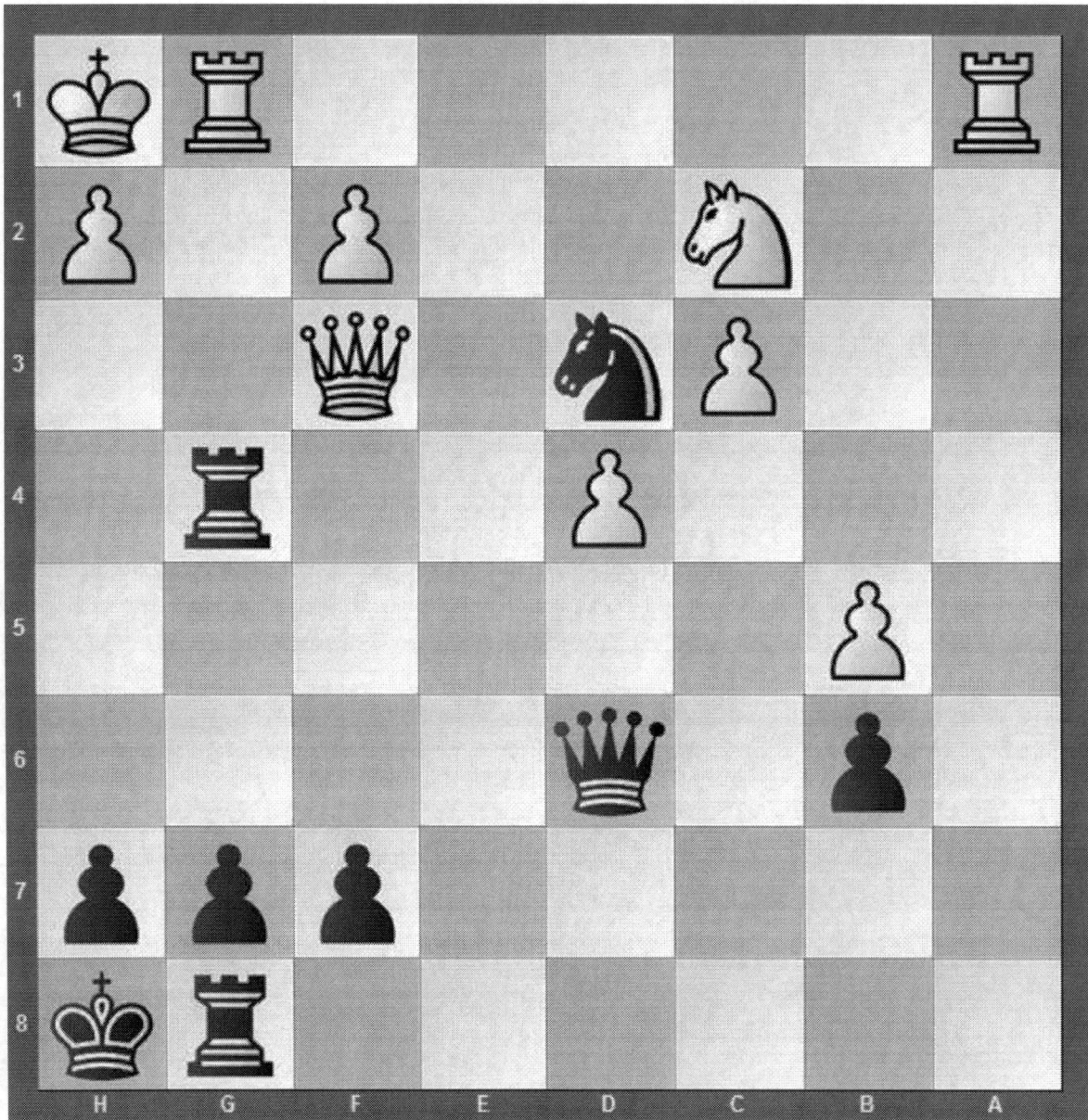

1		
2		

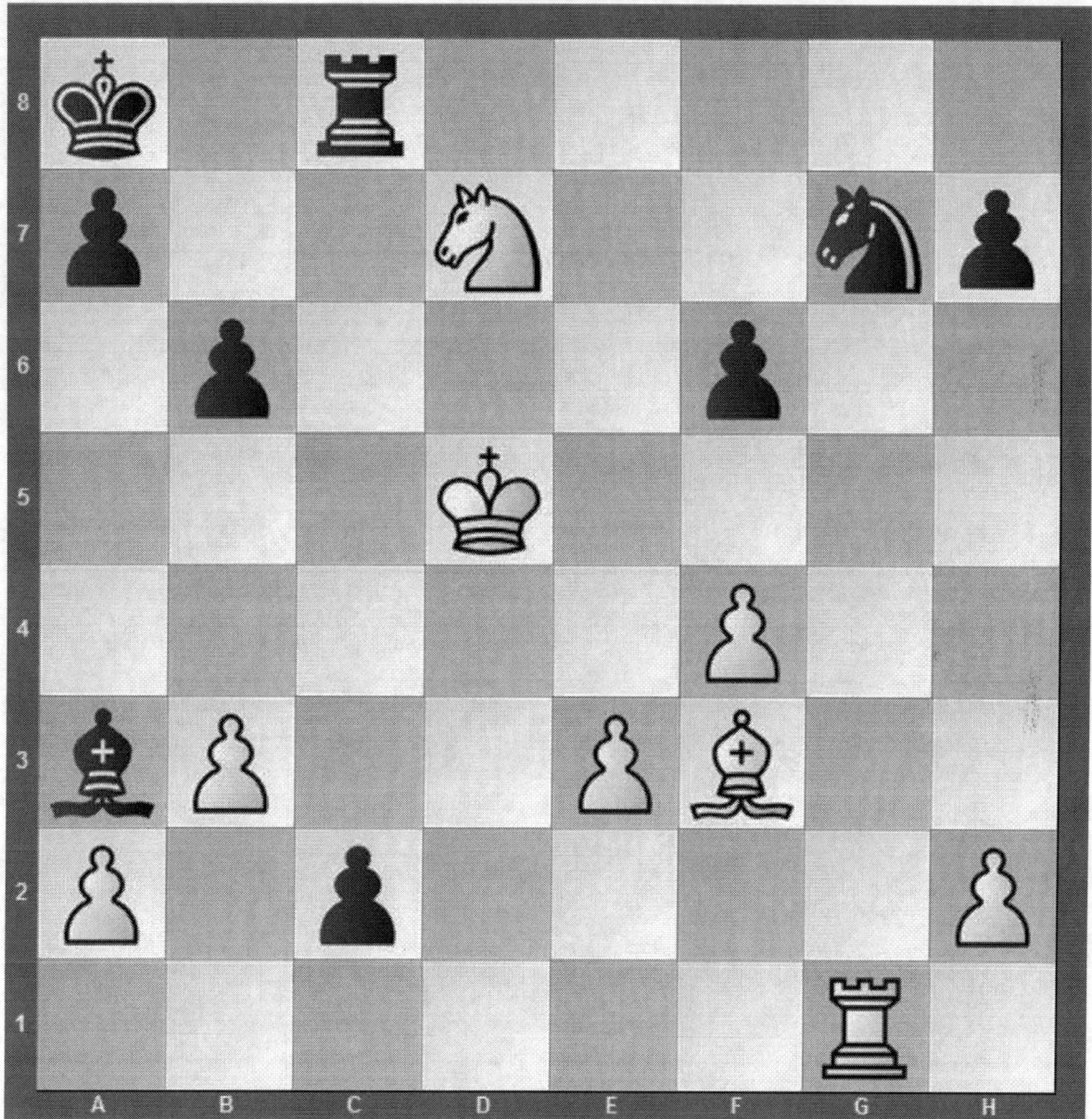

1		
2		

1		
2		

1		
2		

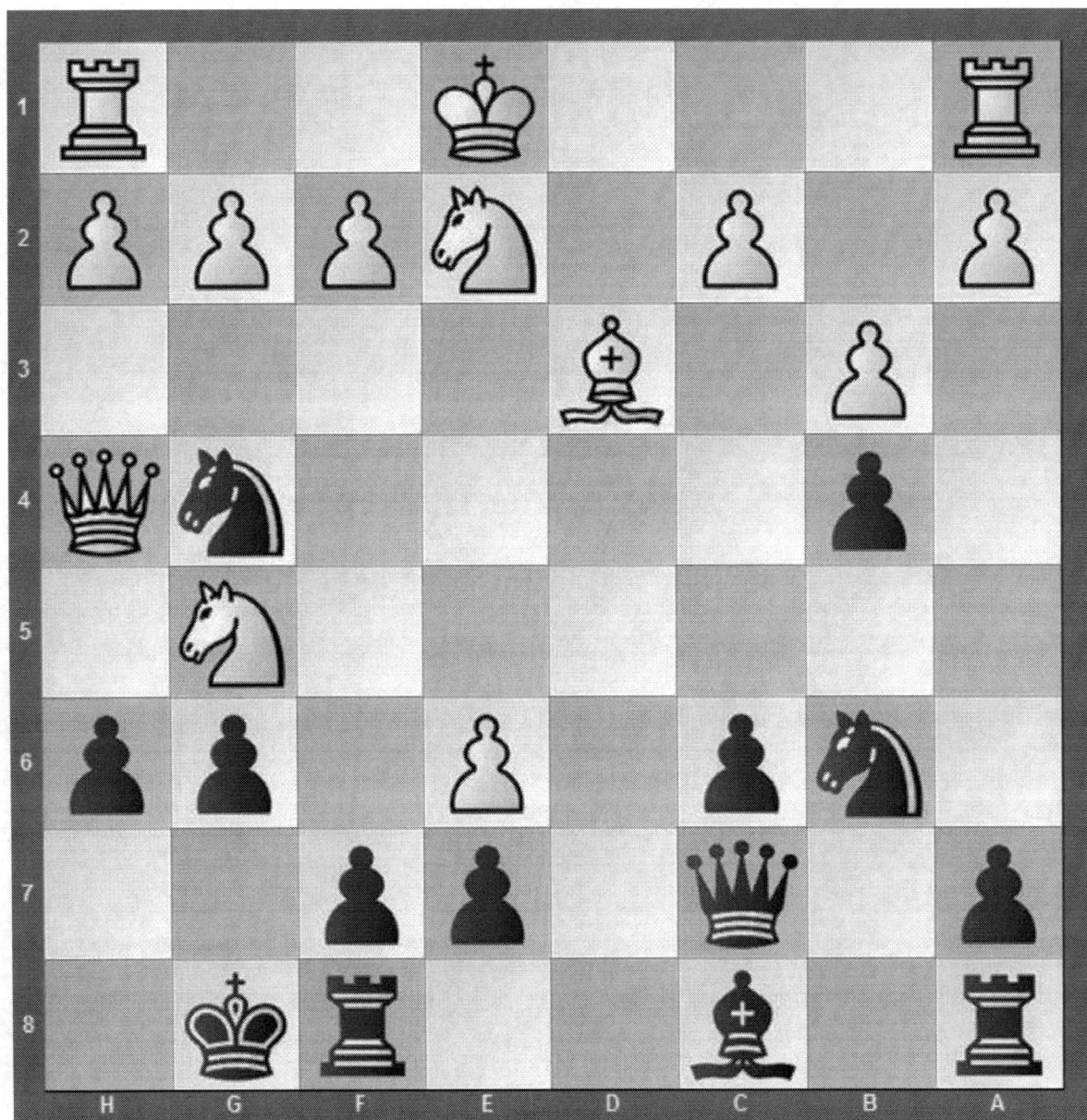

1		
2		

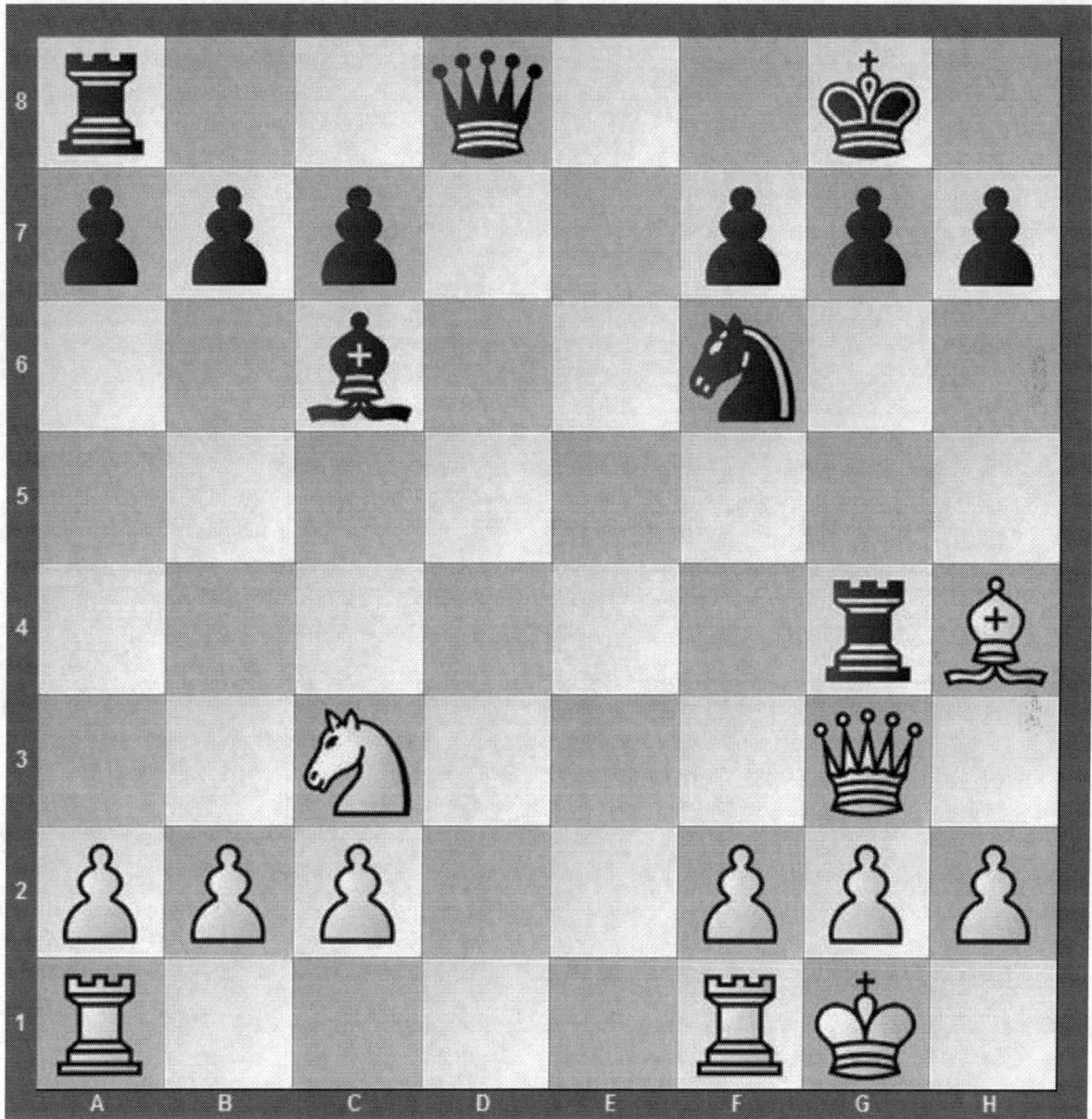

1		
2		

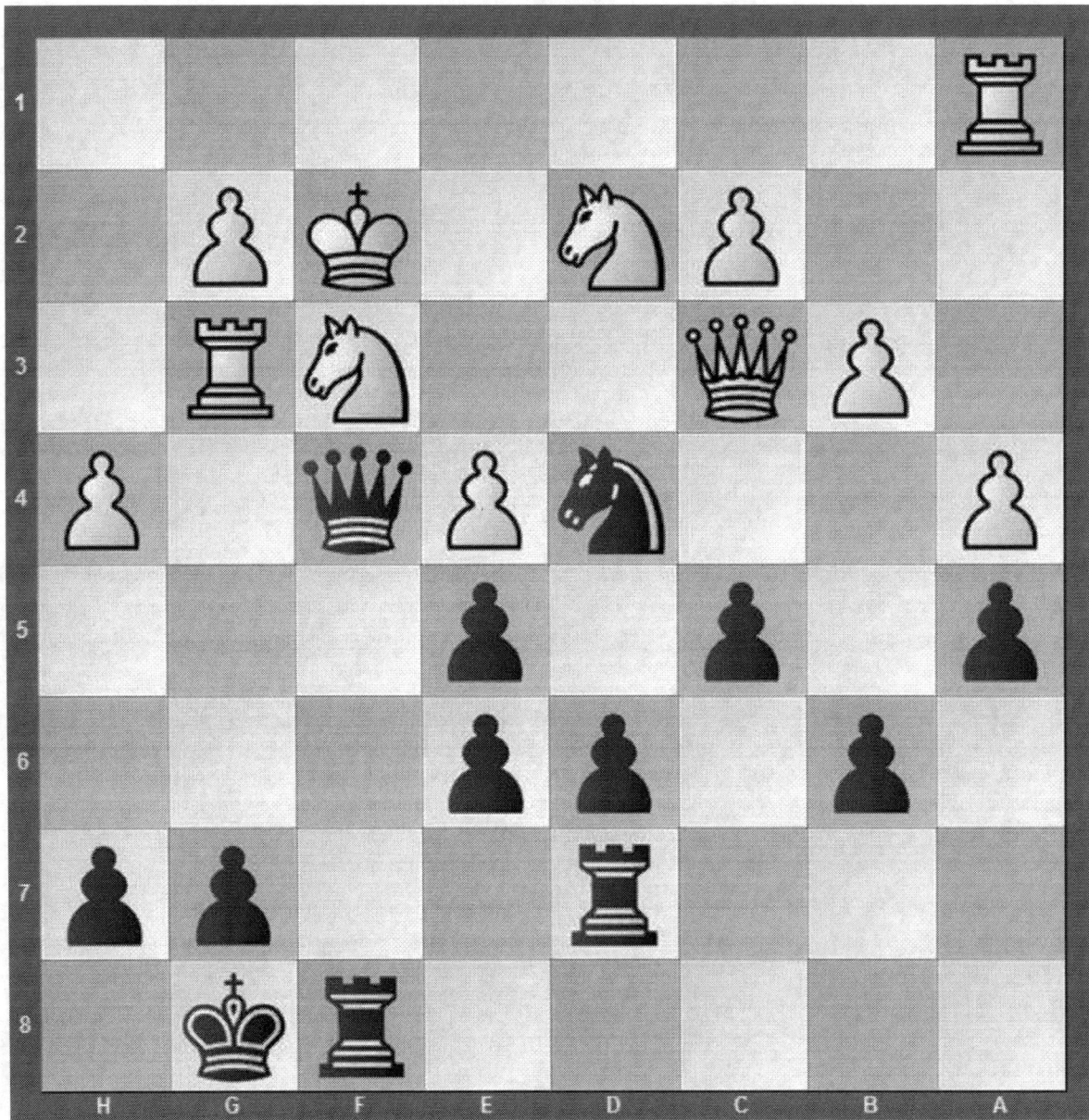

1		
2		

"The human element, the human flaw and the human nobility - those are the reasons that chess matches are won or lost." – **Viktor Korchnoi**

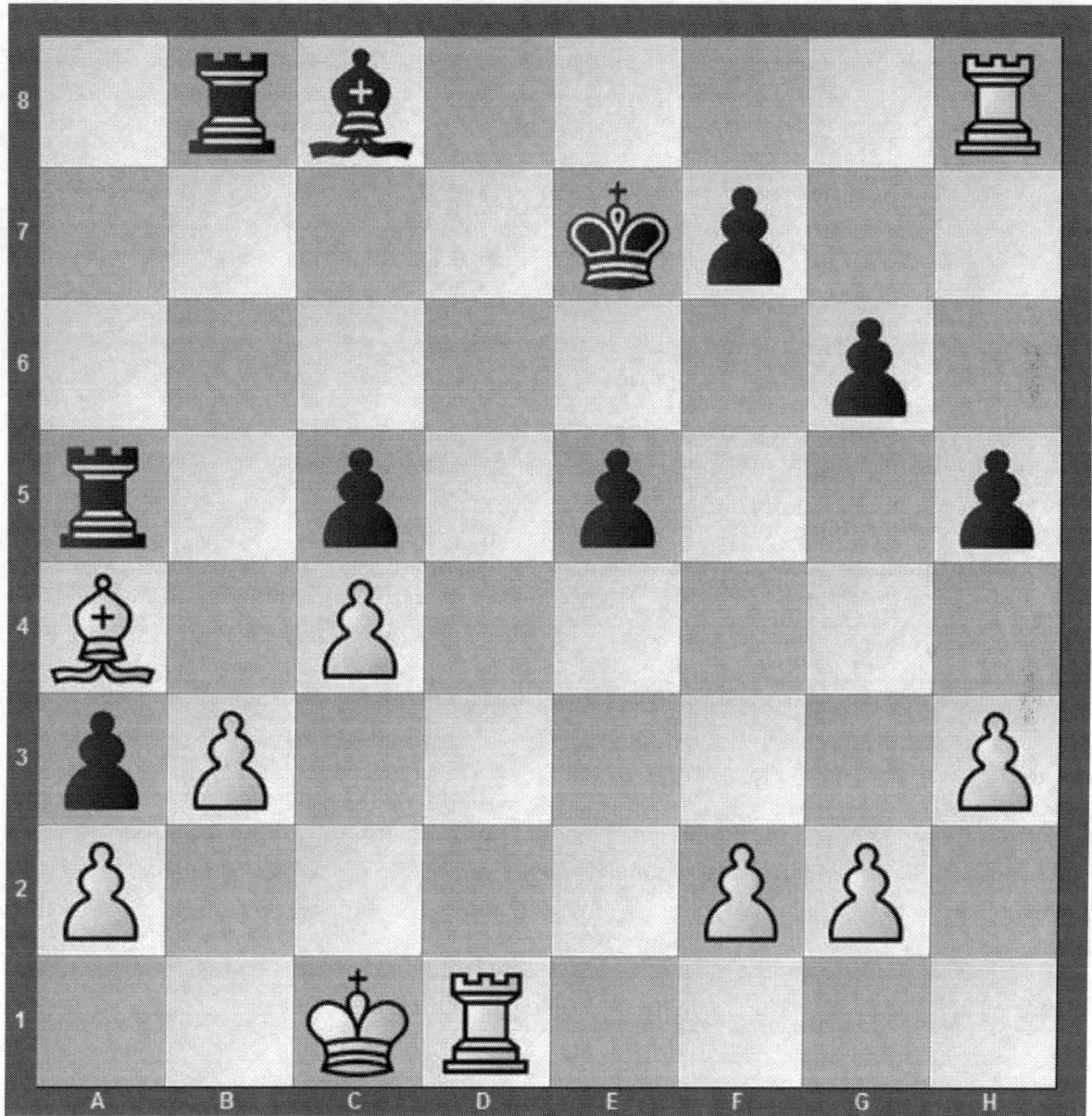

1		
2		

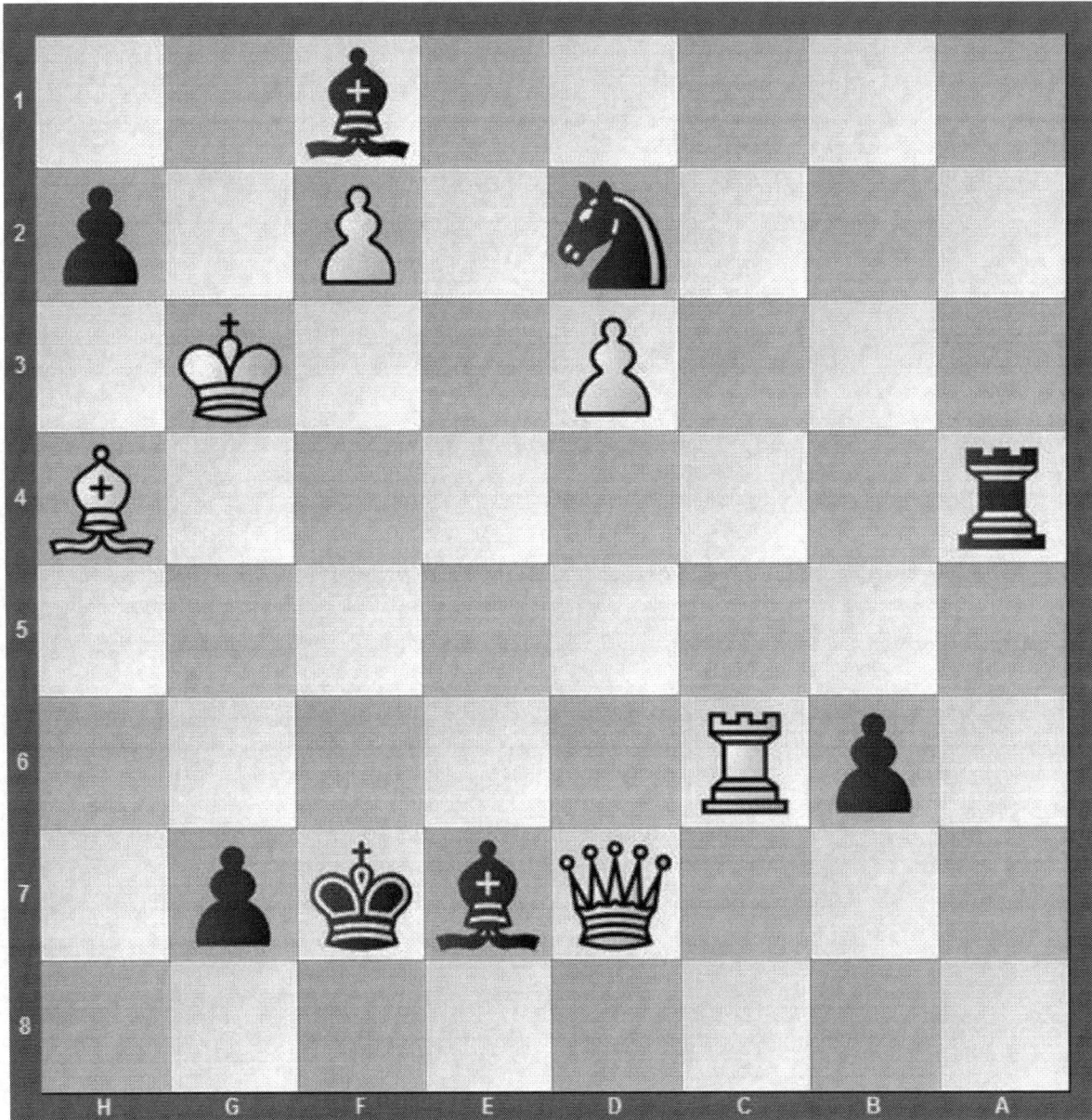

1		
2		

1		
2		

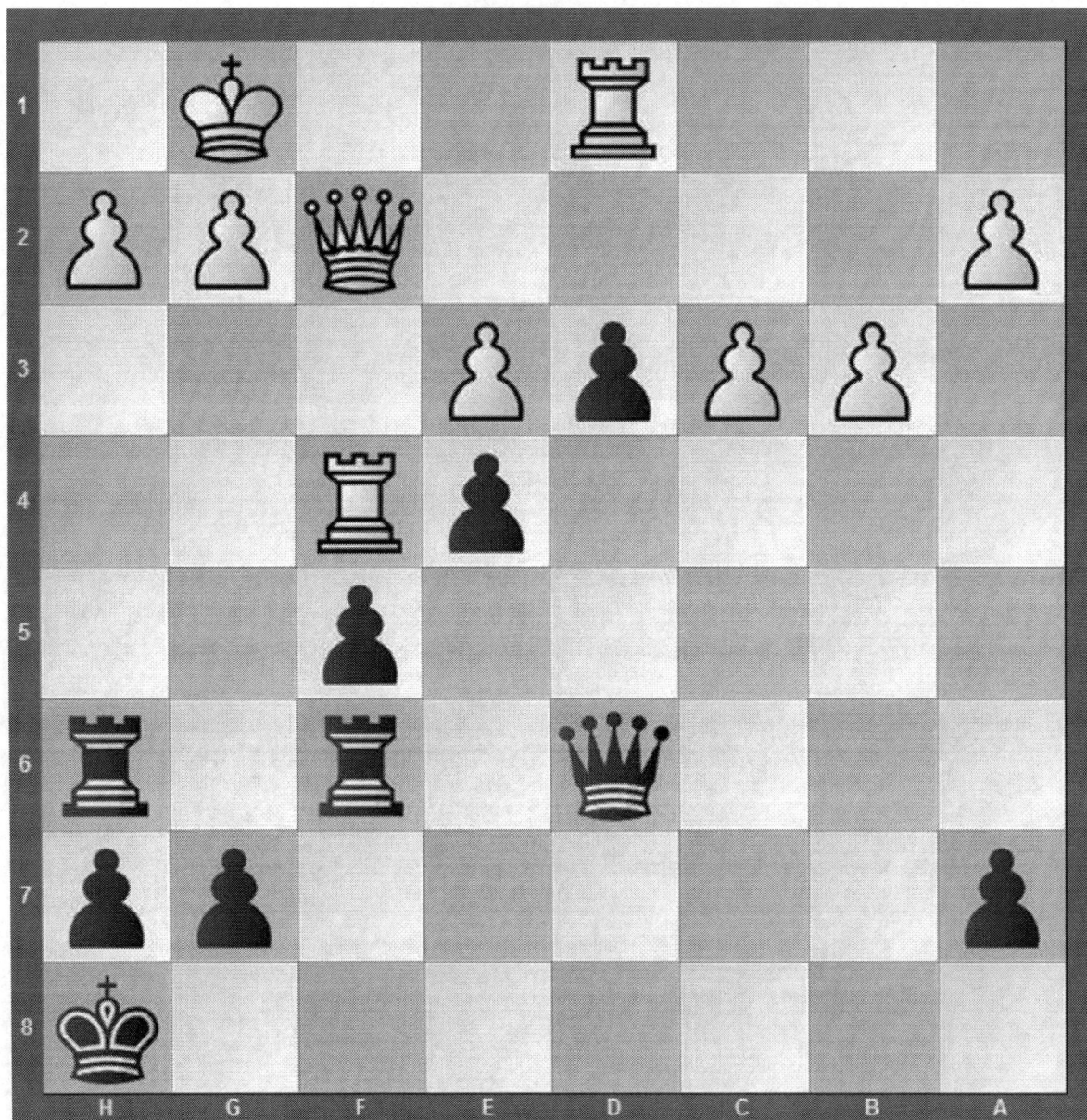

1		
2		

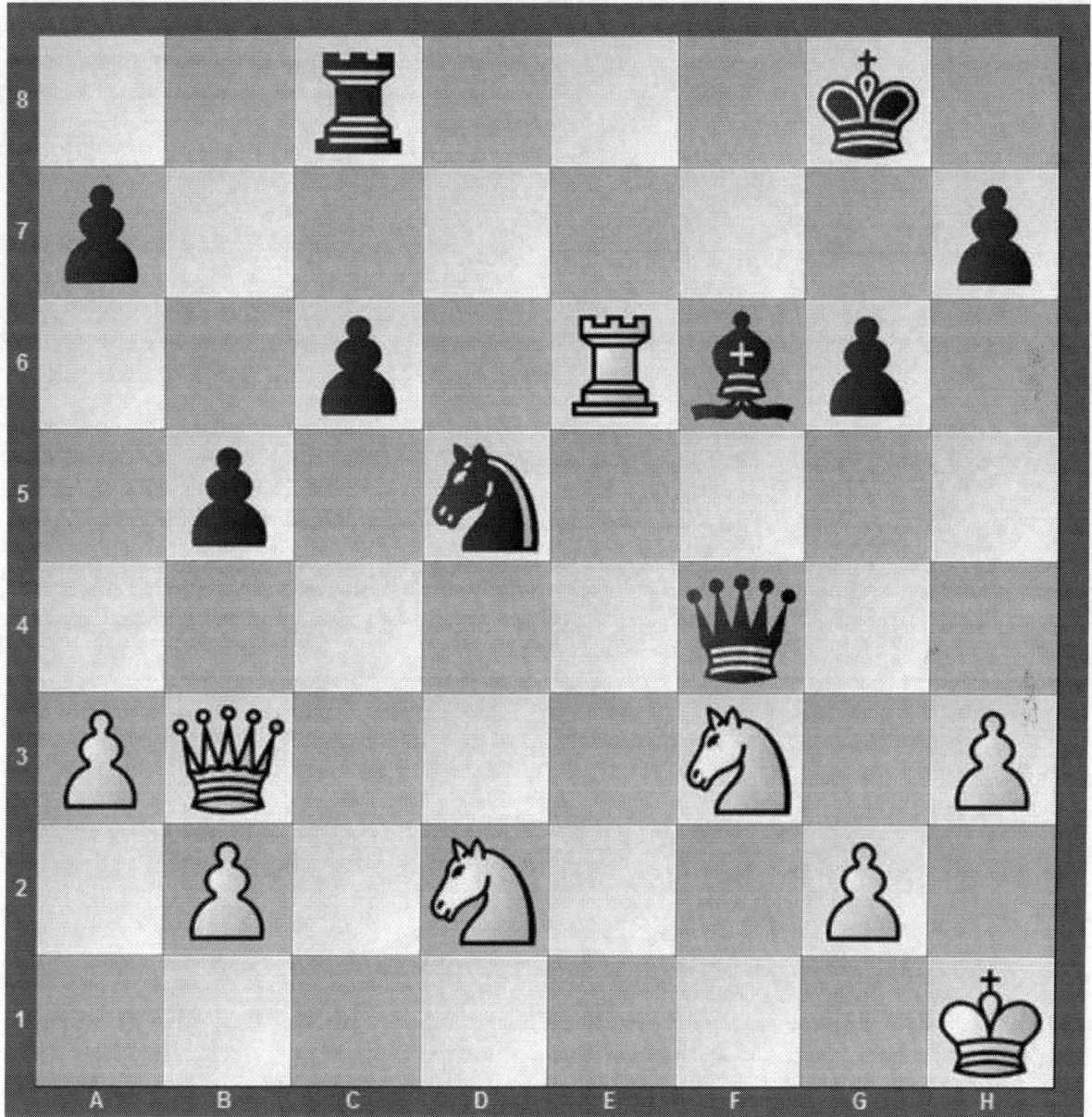

1		
2		

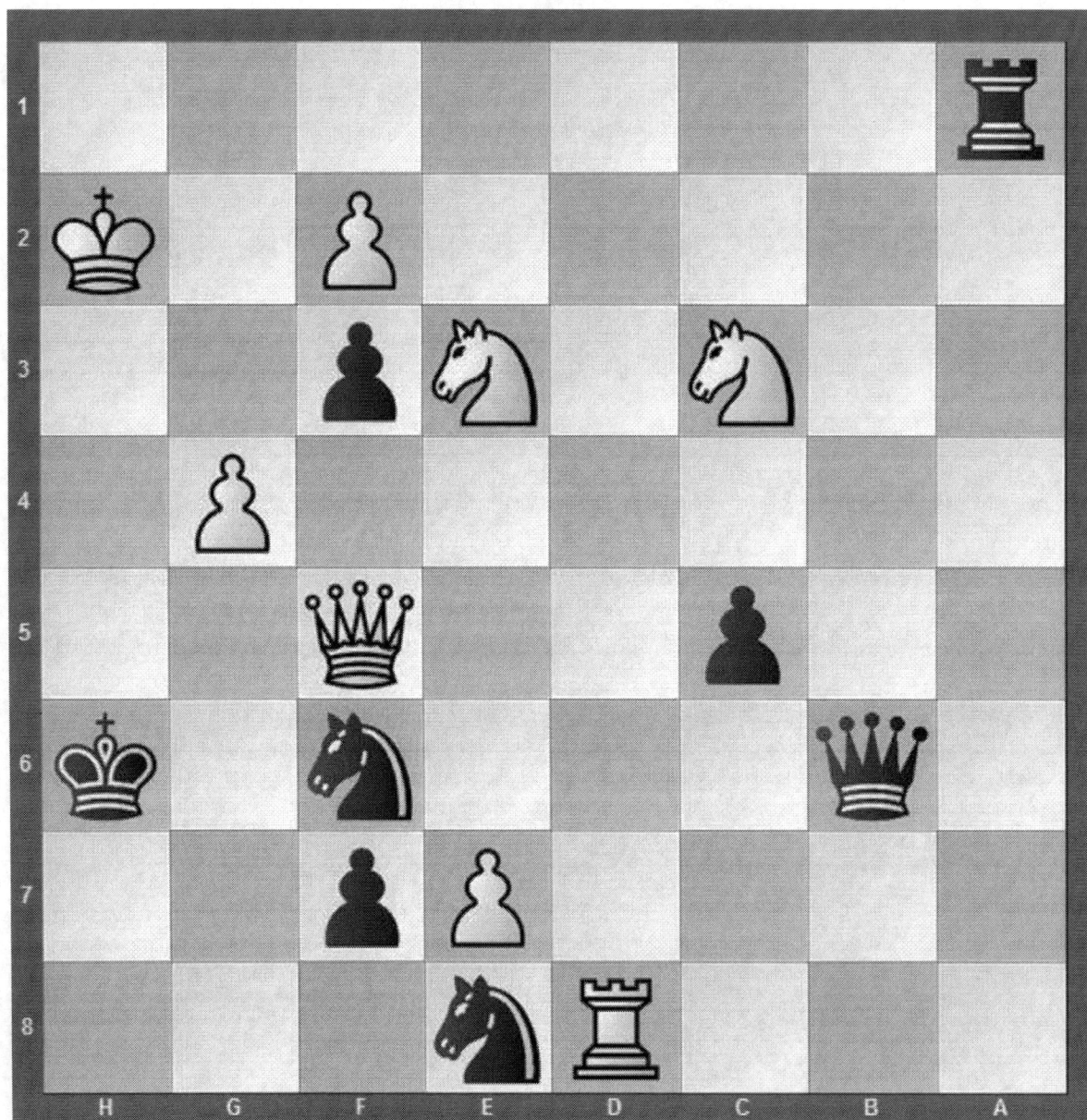

1		
2		

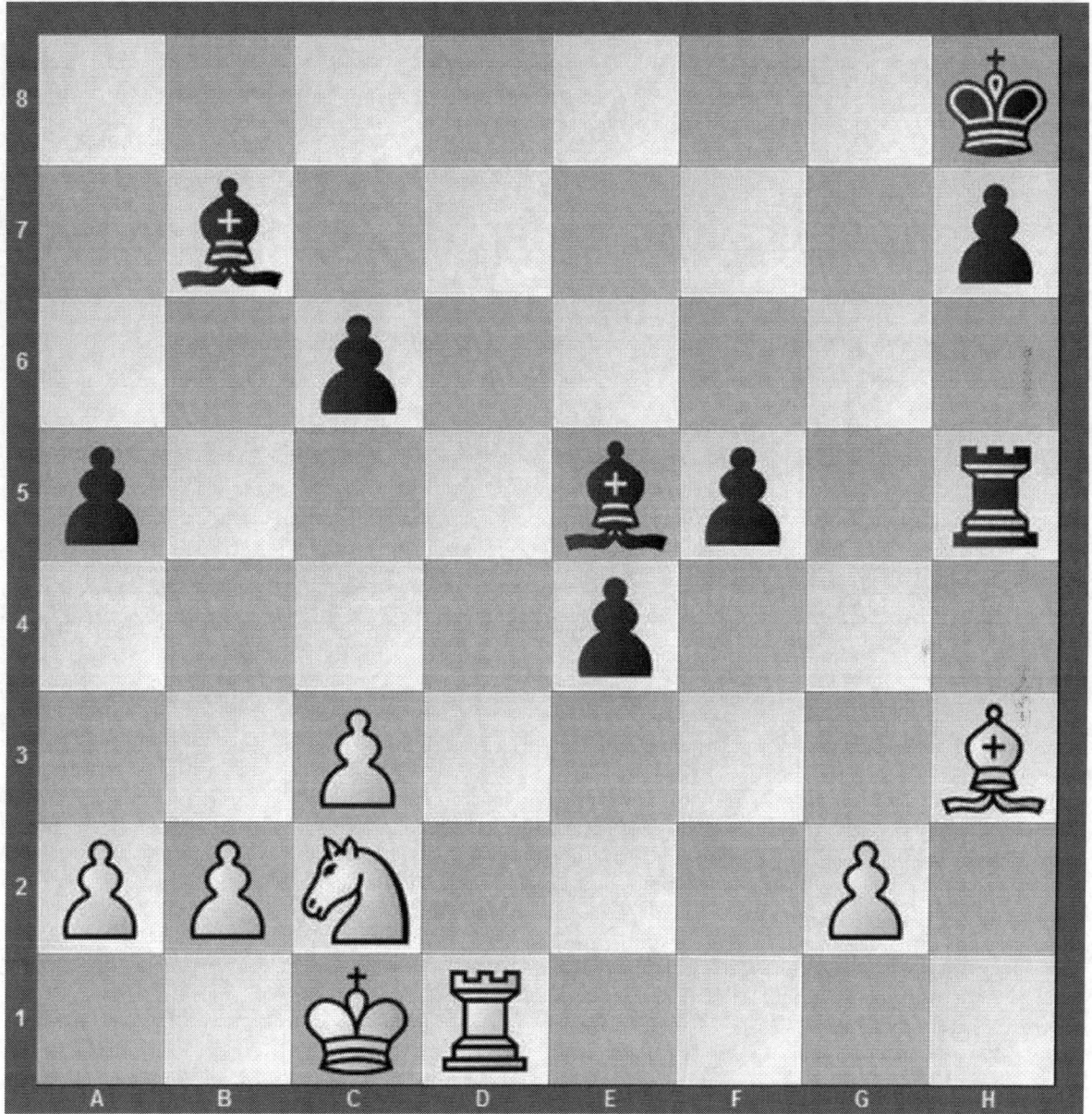

| 1 | | |
| 2 | | |

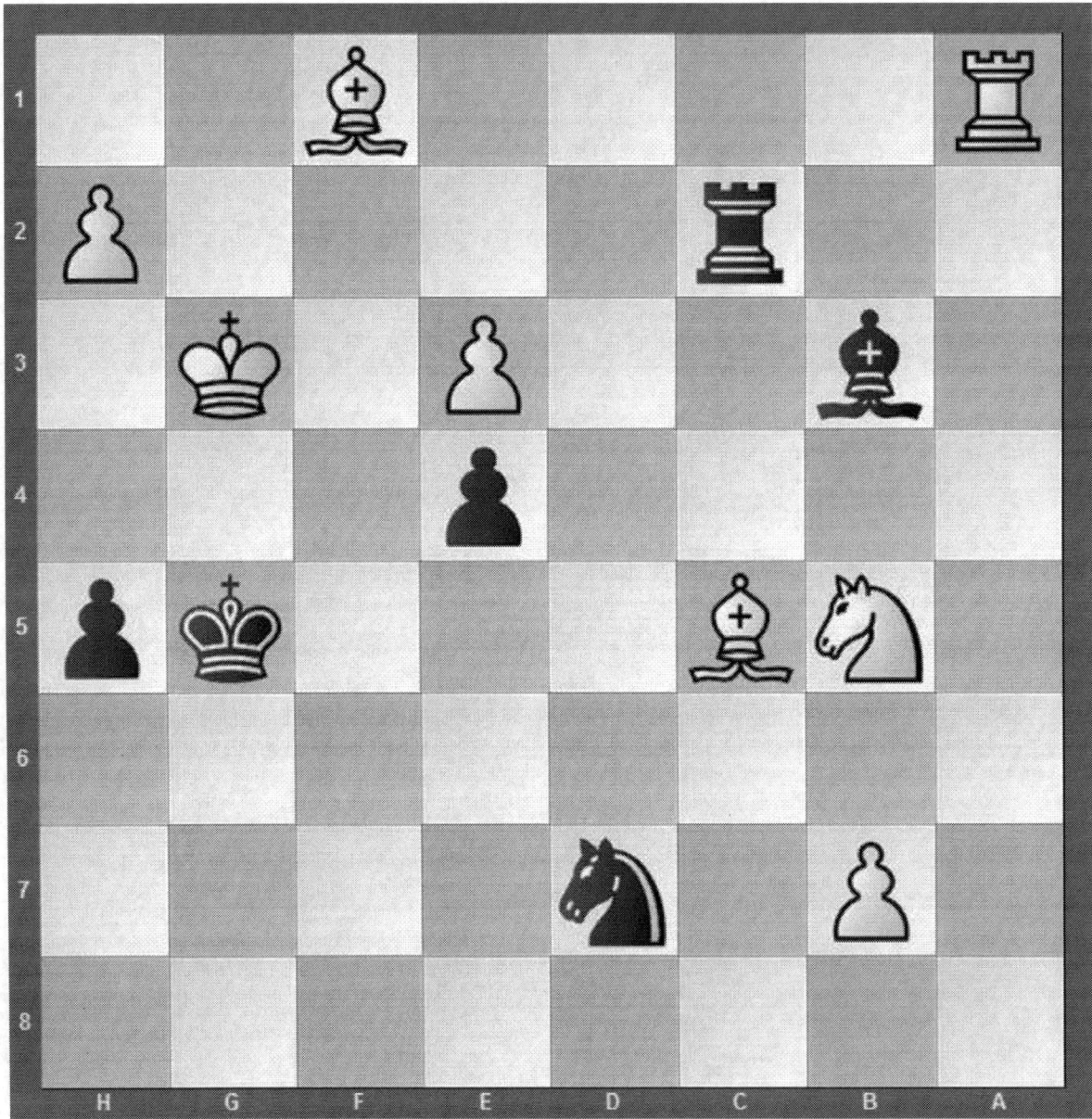

1		
2		

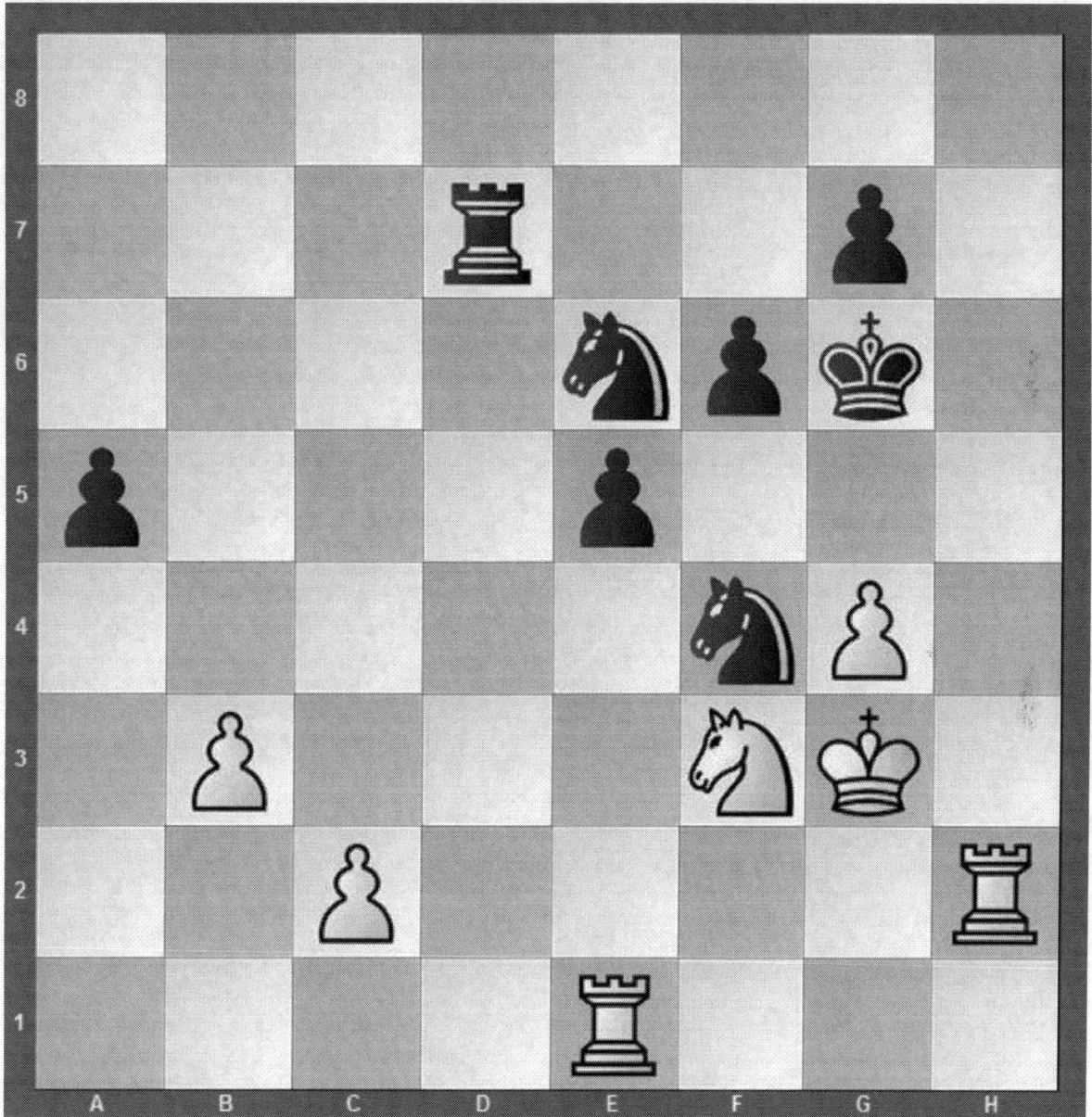

1		
2		

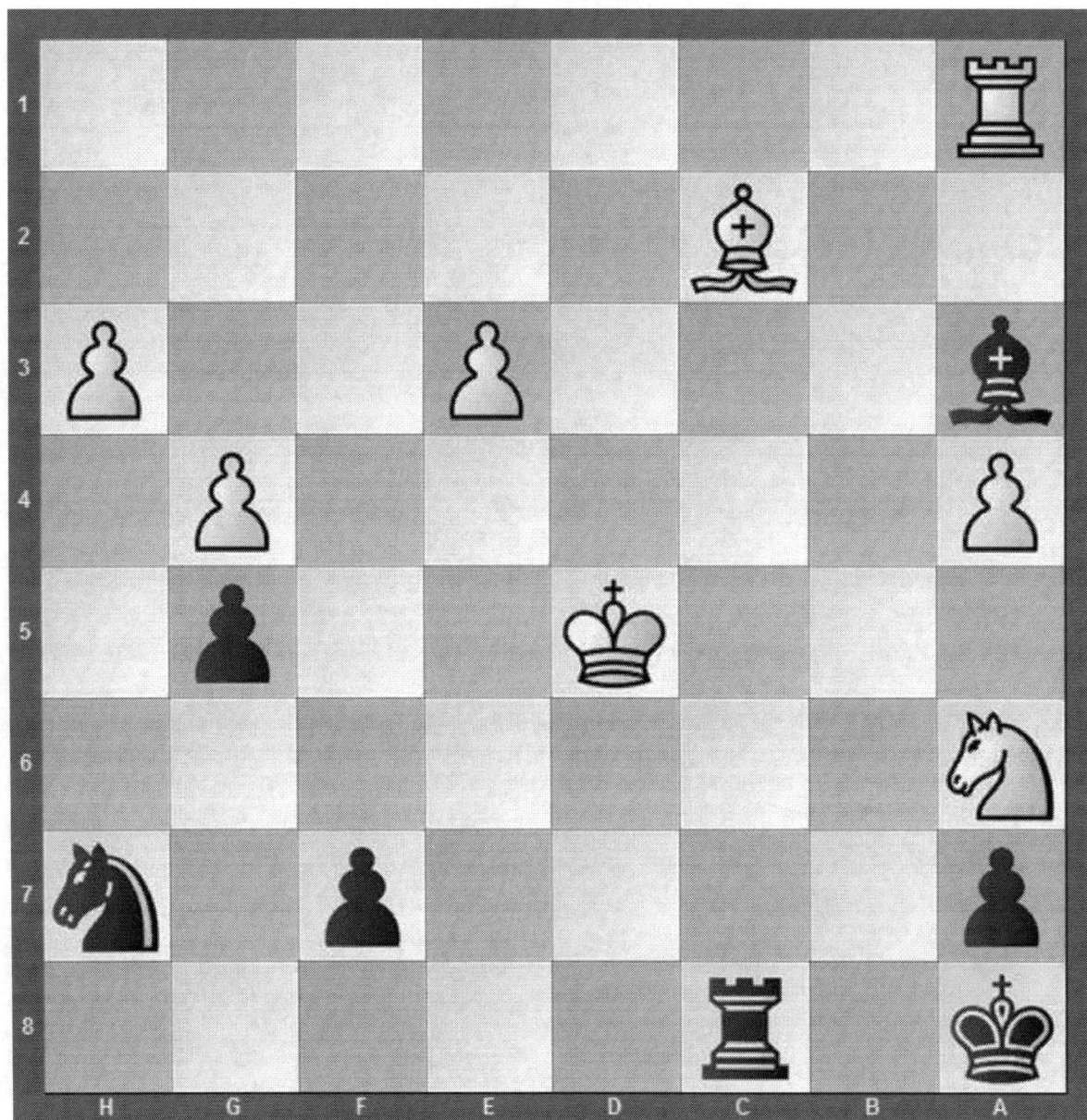

1		
2		

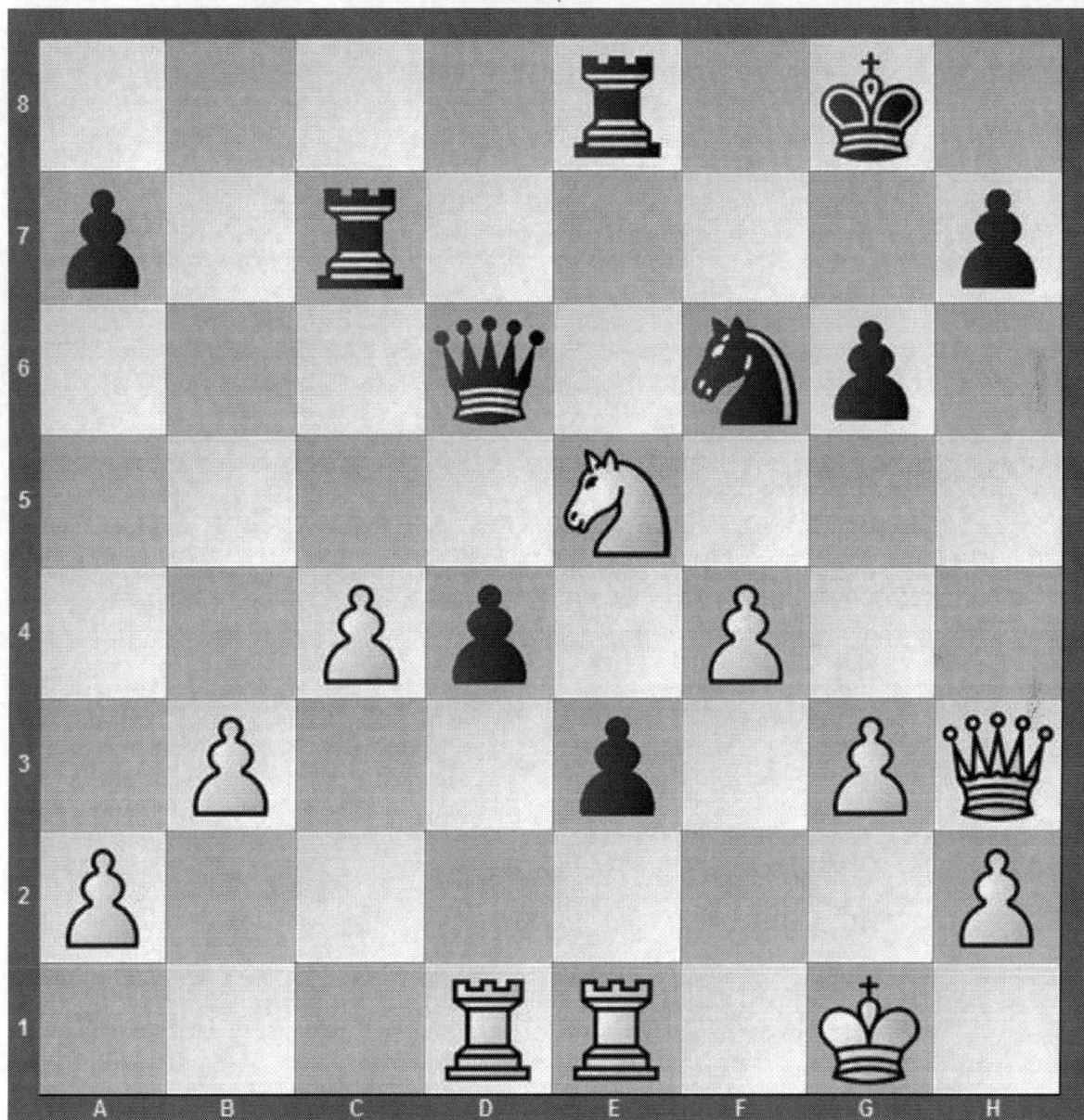

1		
2		

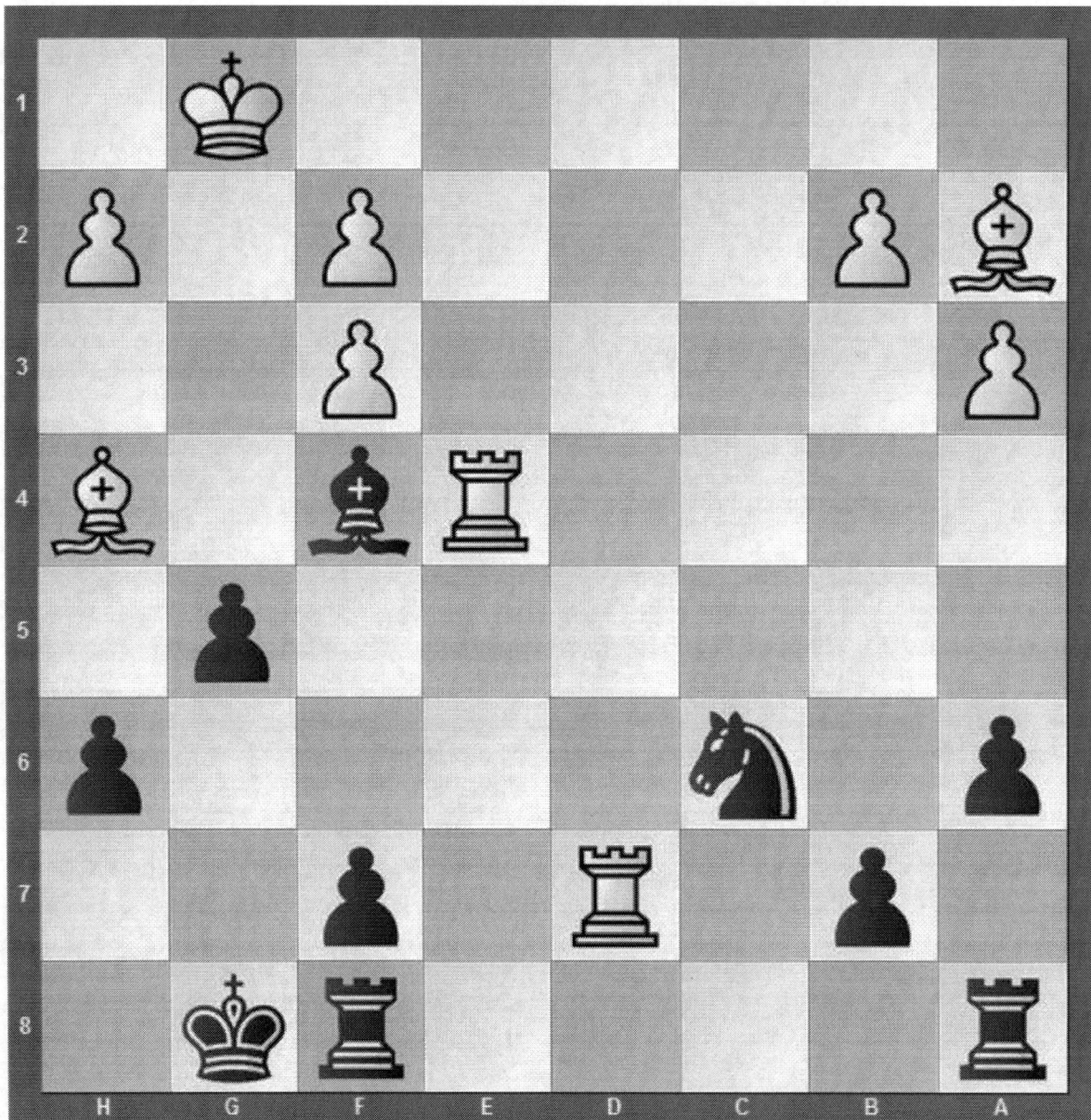

1		
2		

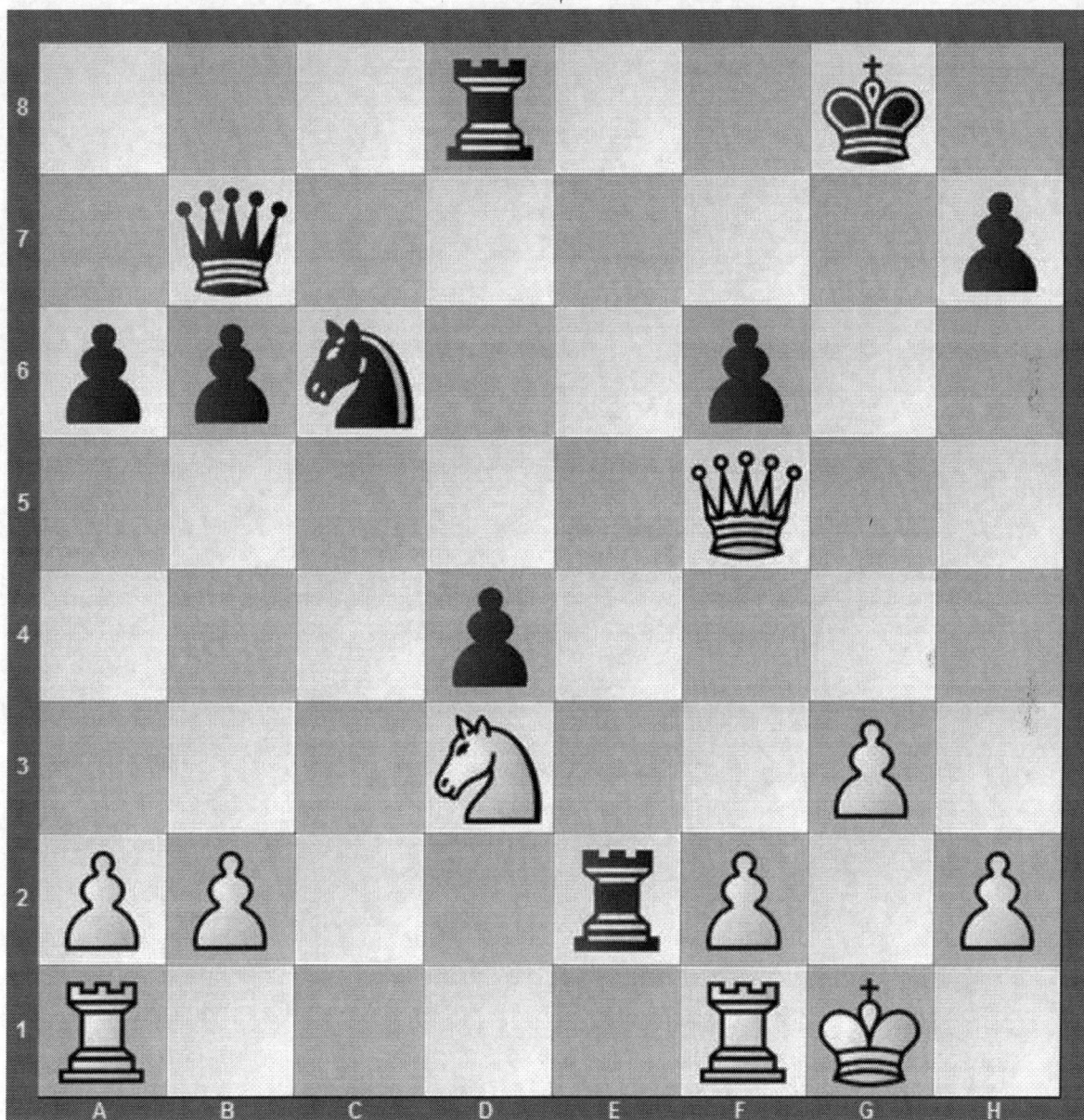

1		
2		

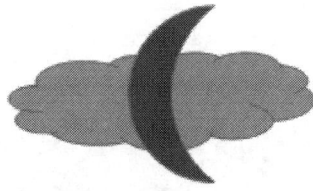

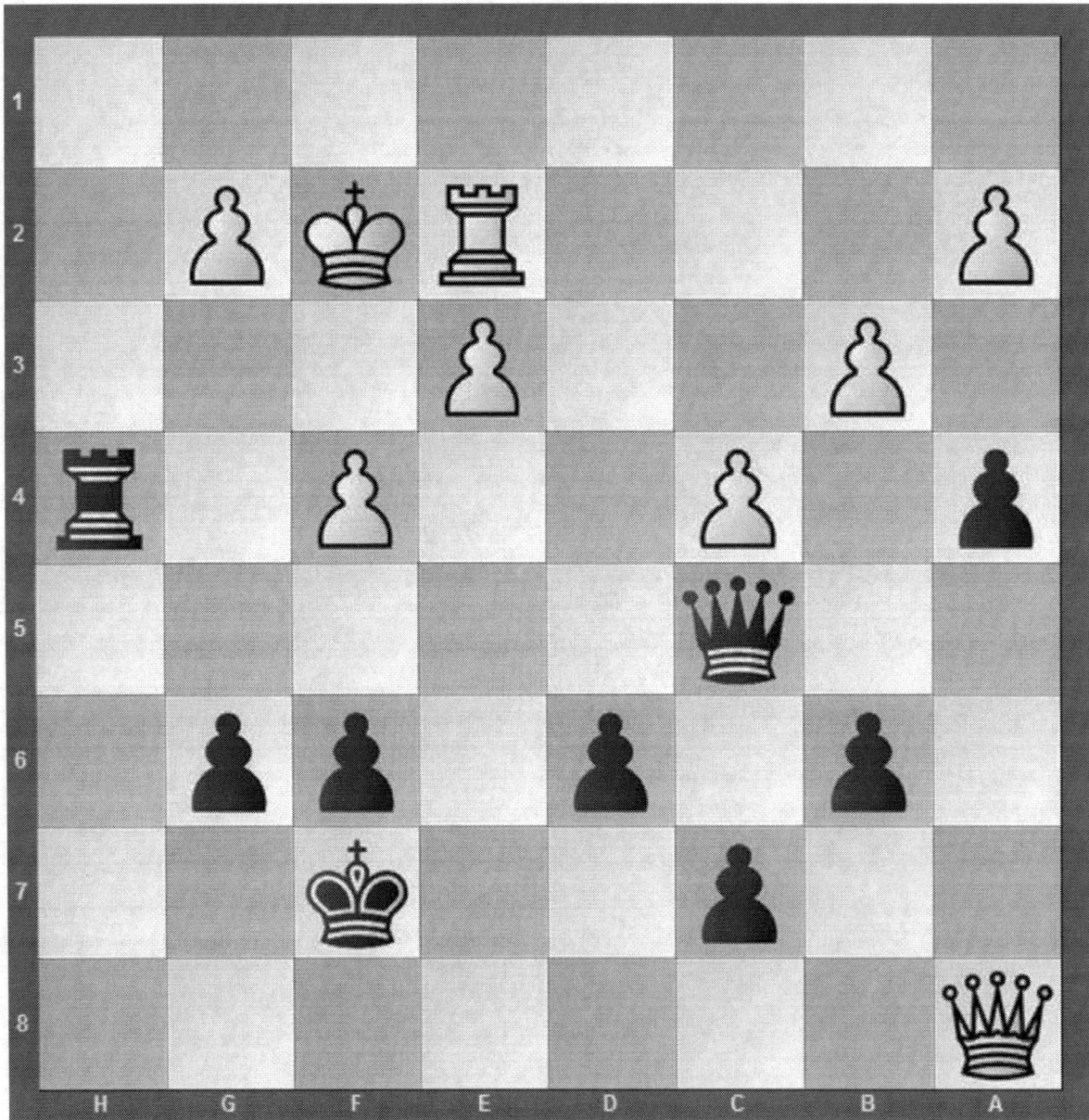

1		
2		

"Chess is played with the mind and not with the hands!" – **Renaud and Kahn**

1		
2		

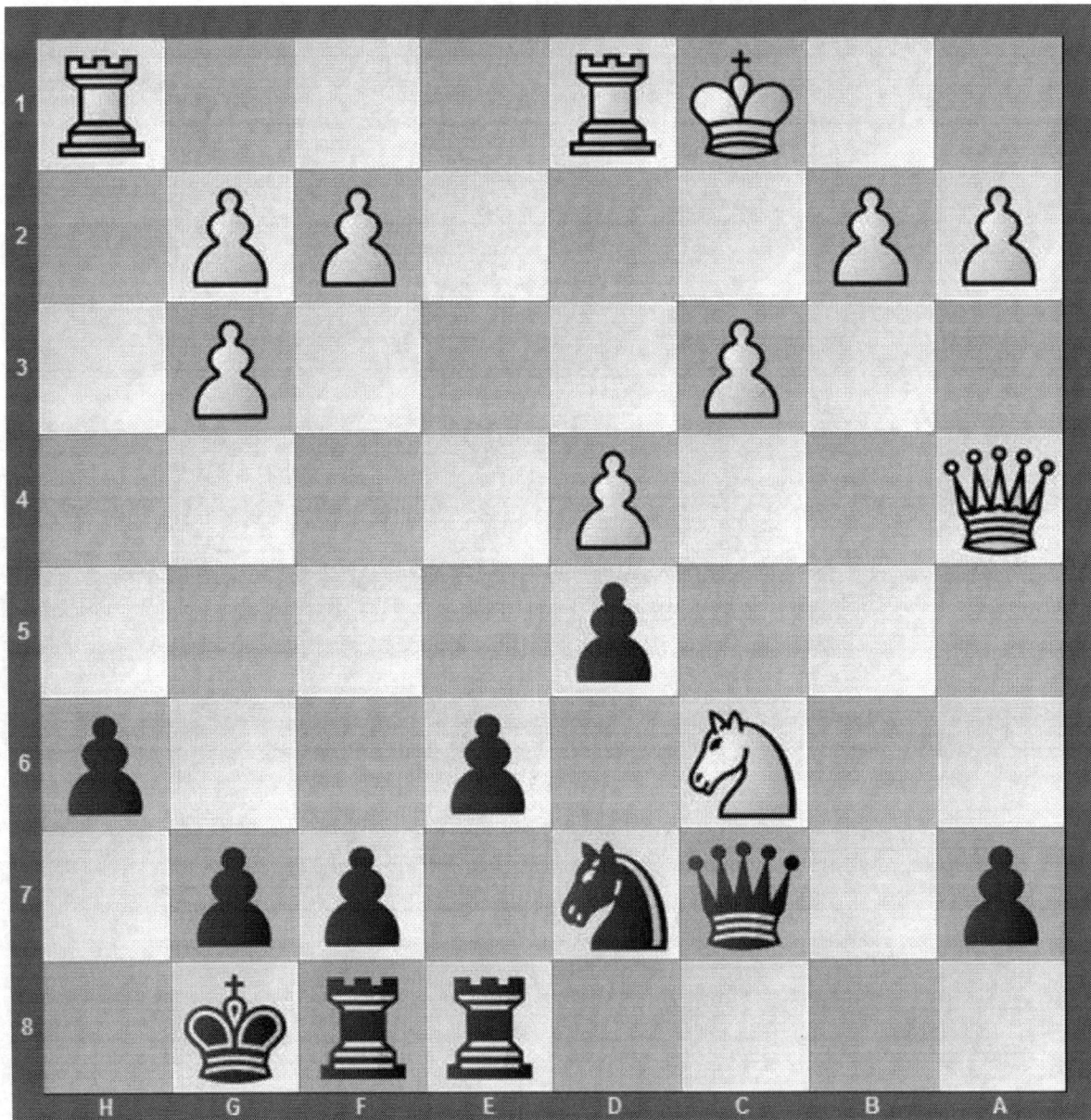

1		
2		

1		
2		

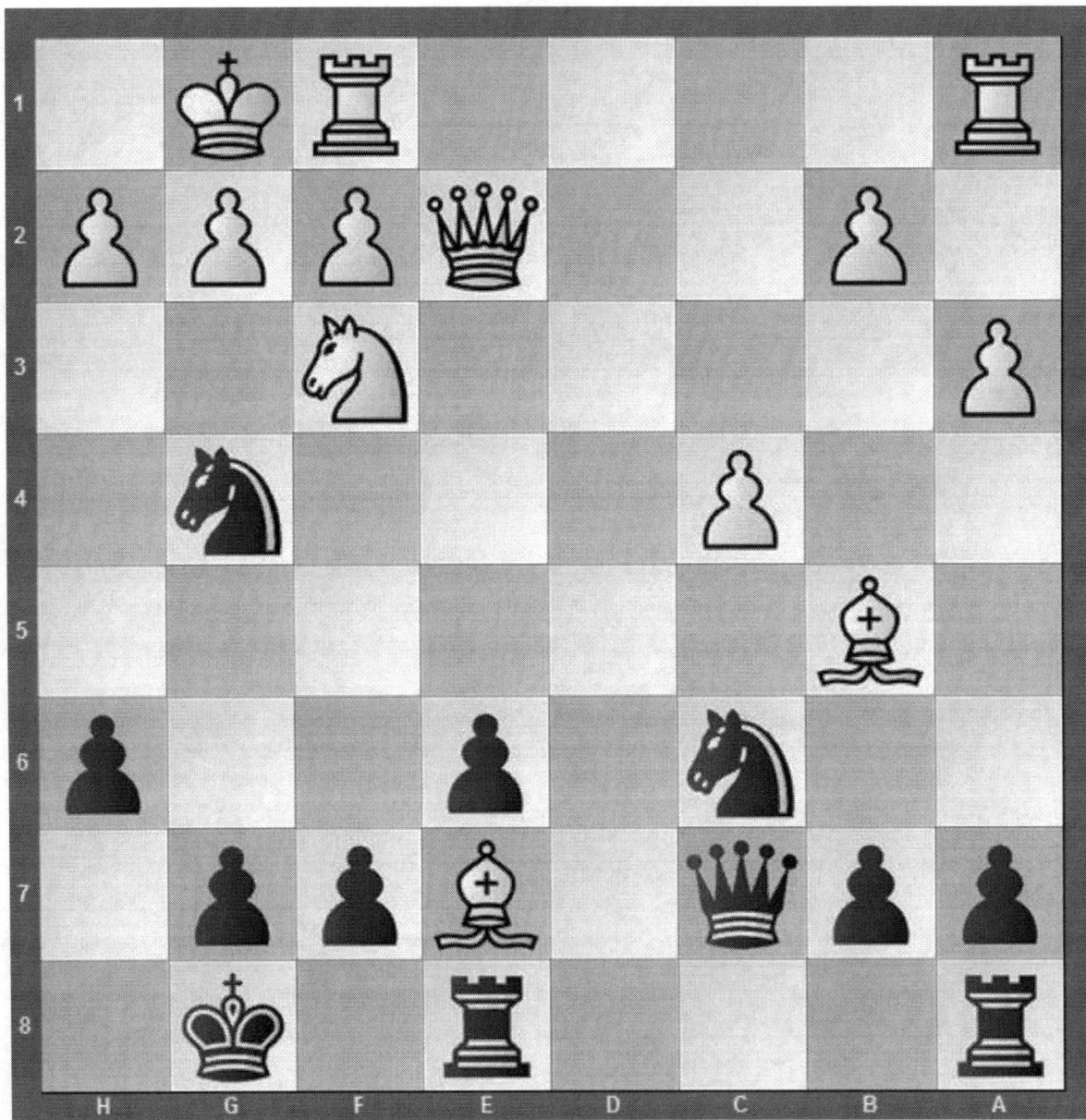

1		
2		

1		
2		

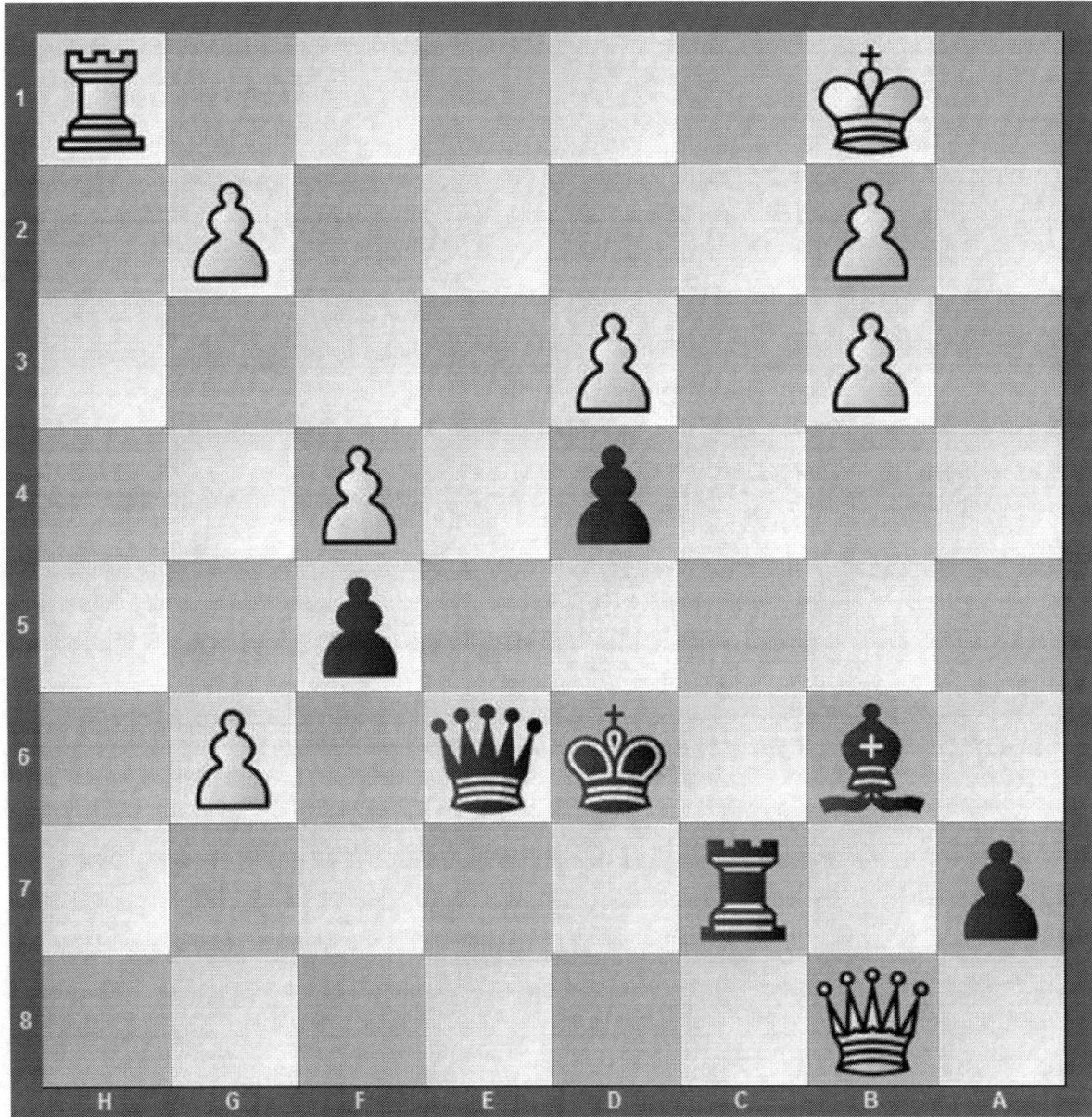

1		
2		

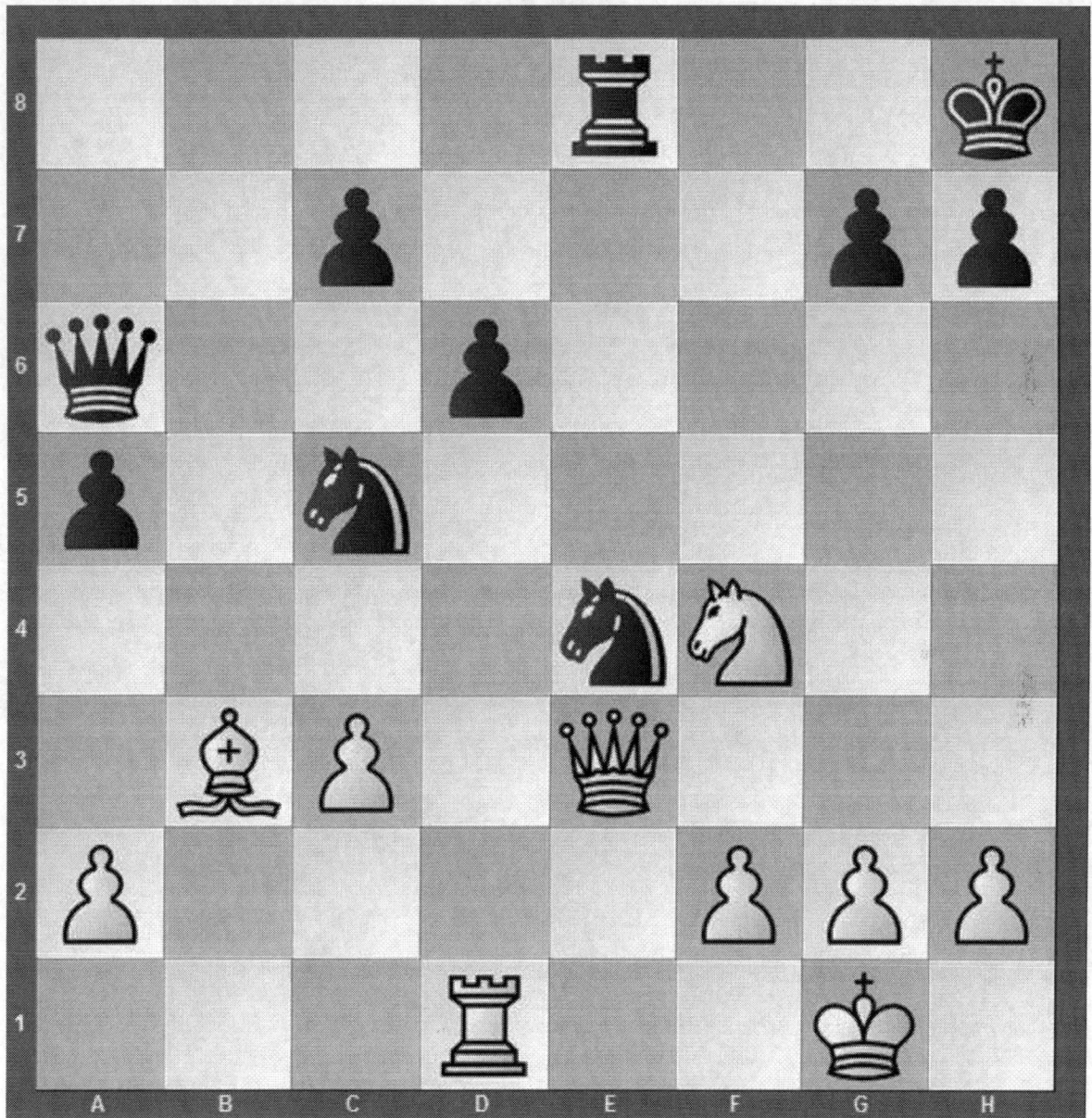

1		
2		

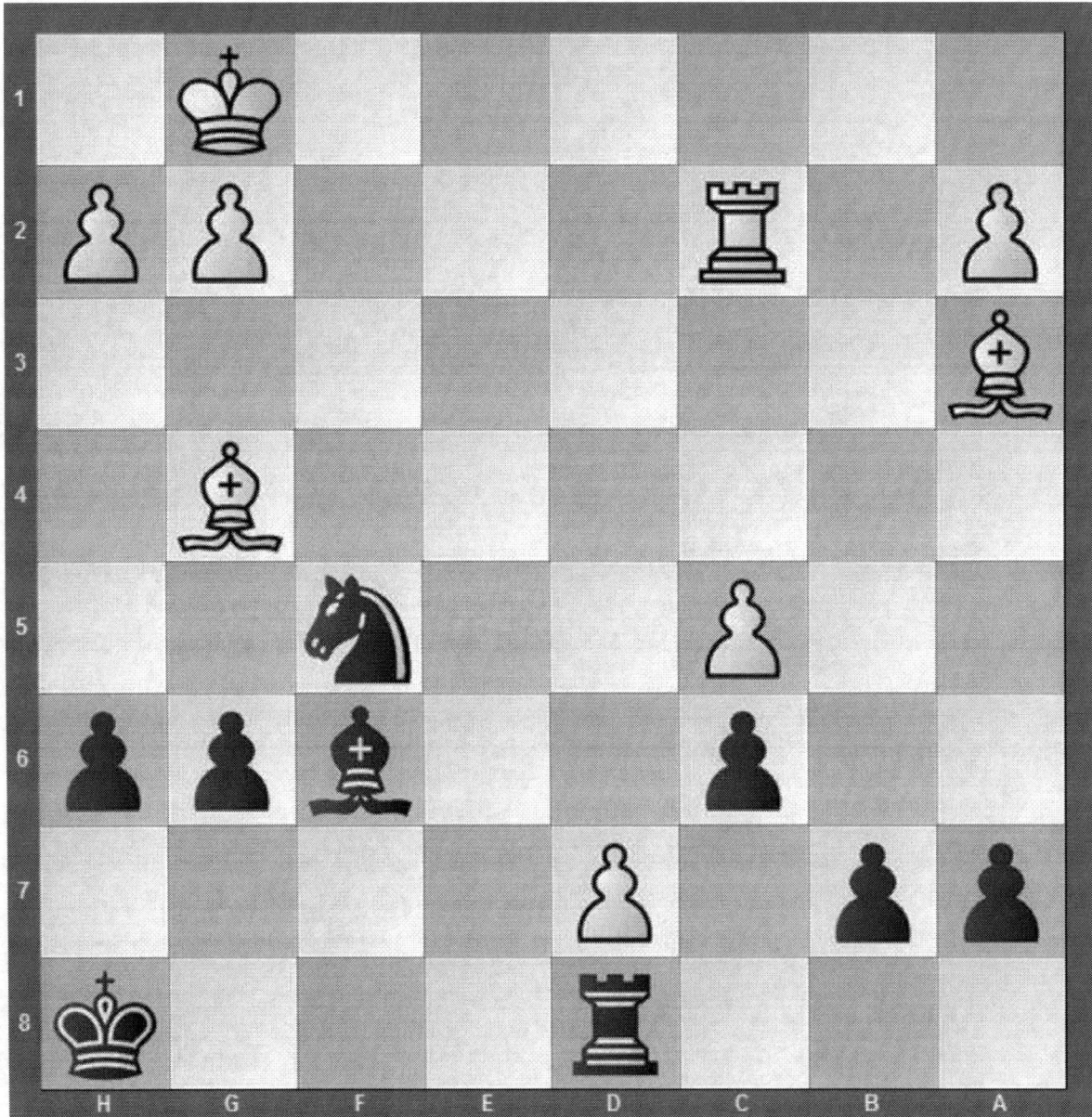

1		
2		

1		
2		

1		
2		

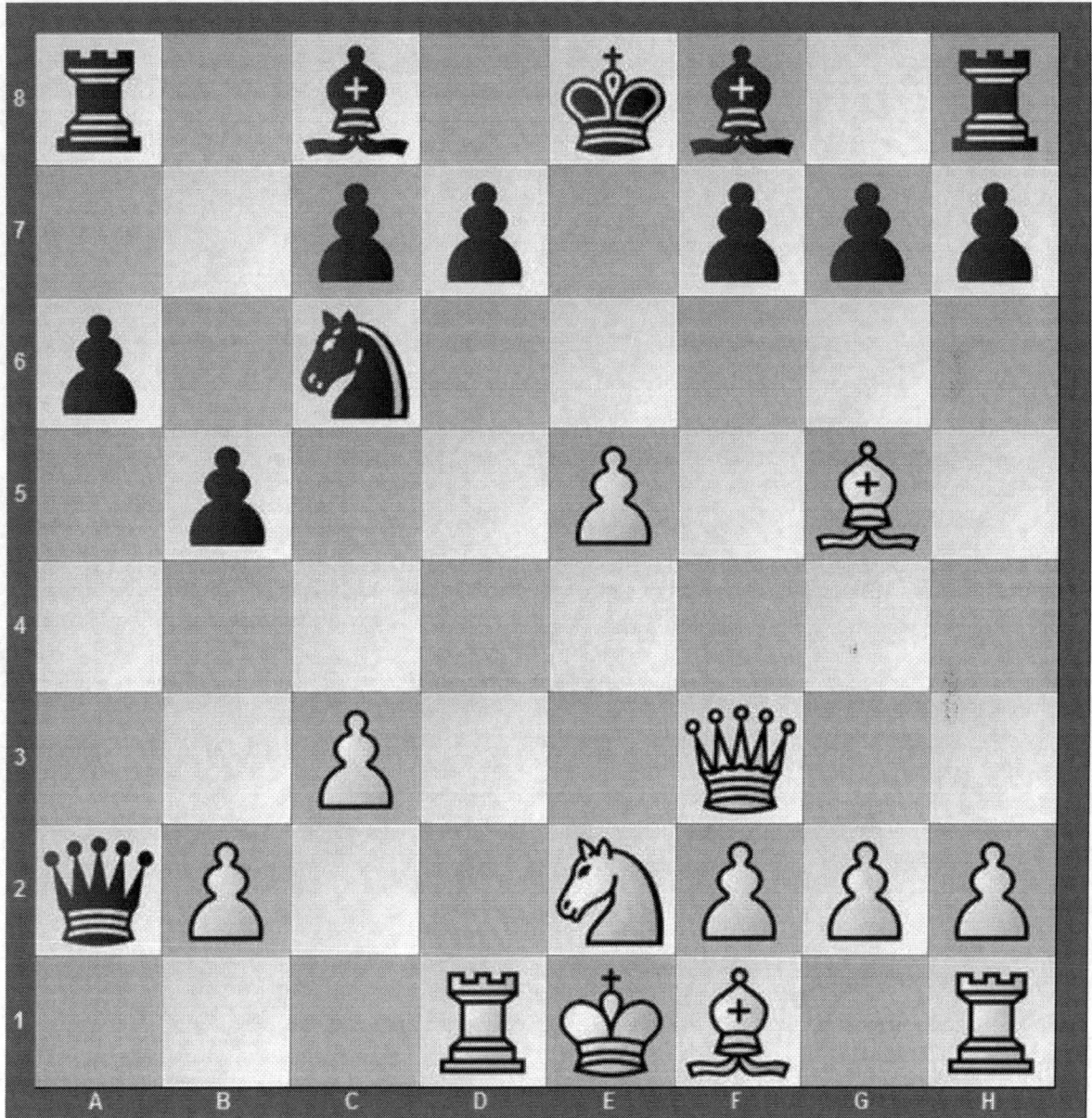

1		
2		

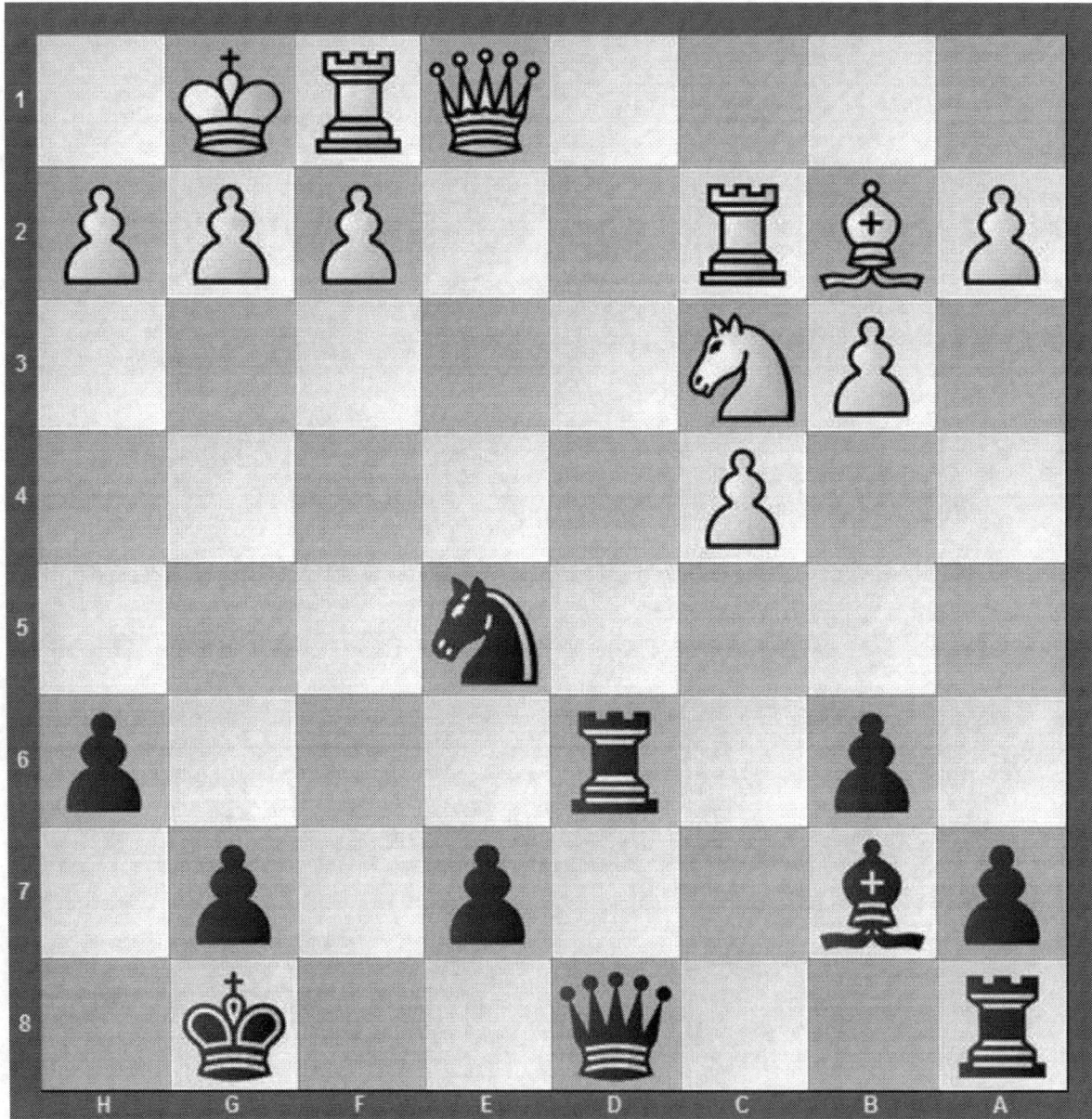

1		
2		

1		
2		

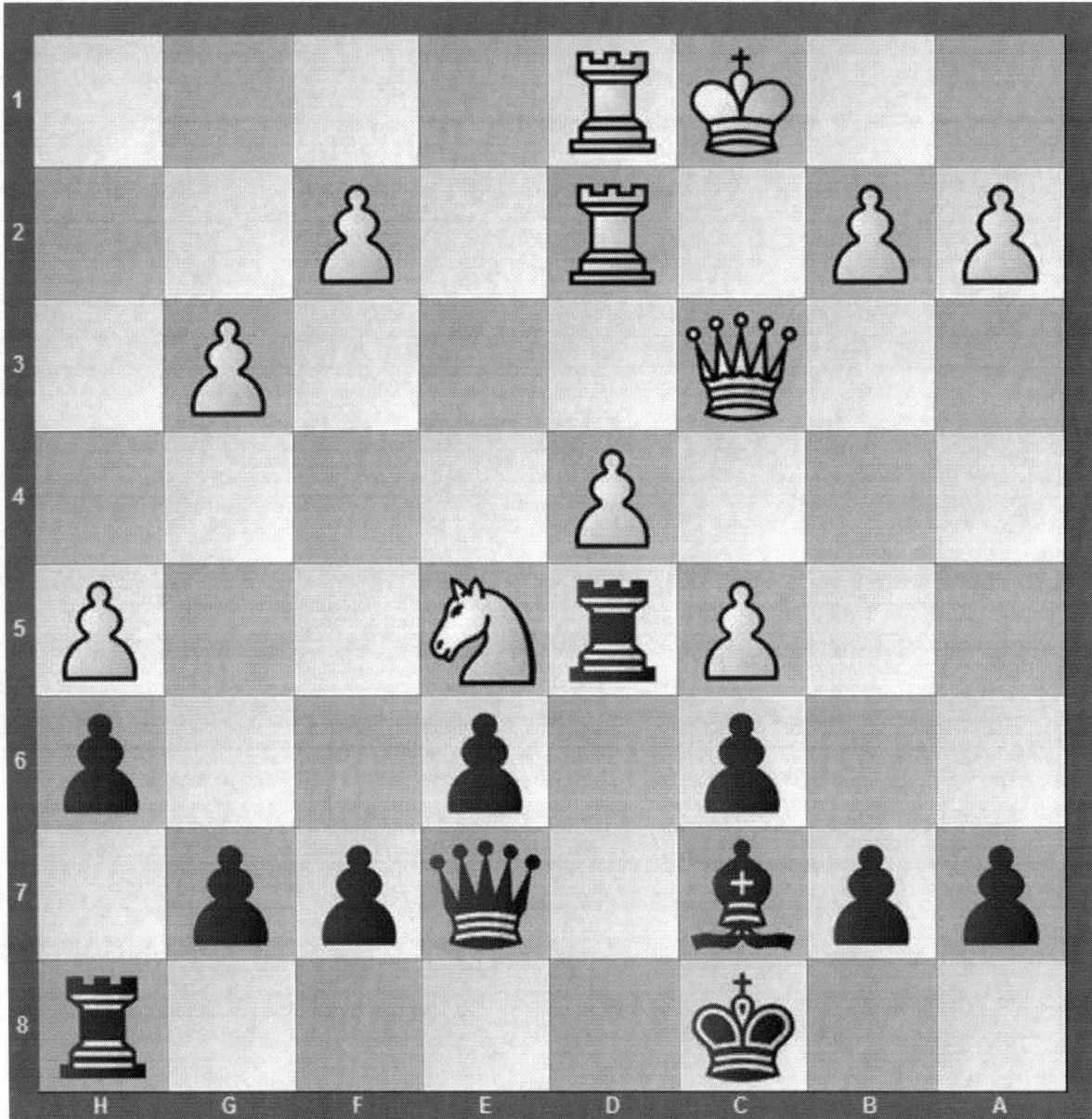

1		
2		

"Chess is my life, but my life is not chess." – **Anatoly Karpov**

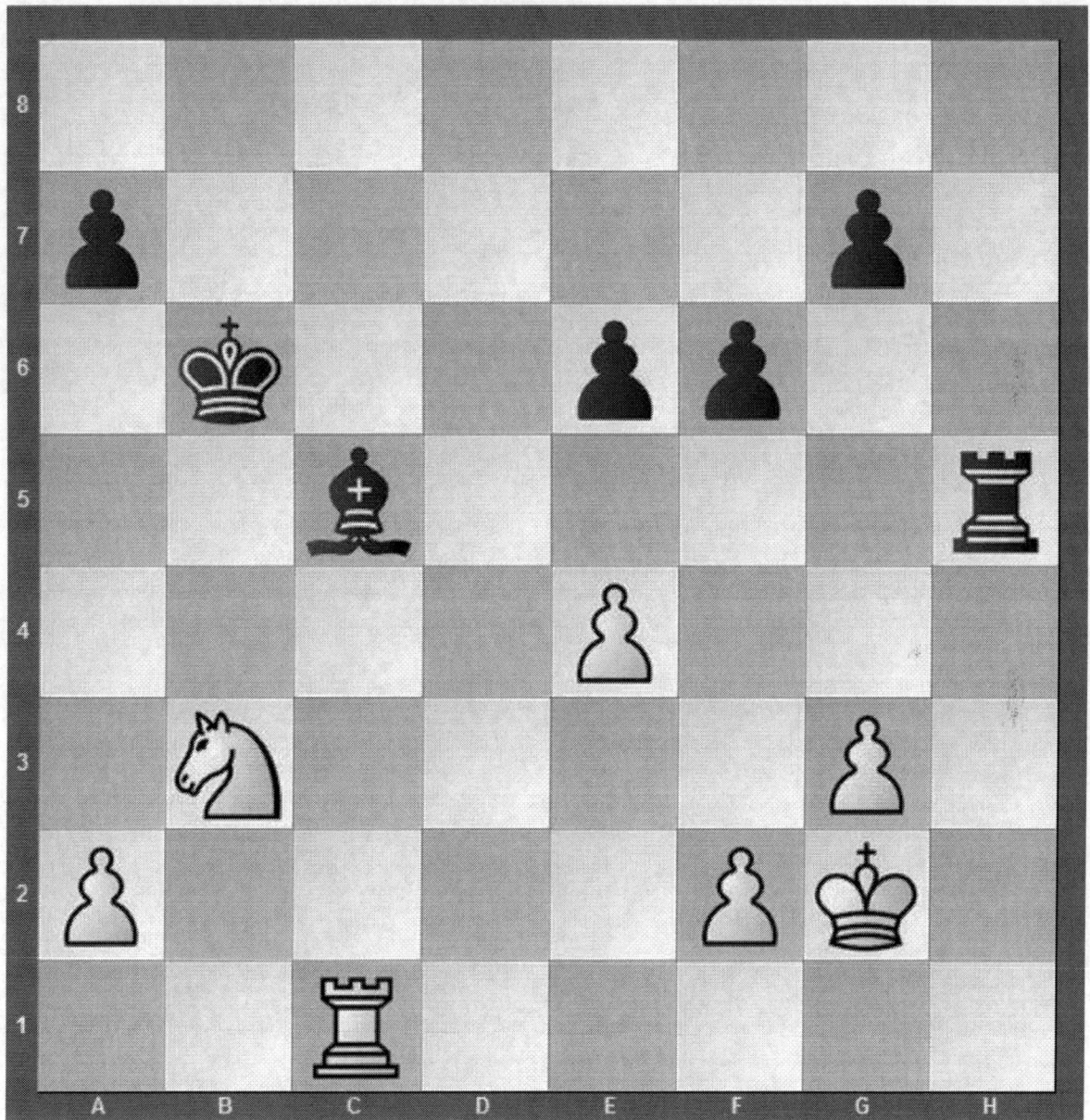

1		
2		

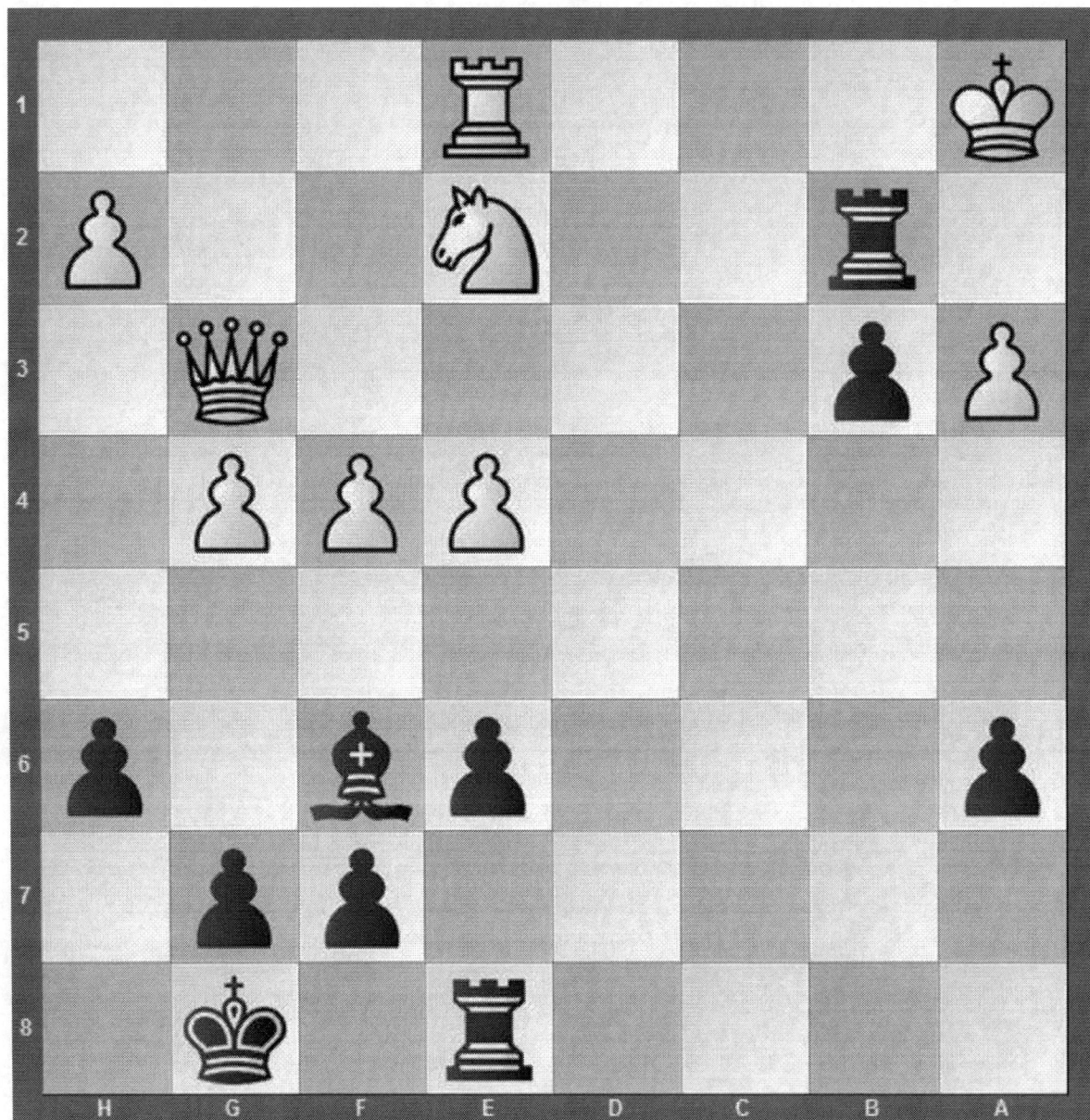

1		
2		

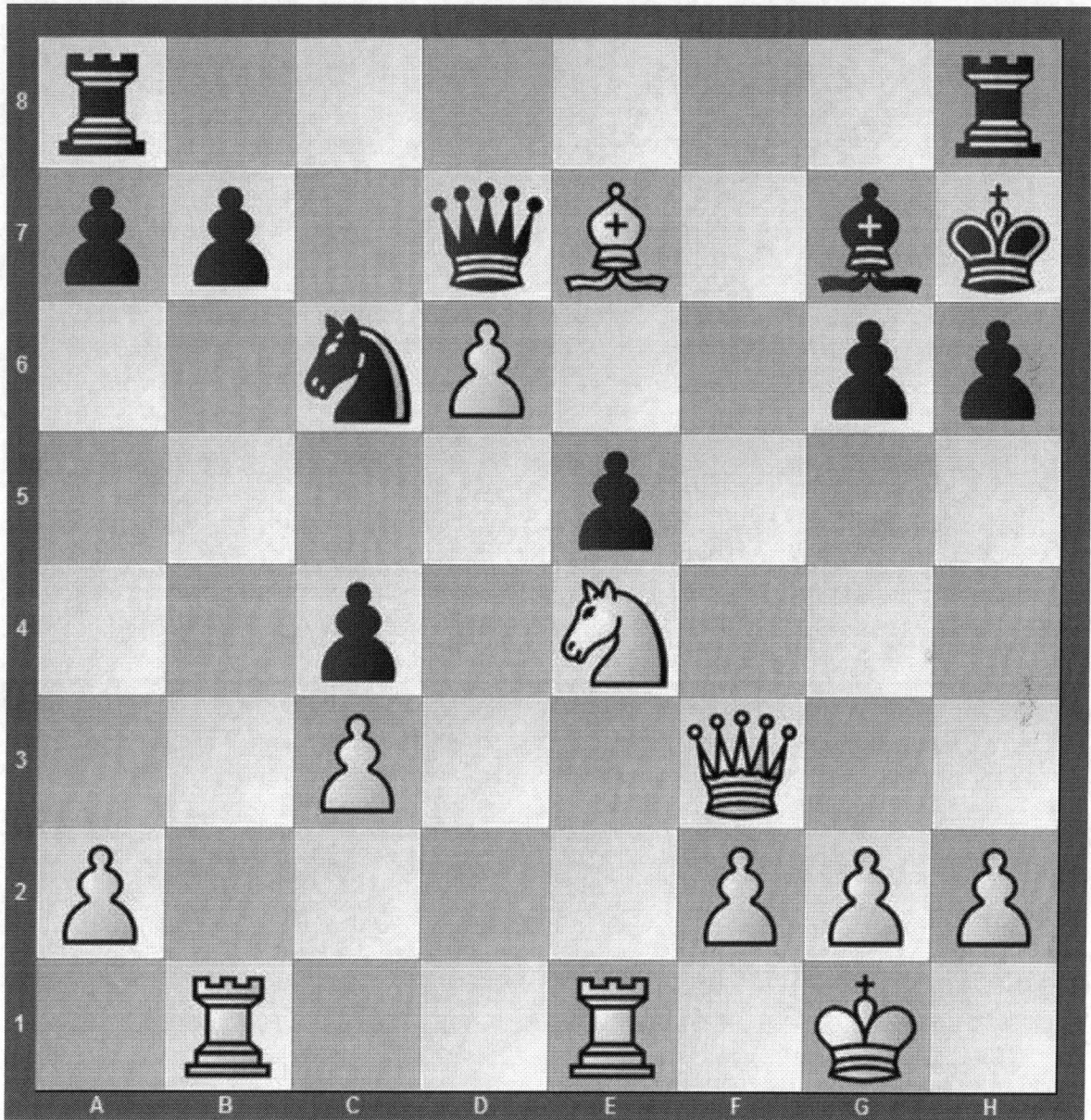

1		
2		

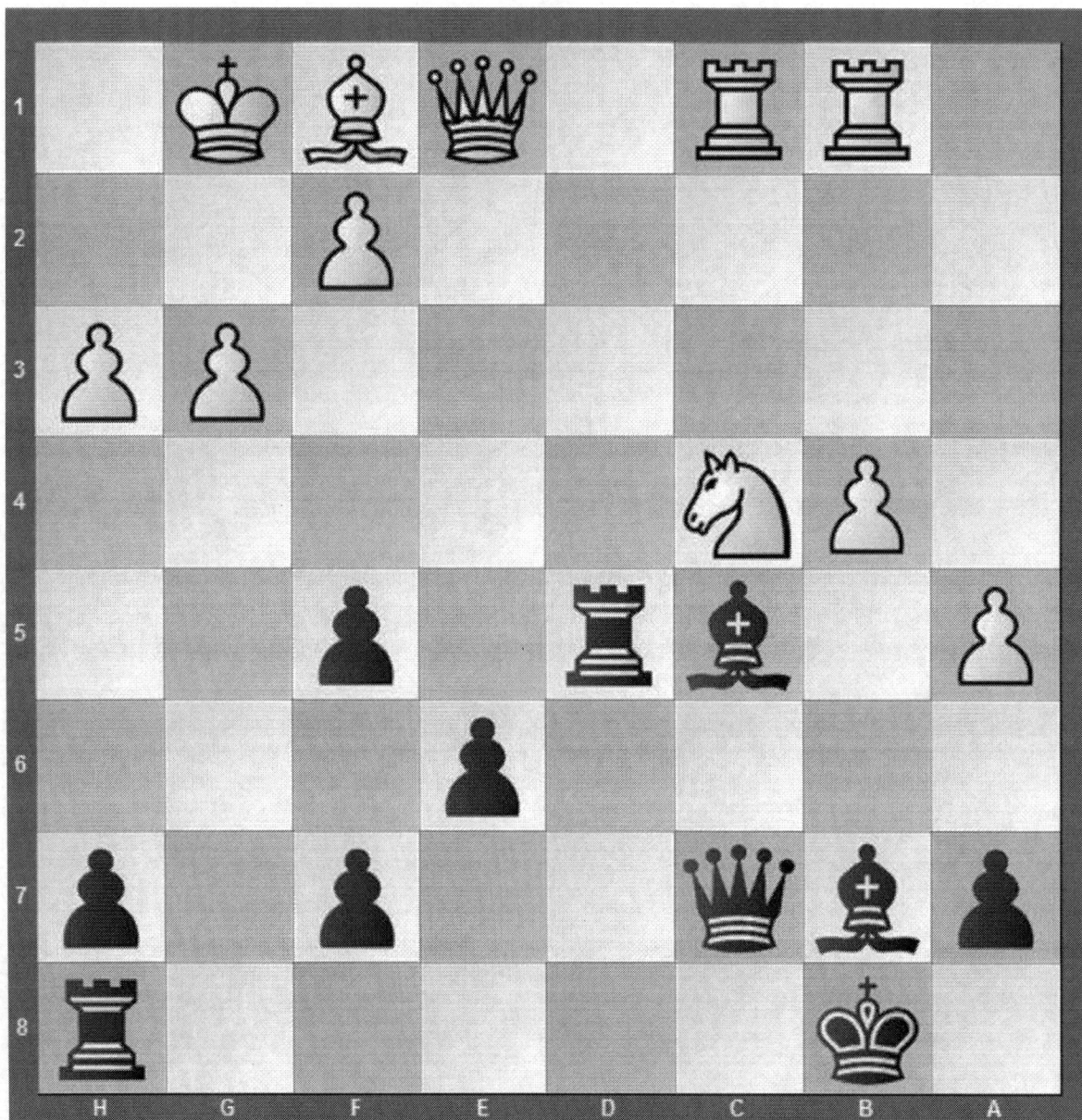

1		
2		

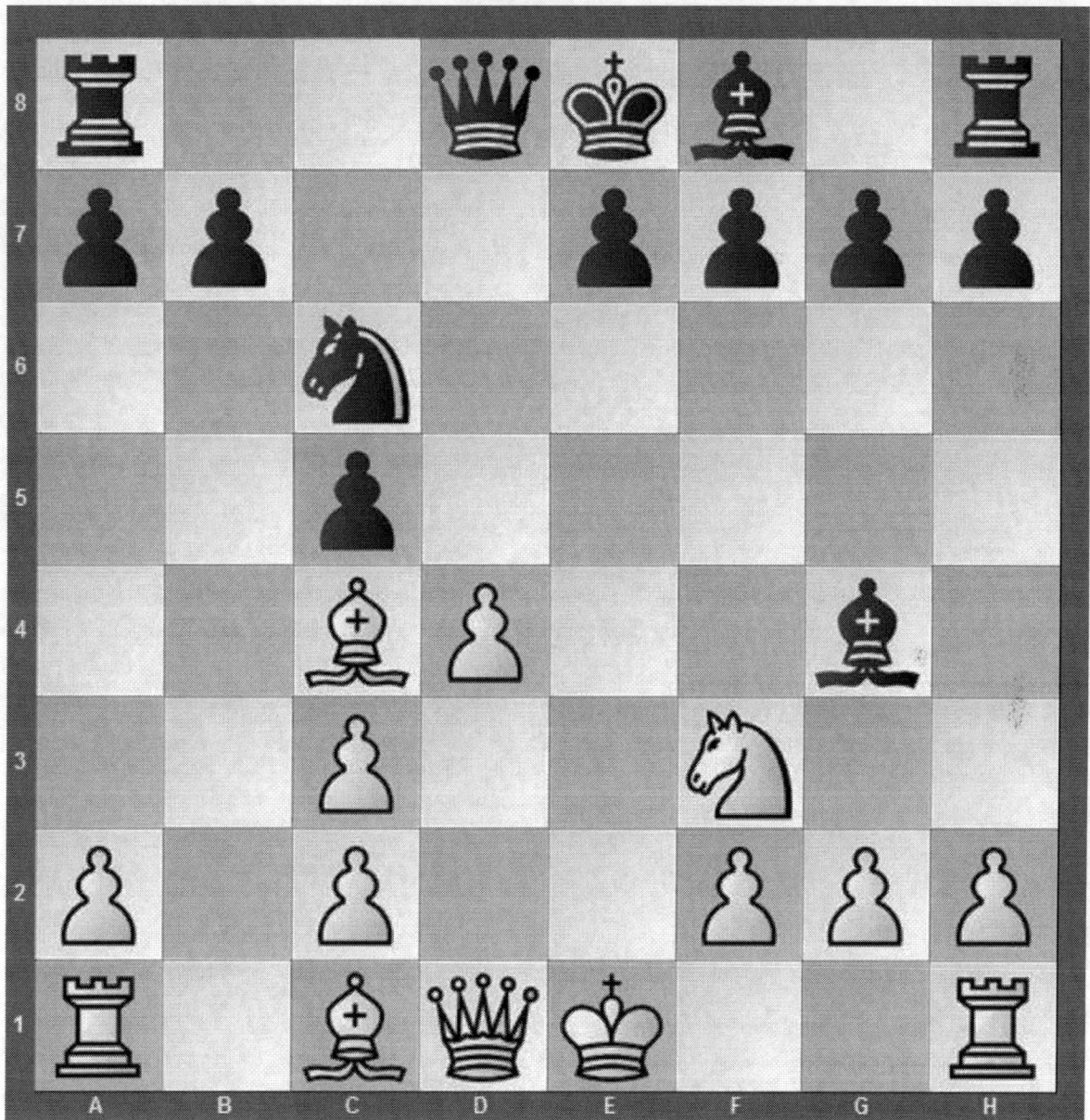

1		
2		

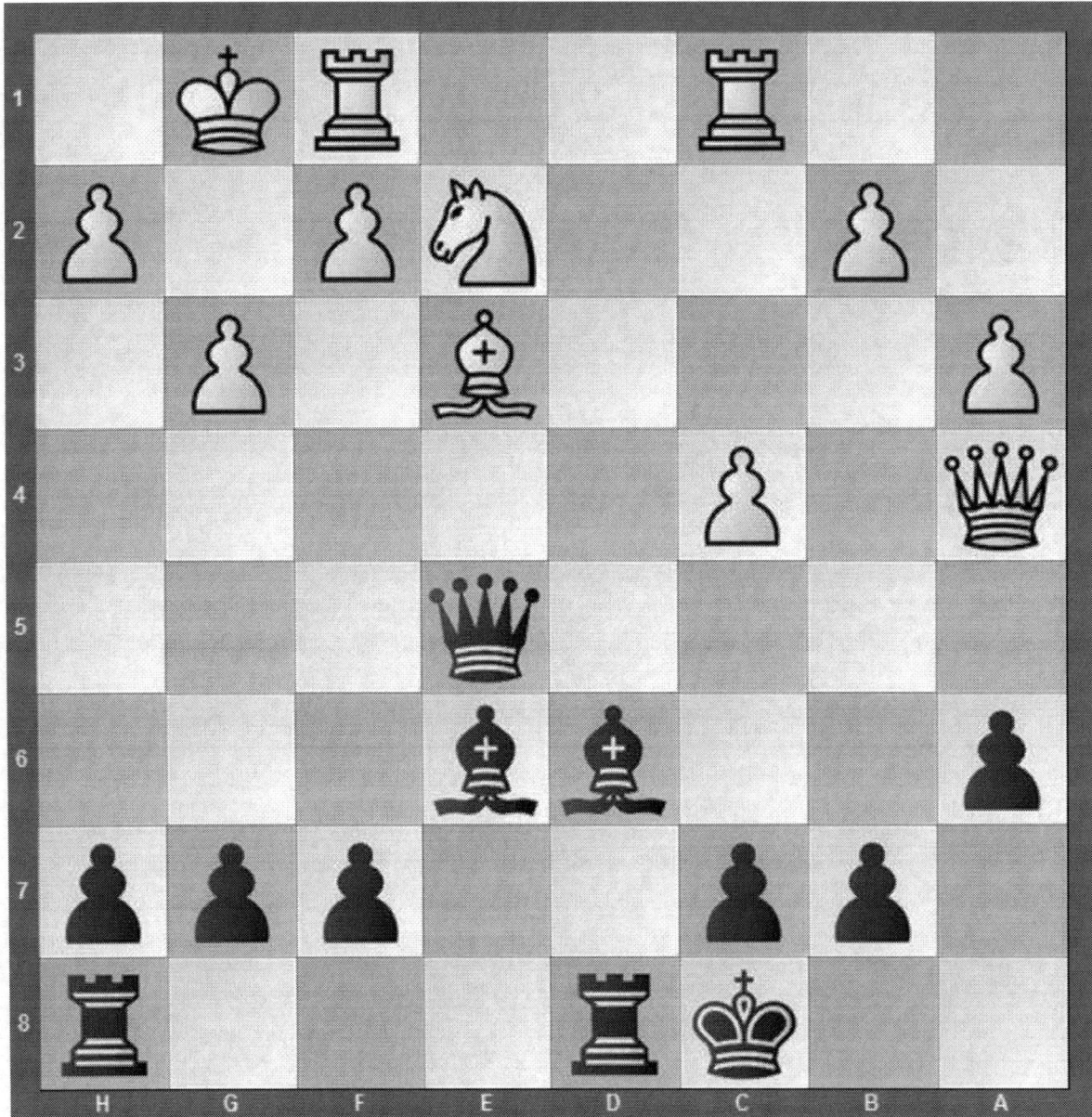

1		
2		

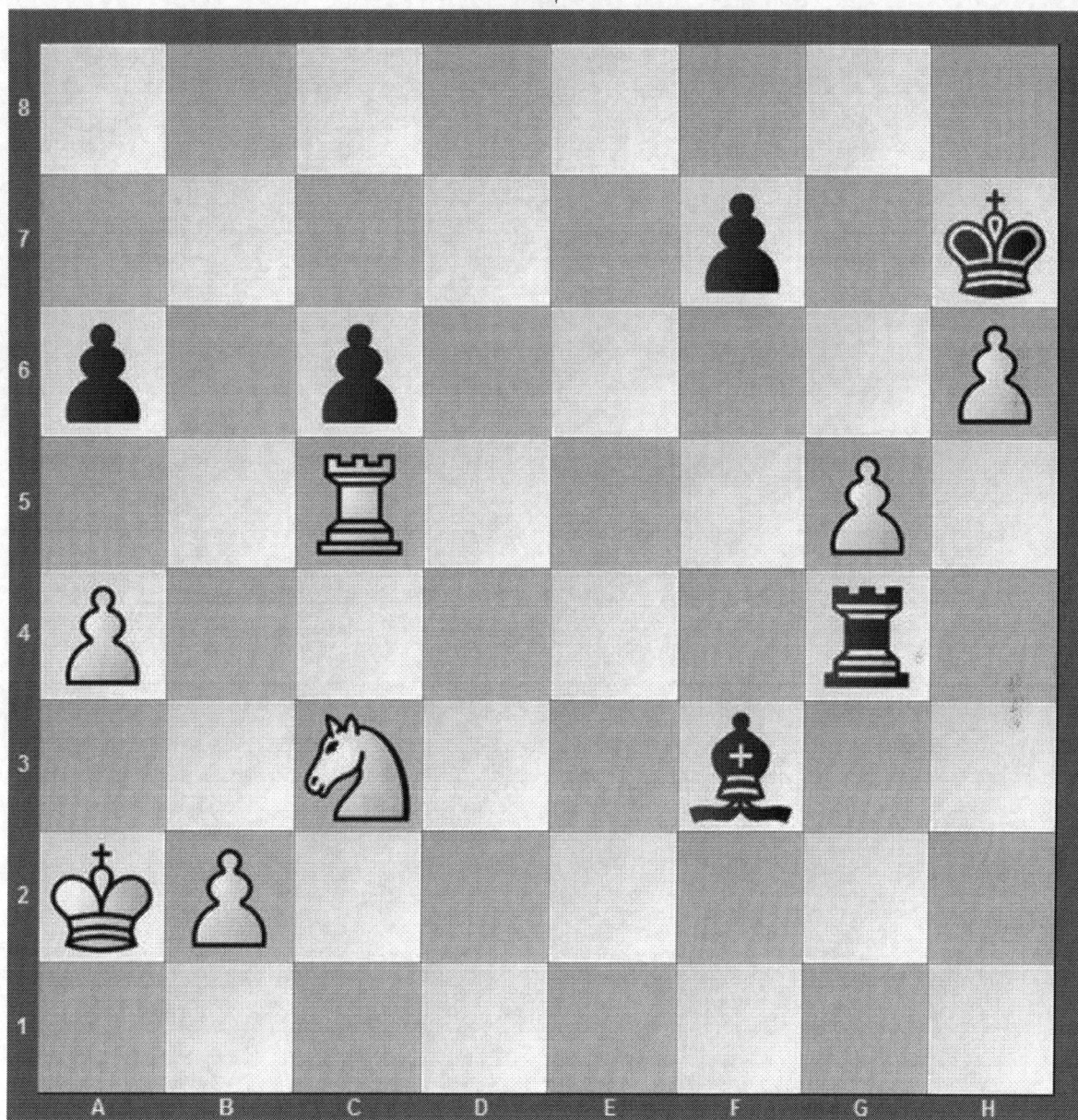

1		
2		

1		
2		

1		
2		

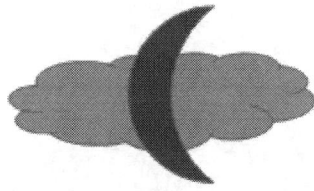

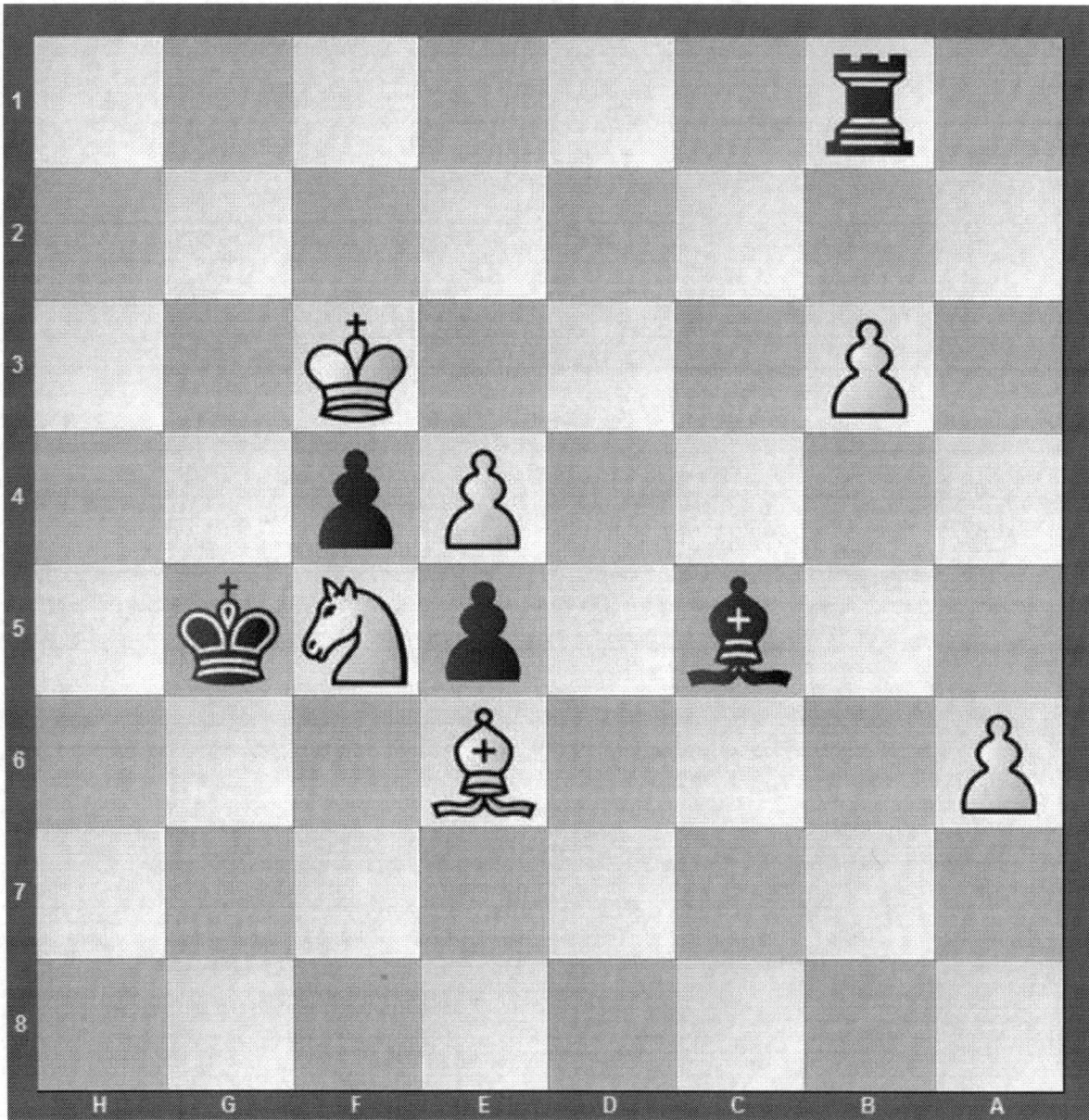

1		
2		

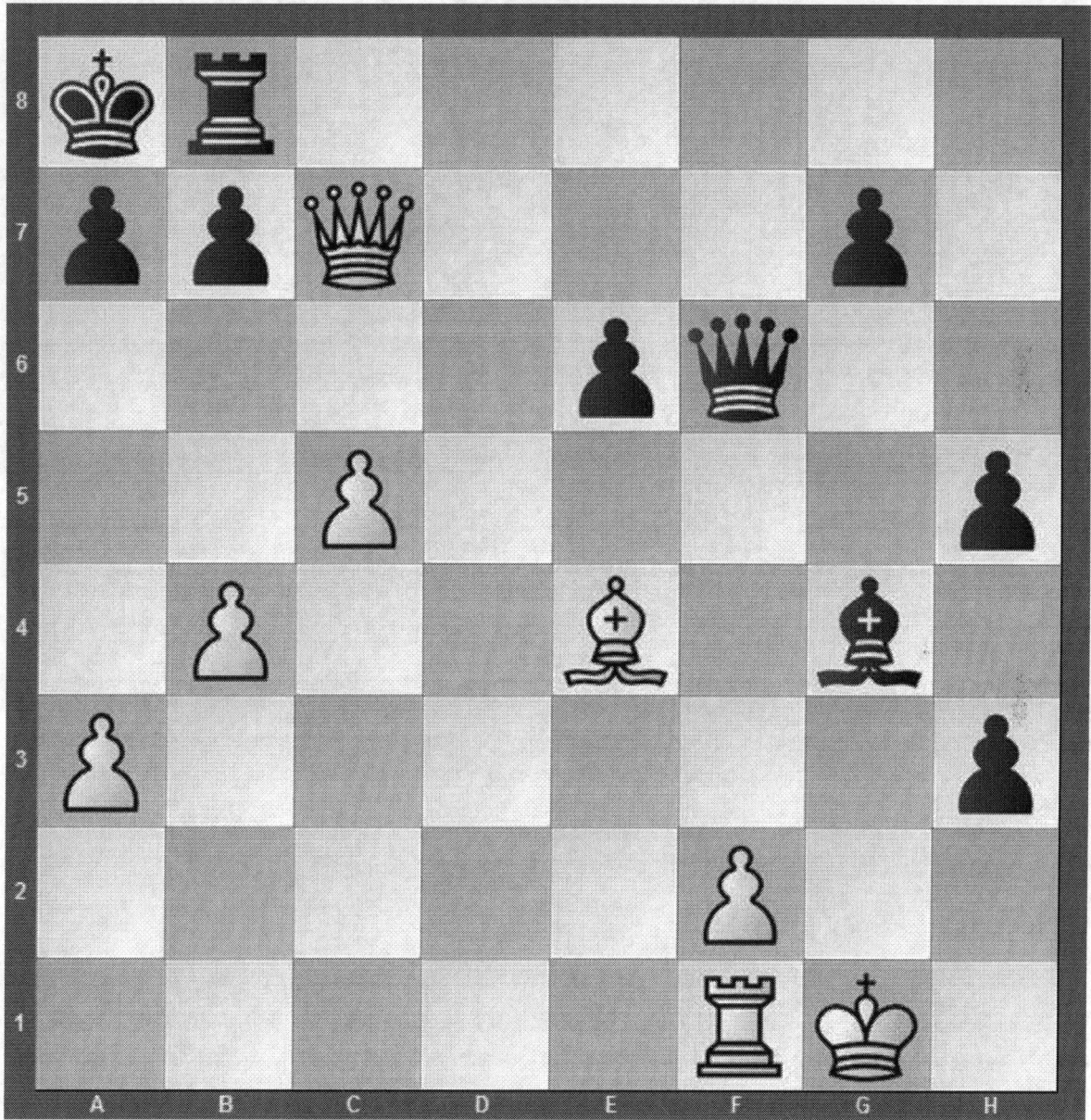

1		
2		

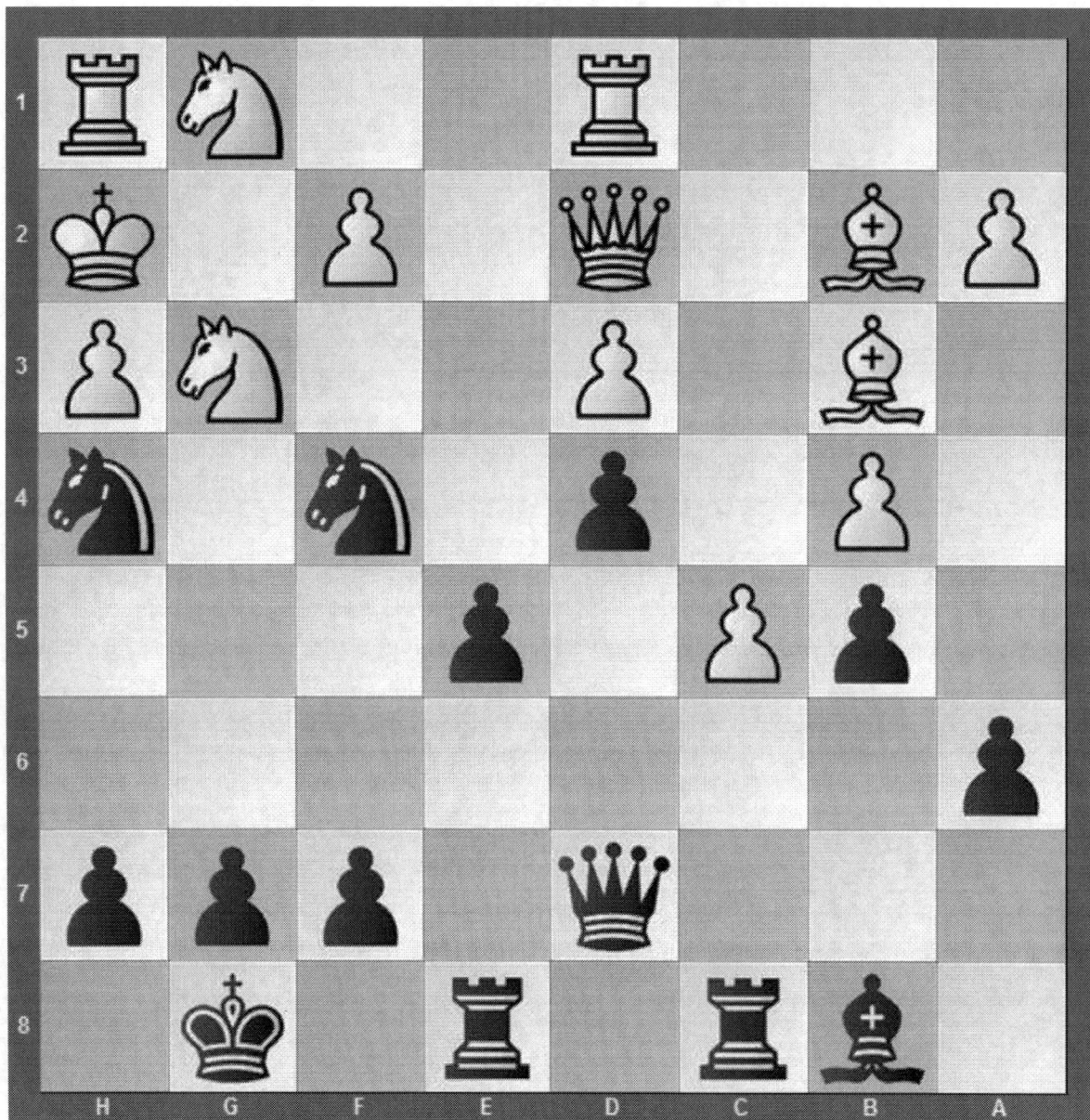

1		
2		

1		
2		

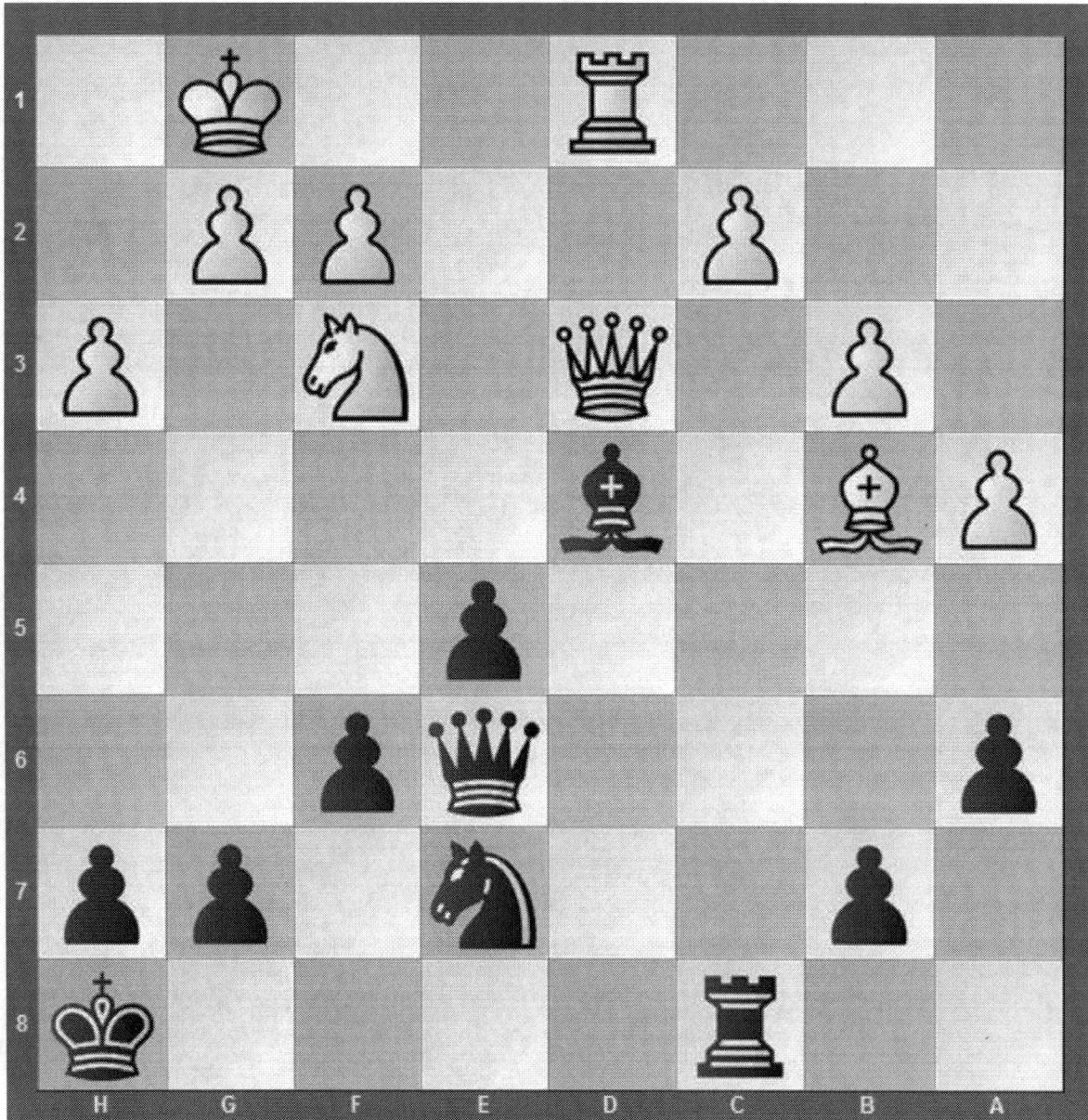

1		
2		

"I don't believe in psychology. I believe in good moves." – **Bobby Fischer**

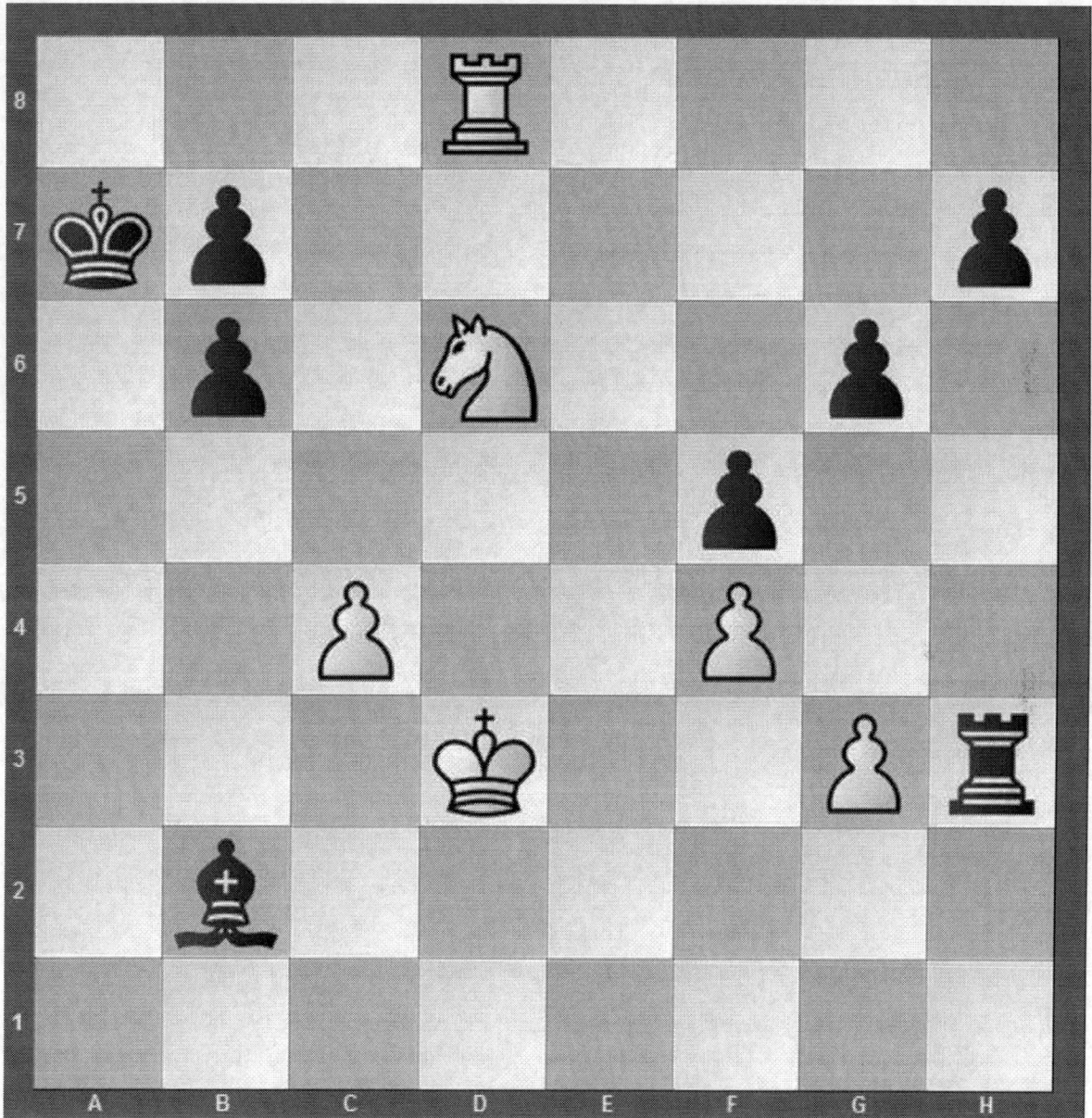

1		
2		

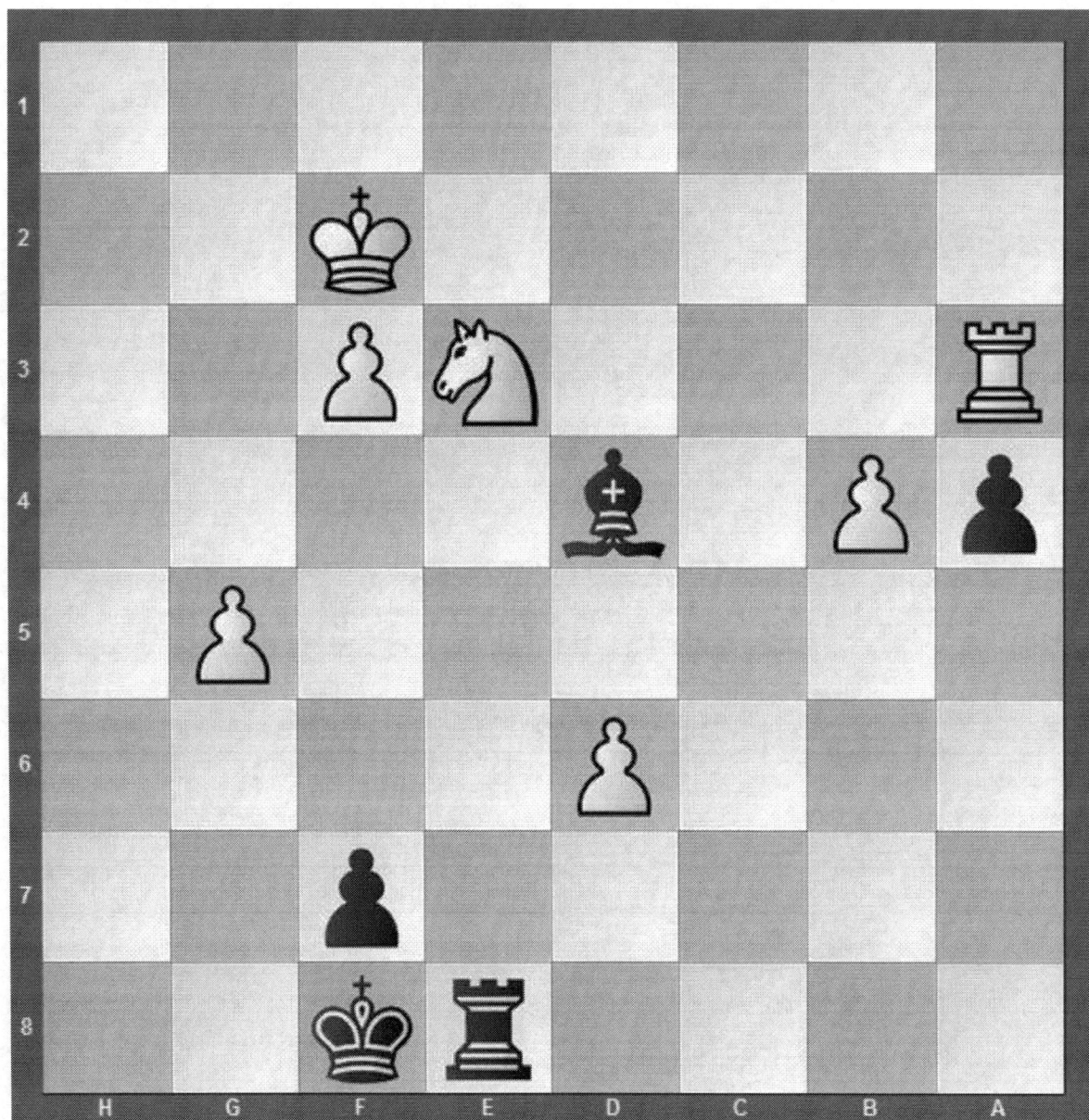

1		
2		

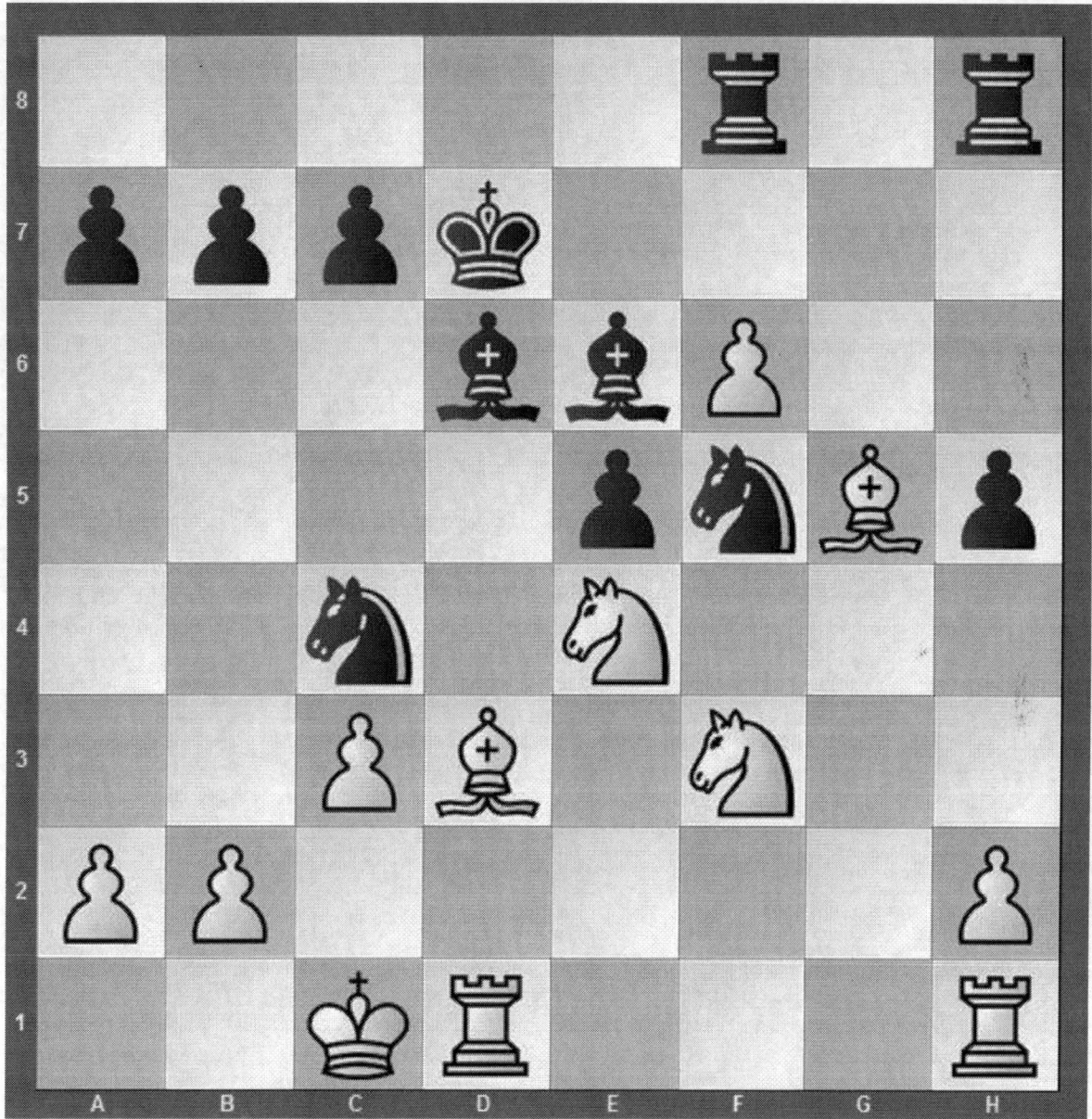

1		
2		

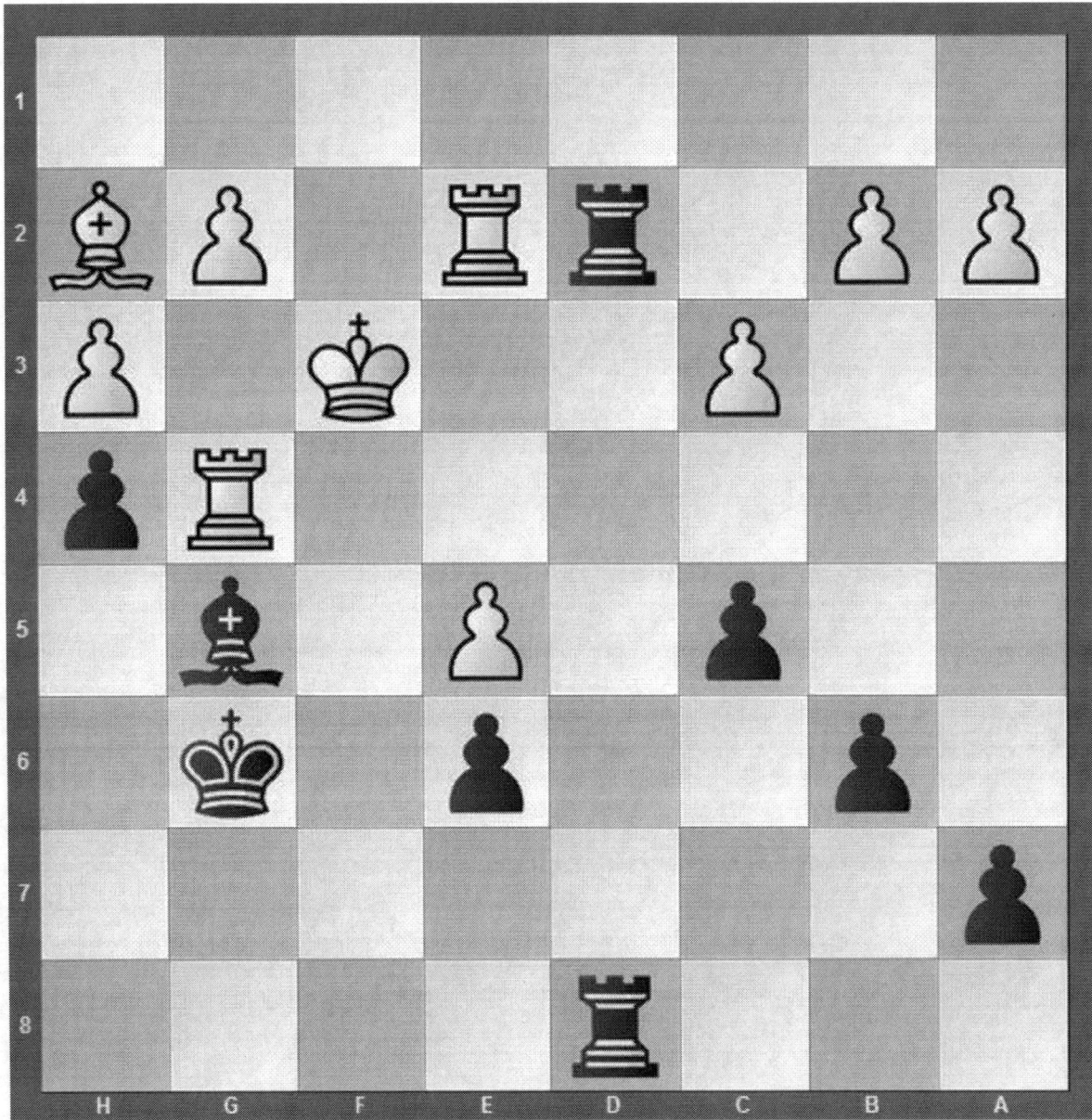

1		
2		

1		
2		

1		
2		

1		
2		

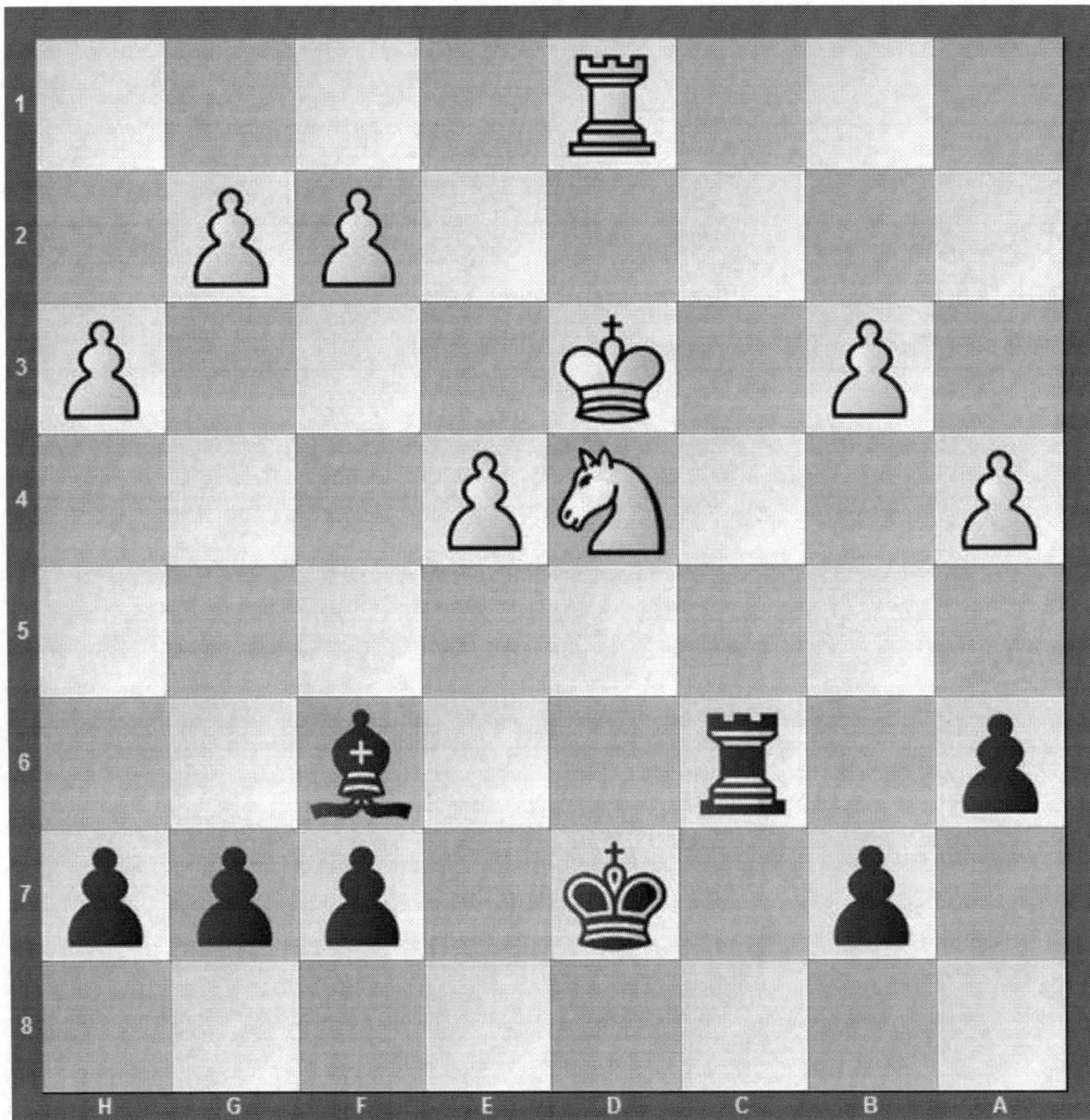

| 1 | | |
| 2 | | |

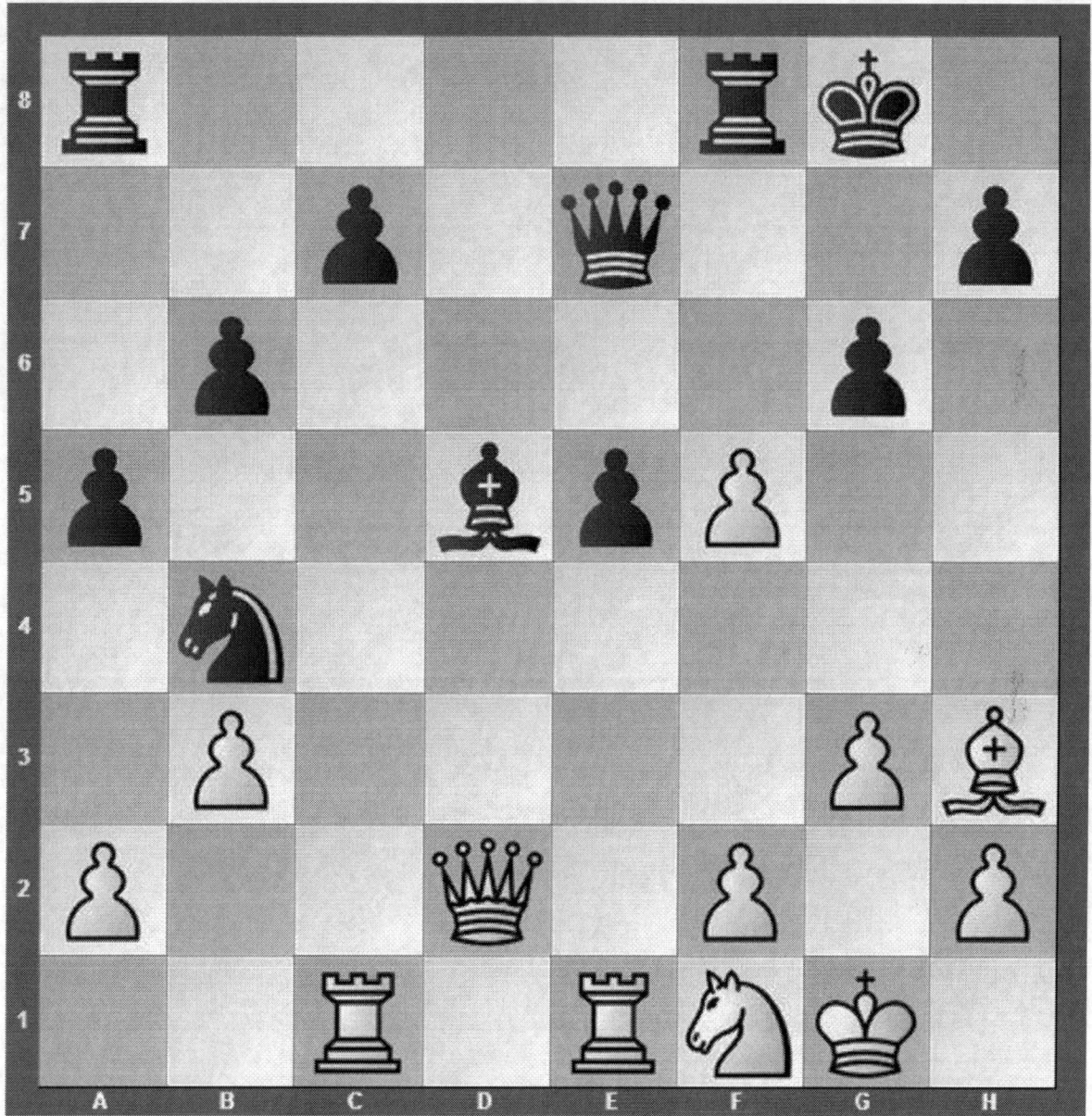

1		
2		

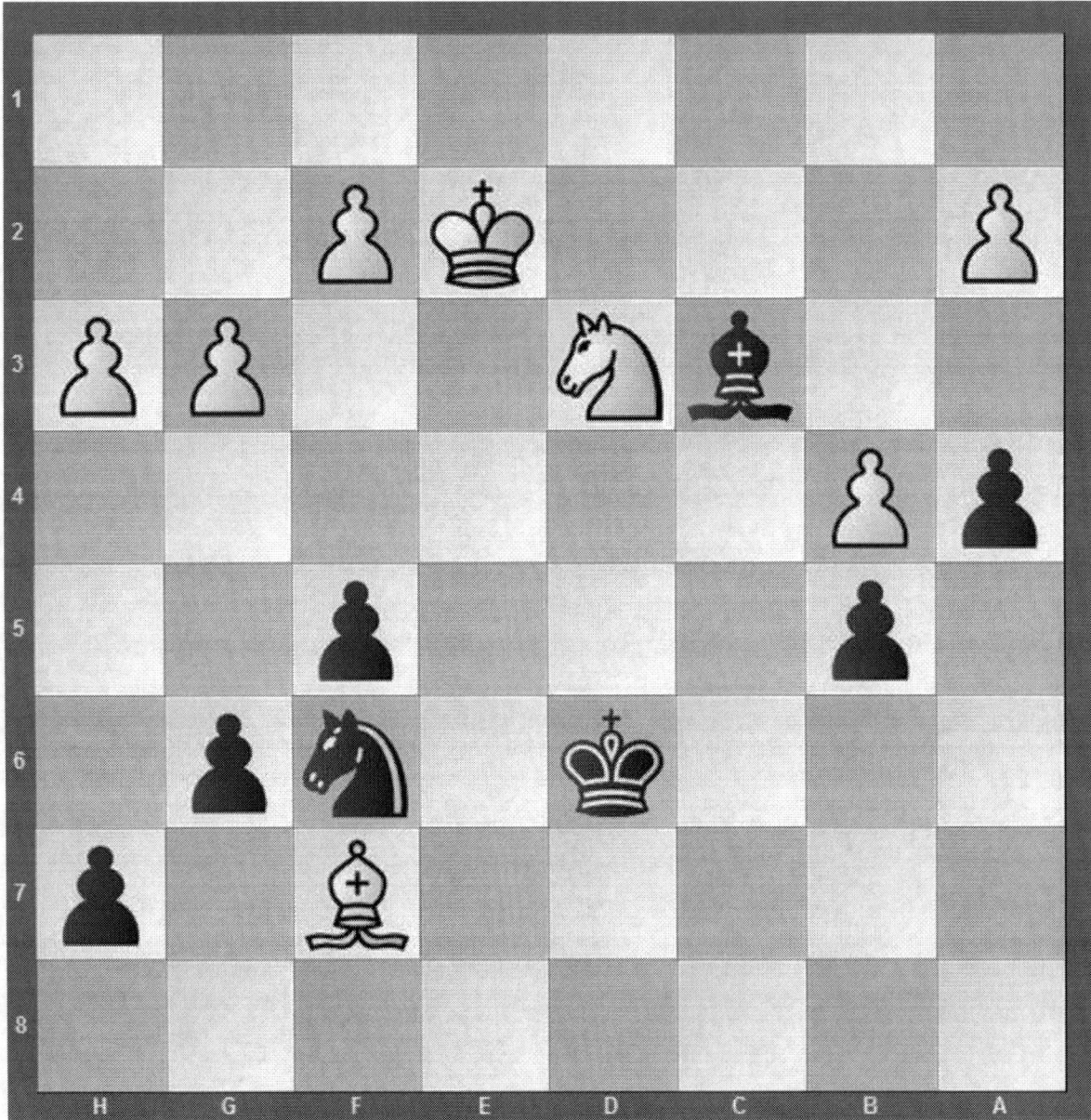

1		
2		

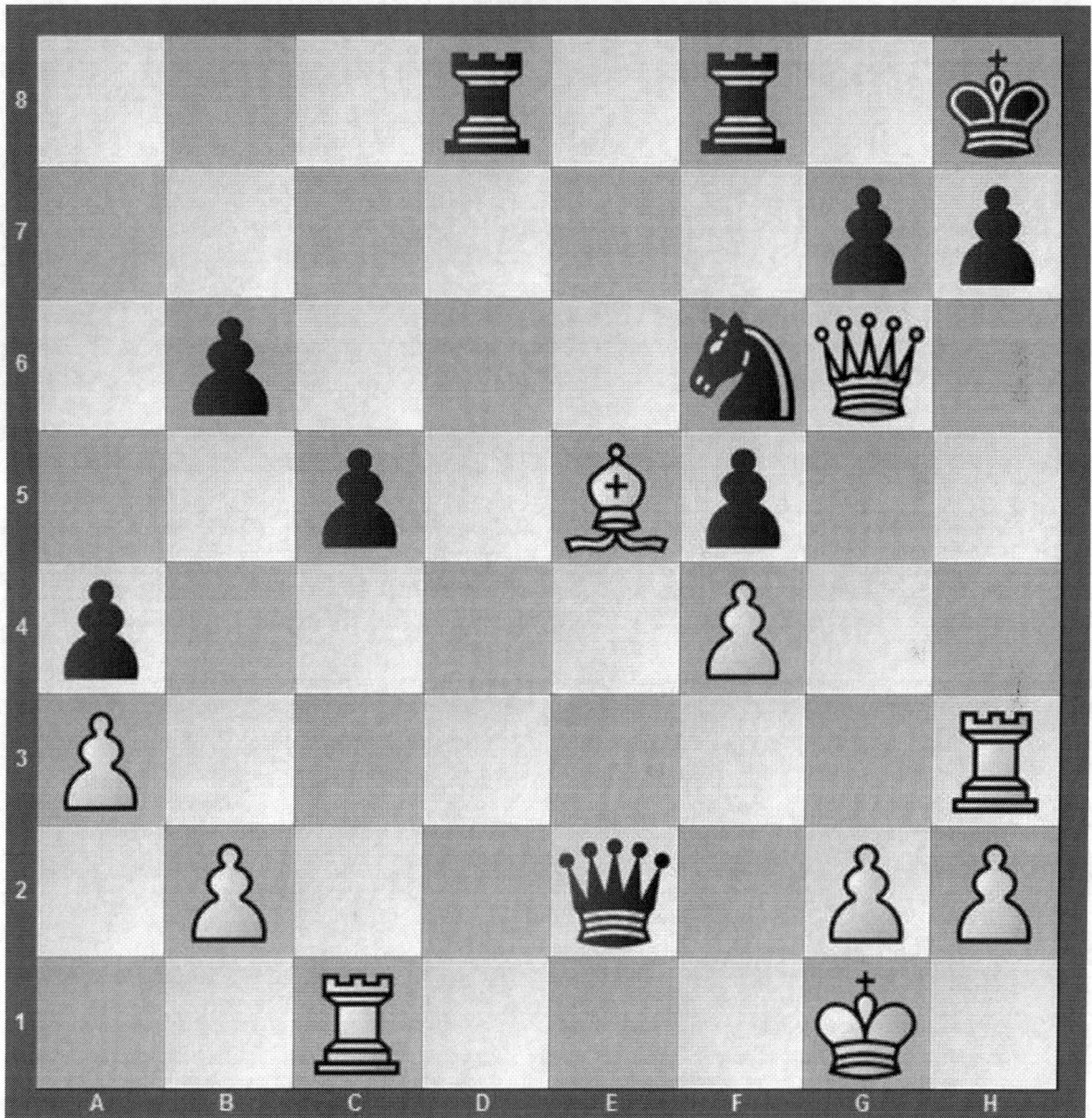

1		
2		

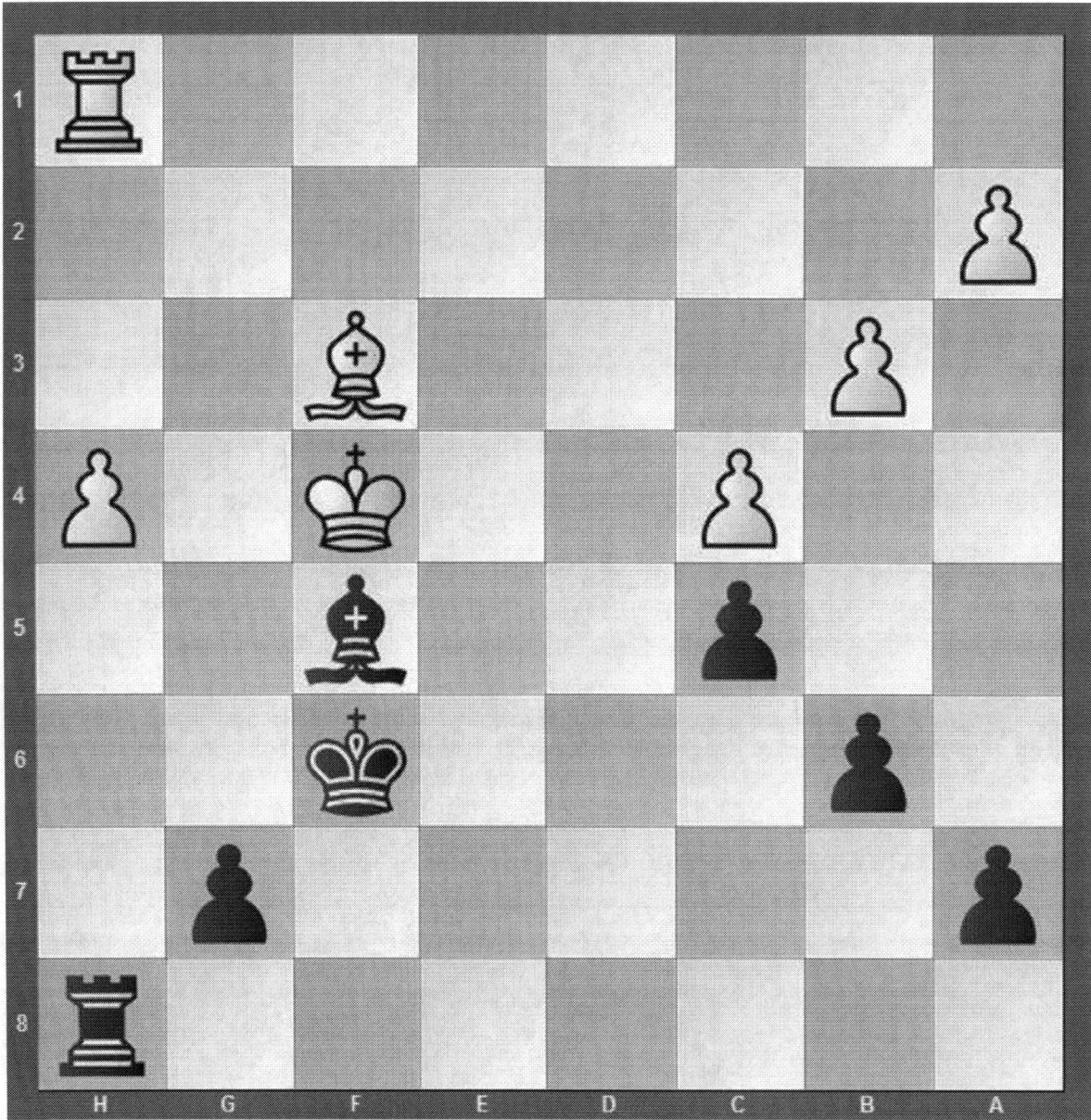

1		
2		

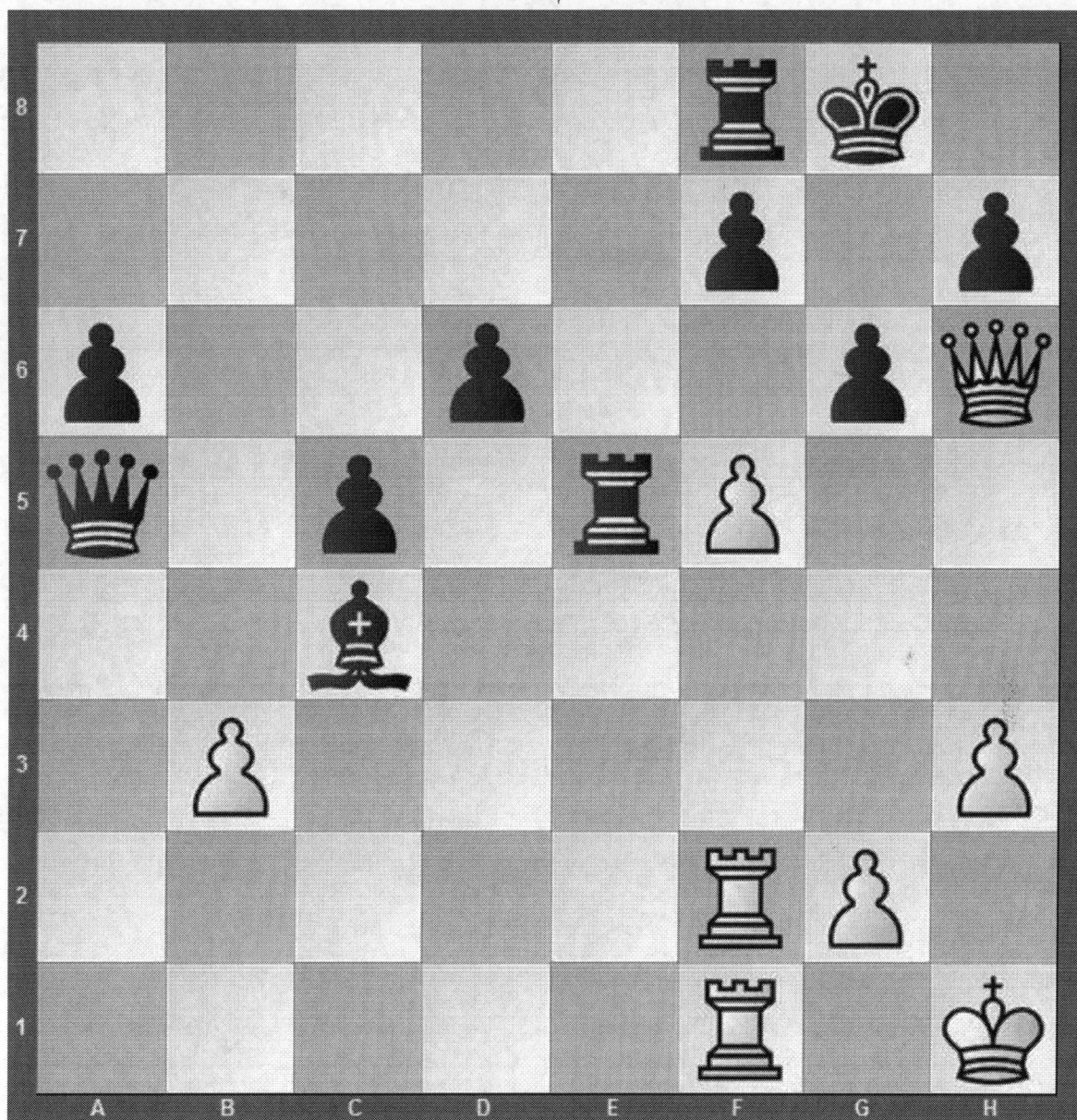

1		
2		

1	
2	

"*I have added these principles to the law: get the Knights into action before both Bishops are developed.*" – **Emanuel Lasker**

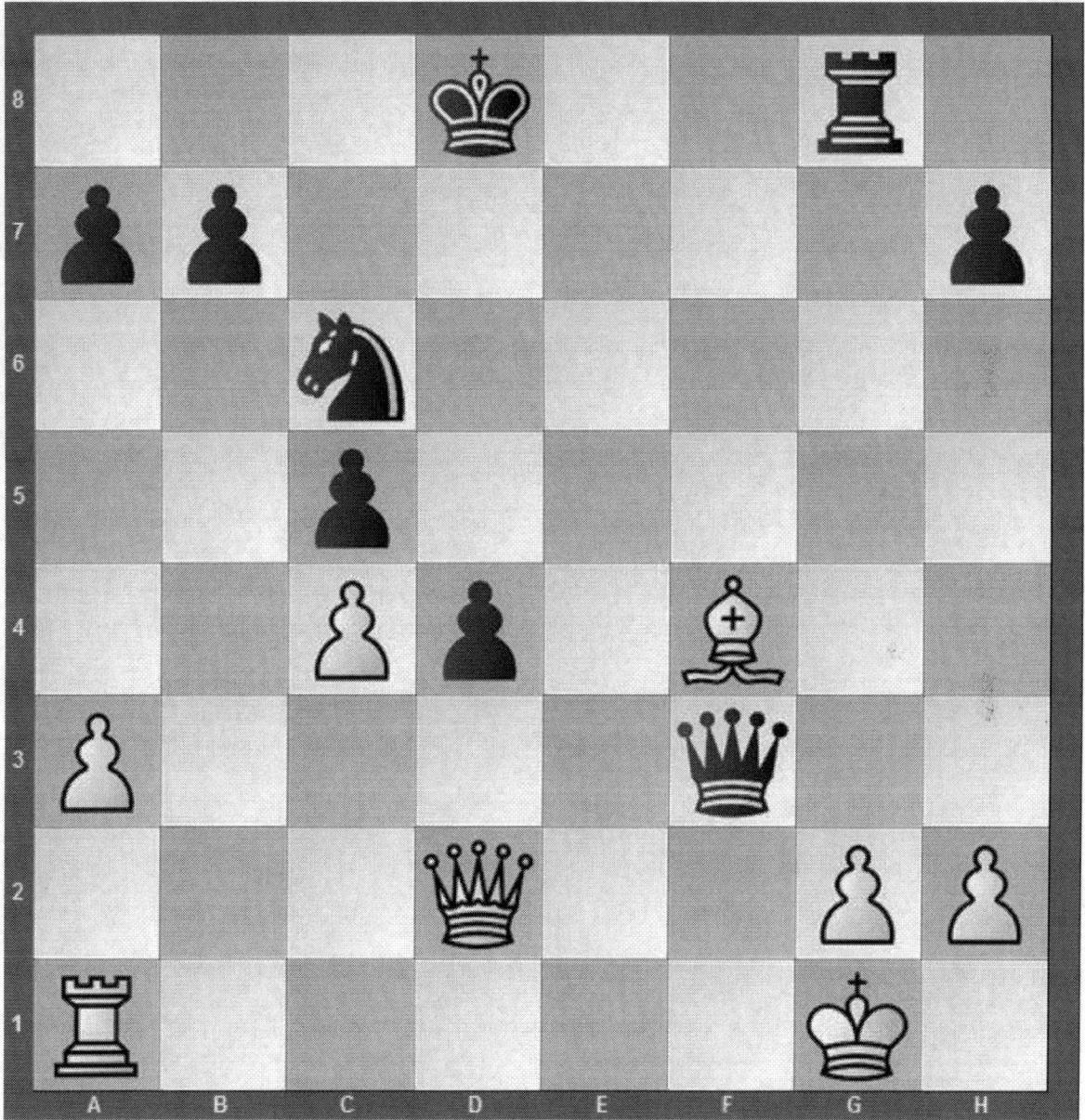

1		
2		

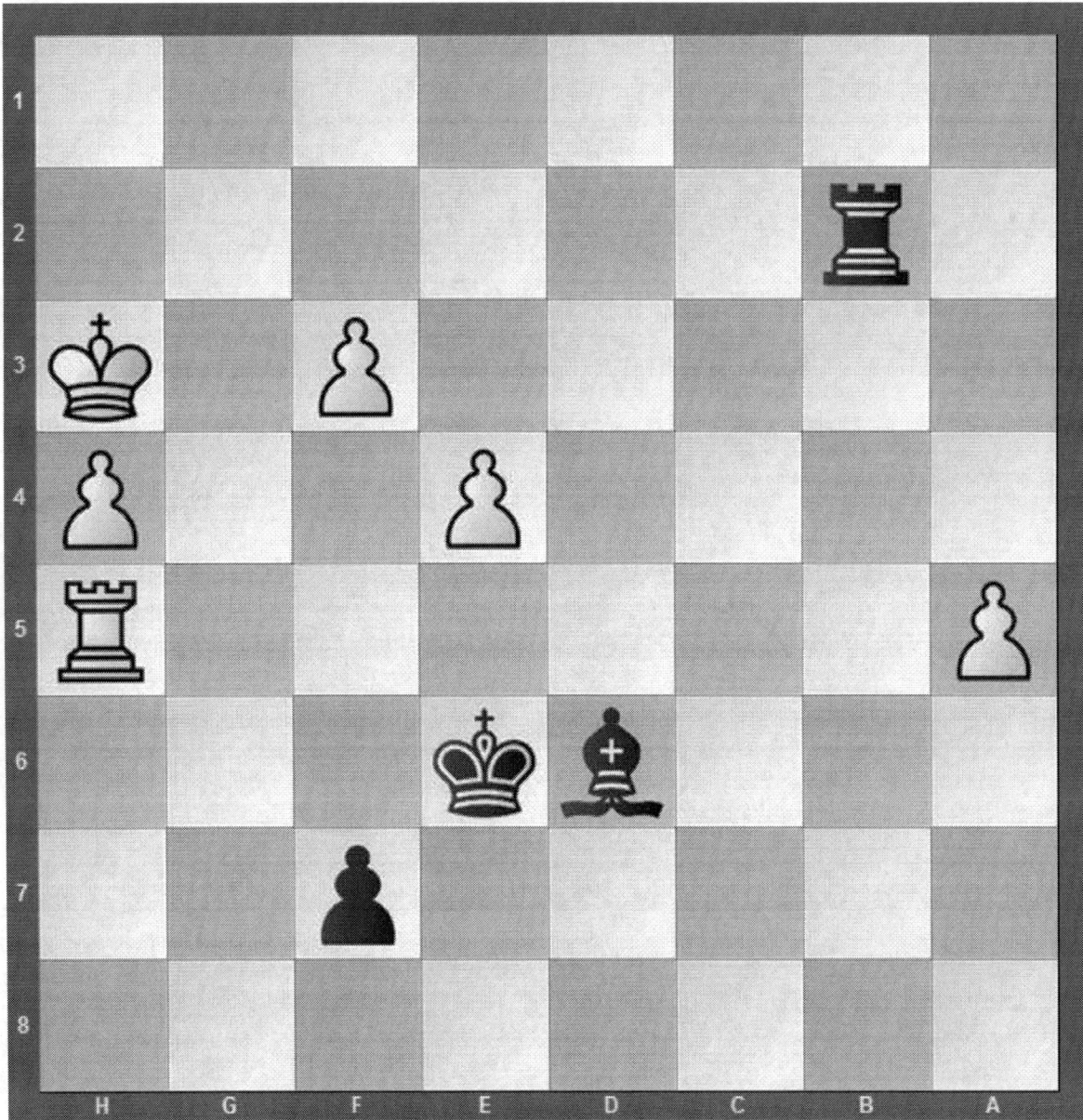

1		
2		

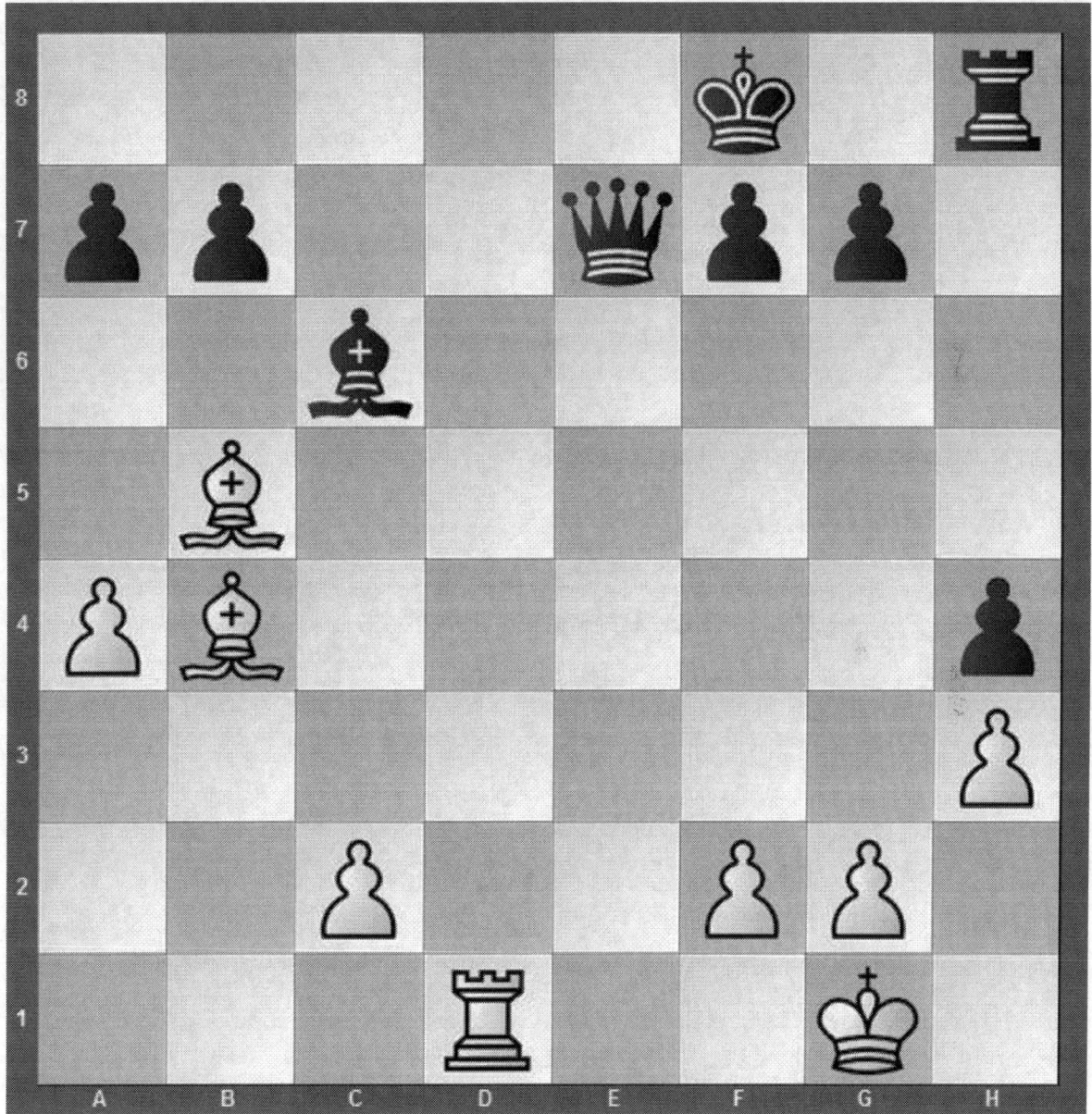

1		
2		

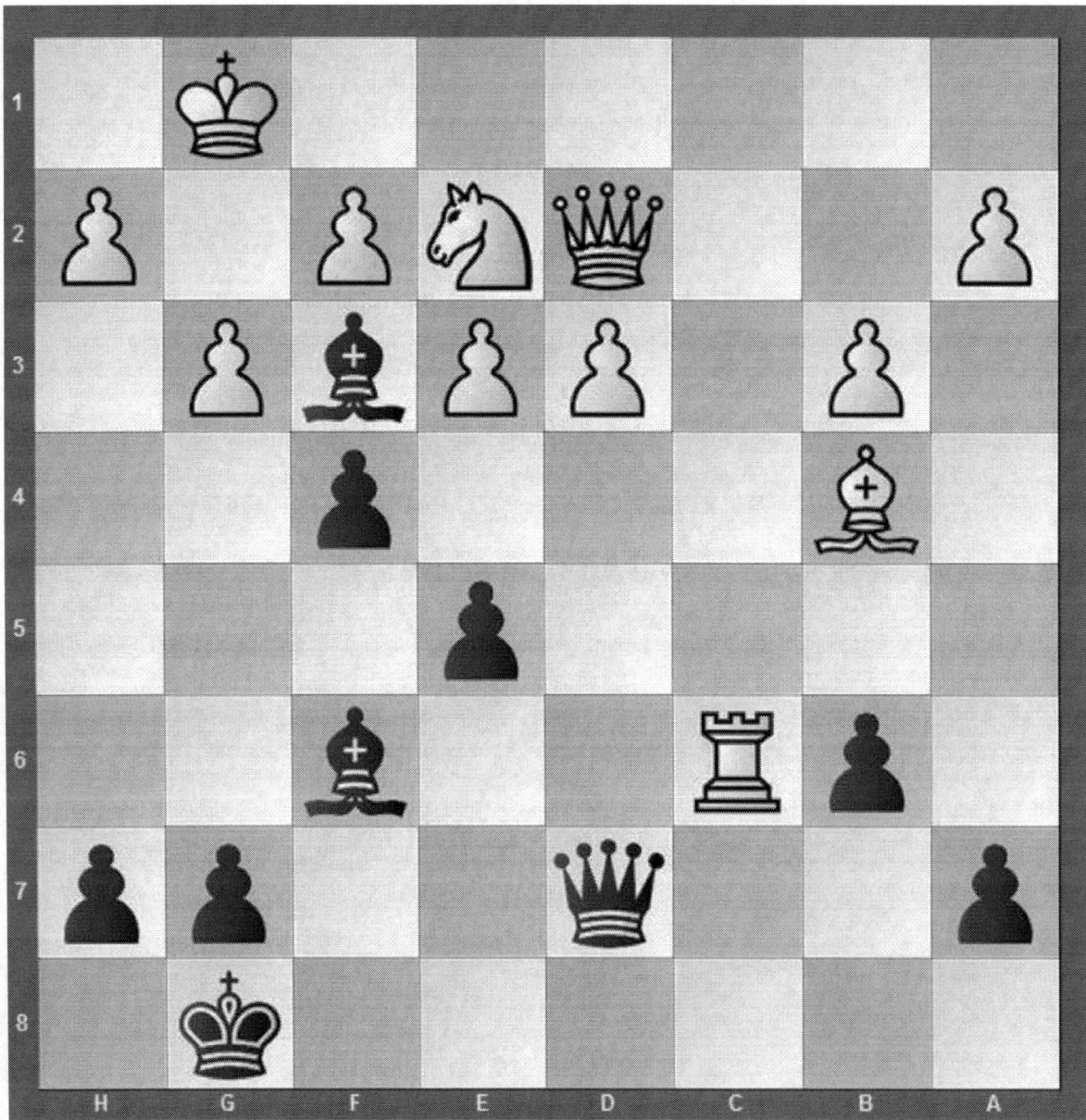

1		
2		

| 1 | | |
| 2 | | |

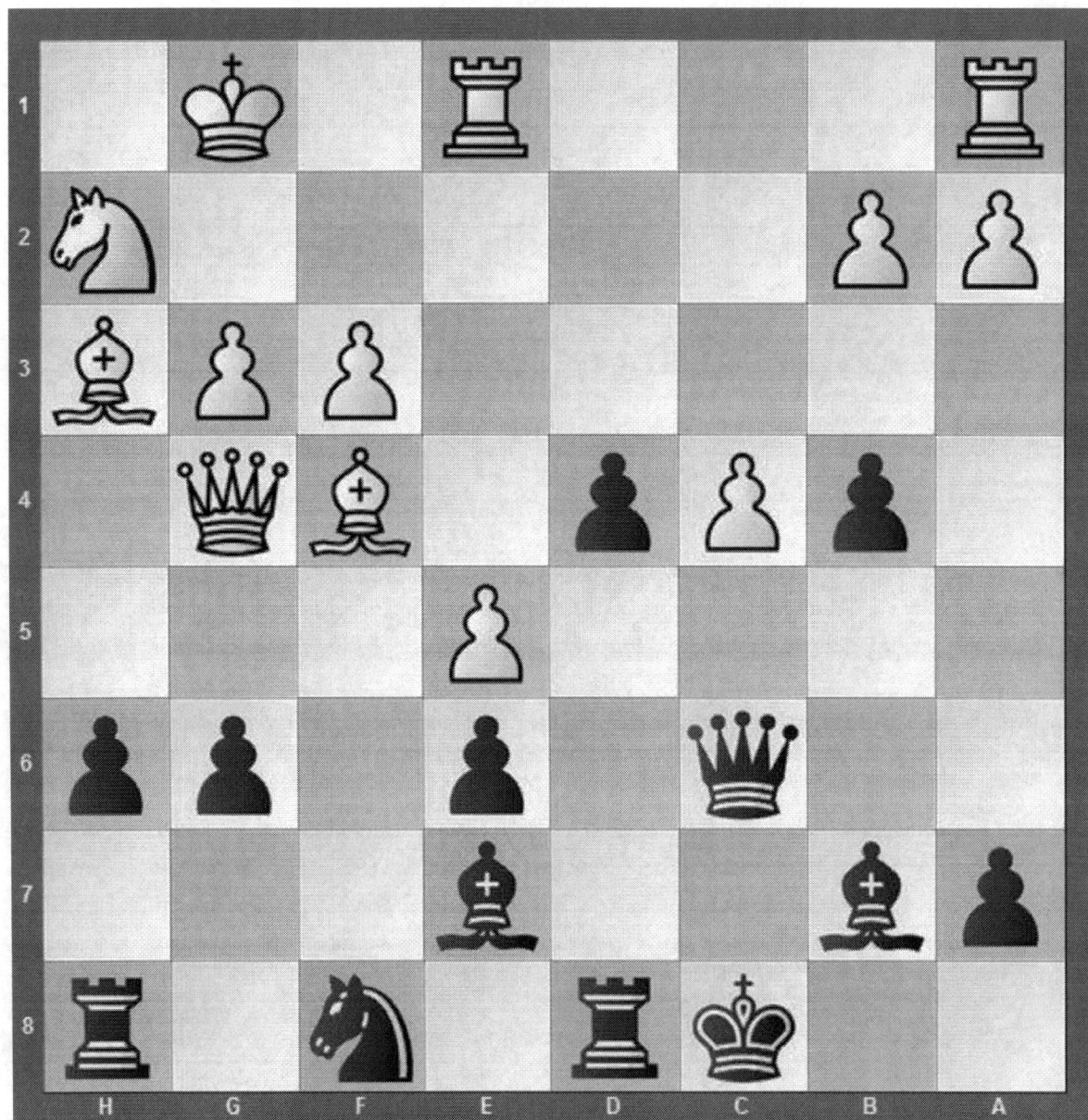

1		
2		

1		
2		

1		
2		

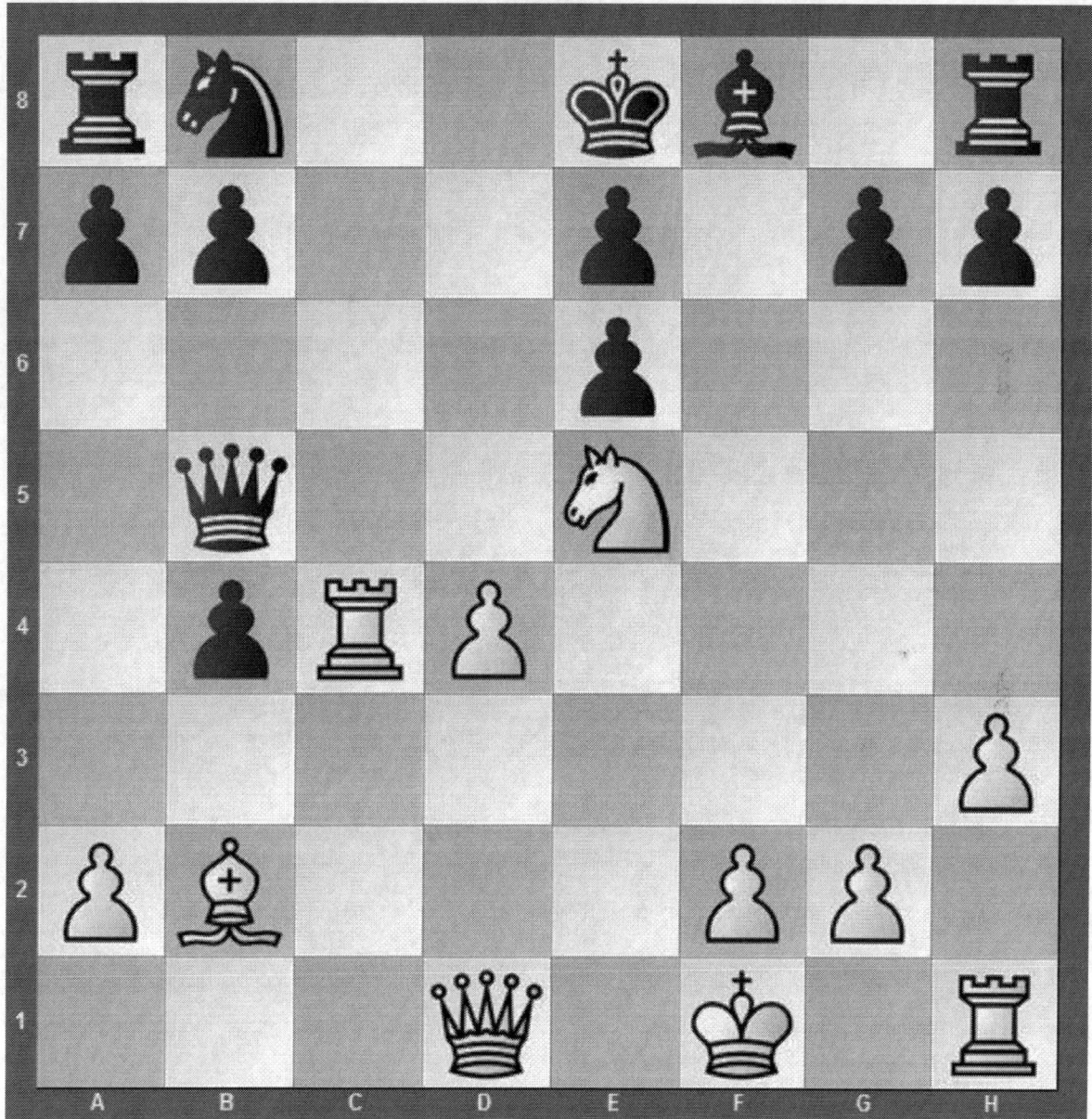

1		
2		

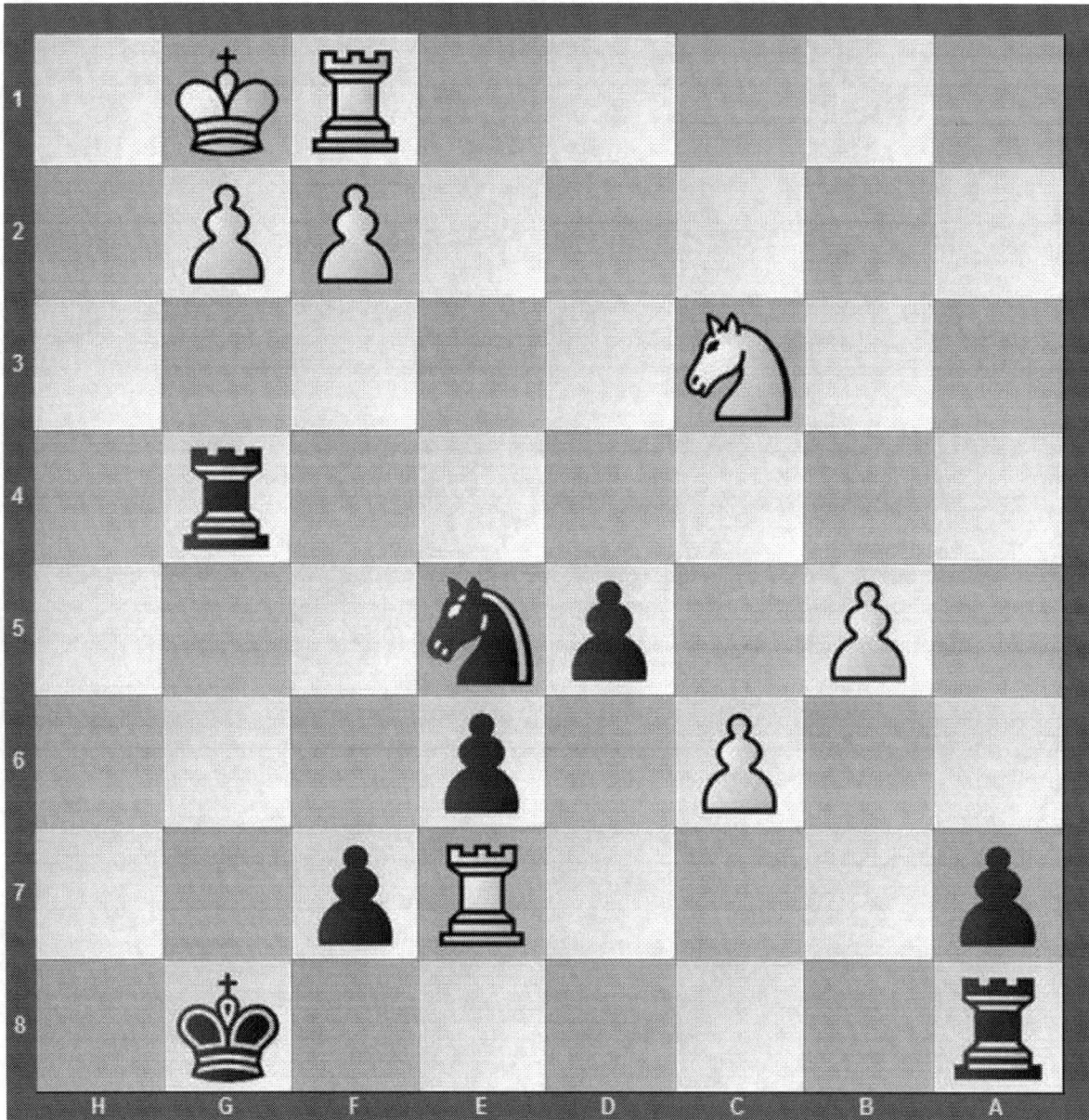

1		
2		

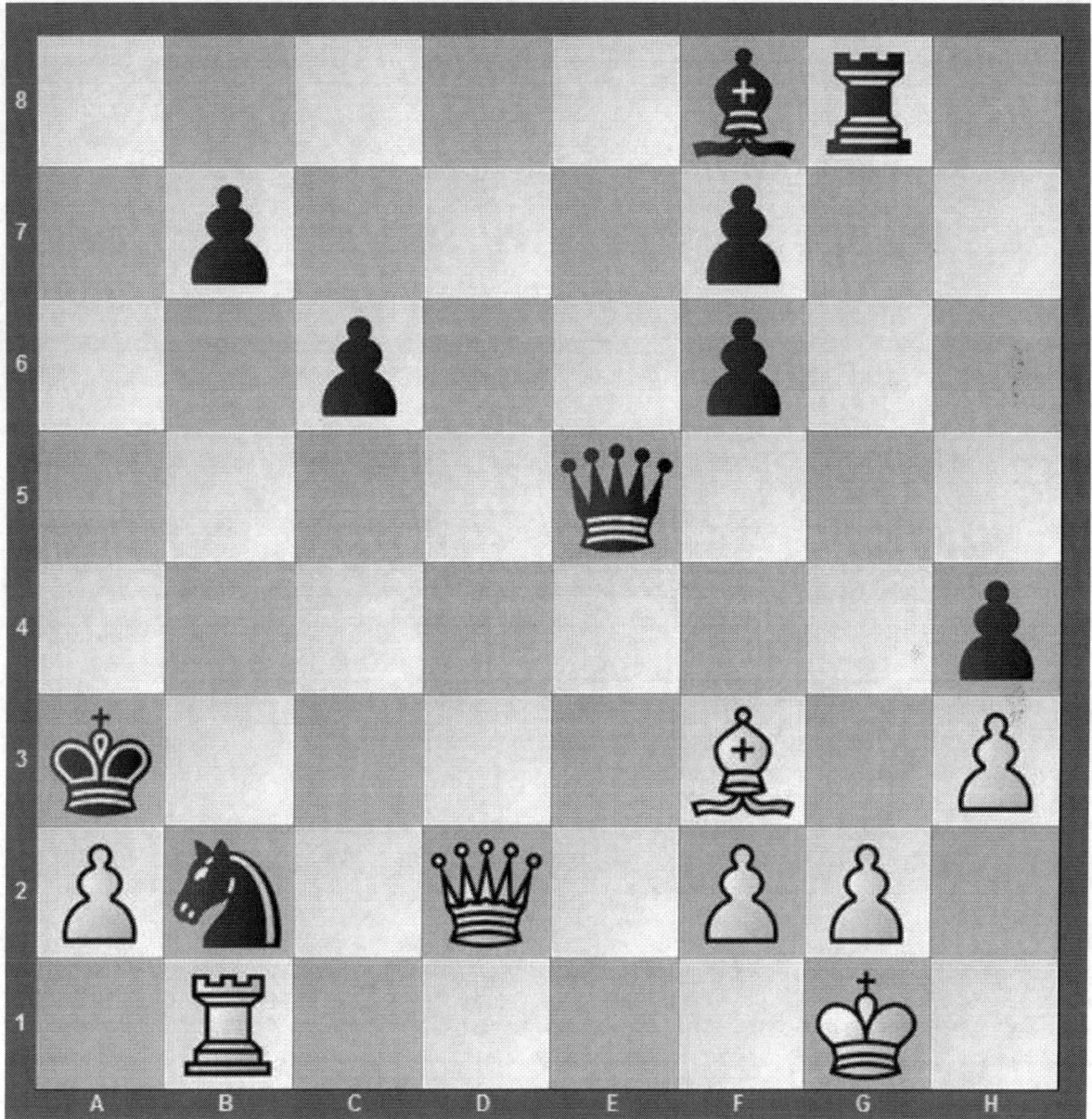

1		
2		

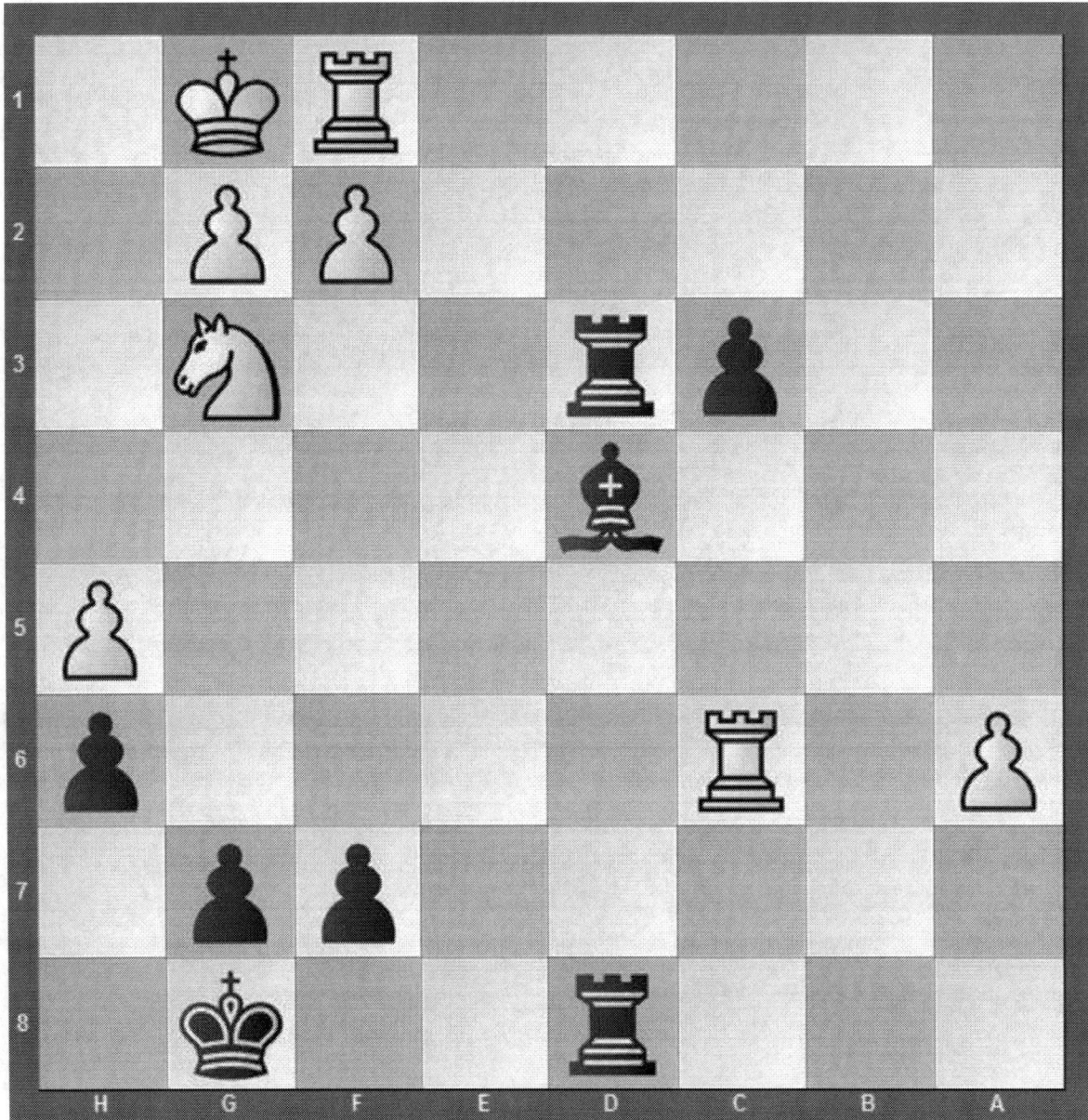

1		
2		

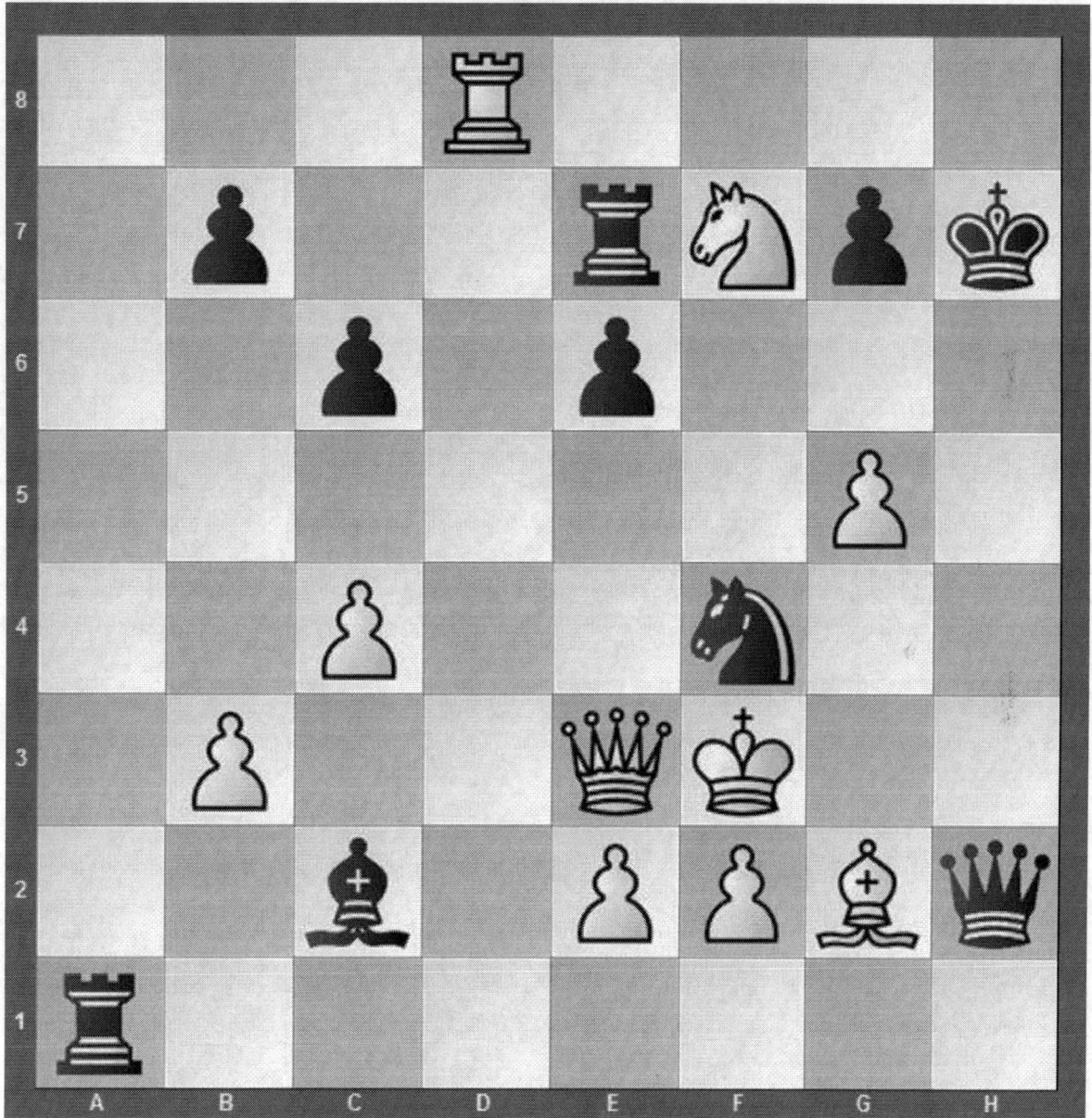

1		
2		

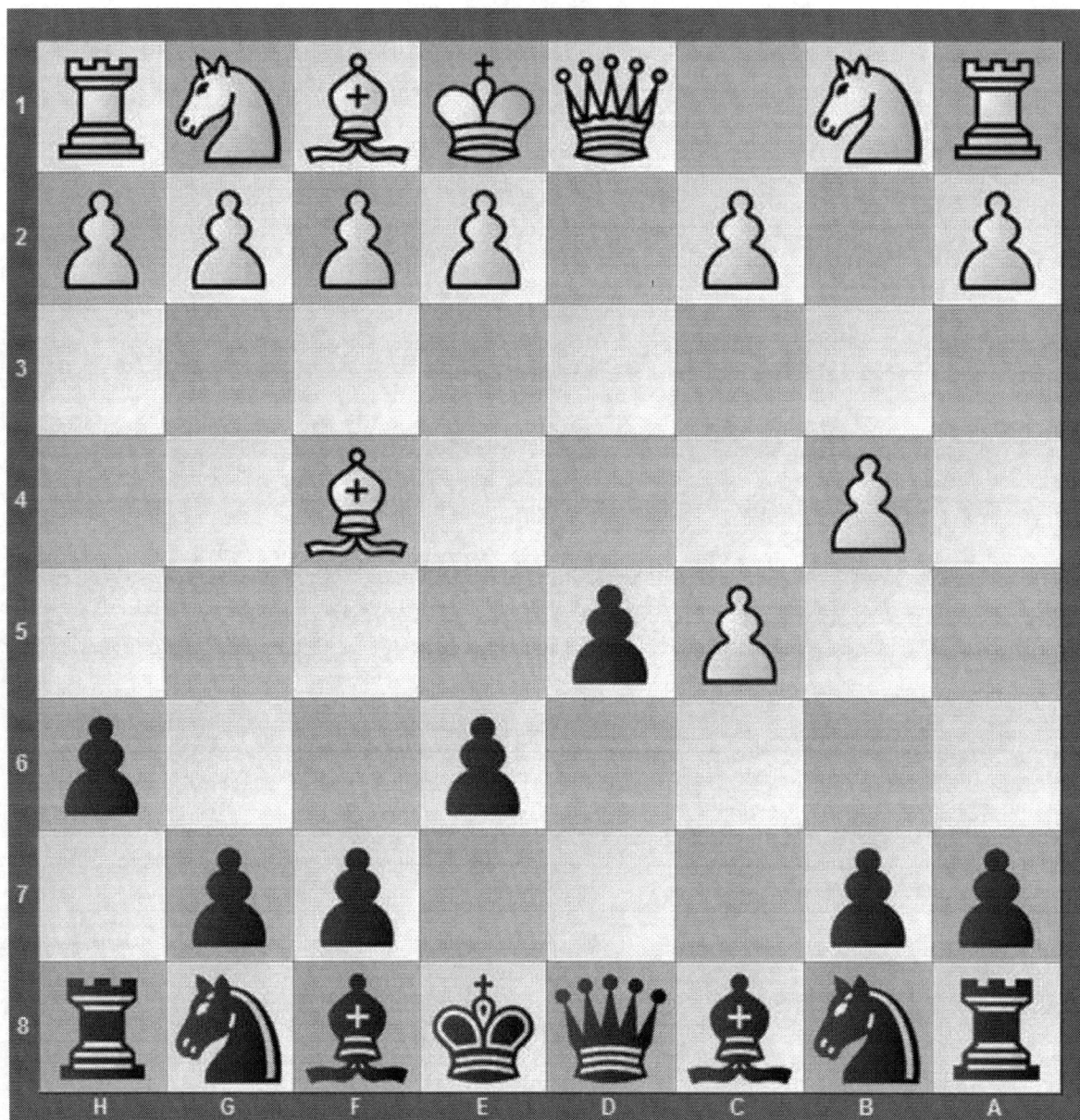

1		
2		

"When you see a good move, look for a better one." – **Emanuel Lasker**

1		
2		

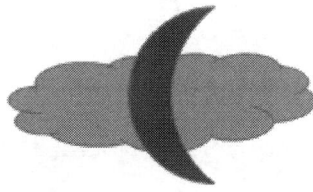

1		
2		

1		
2		

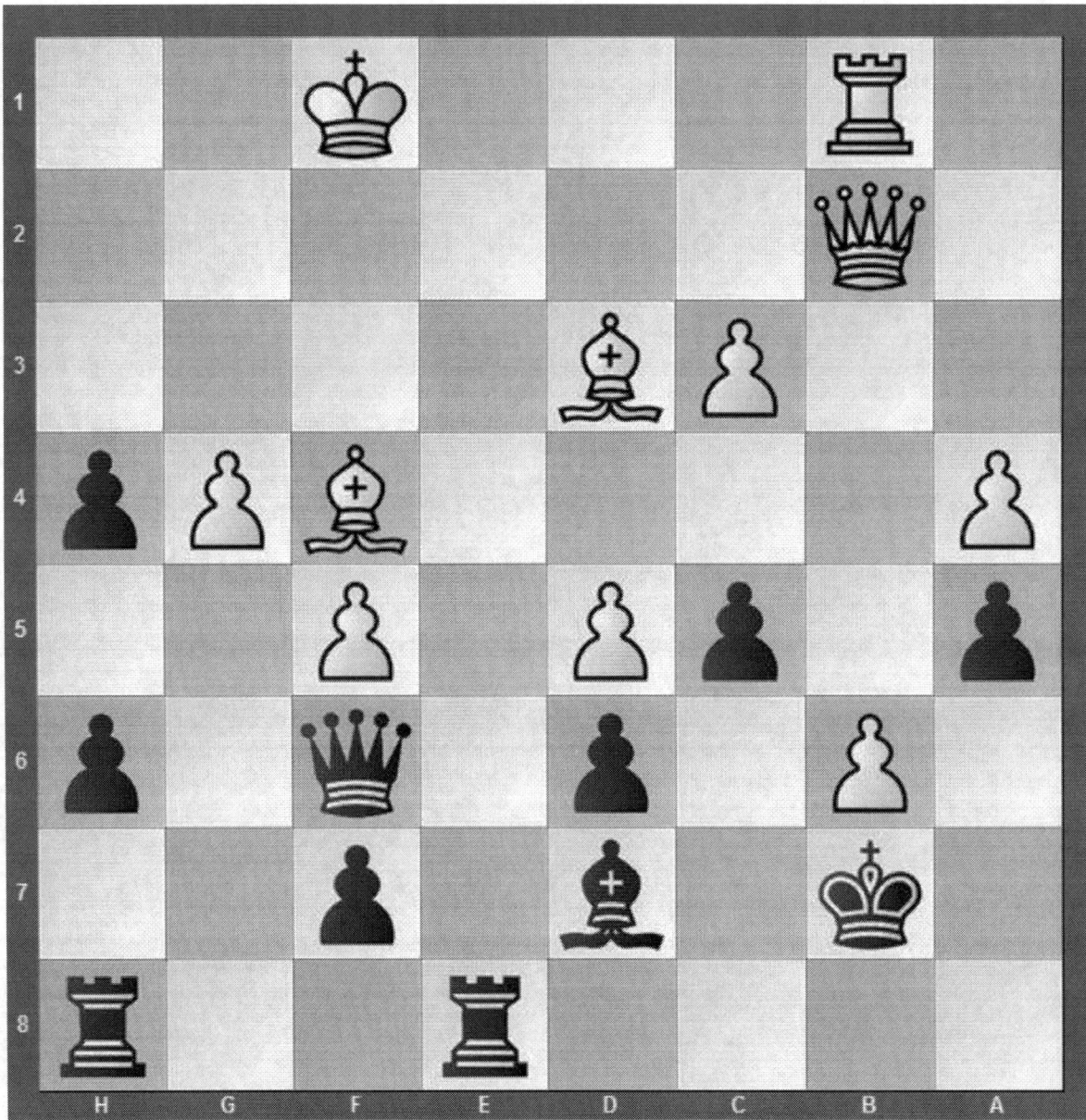

1		
2		

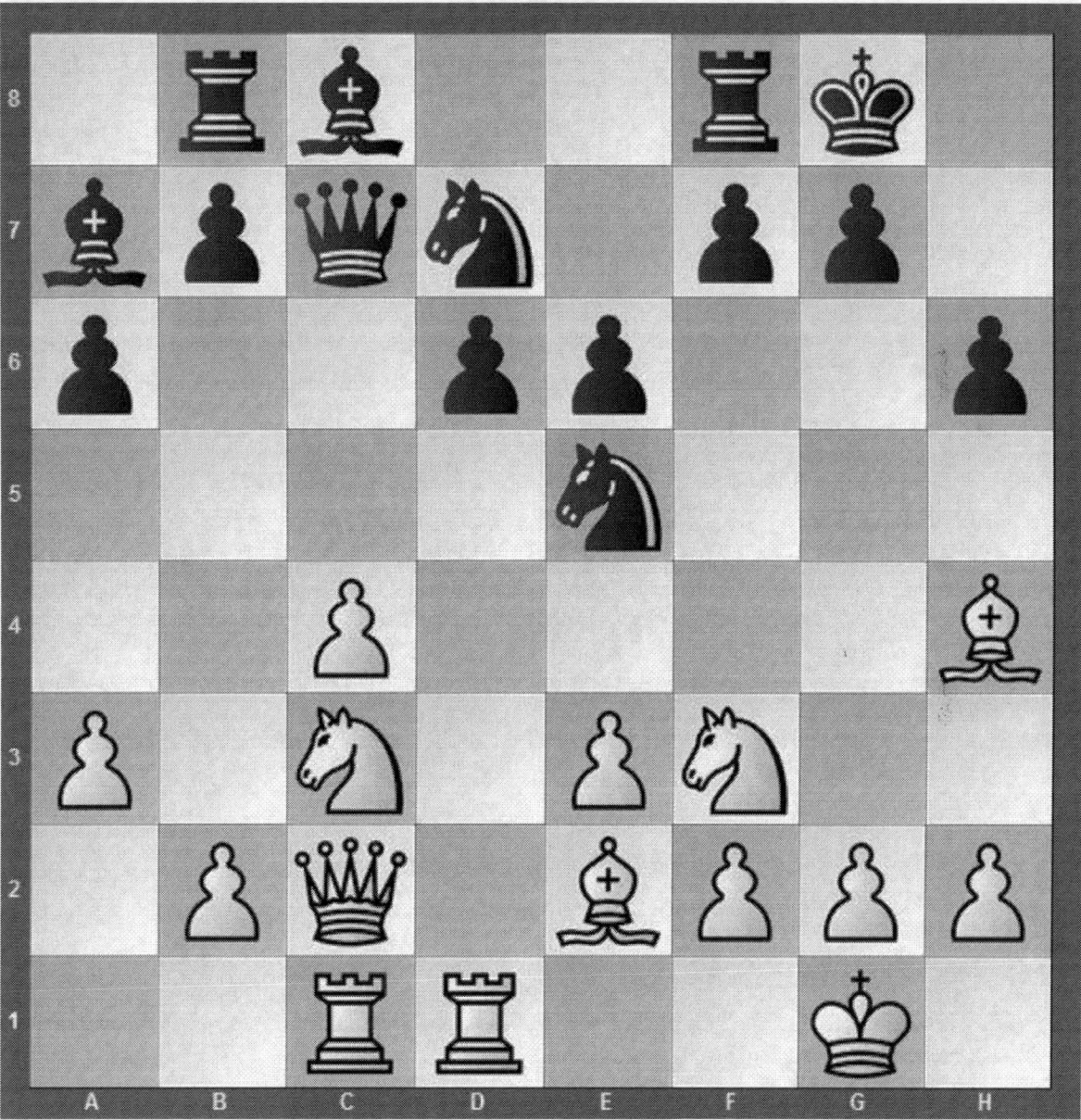

1		
2		

1		
2		

1		
2		

1		
2		

1		
2		

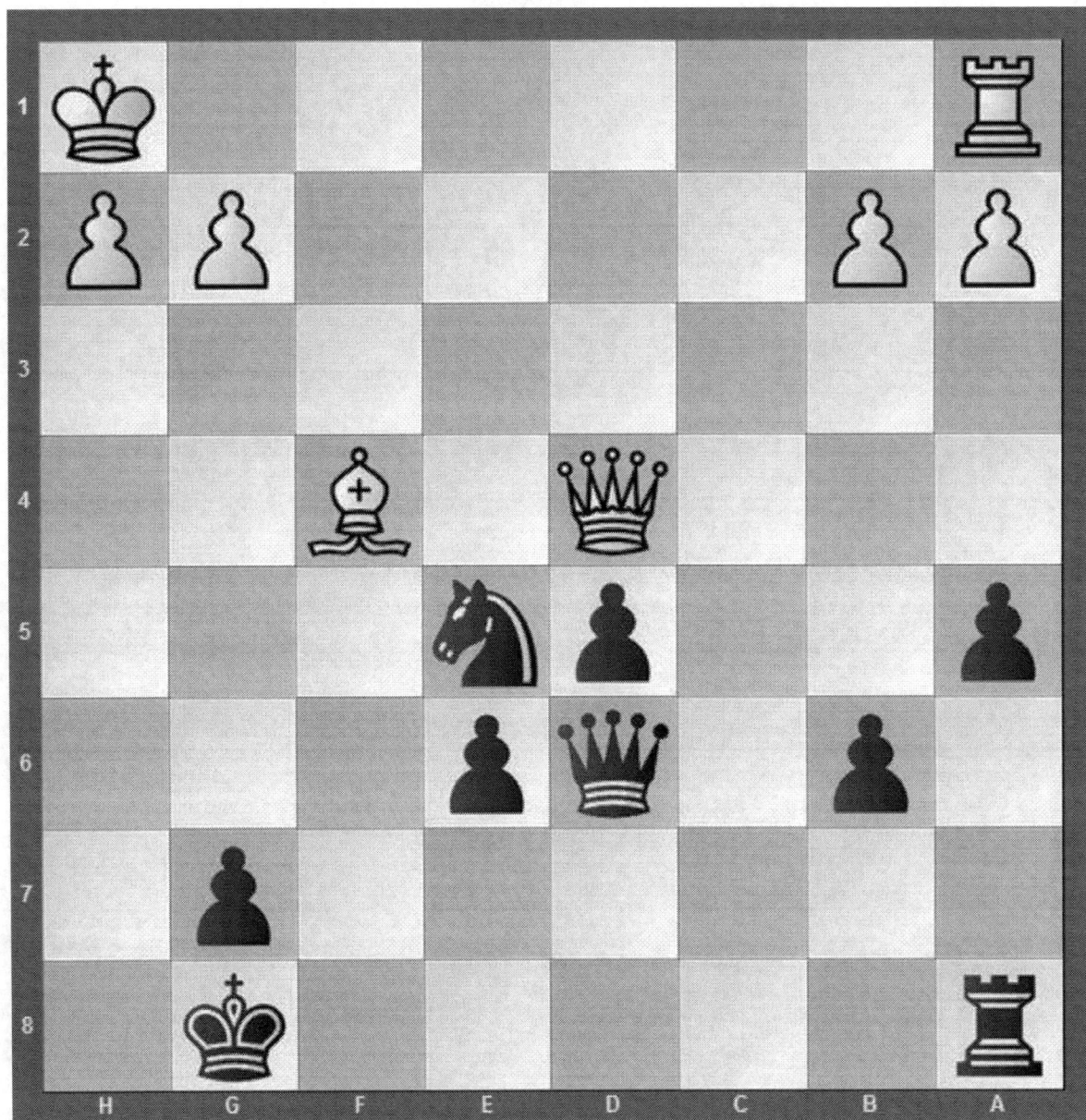

1		
2		

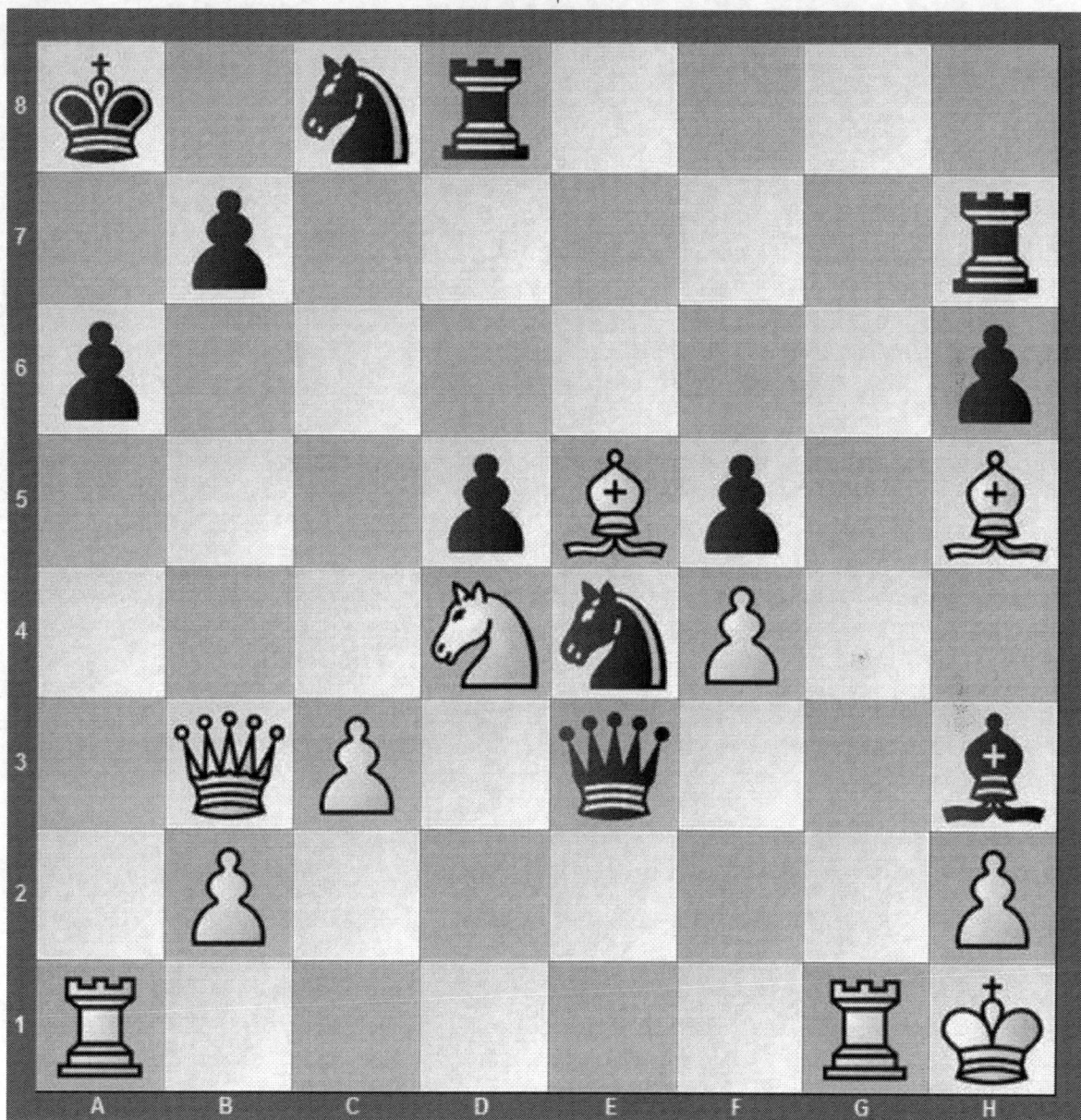

1		
2		

1		
2		

1		
2		

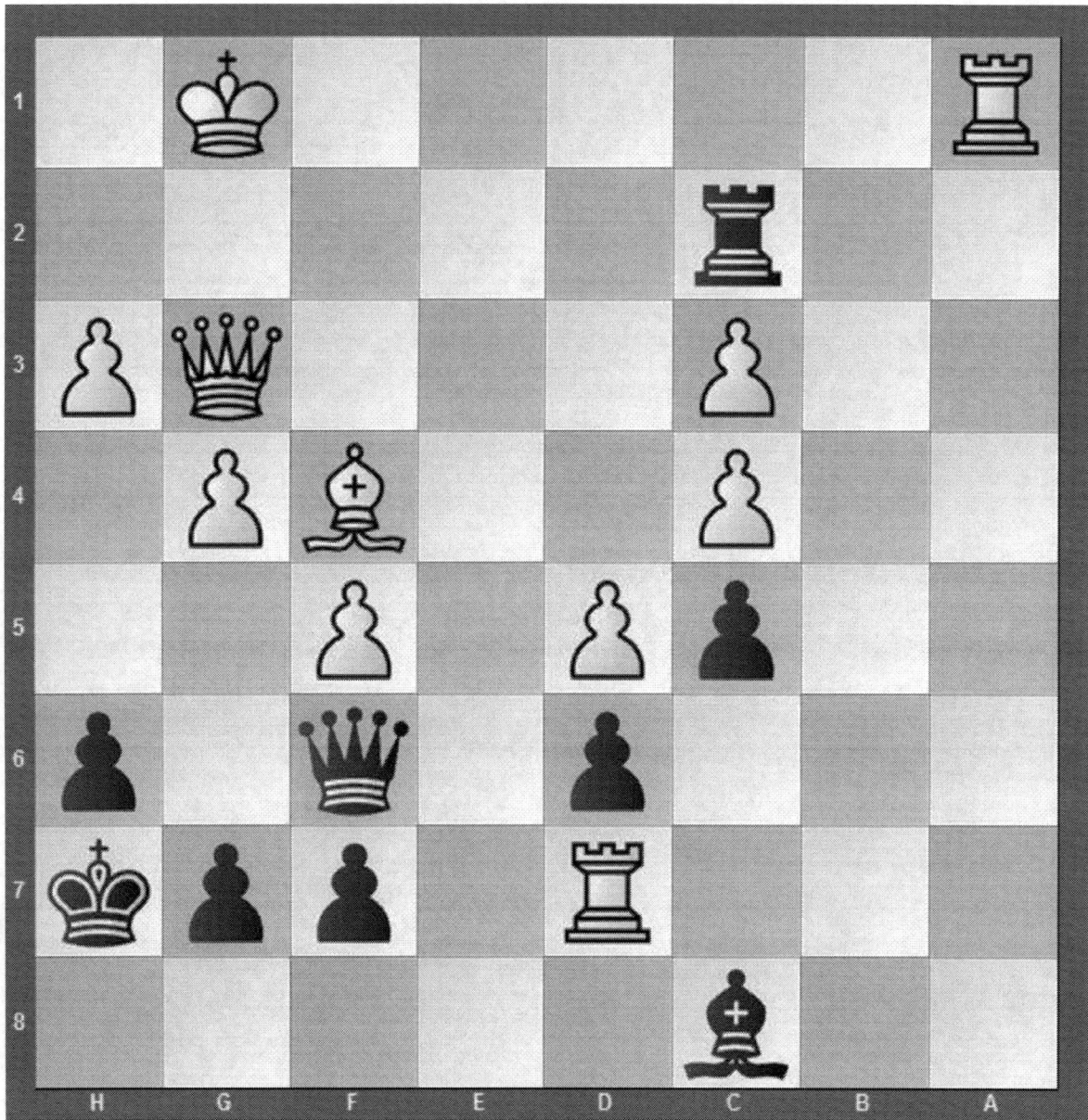

1		
2		

"Some part of a mistake is always correct." – **Savielly Tartakover**

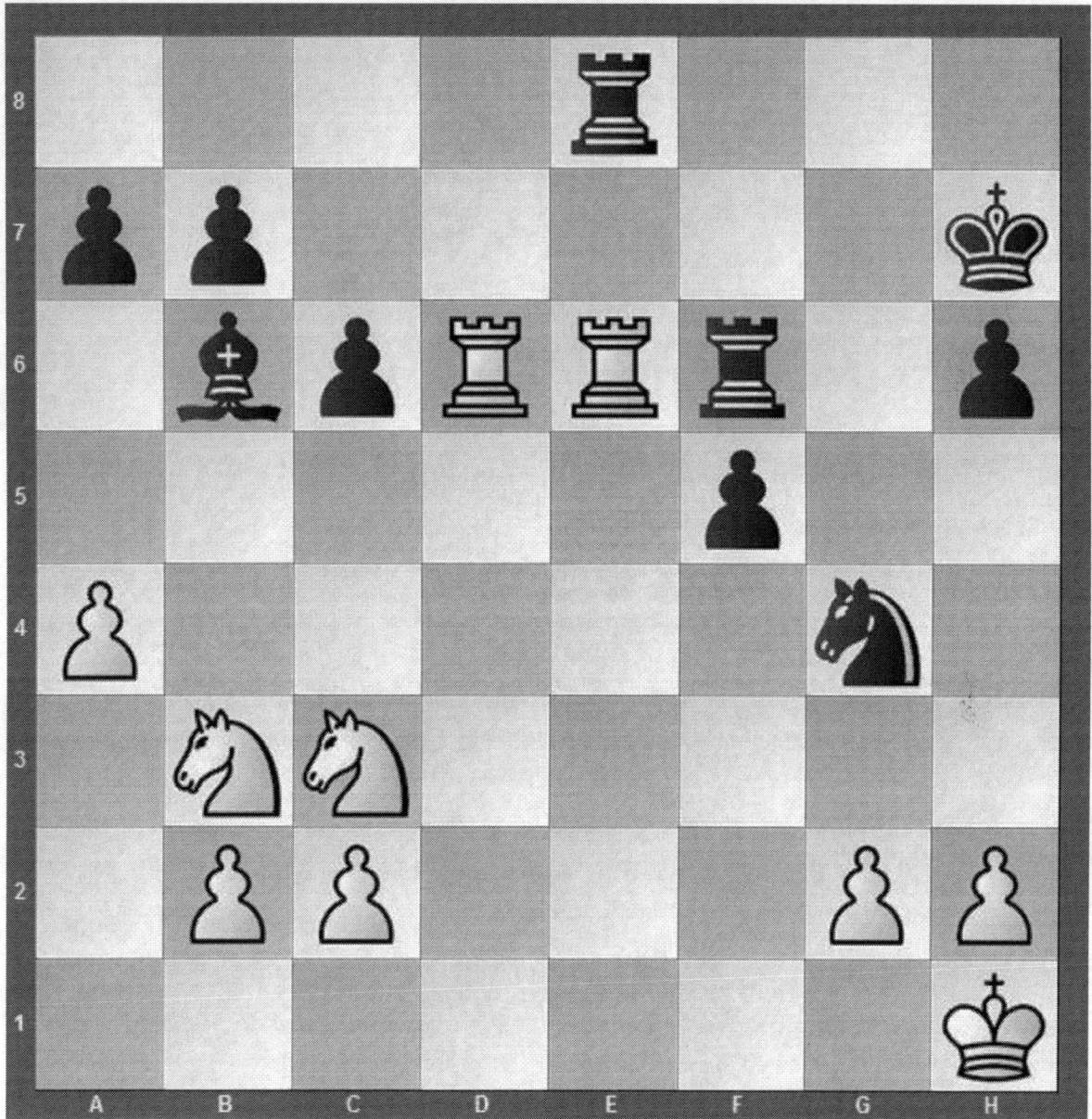

1		
2		

1		
2		

1		
2		

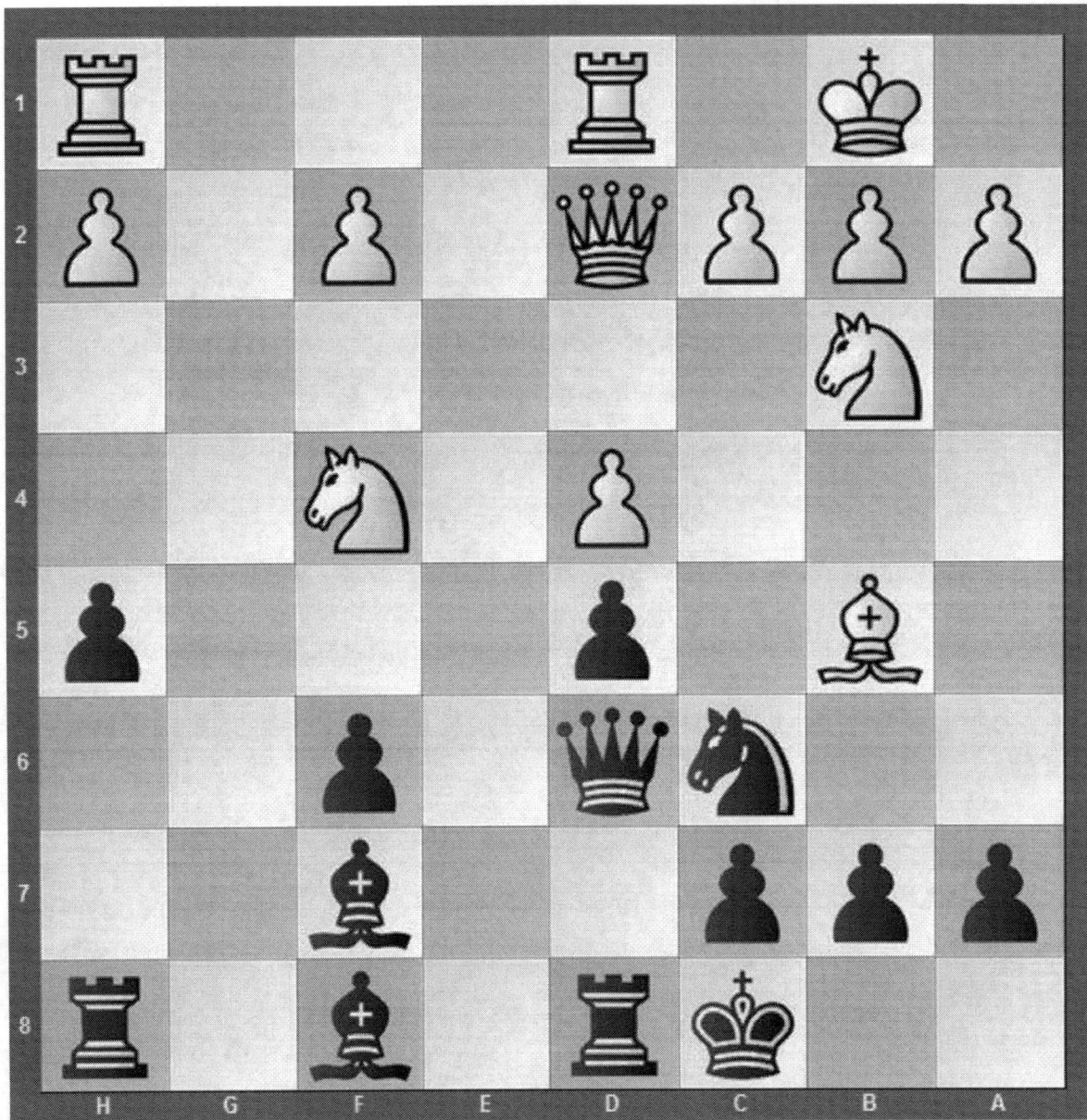

1		
2		

1		
2		

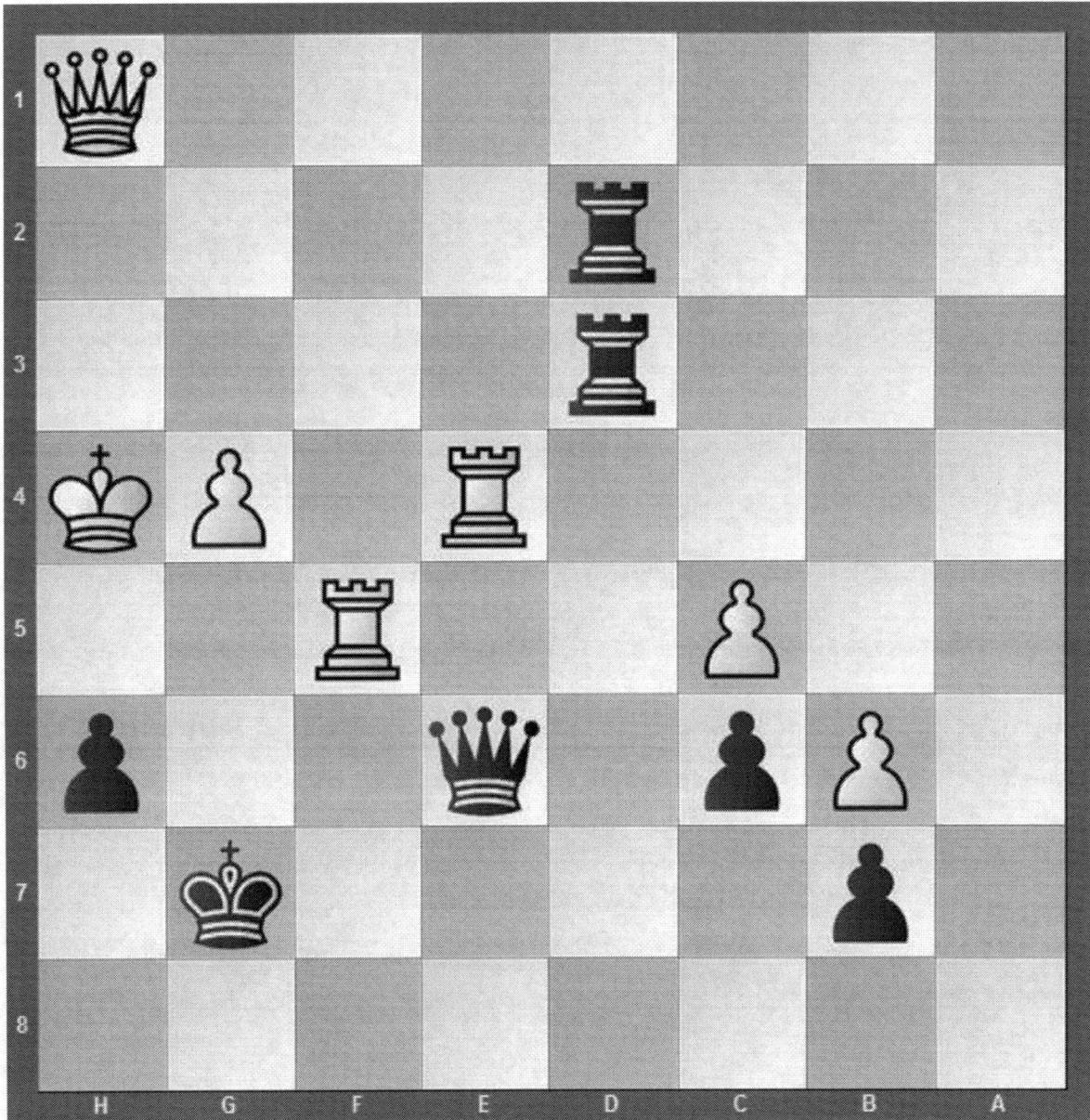

2 Mastering chess sight

1		
2		

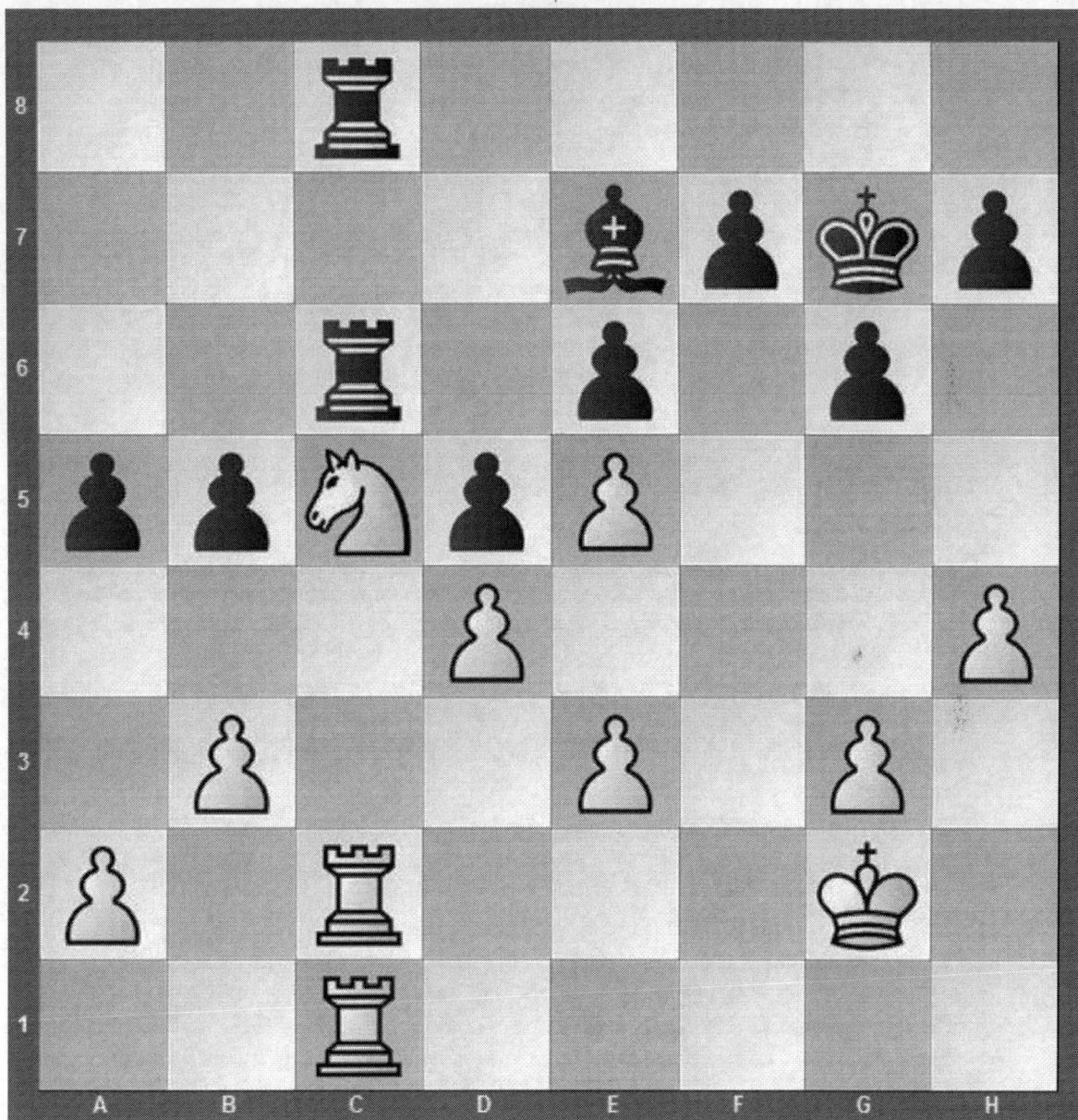

1		
2		

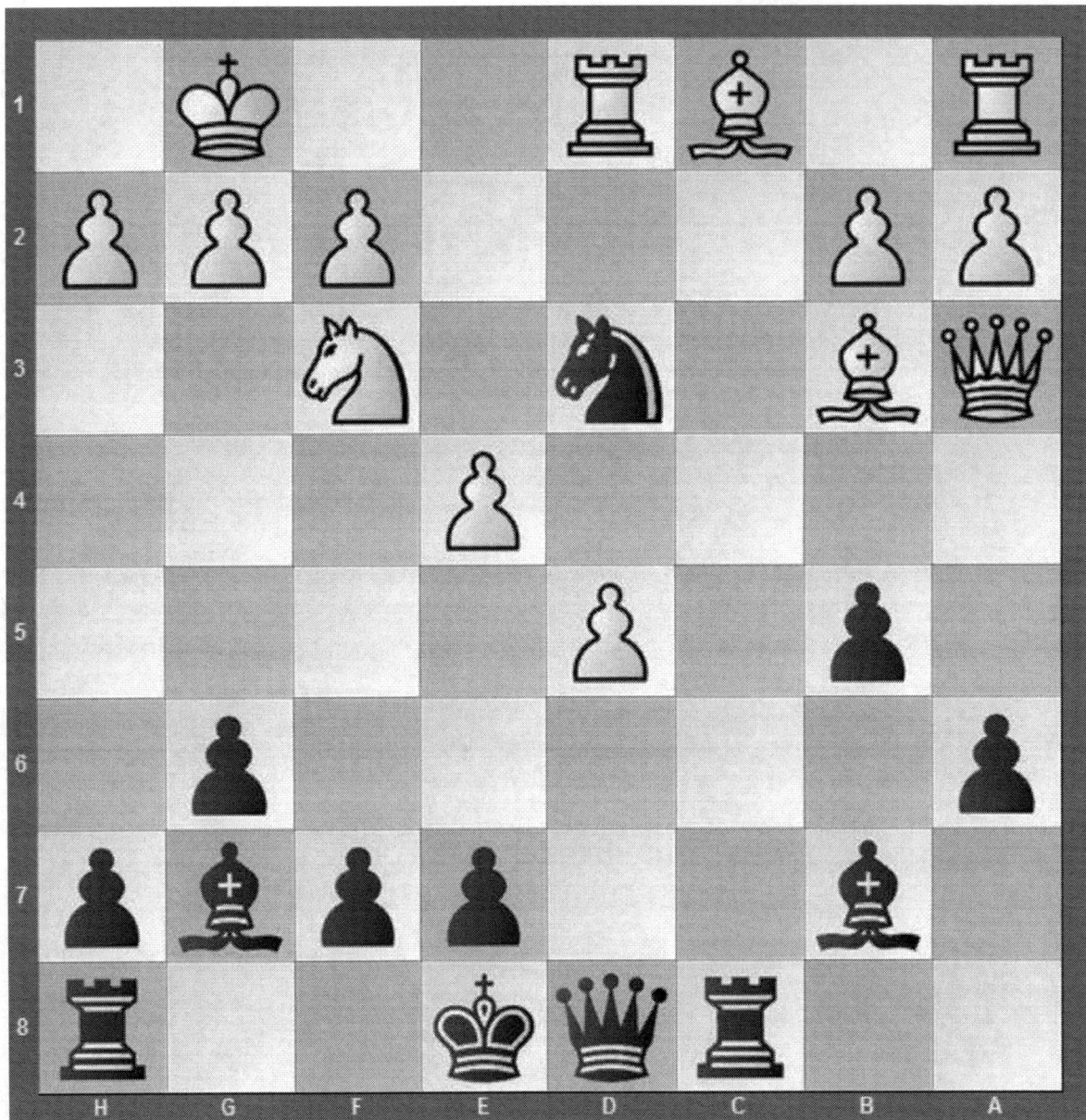

1		
2		

1		
2		

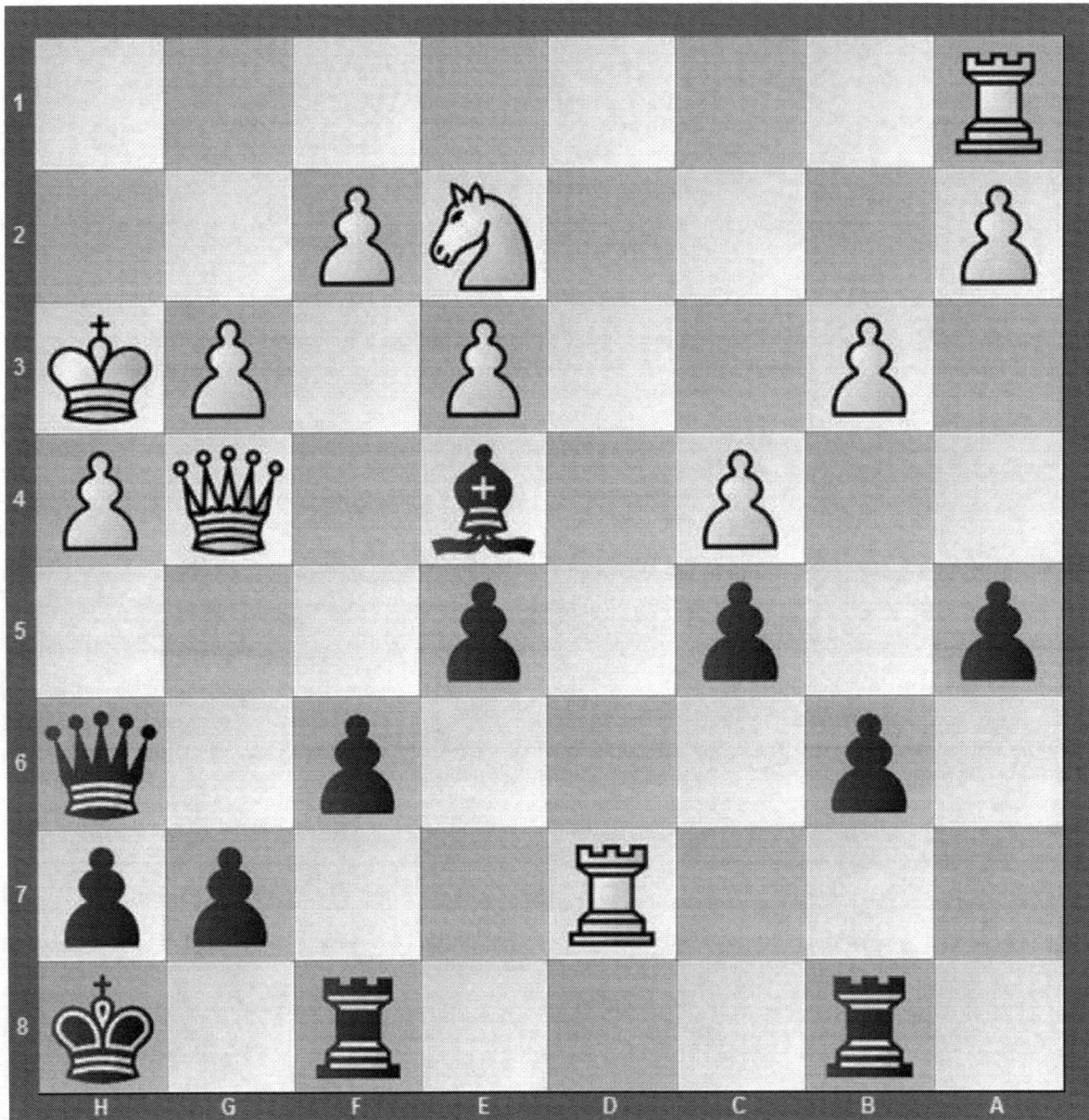

1		
2		

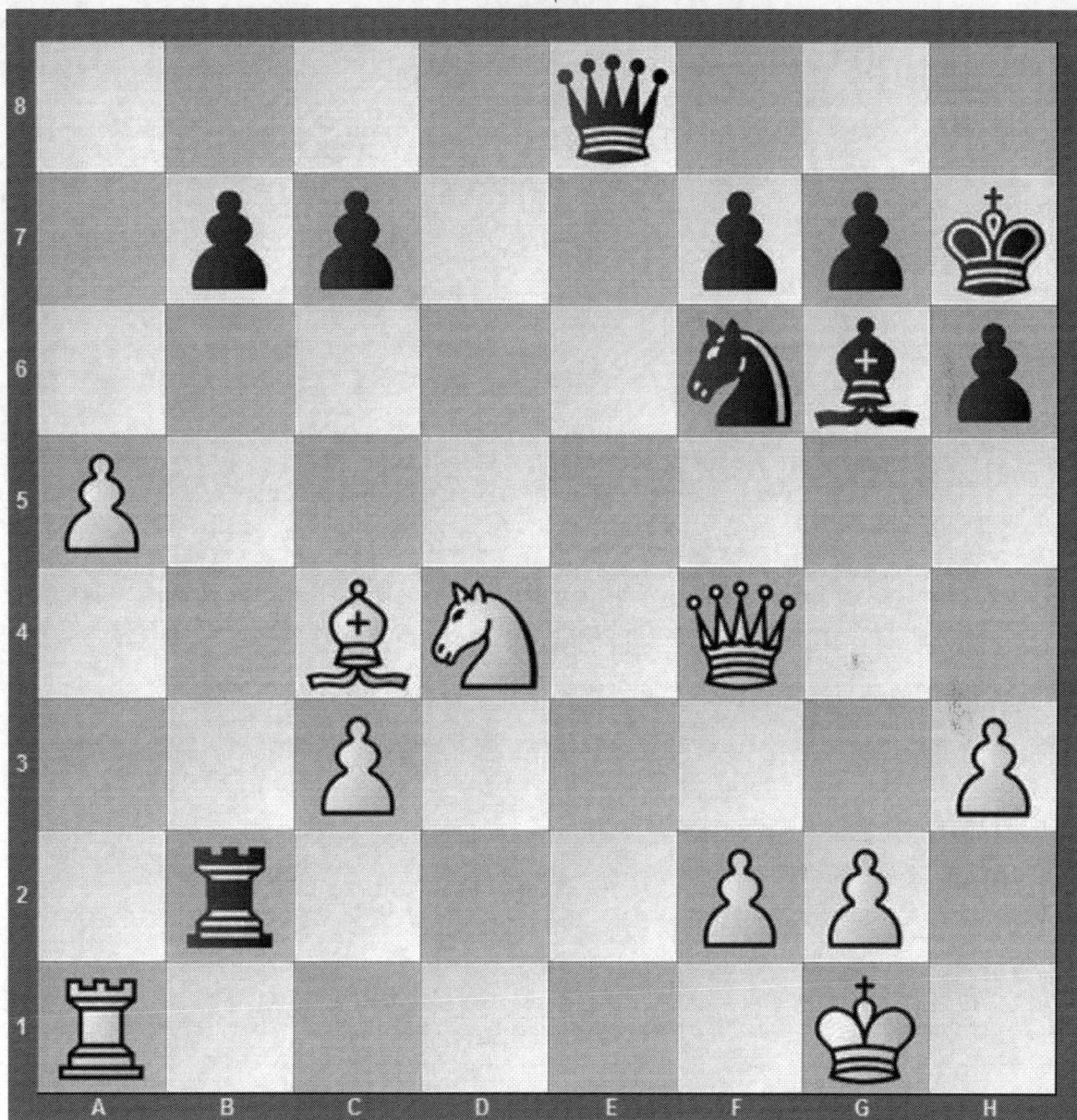

| 1 | | |
| 2 | | |

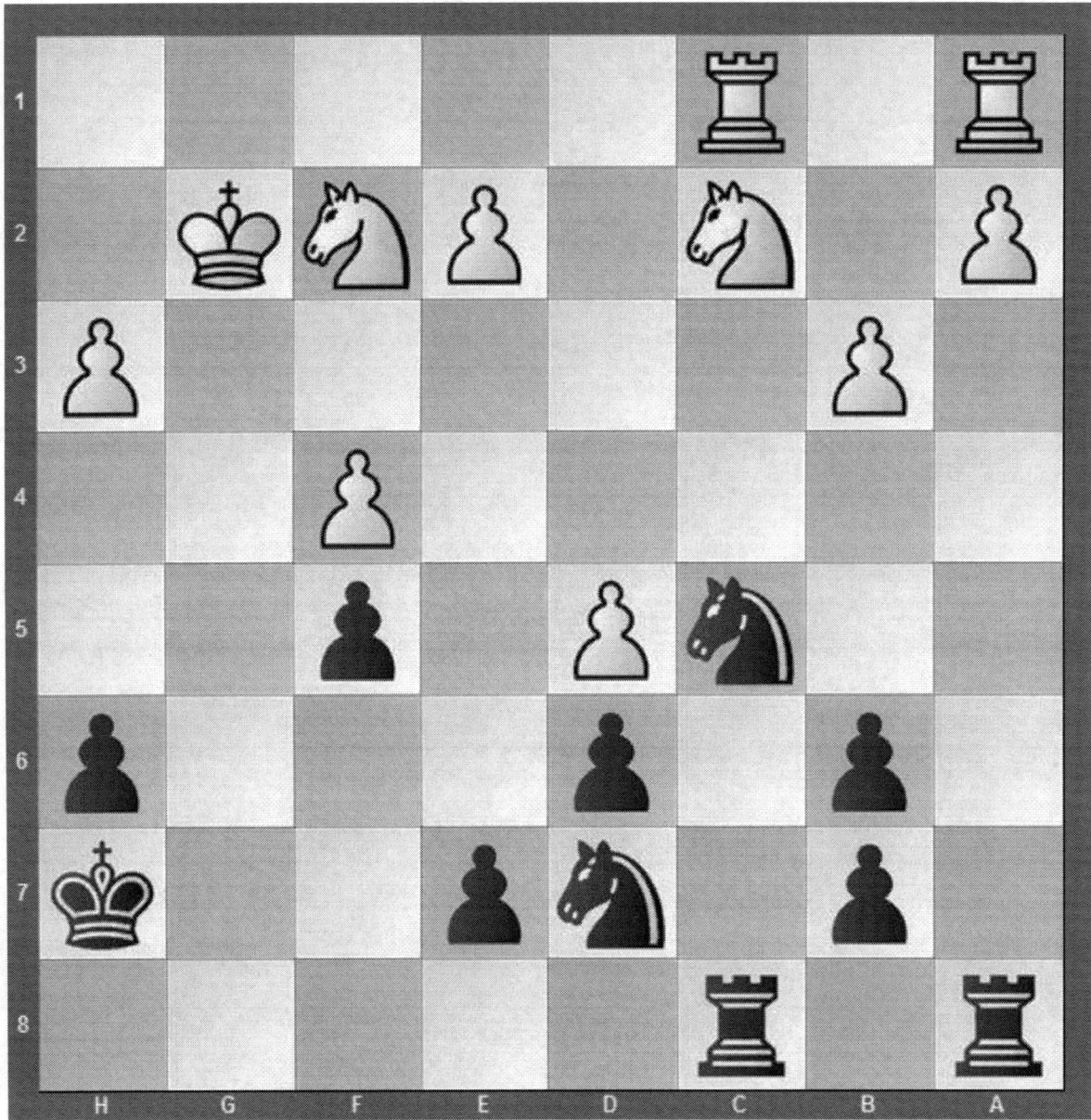

1		
2		

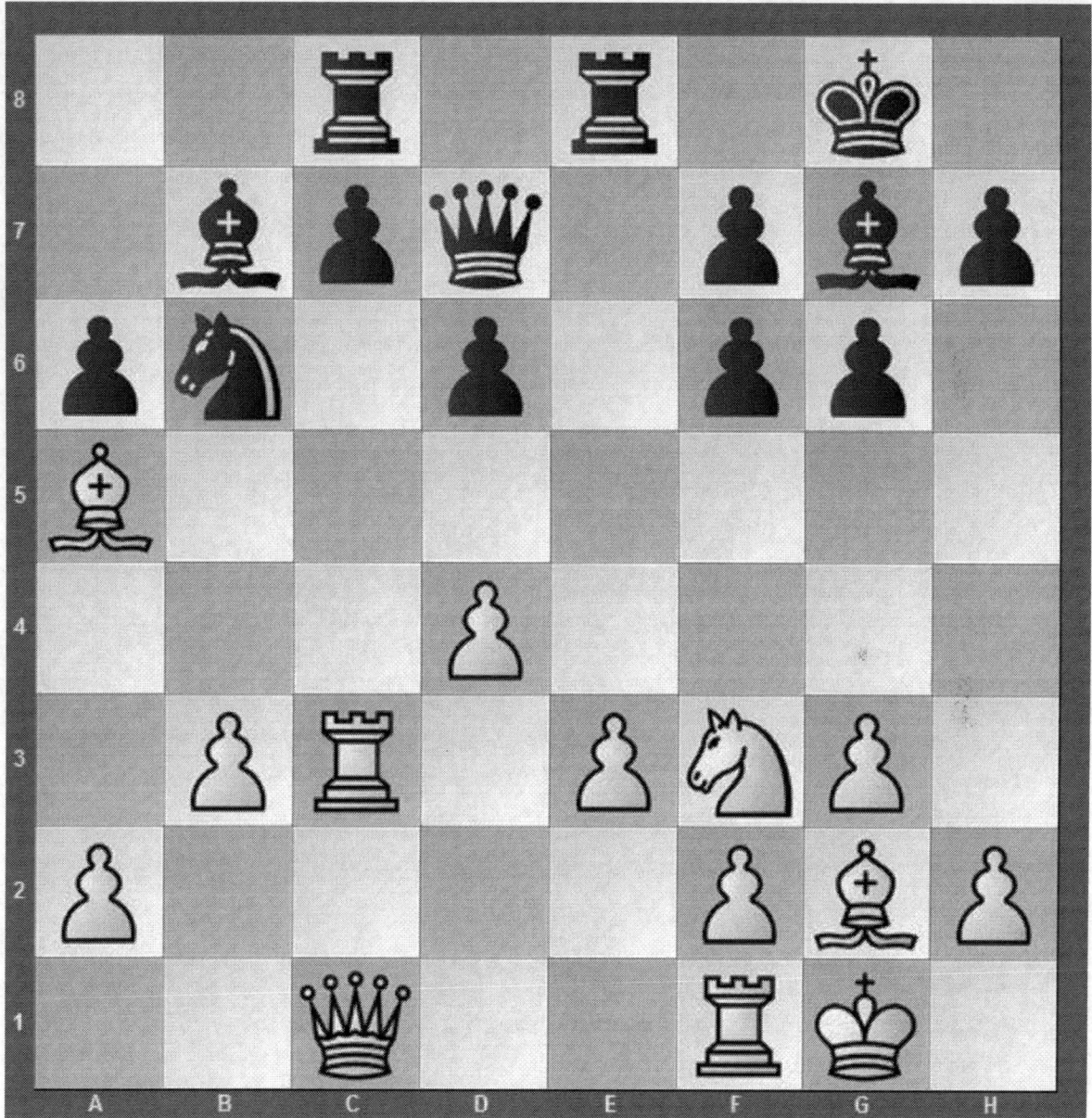

1		
2		

325

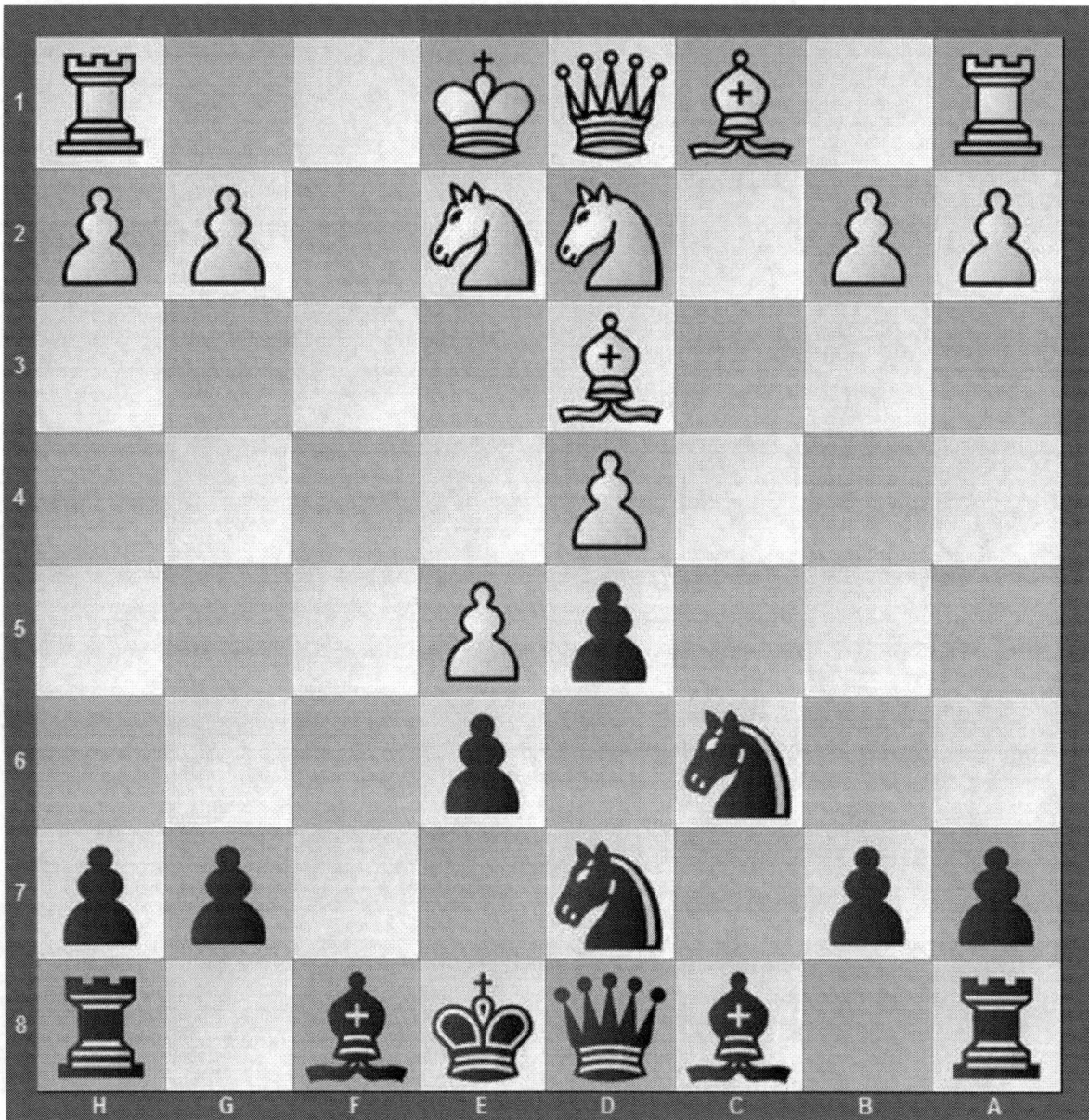

1		
2		

"*My opponents make good moves too. Sometimes I don't take these things into consideration.*" – **Bobby Fischer**

1		
2		

1		
2		

1		
2		

1		
2		

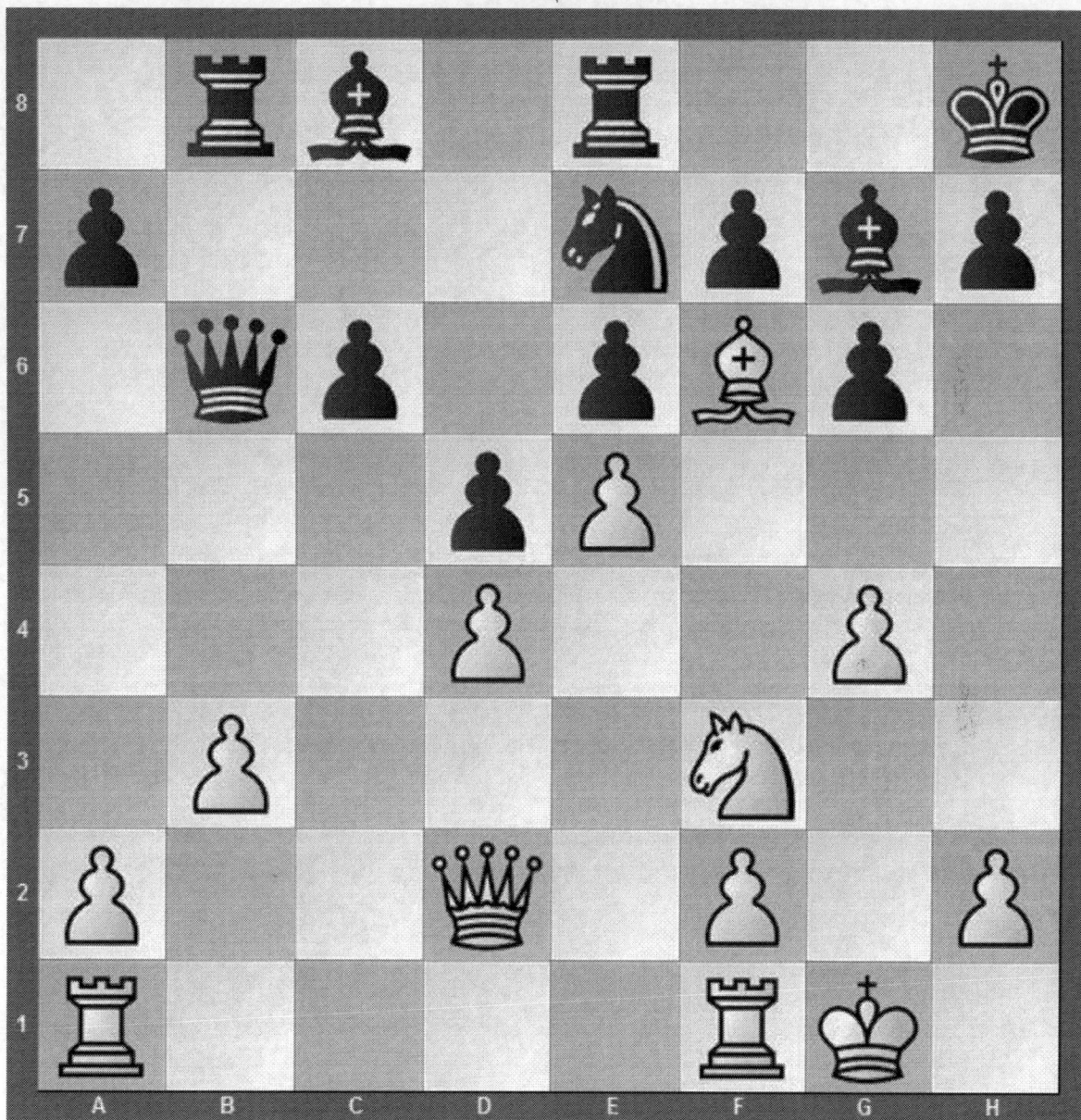

1		
2		

1		
2		

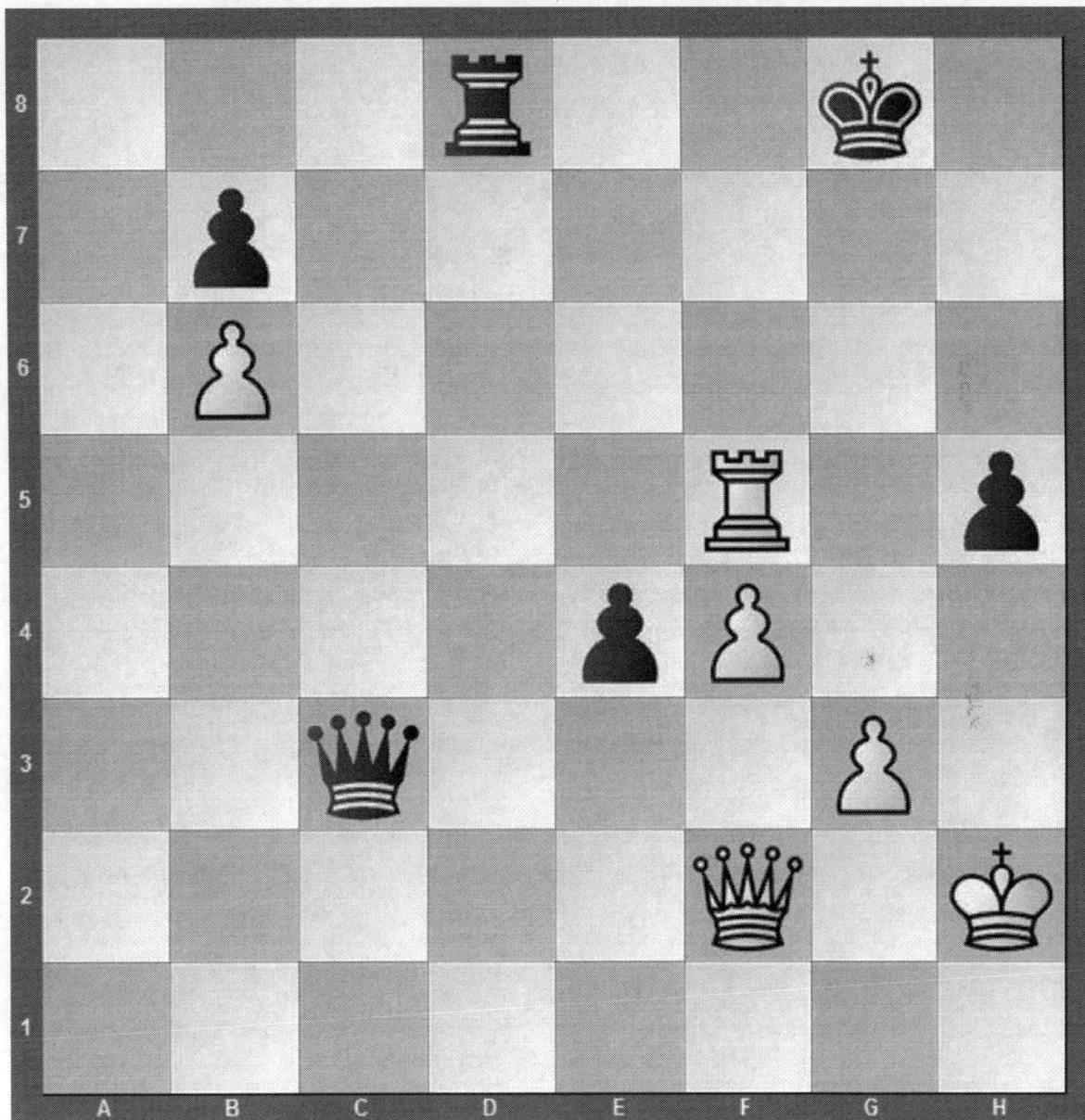

| 1 | | |
| 2 | | |

1		
2		

1		
2		

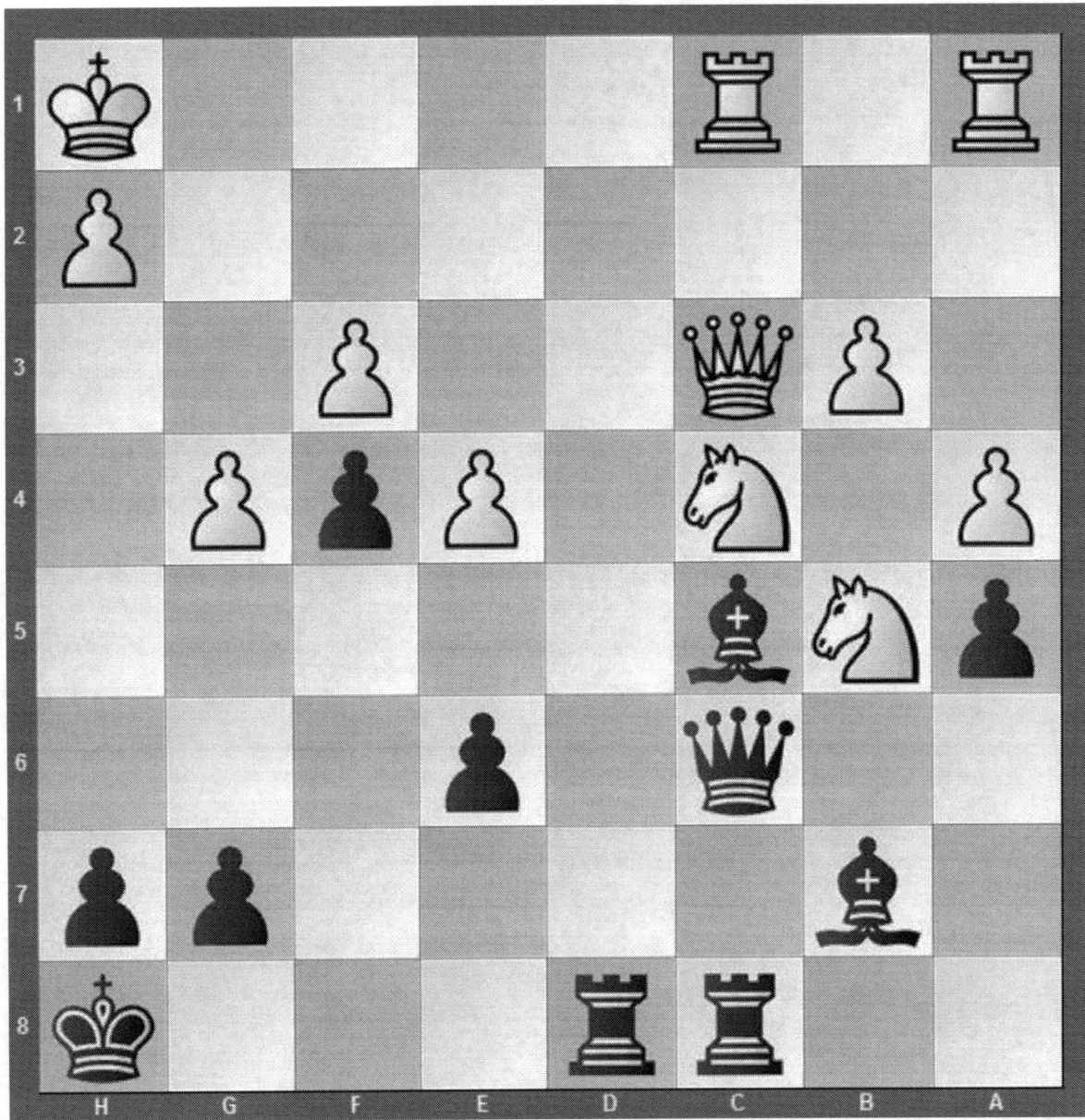

1		
2		

1		
2		

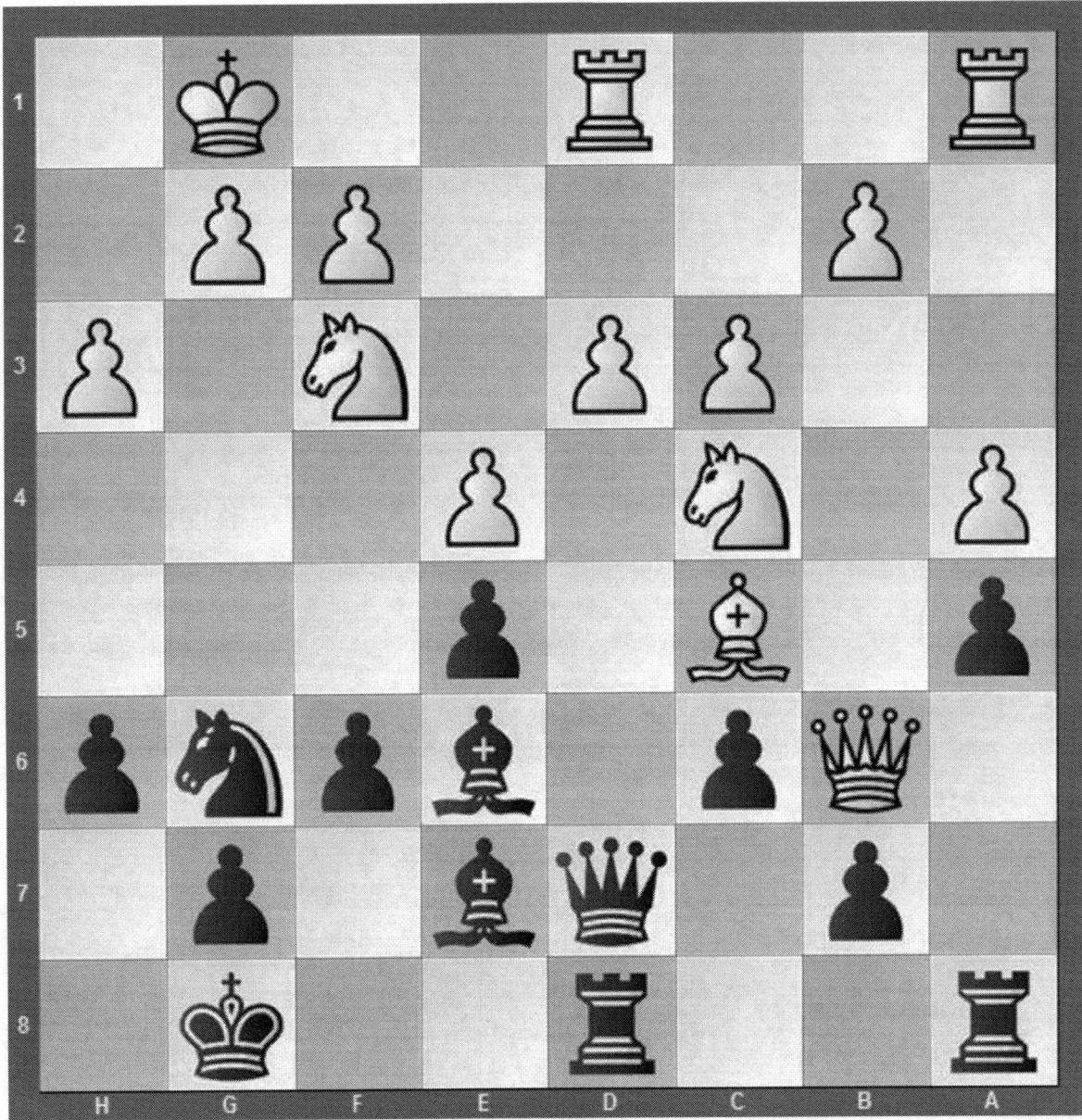

1		
2		

1		
2		

1		
2		

"Chess is a terrific way for kids to build self-image and self-esteem." – Saudin
Robovic

1		
2		

1		
2		

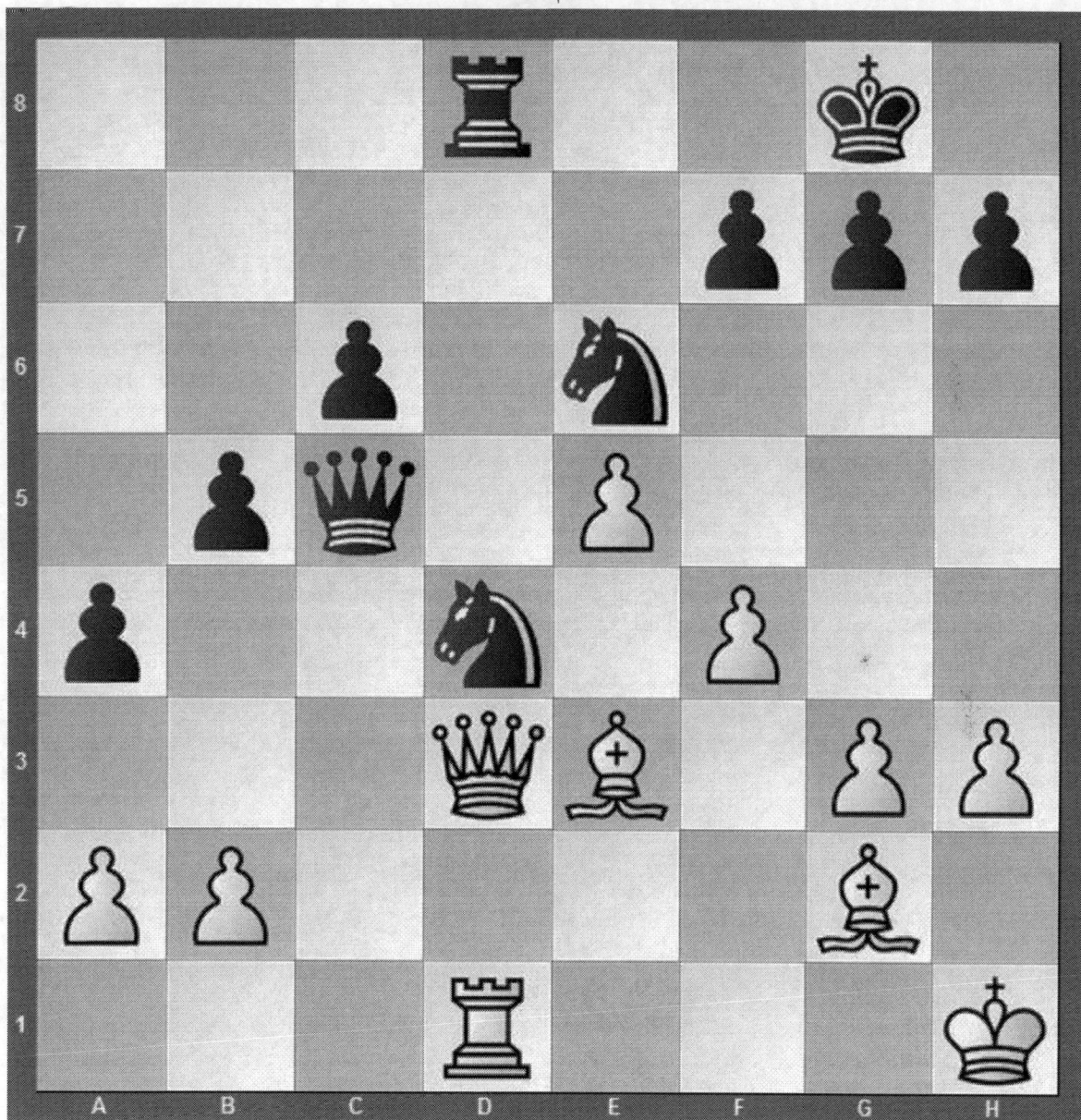

1		
2		

H G F E D C B A

1		
2		

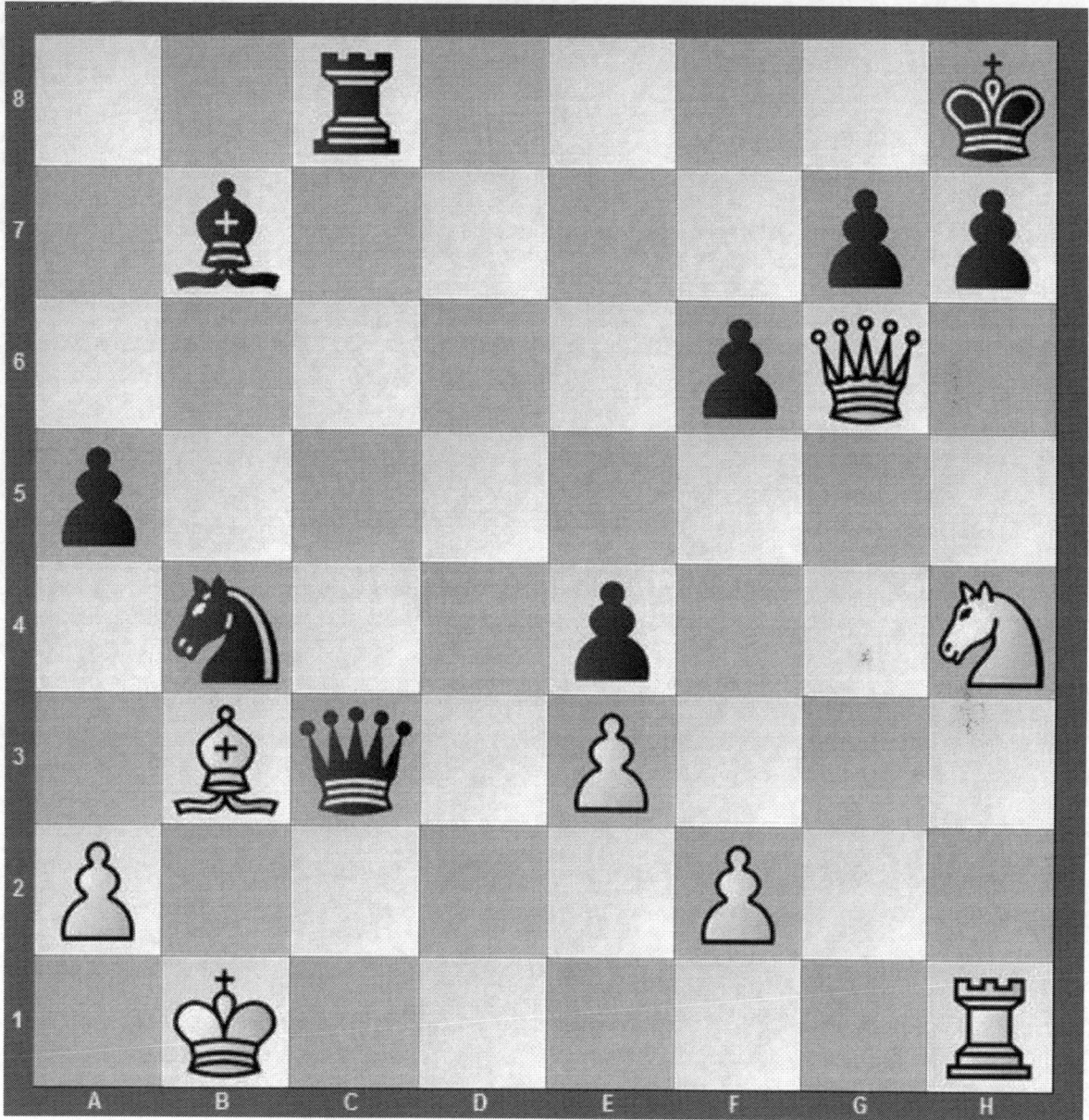

1		
2		

1		
2		

1		
2		

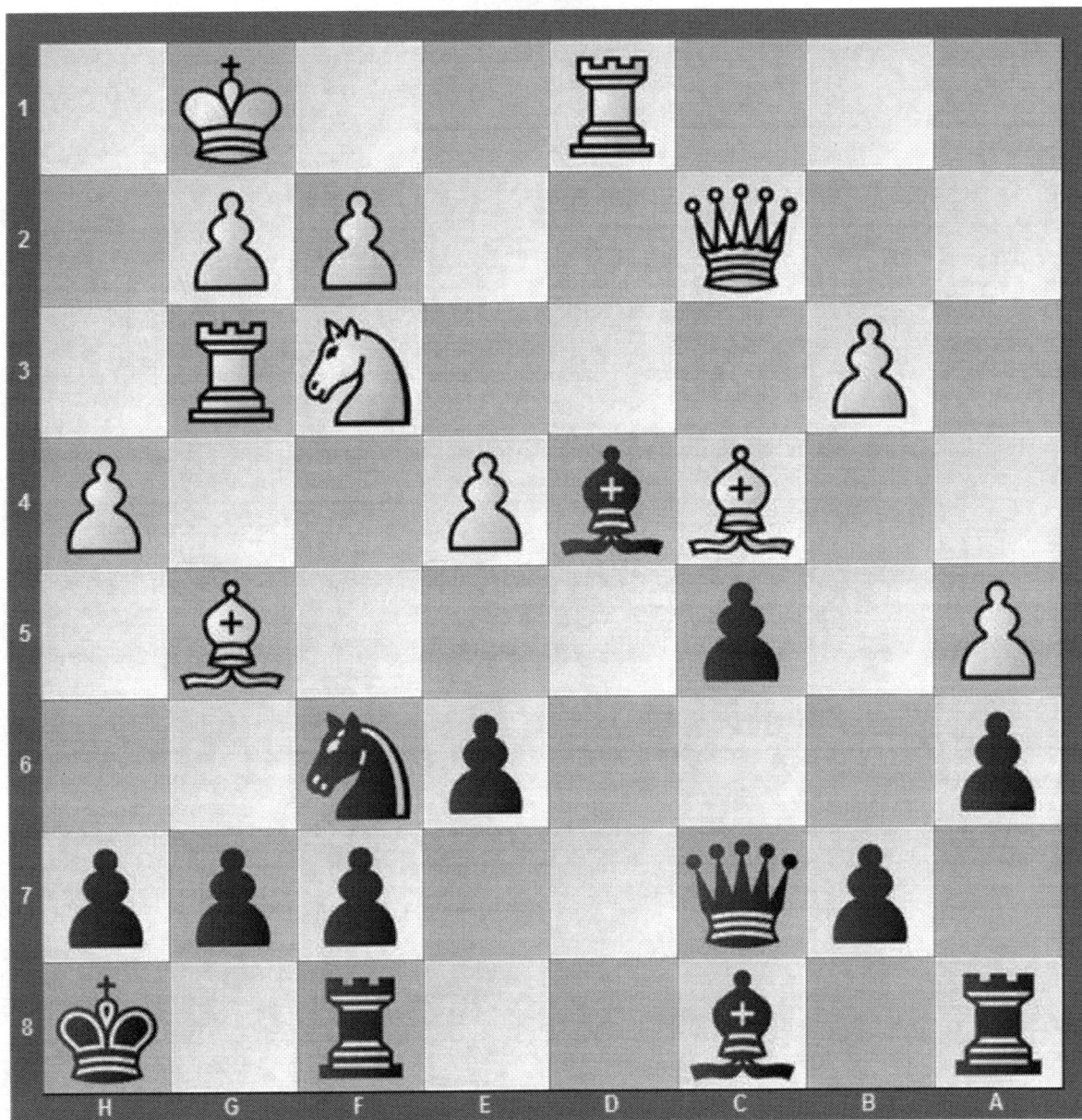

1		
2		

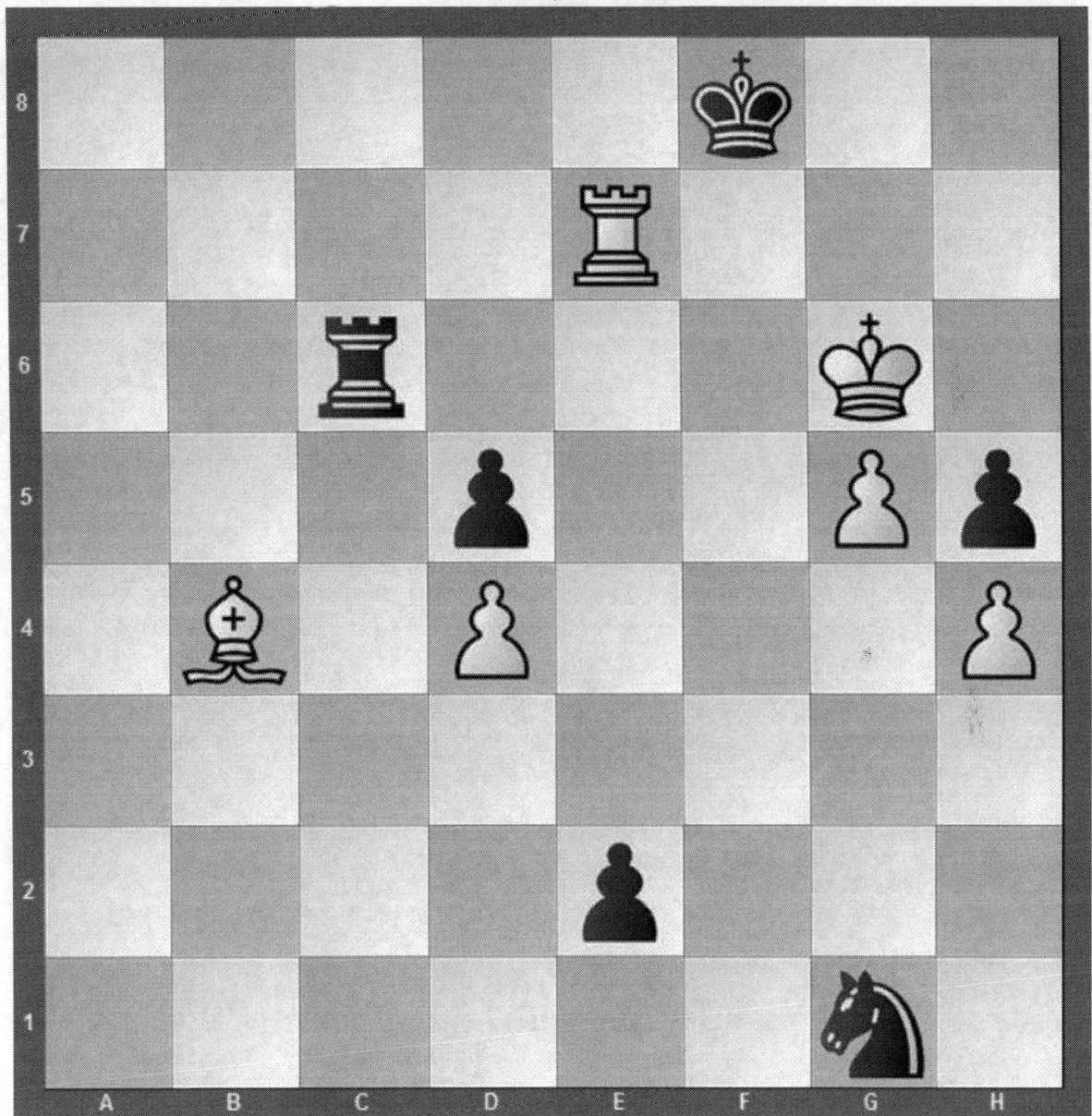

1		
2		

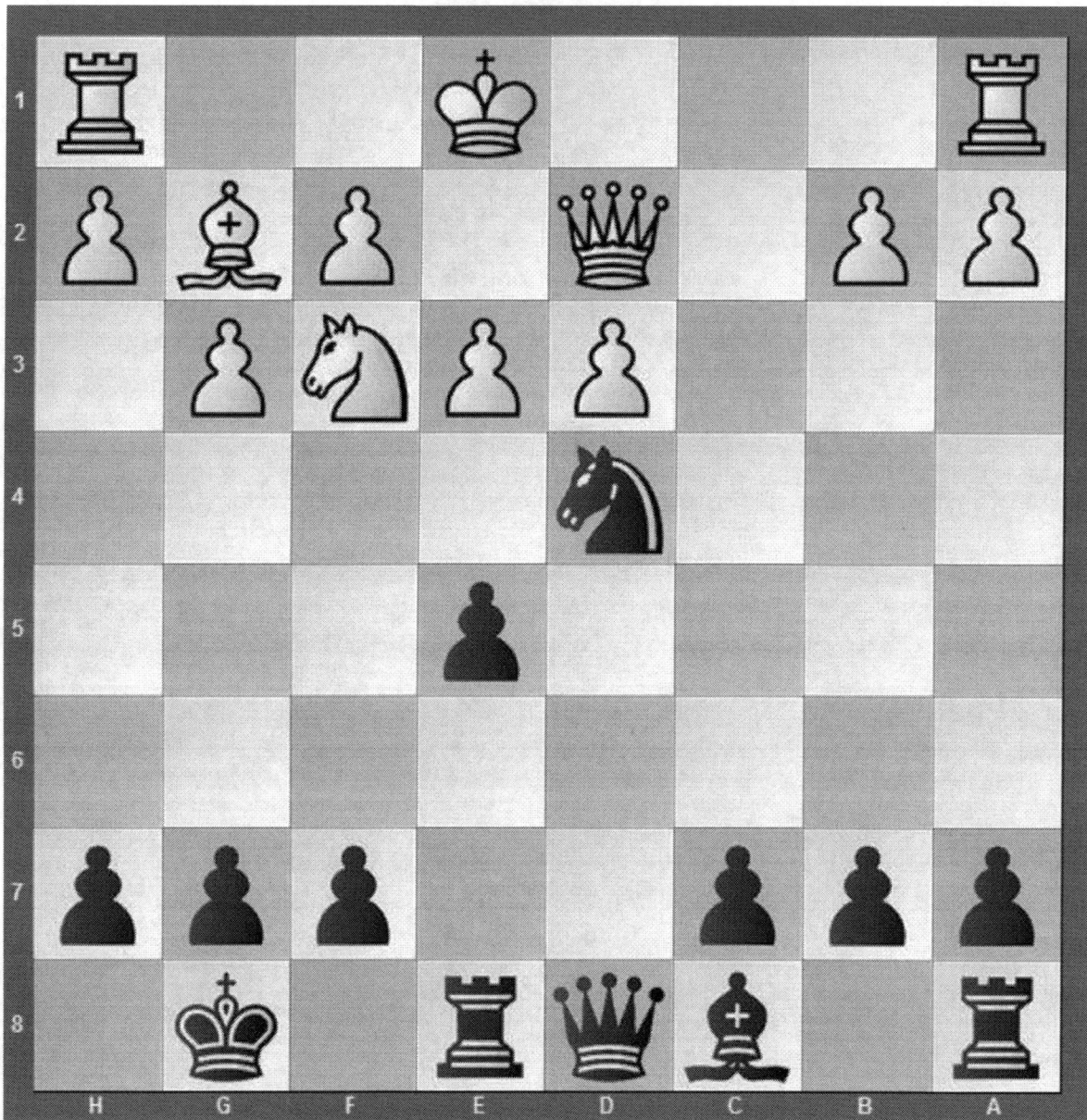

1		
2		

1		
2		

1		
2		

1		
2		

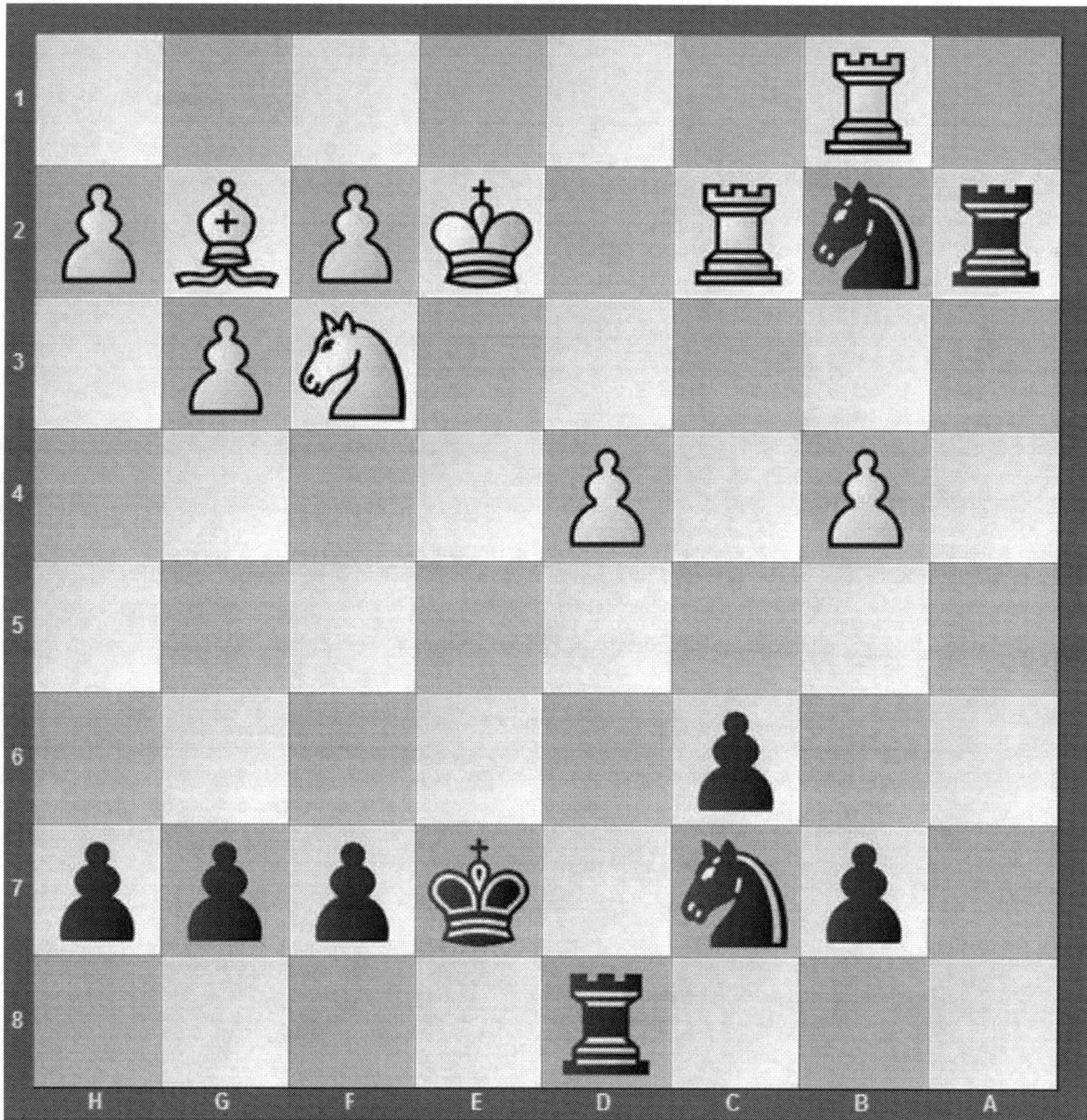

1		
2		

"I'm convinced, the way one plays chess always reflects the player's personality. If something defines his character, then it will also define his way of playing." – **Vladimir Kramnik**

Solutions

Page #		Page #	
5	1. Rd8 Bxd8 2. Qf8#	40	1. ... Qe6 2. Rb2 Qxg4
6	1. ... Rxh2+ 2. Kxh2 Rh8+	41	1. Bc7 Rxc7 2. Re8+
7	1. Nf6+ Kf8 2. Rf7#	42	1. ... Qc2 2. Rf1 Qxc3
8	1. ... Rd8	43	1. f6 Qd8 2. Bxh6
9	1. Rxg7+ Kxg7 2. Bxe5+	44	1. ... Ndxe4 2. fxe4 Nxe4+
10	1. ... Rxf5 2. exf5 Qf3	45	1. Qg2 Rxg2 2. Rc8#
11	1. Ne5 Qc7 2. Nxc6 (3. Bb5)	46	1. ... Qf1+ 2. Qxf1 d3#
12	1. ... Qxe1+ 2. Rxe1 Nf2+	47	1. Nh6+ Kh8 2. Nf7+
13	1. Qh1 Qxa2 2. Qh8#	48	1. ... Nxe4 2. fxe4 Bh4
14	1. ... Ng4+ 2. hxg4 Qh4#	49	1. Rd8+ Kh7 2. Qxb7
15	1. Qxe6+ Kxe6 2. Nf4+	50	1. ... Bg4 2. Qd2 Bxd1
16	1. ... Nxe4 2. Nxe4 Qa5+	51	1. Rxg7+ Kxg7 2. Bxd4
17	1. Qxf8+ Kxf8 2. Nxg6	52	1. ... Bb4
18	1. ... Qxh4	53	1. Nf6+ gxf6 2. Bxc6
19	1. Bb6 Qb4 2.a3	54	1. ... Rxa2 2. Kxa2 Qxc2+
20	1. ... Rg3 2. Kc2 Rxd3	55	1. Qxe2 Rxc1+ 2. Rxc1
21	1. Bxf7 Kxf7 2. Qc4+	56	1. ... Rh1+ 2. Kxh1 Qb1+
22	1. ... Qxg2 2. Kxg2 Ne1+	57	1. Qxh7+ Qxh7 2. Nf7#
23	1. Rxf7 Kxf7 2. Qxg6	58	1. ... Qxd6 2. exd6 Re1+
24	1. ... Nxd4 2. exd4 Rxc2	59	1. Qd4
25	1. Rb7 Rxb7 2. Rf8#	60	1. ... Qxf2 2. Rxf2 Rb1+
26	1. ... Bg4 2. Qxc6 Qd1#	61	1. Qg1#
27	1. Qf4 Be4 2. Rc7	62	1. ... Ng4 2. Nxg4 Qg2#
28	1. ... Rxe3 2. Qxe3 Qxc2+	63	1. Qh8+ Kd6 2. Qb8+
29	1. Qxf8 Rxf8 2. Ne7+	64	1. ... Qe8+ 2. Rxe8 g6#
30	1. ... Ne3+ 2. Kh3 Nxg4	65	1. Rh8+ Kf7 2. Qg6+
31	1. Re8+ Kh7 2. Qxh5#	66	1. ... Nxe3 2. dxe3 Qxc3
32	1. ... Qxc1+ 2. Qxc1 Rxa2#	67	1. Qxh6+ Rh7 2. Qxh7#
33	1. g6+ Kf6 2. Rf8#	68	1. ... Nf3 2. gxf3 Qxf3+
34	1. ... Qxe3+ 2. Rxe3 Rd1+	69	1. Nc4
35	1. d6 Qxd6 2. Qxa8+	70	1. ... Nb4 2. Qd1 Nd3+
36	1. ... c3 2. Qxc3 Qxc3	71	1. Rc8+ Kxc8 2. Nb6#
37	1. Qh5	72	1. ... Bf8 2. Qe3 Bxa3
38	1. ... Qxg2 2. Kxg2 Re1#	73	1. Nh4+ Kg7 2. Qg5+
39	1. Ne7+ Kh8 2. Qxb7	74	1. ... Rxc1+ 2. Kxc1 Nd3+

Solutions

Page #			Page #	
75	1. Bxh7+ Kxh7 2. Qh3+		110	1. ... Qe5 2. f4 Qxd5
76	1. ... Qh4		111	1. Bc7 Kg7 2. a4
77	1. Bg5		112	1. ... Qxf1+ 2. Kxf1 Nd2+
78	1. ... Bg5 2. Rdd1 Bxc1		113	1. Nxe5+ fxe5 2. Nxe5+
79	1. Rb5 cxb5 2. b7		114	1. ... Rxe5 2. Rxe5 Qxe5
80	1. ... Bh4 2. Qg4 Bxe1		115	1. Nc6 Kxb7 2. Nd8+
81	1. Rxe6 Qxe6 2. Qxg7#		116	1. ... Rh1+ 2. Kxh1 Qh8+
82	1. ... Qg4+ 2. Qg2 Rxf1+		117	1. Qe7 Rf7 2. Bxe6
83	1. Nxc4 dxc4 2. Bxb7		118	1. ... h3+ 2. Kxh3 Qxf2
84	1. ... Ng3 2. Rf7 Rh1#		119	1. Nd6 Kf8 2. Nxf5
85	1. Ne6 Re8 2. Rd4+		120	1. ... Rxc3 2. bxc3 Qxb8
86	1. ... Bxe3 2. Rxc7 Bb6+		121	1. Nh4
87	1. Qxh5+ Kg8 2. Qh6		122	1. ... Bb2 2. Nb5 Bxe5
88	1. ... Rxc2 2. Qxc2 Qh1#		123	1. Nxe4 dxe4 2. d5
89	1. Kb6		124	1. ... Rgxe3+ 2. Kd1 Rxe1#
90	1. ... Bxc5+ 2. bxc5 Rxb2		125	1. Qxc8 Qxc8 2. Nxe7+
91	1. Nxe6 fxe6 2. Qxe6+		126	1. ... Rxf3 2. Qxf3 Nxd2
92	1. ... Nxd4 2. cxd4 Qe3#		127	1. Rxe6
93	1. Qxf6 gxf6 2. Nxd7#		128	1. ... Qe1+ 2. Kh2 g3#
94	1. ... Qc2		129	1. Rc8 Re8 2. Rxe8
95	1. Nxe4+ fxe4 2. Nxe4+		130	1. ... d4 2. Bxd4 Bd5+
96	1. ... Rb2		131	1. a6 Bxa6 2. Kb8 =
97	1. a5 bxa5 2. Kxc5		132	1. ... Bg2+ 2. Kg1 Nxf3#
98	1. ... Bf4 2. Rc2 Rh6#		133	1. Ra1+ Kb7 2. Ra7+
99	1. Nc4 Qc7 2. Bf4		134	1. ... Qxg3+ 2. Rxg3 Rf1#
100	1. ... Qg3+ 2. fxg3 fxg3+		135	1. Rxg6 fxg6 2. Qxd3
101	1. Rxg6 Rxe3 2. Rxg7		136	1. ... Rc2
102	1. ... exd4 2. Kxd4 Rxc5		137	1. Ne7+ Kg7 2. Nc6
103	1. Rxg7+ Kxg7 2. Rg1+		138	1. ... Qd5+ 2. Kg1 Bh3
104	1. ... Bb4 2. Bxf6 Nxf6		139	1. Nxf6 Qxf6 2. Bxe5
105	1. Bxf7+ Kxf7 2. Qb3+		140	1. ... g5
106	1. ... Qxd4 2. Qxd4 Ne2+		141	1. Nxg6
107	1. Ne6 fxe6 2. Qxe8		142	1. ... Be4 2. Rb8+ Kxf7
108	1. ... Qf3+ 2. Bxf3 Nf2#		143	1. Rxg7 Bxg7 2. Qg3
109	1. Rxf6 Kxf6 2. Nd5+		144	1. ... Qxf1 2. Kxf1 Rd1#

Solutions

Page #			Page #	
145	1. e8=N+ Kf8 2. Nxd6		180	1. ... f3 2. gxf3 Nf4+
146	1. ... Qb1+ 2. Kf2 Rf8+		181	1. Rd8+ Kh7 2. Rxc8
147	1. Rxf6+ Qxf6 2. g7+		182	1. ... Rxh2+ 2. Kxh2 Qf2+
148	1. ... Rxb2 2. Rxb2 Qe5		183	1. Ng5 Rf6 2. e5
149	1. f5 Nd6 2. Rf8#		184	1. ... Rxe3 2. Nxe3 Qxe3+
150	1. ... Qg5+ 2. Kb1 Qxd5		185	1. Bb7
151	1. Qb4 Qxd2 2. Qc5+		186	1. ... Rxh2 2. Kxh2 Rh6+
152	1. ... Rxf2+ 2. Kxf2 Qxd1		187	1. Rh6 d2 2. Rh7+
153	1. Ng5 Nxg5 2. Qf8+		188	1. ... Rxh3 2. Kxh3 Qh8+
154	1. ... Rxg3+ 2. fxg3 Qf2+		189	1. Qh5 gxh5 2. Rg3+
155	1. Qxe6+ Qxe6 2. d7		190	1. ... Rxc4 2. Qxc4 Bd5
156	1. ... Rxf2+ 2. Qxf2 Qxa1+		191	1. e4
157	1. Rexe7 Rxe7 2. Rxa8+		192	1. ... Qxd5 2. Qxd5 stalemate
158	1. ... Qxh2+ 2. Kf1 Qh1#		193	1. g5 Nh5 2. Nd5
159	1. Ne5+ Qxe5 2. Qf7+		194	1. ... Qc1+ 2. Nxc1 Rd1+
160	1. ... Qg4 2. Qxc3 Qxd7		195	1. Rxb5 Qxa3 2. Rb7+
161	1. Qc8+ Kh7 2. Qxc3		196	1. ... Bc5 2. Kf2 Rxd2+
162	1. ... Nf3+ 2. Qxf3 Qh2+		197	1. a5
163	1. Rc5 Qg6 2. Qxh5		198	1. ... Qxg1 2. Kxg1 Re1#
164	1. ... Nf3+ 2. Bxf3 Bc3		199	1. Qxg7+ Rxg7 2. Rd8+
165	1. Nxf7 Rxf7 2. Qxe6		200	1. ... Bxe2
166	1. ... Nd5 2. Qxc4 Nxe3+		201	1. Rf8+ Bxf8 2. Qg8#
167	1. Nc4 Qc5 2. Ncxe5		202	1. ... Qb1+ 2. Nxb1 Rc1#
168	1. ... Nd4 2. Qe4 Qxd5		203	1. Nxe6 dxe6 2. Bxc5
169	1. Qe8+ Rxe8 2. Rxe8#		204	1. ... Nf6
170	1. ... Rxe1+ 2. Kxe1 Nxg2+		205	1. Bf8 g6 2. Qh6+
171	1. Rh1 Nh4 2. Kg1		206	1. ... Rxe3 2. fxe3 Qxe3+
172	1. ... Bxh4 2. gxh4 Nf4+		207	1. Nxd6 Qxd6 2. Bf4
173	1. Bd5 Qxd5 2. Ne7+		208	1. ... g5 2. h4 f6
174	1. ... Bf4		209	1. Qb2+ Kf7 2. Nh6+
175	1. Rxd6 cxd6 2. Qxb4		210	1. ... c1=N+ 2. Kd1 Nxd3
176	1. ... Bxg2 2. Kxg2 Qb7+		211	1. Ra6+ bxa6 2. b6+
177	1. Rxe8+ Rxe8 2. Rxa4		212	1. ... Rxd3 2. cxd3 Rc8
178	1. ... Qxg3 2. fxg3 Bxh6		213	1. Qh2 Rxe1 2. Qh5#
179	1. Bb6 c5 2. Rd8+		214	1. ... Re8 2. Kh2 Rg8

Solutions

Page #			Page #	
215	1. Bxf6 Bxf6 2. e5		250	1. ... Ne3
216	1. ... Qxb7 2. Qxb7 Bc6+		251	1. Qa3+ Qd6 2. Qxd6#
217	1. Nxc7 Bxb3 2. Nxe8+		252	1. ... Rd5 2. Qf4 Rh5+
218	1. ... Ra3+ 2. Ke2 Rxe3+		253	1. Qxc6 dxc6 2. Rd8#
219	1. Rh7+ Kxh7 2. Qg7#		254	1. ... Nf3+ 2. gxf3 Rg6+
220	1. ... Bxh2+ 2. Kh1 Bf4		255	1. Qg8+ Kh6 2. Bg5#
221	1. Nf6+ Bxf6 2. Qxd3		256	1. ... Bxe5 2. dxe5 Rxc5
222	1. ... Qd5 2. Qxd5 Nxf2#		257	1. g4 Rg5 2. f4
223	1. Kd4+ Rc6 2. Bxc6#		258	1. ... Ra2+ 2. Kb1 Ra1#
224	1. ... g4+ 2. Qxg4 Qxg4+		259	1. Qf7 Nxe7 2. Nf6#
225	1. Nf8+ Rxf8 2. Qg6+		260	1. ... Qxg3+ 2. Bg2 Rd1
226	1. ... Qe5 2. Rd1 Qxg5		261	1. Bxf7+ Kxf7 2. Ng5+
227	1. Qxg4 Nxg4 2. Bxd8		262	1. ... Bh3 2. Rfd1 Qe4
228	1. ... Qxg3 2. Kxg3 Ne2+		263	1. Rf5 Bd5+ 2. Nxd5
229	1. Rdd8 Raa8 2. Bd7		264	1. ... Nxe4 2. dxe4 Bxg5
230	1. ... h1=N+ 2. Kh2 Rxh4+		265	1. Ng5 Qe7 2. Nxe6
231	1. Rf5		266	1. ... Rb2 2. Bc4 Rf2#
232	1. ... g5 2. Rxf5 Qxh2+		267	1. c6
233	1. Rxc6 Rxc6 2. Qxd5+		268	1. ... Qxh3+ 2. Nxh3 Nf3#
234	1. ... Qc7+ 2. Kh3 Rh1#		269	1. Qxc6 Qxc6 2. Rxd8+
235	1. Rd8+ Kg7 2. Rd7+		270	1. ... Bxf2+ 2. Kxf2 Qb6+
236	1. ... h4+ 2. Kh3 Be6#		271	1. Nb5+ Ka6 2. Ra8#
237	1. Rxe5 fxe5 2. Nxe5+		272	1. ... Rxe3 2. Rxe3 Bxe3+
238	1. ... Nf6+ 2. Ke5 Bb2+		273	1. Bxc4 Bxc4 2. Nxe5+
239	1. Rxe3		274	1. ... Rf8+ 2. Bf4 Rxf4+
240	1. ... Ne5 2. Rxe5 Bxe5		275	1. Qxh6+ gxh6 2. Nf6+; Rg8#
241	1. Qg4+ Qg7 2. Qxe2		276	1. ... Rd8
242	1. ... Rxf4+		277	1. Nxc6 bxc6 2. Rxc6
243	1. Kf2 bxc4 2. Rh1		278	1. ... Bxd4 2. Kxd4 Rd6+
244	1. ... Nb6 2. Qb5 a6; Qc5 Na4		279	1. a3 Rad8 2. axb4 Bg2; Qh6
245	1. Bg7+ Kg8 2. Rxd7		280	1. ... Ke7
246	1. ... Nd4 2. Qd3 Nxf3+		281	1. Rxh7+ Nxh7 2. Qxg7#
247	1. Qg5+ Kxg5 stalemate		282	1. ... Rxh4 2. Rxh4 g5+
248	1. ... Qc8 2. Qxc8 Rxc8		283	1. f6 Bxf1 2. Qg7#
249	1. Ng6+ hxg6 2. Qh3#		284	1. ... Rxc3+ 2. Kxc3 Bg7

Solutions

Page #			Page #	
285	1. Bg5+ Kc8 2. gxf3		320	1. ... Rxc1 2. Raxc1 Bxb2
286	1. ... Rh2+ 2. Kg4 Rg2+; Rg3+		321	1. Bxg5 fxg5 2. Qxe5
287	1. Rd8+ Be8 2. Rxe8#		322	1. ... Bb7 2. Kh2 Bc8
288	1. ... Qh3		323	1. Qc1 b5 2. Bf1
289	1. Nf6+ Bxf6 2. exf6		324	1. ... Nxb3 2. axb3 Rxa1
290	1. ... h5		325	1. Ne5 fxe5 2. Bxb7
291	1. Bc4 Nf4 2. Bxf7+		326	1. ... Nxd4 2. Nxd4 Qh4+
292	1. ... Qxe1+ 2. Bxe1 Rxe1+		327	1. c4
293	1. Qa4 Qxa4 2. Rc8#		328	1. ... Bxe4 2. dxe4 Rxd2
294	1. ... Nf3+ 2. Kh1 Rh4#		329	1. Nf6+ gxf6 2. Qg4+; 3. Qxc8
295	1. Rxb2 Qxb2 2. Qa5#		330	1. ... Qb1+ 2. Kg2 Qxe4+
296	1. ... Rxg3		331	1. Qh6 Bxf6 2. exf6
297	1. Rh8+ Kg6 2. Rxh2		332	1. ... Ra8
298	1. ... Qf6 2. Bxb8 Qxa1		333	1. Qa2+ Kh8 2. Rxh5+
299	1. Qxh7+ Kxh7 2. Rh1+		334	1. ... Ng4+ 2. hxg4 Qh4+ =
300	1. ... Ng4+ 2. Kh3 Nf2+=		335	1. cxb5 axb5 2. c7
301	1. Be8 Rxe8 2. Qxf8+		336	1. ... Qxe4 2. fxe4 Bxe4+
302	1. ... c4 2. Bxc4 Re4		337	1. c8=R+ Nb8+ 2. Kd6
303	1. Be7 Re8 2. Bxd6		338	1. ... Ra6 2. Qb3 Bxc5
304	1. ... Nxf3+ 2. Rxf3 Bxe4		339	1. Rxe7 Rxe7 2. Bxd6
305	1. Rb8 Rxb8 2. Bxe5+		340	1. ... Qxe4 2. Bxc3 Nxd1
306	1. ... Qxf4+ 2. gxf4 Rxh3		341	1. Nd4 Qd7 2. Nxe6
307	1. Bg5 Ne5 2. Bf6+		342	1. ... Rxg4+ 2. hxg4 Ne4+
308	1. ... Nc6 2. Bxd6 Nxd4		343	1. f5 Nxf5 2. Qxd8+
309	1. Rxa6+ Na7 2. Rxa7+		344	1. ... Nxe3 2. fxe3 Rxe3
310	1. ... Rb1+ 2. Kxb1 Qb8+		345	1. Qe8+ Rxe8 2. Ng6#
311	1. Nd6+ Kf8 2. Nxb7		346	1. ... Qxc3 2. Qxc3 Nxe2+
312	1. ... Rxc3 2. Qe1 Bxd7		347	1. Nxe4 Nxe4 2. Qxc4
313	1. Rd7+ Kg6 2. Rxe8		348	1. ... Qxg3 2. Rxd4 Qc7
314	1. ... Qxa2+ 2. Bxa2 Nxc2#		349	1. Re6+ Kg8 2. Rxc6
315	1. Rxf6 gxf6 2. Qxf6		350	1. ... Bh3 2. Nxd4 Bxg2
316	1. ... Bh6 2. Nc5 Bxf4		351	1. Rf4+ Kb3 2. Rf3+ Ka2; Rxa3
317	1. Qg6 fxg6 2. Rxg7+; 3. Ng6#		352	1. ... Qd4 2. c3 Rxc3
318	1. ... Qxe4 2. Qxe4 Rh2#		353	1. c4 Bd7 2. Rxa6
319	1. Nxe6+ fxe6 2. Rxc6		354	1. ... Na4 2. Rxa2 Nc3+; Nxa2